Systematic Reviews of Research in Basic Education in South Africa

Published by African Sun Media under the SUN PReSS imprint

All rights reserved

Copyright © 2021 African Sun Media and the editor

This publication was subjected to an independent double-blind peer evaluation by the publisher.

The author(s)/editor(s) and the publisher have made every effort to obtain permission for and acknowledge the use of copyrighted material. Refer all enquiries to the publisher.

No part of this book may be reproduced or transmitted in any form or by any electronic, photographic or mechanical means, including photocopying and recording on record, tape or laser disk, on microfilm, via the Internet, by e-mail, or by any other information storage and retrieval system, without prior written permission by the publisher.

Views reflected in this publication are not necessarily those of the publisher.

First edition 2021

ISBN 978-1-991201-14-0
ISBN 978-1-991201-15-7 (e-book)
https://doi.org/10.18820/9781991201157

Set in Adobe Caslon Pro 11/14

Cover design, typesetting and production by African Sun Media

SUN PReSS is an imprint of African Sun Media. Scholarly, professional and reference works are published under this imprint in print and electronic formats.

This publication can be ordered from:
orders@africansunmedia.co.za

Takealot: bit.ly/2monsfl

Google Books: bit.ly/2k1Uilm
africansunmedia.store.it.si (e-books)
Amazon Kindle: amzn.to/2ktL.pkL

Visit africansunmedia.co.za for more information.

SYSTEMATIC REVIEWS OF
RESEARCH IN BASIC EDUCATION
IN SOUTH AFRICA

FELIX MARINGE (ED)

SUN PRESS

Contents

Contributors ix
Acknowledgements xv
Preface xvi

Chapter 1
Systematic reviews in basic education in South Africa:
The gold standard of evidence for educational decision-making 1
Felix Maringe and Otilia Chiramba

Abstract 1
Introduction and context 1
What are systematic reviews? 2
Types of systematic reviews 3
Systematic reviews: Approaches and purposes 4
Key steps in conducting a systematic review 5
The context of education under apartheid 6
Post-apartheid educational reform: Successes and failures 8
The need for education improvement 11
The role of education in development 12
Contribution of the education sector to development 13
Hierarchies of knowledge from research 13
The Quantitative/Qualitative debate 15
A synopsis of chapters in the book 16
References 21

Chapter 2
Interventions to improve learner achievement in South Africa:
A systematic meta-analysis 27
Neissan Alessandro Besharati, Brahm Fleisch and Khotso Tsotsotso

Abstract 27
Introduction 27
Challenges in evaluating education interventions 31
Method 34
Results 39
Discussion 54
References 57

Chapter 3
The impact of poverty on basic education in South Africa:
A systematic review of literature 69
Vitallis Chikoko and Pinkie Mthembu

Abstract 69
Introduction 69
Methods 71
Understanding the term 'poverty' 72
Highlights of the education–poverty interface 74

Poverty as a trigger for self-emancipation 85
Learning from the evidence 86
Conclusion 88
References 89

Chapter 4
Review and evaluation studies of school effectiveness and improvement in South Africa: A systematic and critical appraisal 91
Francine de Clercq and Yael Shalem

Abstract 91
Introduction 91
International lens on school effectiveness and improvement research 93
Historical lens on school effectiveness and improvement research in SA 94
Eight review and evaluation studies: What do they tell us about school
    effectiveness and improvement factors, accountability and support? 96
In search of a theory: Importance and role of theories of schooling and learning . 103
Conclusion: Towards new theories? 109
References 111

Chapter 5
Research on school leadership in South Africa: A systematic review 115
Tony Bush and Derek Glover

Introduction 115
Policy on school leadership 116
Leadership styles and models 117
Leadership roles in South African basic education 119
School management teams 120
Curriculum management and instructional leadership 121
Management of finance and resources 123
School governance 124
Leadership and management of people 126
Leadership and diversity 128
Leadership culture and structures 130
Leadership and student outcomes 131
Leadership preparation and development 131
Research gaps 132
Implications and conclusion 133
References 134

Chapter 6
A Systematic review of trends in teaching and learning research in South African schools 141
Dr Laura Dison and Dr Alison Kearney

Abstract 141
Introduction 141
Methodology 142
Emergent themes 144

Socio-economic conditions affecting learning and teaching 144
Culture of teaching and learning in schools 146
Effects of curriculum change 148
Teacher activities 151
Learner-centred approaches to teaching and learning 154
Conclusion 157
References 159

Chapter 7
Science teacher professional development in post-apartheid South Africa: A systematic review of the literature on basic education ... 163
Elaosi Vhurumuku

Abstract 163
Introduction 163
Purpose of the review 165
Effective teacher professional development 166
Teaching effectiveness 171
Method 172
Results 175
Discussion 179
Conclusions and recommendations 182
References 183

Chapter 8
Dealing with difference: A scoping review of disability in education in South Africa 189
Judith McKenzie, Brian Watermeyer and Kyla Meyerson

Introduction 189
Background and rationale 189
Aims and objectives of the chapter 191
Methodological approach 191
Thematic categories 194
Conclusions 203
References 205

Chapter 9
Research on mathematics teacher knowledge in Southern Africa: A 2010-2018 systematic review 215
Judah P. Makonye

Abstract 215
Background and rationale 216
Problem Scoping: Mathematics teacher knowledge problem in South Africa 217
Mathematics education research in Southern Africa 219
Purpose of the review 220
Methodological approach and data collection 220
Findings and discussion 222
Emerging patterns on the number of publications per journal over the period 223
Trends on research on different MKT domains over the period 223

Mathematics teacher knowledge research published abroad by
   Southern African Researchers 224
Research on errors and misconceptions 225
Other trends 226
Who does research on mathematics teacher knowledge? Journal articles and
   first author affiliation 227
Summary of strong evidence in the area 229
Summary of persistent gaps 229
Recommendations for further research, policy and practice 230
Further notes 230
References 231

Chapter 10
Systematic literature review of literacy and reading in South Africa 235
Geeta Motilal

Abstract 235
Introduction 235
Methodology 235
Literacy and reading 238
Literacy and reading theories frameworks 238
The South African literacy and reading landscape 239
Causal factors of literacy and reading challenges 241
Reading as oral performance 242
Literacy as a social practice 243
Role of the family in literacy and reading development 243
Reading ability and academic performance 245
Reading and teacher education in South Africa 249
Summary of findings 250
Gaps in literature and implications for future research 251
Conclusion 252
References 253

Chapter 11
Imperatives for educational improvement in South Africa's basic education system 257
Felix Maringe and Otilia Chiramba

Abstract 257
Evidence from the systematic reviews reported in this book 258
Conclusion 263
Key recommendations 264
References 270

TABLES AND FIGURES

Table 1.1	Comparing the racial bases of apartheid education in South Africa	8
Table 1.2	Hierarchies of knowledge from research	14
Table 2.1	Categories of education interventions	30
Figure 2.1	Funnel plot SA education meta-analysis	41
Figure 2.2	Graphical illustration of SA education Multi-Treatment Meta-analysis (MTMA)	46
Figure 2.3	Regression of effect size on school grade	46
Figure 2.4	Impact of interventions to improve language abilities	49
Figure 2.5	Impact of interventions to improve mathematics abilities	50
Figure 2.6	Impact of interventions to improve science and other FET subjects	50
Figure 2.7	Impact of LTSM provision	51
Figure 2.8	Impact of whole school development programmes	52
Figure 2.9	Impact of government programmes versus academic experiments	53
Table 4.1	Our own compilation of a summary of effectiveness factors, pressure and support coming from different levels of the education system	101
Table 7.1	Models of continuous professional development	168
Figure 7.1	A summary of the literature search and selection procedure	174
Table 7.2	A summary of the main features and characteristics of the reviewed studies	176
Figure 8.1	Flow chart representing article selection	193
Table 9.1	Number of papers from South African universities on PCK and MKT (2010-2018)	222
Figure 9.2	Frequencies of segments of research on MKT (2010-2018)	224
Table 9.2	Mathematics Teacher Knowledge Theme Publications by Journal by Southern African Mathematics Education Researchers	225
Figure 9.3	Number and proportion of articles relating to research on errors and misconceptions in two Southern African mathematics education journals	226
Figure 9.4	Number of articles on errors and misconceptions research in Pythagoras versus ARJMSTE	226
Figure 9.5	Number of articles published and first author affiliation in the ARJMSTE journal	227

Contributors

Felix Maringe is a Professor of Higher Education at the University of the Witwatersrand Johannesburg where he has been the Head of the Wits School of Education until December 2020. He has worked in three Higher Education systems in Zimbabwe, the UK and South Africa. Felix did his undergraduate and Masters degree studies at the University of Zimbabwe and completed his PhD Degree at the University of Southampton in 2003.
Felix has published extensively in refereed journals, has 8 co-authored and edited books, several book chapters, and high-profile commissioned research reports. He has editorial board membership in several journals and is currently Editor in Chief of the South African Journal of Educational Studies (JES). Felix is also a consultant in the College of Education at the University of South Africa (UNISA). He researches primarily in three areas of educational leadership, the internationalisation of Higher Education and in the Decolonisation of Higher Education.
He is currently working on two edited book on the impact of the Covid-19 pandemic which are due to be published in 2021. ORCID: 0000-0002-7992-9079

Otilia Chiramba holds a PhD in Educational Leadership and Policy Studies at the University of the Witwatersrand. Her specialisation is in higher education specifically focussing on under privileged groups like refugees and young researchers. She has also developed interest in basic education studies. At present, she is working as a researcher at Wits School of Education. Her work involves managing projects and co-authoring articles and book chapters. She has published articles and book chapters in the areas of higher education in South Africa. She has also presented her work at local and international conferences. ORCID: 0000-0003-4668-8536

Neissan Alessandro Besharati is the Director for Deloitte Development Africa. He also serves as a senior research associate at many prominent international development think-tanks and visiting professor at several universities in Africa and internationally. Dr. Besharati provides regular advisory services to governments, bilateral donors, regional institutions, private foundations, and sits on various United Nations, World Bank, African Union and OECD expert groups and committees. His areas of expertise include monitoring and evaluation, education policy, international development, emerging economies, public-private partnerships, development finance, and South-South cooperation. ORCID: 0000-0001-7061-6271

BRAHM FLEISCH is Professor of Education Policy in the Division of Education Leadership, Policy and Skills at the University of the Witwatersrand, Johannesburg. Brahm did his graduate studies at Columbia University in New York. After moving back to South Africa in 1990, he has lectured in education in the Wits School of Education, served as a district director in the newly formed Gauteng Department of Education and advised the national Department of Basic Education and the provincial education departments. His books include: Primary Education in Crisis: Why South African Schoolchildren Underachieve in Reading and Mathematics and (co-authored with Stu Woolman) The Constitution in the Classroom: Law and Education in South Africa, 1994-2008 and The Education Triple Cocktail: System-wide Instructional Reform in South Africa. His current research and professional work focuses on successful system-wide instructional reform. ORCID: 0000-0001-9952-1209

KHOTSO TSOTSOTSO is currently the head of M&E at New Leaders Foundation. Before this, he was an M&E Technical Specialist and Researcher at the Centre for Learning on Evaluation and Results for Anglophone Africa (CLEAR-AA), based at Witwatersrand University (Johannesburg). His academic background is in Economics, Management and Finance, with a strong aptitude for statistical analysis. He has completing his MA in Evaluation at Saarland University, Germany.
Khotso has led the CLEAR Center's work on technical evaluation, assisting strategic clients to strengthen their organizational capacities to design and implement evaluations, and build systems and processes to generate and use quality evidence in decision-making. Over the past 8 years, Khotso has both co-delivered, and led a total of 16 programme evaluations. He has also published multiple papers mostly in evaluation capacity development and education. ORCID: 0000-0001-7152-6622

VITALLIS CHIKOKO is a professor of Educational Leadership and Management at the University of KwaZulu-Natal. He is co-editor of the book: 'Education Leadership, Management and Governance in South Africa' (Nova Publishers, 2011); assistant editor of the book: 'International Handbook of Leadership for Learning' (Springer, 2011); and editor of the books: 'Leadership that works in deprived school contexts of South Africa' and 'Africa Handbook for School Leadership' (Nova Publishers, 2018 and 2019 respectively). His areas of research include: leadership in deprived school contexts; leadership development; and school leadership in Africa. ORCID: 0000-0001-6135-6172

PINKIE MTHEMBU holds a PhD in Educational Leadership Management and Policy, which focusses on the district leadership role in supporting teaching and learning in South African schools. Pinkie is a lecturer at the School of Education at the University of KwaZulu Natal. She teaches and supervises students at a postgraduate level in the Discipline of Educational Leadership Management and Policy. Before joining the university, her work experience spans over 20 years in secondary education as a teacher and a head of department (HOD) and a deputy principal. Pinkie's research interests are school district leadership, gender and leadership, school leadership and management as well as leading and managing teaching and learning in the context deprived communities. Together with her colleagues, she is currently working on the research/practice partnership with one rural school district in KwaZulu-Natal Province, South Africa. ORCID: 0000-0003-0586-4898

FRANCINE DE CLERCQ is an Honorary Senior Researcher in the Division of Educational Leadership and Policy Studies (ELPS), School of Education, University of the Witwatersrand. She does research in Teacher Education, Teacher Development, Educational Policy/Policy Implementation and Educational Leadership. Her current project with colleagues of the School of Education is on a critical analysis of large scale system-wide instructional interventions such as the GPLMS and PILO intervention in South African schools'. ORCID: 0000-0001-9209-059X

YAEL SHALEM is an honorary fellow at the Wits School of Education. Her research interests include professional knowledge, curriculum, teacher education and teacher work. She is one of two editors (Yael Shalem and Shirley Pendlebury) of Retrieving Teaching: Critical Issues in Curriculum Pedagogy and Learning, which was written in memory of Wally Morrow, the founder of educational theory in South Africa. Her recent book is Knowledge, Curriculum, and Preparation for Work, co-edited with Stephanie Allais (Brill Sense, 2018). ORCID: 0000-0001-6710-7150

TONY BUSH is Professor of Educational Leadership at the University of Nottingham, UK, and President of the British Educational Leadership, Management and Administration Society (BELMAS). He is also the editor of the leading international journal, Educational Management, Administration and Leadership (EMAL). He is a prolific author with more than 100 books and refereed journal articles. His bestselling text, Theories of Educational Leadership and Management is now in its fifth edition. His extensive international work includes research, consultancy and invited keynote presentations in 23 countries. ORCID: 0000-0001-8995-6057

DEREK GLOVER taught economics and geography in schools in the Midlands following his undergraduate years at LSE. He then had twenty years as head of Burford School, Oxfordshire. Since 1990 he has worked in higher education researching in leadership, financial management, anti-bullying and new technologies and teaching using distance learning approaches. He is an associate at the UCL Institute of Education, London, an Hon. Prof at Keele University and has worked with Prof. Bush since 1992, currently at Nottingham University. He has co-authored over sixty journal articles and seven texts including the widely used 'Educational Resource Management'. ORCID: 0000-0001-9892-361X

LAURA DISON has worked as a teaching and learning specialist at Wits for more than 25 years. She started as an Academic Development Advisor in the Faculty of Humanities before establishing the Wits School of Education Writing Centre in 2010. She co-edited a book on writing centres in South Africa in 2017 entitled Writing Centres in Higher Education: Working In and Across the Disciplines. Since 2015, she has been the Co-coordinator of the Post Graduate Diploma in Education (in the field of Higher Education), a professional qualification for lecturers to enhance their teaching practices. She currently lectures and supervises students in the Curriculum Division at the Wits School of Education and was appointed Assistant Dean for Teaching and Learning in the Faculty of Humanities in 2020. She is involved in collaborative research projects on innovative assessment in higher education and writing intensive courses at the School of Education. ORCID: 0000-0001-1626-4954

ALISON KEARNEY is an artist, art historian and art educator based in Johannesburg, South Africa. She is senior lecturer in arts education and head of the Curriculum Division in the Wits School of Education. Since July 2018 Dr Kearney is president of the South African Visual Arts Historians Association (SAVAH), and serves on the editorial board of the Taylor and Francis published, South African Art History Journal De Arte. In her multifaceted research practice, Dr Kearney explores learning in and about art, through making artworks, theorizing about contemporary African art and working with different audiences to promote visual literacy through engaging with art in the art museum. For the past seven years she has worked closely with the education curator at the Wits Art museum to develop teaching and learning resources, and regularly facilitates skills development workshops with teachers and learners in the art museum. ORCID: 0000-0001-9974-0268

ELAOSI VHURUMUKU is an Associate Professor of Science Education, in the School of Education, University of Witwatersrand. He has researched and published several works in a variety of areas including: investigating and developing teachers' and learners' understandings of the nature of science and nature of scientific inquiry; laboratory work in Chemistry Education; indigenous knowledge systems in the African context; and education for sustainable development in science and technology teacher education. He has a passion for professional development of science teachers. ORCID: 0000-0001-9360-1769

JUDITH MCKENZIE is head of the Disability Studies Division at the University of Cape Town in the Department of Health and Rehabilitation Sciences. She is the principal investigator responsible for the Teacher Empowerment for Disability Inclusion (TEDI) project and director of the newly established accredited research unit at UCT, Including Disability in Education in Africa (IDEA). She has worked in the field of inclusive education for over 20 years and is the mother of a young man with Down Syndrome, causing her to have a deep interest in disability inclusion at a personal as well as a professional level. ORCID: 0000-0002-2575-7718

BRIAN WATERMEYER trained as a clinical psychologist (M.A. {Clin. Psych.}) at UCT, before completing a doctorate in psychology (D. Phil), focusing on disability studies, at Stellenbosch University. He was first editor of South Africa's first major text in disability studies, entitled Disability and Social Change: A South African Agenda, published in 2006 (HSRC Press). His second book, Towards a Contextual Psychology of Disablism, was published internationally by Routledge in 2013. His most recent book is The Palgrave Handbook of Disability and Citizenship in the Global South (New York: Palgrave), edited by B. Watermeyer, J. McKenzie and L. Swartz (2019). Dr Watermeyer has an extensive list of international journal publications, book chapters, and media appearances as a disability scholar and activist. He teaches on postgraduate programmes in disability and clinical psychology, as well as guest lecturing in medicine and rehabilitation science. ORCID: 0000-0001-7671-4323

KYLA MEYERSON is currently a student clinical psychologist in training at the University of Johannesburg. Kyla's background lies in social science research specifically in the field of psychology. She recently completed her Masters in psychology, at Stellenbosch University. In her thesis, she examines the psychological effects of caregiver-child separation during long-term hospitalisation for paediatric MDR-TB. Kyla worked as a research assistant as part of the Sociobehavioural Sciences team at the Desmond Tutu TB Centre, Stellenbosch University. In this role, she contributed to various studies on the acceptability of paediatric antituberculosis treatment. Kyla has also recently conducted research, as a research assistant, for the Division of Disability Studies at the University of Cape Town. ORCID: 0000-0002-6038-7425

JUDAH PAUL MAKONYE is an Associate Professor in Mathematics Education, University of the Witwatersrand, South Africa. He has published widely on mathematics education research and presented in many local and international conferences. At the heart of his research is building mathematics teaching professionally situated knowledge through carefully observing learner errors and misconceptions through what they say and do when engaging with mathematics tasks. He seeks further insight into learner thinking by conducting interviews. He believes that with the help of high leverage mathematics teaching and learning practices informed by research; such as productive struggle, and high expectations for all learners, all learners can realise mathematics success. Prof Makonye has supervised many post graduate students including PhDs. Presently, he is the head of the masters programme at the University of the Witwatersrand School of Education. He has taught at all levels of the education system; primary and high school, teachers' college and university in Zimbabwe and South Africa. ORCID: 0000-0001-7437-8856

GEETA MOTILAL is the Head of Foundation Studies, lecturer, teacher trainer and researcher at the Wits School of Education, University of Witwatersrand. She has lectured in Literacy in Foundation Phase and in the Leadership and Management of Teaching and Learning in the Educational Leadership Masters Programme and was a facilitator of the Executive Leadership programme to train principals to lead schools. She is a researcher in instructional leadership, instructional practices and in Early Grade Reading in Foundation Phase. She is also a Hubert Humphrey Fellowship alumni and in 2014/15 she completed a yearlong programme in Leadership at Vanderbilt University, Nashville, Tennessee. Her PhD study focused on instructional leadership of school heads in primary schools. She has supervised and examined many MEd and PHD students, published several book chapters and journal articles. She has obtained a grant to research an alternative reading strategy for the teaching of reading in an Additional language in South Africa. ORCID: 0000-0002-7976-8252

Acknowledgements

Putting this book together was an achievement of the many authors who bought into the idea of systematic reviews as a basis for garnering the most powerful evidence that speaks to the successes and failures of the Basic Education system in South Africa. The names of the authors appear elsewhere in the book and I shall not repeat them. The methodology of systematic reviews itself is alien and under-developed in the education fields. Therefore, I wish to express a deep sense of gratitude to all the authors who agreed to take the plunge into previously uncharted territory and still produced a manuscripts of a good standard. For us, the intended value to the field of educational research and to the ailing system of Basic Education in South Africa was a strong driving force worth investing time and effort. Thank you colleagues.

I also wish to thank Dr Otilia Chiramba, who started working with me as a research assistant, receiving drafts, logging them, sending material to reviewers, compiling the comments and many other activities, without which this book would have taken substantially longer to complete. In the final analysis, Otilia's work became so substantial in terms of not only helping with literature searches, but also in terms of contributing to the writing and critical engagement with my own drafts. I am convinced that editors must shift from past practices of intellectual capitalism, through which the contribution of project assistants are not acknowledged and remain obscured and anonymised. In the end, Dr Chiramba contributed substantially to this intellectual project and has been rightly included as a co-author in my chapters as editor. Thank you Dr Chiramba.

I acknowledge the efficiency of the Publishing editor Wikus Van Zyl at African Sun Media, for the ways in which he contained disappointments and anxiety when the manuscript experienced many delays, adjustments and redrafting in some cases. Together with the excellent comments we received from blind reviewers, I express on behalf of the authors my deepest gratitude.

Lastly, but perhaps most importantly, I wish to express my deepest gratitude to Professor Patricia McInerney, now retired from the Faculty of Health Sciences at Wits for hosting a full day workshop on the idea of systematic reviews at the start of the project, back in 2018. As indicated earlier, this is a methodology we have read about but which we rarely utilise in the field of educational research. Thank you Trish.

I hope the readers will find the contents of the chapters in this book exciting, meaningful and usable to begin a new generation of research and to improve practice and performance of the Basic Education sector in South Africa.

Professor Felix Maringe

Preface

I am delighted to have been asked to write a few words about a book that is likely to constitute a significant basis for informing school improvement in the South African Basic Education sector and beyond. Although South Africa leads the way in terms of knowledge production on the African continent, the knowledge bases tend to be in disparate places, as little attempts are made, not only to evaluate the strength of the underlying evidence, but also in terms of bringing the knowledge together in accessible forms to inform evidence based practice and policy development in the sector. In addition, much of our knowledge production tends to be small in scale, based on isolated case studies and institutional driven imperatives. This makes it extremely difficult for policy makers and practitioners to develop informed decisions about school improvement.

Led by Professor Maringe, a team of scholars, largely based at the Wits School of Education but also drawing from many universities across the country agreed to search, analyse and synthesise the best evidence we have available about important topics affecting educational performance in the South African context. In 2018, the team met at the Wits SoE in a day long workshop facilitated by Professor Patricia McInerny in the faculty of Health Sciences. Topics we selected which reflected some of the most intractable challenges faced by the Basic Education sector, but which also resonated with the research expertise and interests of the scholars. The team agreed to use the systematic review process as a shared methodology for pulling together what works and does not work in the South African Basic Education sector.

Systematic reviews have their origin in the medical field, where practitioners have to utilise the best available evidence to inform decisions about caring and treating patients. In this sector, evidence based practice is a matter of life and death and systematic reviews are thus the golden standard for determining the best evidence available to determine patient practices and interventions and to inform broad policy interventions too. In education, the situation has never been considered in life and death terms. But it can be argued that, poorly educated citizens constitute a huge risk to the development of any country. Such citizens are unlikely to have the requisite skills, knowledge and understandings which would drive meaningful national development. In the work places, poorly educated citizens are a liability to both organisational and national development. Employers usually and with good reason, shun poorly educated citizens. Consequently, schools that do not churn out well educated citizens are complicit in the poor performance of their countries, in economic terms, in social terms and even in political terms. Systematic reviews retain their value even in this education context as it pulls and represent the best knowledge for the given time.

Acknowledgements

The South African Basic Education sector is arguably one of most well-funded systems of education on the continent and compares favourably in terms of per capita investment with some of the best performing nations in the world. Yet in terms of performance on a variety of scales, such as TIMMS, PIRLS, amongst others, the country is perpetually found at the bottom of the performance league tables. This is hard to explain. In addition, South Africa is also considered to be one of the most unequal societies in the world, with a GINI index of 0.65, way above the 0.2 level which represents equality in wealth distribution. Partly because of the legacy of apartheid, itself a most divisive and discriminatory ideology, and also because of many contemporary failures and systemic inefficiencies, South Africa's education system continues to operate as a bifurcated system catering to the needs of the privileged who attend in well-resourced schools which are efficiently led on one hand and to those of the underprivileged majority in under resourced and poorly led schools.

The book has 11 chapters. The first provides a well argued discussion of the context of Basic Education in South Africa and the importance of systematic reviews as a tool for gathering evidence which can be used for systemic improvement and policy revision. The second chapter assess the usefulness of post 84 educational interventions indicating why some have not been as impactful as intended. The third chapter explores the issue of poverty as an overarching challenge in schools for the underprivileged and also provides an analysis of the successes and failures of the poverty mitigations that have been introduced in South African schools since 1994. The fourth chapter is a meta-analysis of some of the most significant evaluations conducted in Basic Education in South Africa. In the fifth chapter, the role of school leadership and principalship is brought under focus in South Africa and identifies the challenges and weaknesses related to school leadership in the country. Chapter 6 focuses on the role of Teaching and Learning in South Africa and identifies some of the key impediments to successful and impactful teaching and learning in the country. In Chapter 7, the central importance of science teaching is illuminated through research on science teacher professional development. The issue of inclusion and disability is the focus of Chapter 8, which identifies the strengths and weaknesses of various models adopted to develop an inclusive education systems in South Africa. In Chapter 9, focus turns to mathematics teacher knowledge in a subject which routinely experiences the worst examination performances year in year out in South Africa. In Chapter 10, the significant notion of literacy and reading in South African schools is tackled. The final Chapter 11 tries to synthesise the strongest evidence available in South African research on Basic Education, which could drive the next generation of school improvement strategies and new research in the coming decades.

As Head of research at the Wits SoE, and as a keen scholar of school improvement, I strongly recommend this book to policy makers at the DBE, researchers in Schools and Faculties of Education across the country and to post graduate researchers undertaking doctoral studies in wide areas of educational development and more specifically on school improvement. I also recommend that the book more widely marketed outside the country as many countries, especially on the African continent, are likely to be experiencing similar challenges.

I would like to congratulate Professor Felix Maringe and his team for what I consider to be a substantial contribution to knowledge to the field of educational research and practice in South Africa.

Professor Elizabeth Mavhunga
Associate Professor in Science Education and
Deputy Head of School for Research at the Wits SoE

CHAPTER 1

Systematic reviews in basic education in South Africa: The gold standard of evidence for educational decision-making

Felix Maringe and Otilia Chiramba

Abstract

There is growing evidence based on practice and research-led development that informs decision-making in education in general and basic education in particular in South Africa. Much inspired transformation has happened in education since 1994 with notable improvement of the system. Even though the apartheid regime was discontinued in 1994, we continue to see the existence of two systems of education: one that serves the affluent minority communities and the other that serves the underprivileged majority. Secondly, despite the considerable financial budget spend on education, South Africa continues to be at the bottom of performance league tables, outperformed by countries that spend less on education with substantially limited resources. The purpose of the chapter is to highlight how the following chapters contribute to the knowledge base by conducting systematic reviews in selected areas in basic education. This methodology is most likely to provide the best evidence that is available in South Africa upon which school improvement and learning outcomes can be enhanced. We conclude by giving a synopsis of each chapter's contribution, outlining the purposes and how a systematic review is to be carried out in each.

The overarching concern of this book is to condense the increasing, broad literature base to highlight the best evidence that tells us where the education system is doing well and where it continues to falter. The book is thus purposed at creating a valid basis for future work that can be used to drive qualitative improvements in the basic education sector.

Introduction and context

Basic education in South Africa is designed for learning that takes place in primary and secondary schools over twelve years, from Grade 1 (6 - 7-year-olds) to Grade 12 (18 - 20-year-olds). Learners who succeed in year 12 exit with a matriculation certificate, which enables them to transition to different forms of tertiary level education and into employment.

This book focuses on obtaining the best available evidence on which school improvement and learning outcomes can be further developed and enhanced in South Africa. However, the areas of research included depended, to a large extent, on the availability and willingness of the authors to undertake complex systematic reviews in the areas. It centres on some of the most enduring issues about basic education in South Africa. We were keen to create a one-stop resource that policymakers, practitioners, researchers and students could use as a reference for the best available evidence that will inform their decisions around improving the quality of teaching and learning, as well as learner outcomes.

There is widespread agreement that systematic reviews provide the best testament to support practise and aid decision-making (Moher et al., 2015). As a team of authors, we decided to follow this protocol to unequivocally direct new areas for research and knowledge generation.

A key reason for undertaking this project is that the South African education system is in crisis (Fleisch and Schöer, 2014). One of the factors contributing to this crisis is that, despite overturning apartheid in 1994 (a system that was based on differentiated access to resources based on race), a bifurcated system persists. Two systems of education exist: one that serves learners of the minority affluent communities and another that serves the majority underprivileged communities. These systems are vastly different in terms of resource endowment, quality of teachers and nearness to factors of poverty. The schools for the privileged, a small segment of the country's schools, contribute nearly 90% of the children who proceed to a university. On the other hand, the majority learn in poorly resourced schools with poorly qualified teachers and deliver the least valuable outcomes for learners, such as the highest numbers of school dropouts, failures, repeaters and children who finish school without being able to read and write.

The chapter begins by providing the context of education under apartheid. With knowledge of how apartheid education degraded the majority, we move on to briefly explore post-apartheid education, both the success in alleviating inequality as well as its failure in doing so. We progress to explore literature that emphasises the need for education improvement. We also focus on the role and significance of education in development. We start with some definitions. We end by giving a synopsis of chapters in this book, justifying the selection of the areas of education represented by each chapter. Before providing the context of education in South Africa, we explore the notion of systematic review as it provides a basis for the work that is reported in the chapters of this book.

What are systematic reviews?

Systematic reviews differ from ordinary reviews of literature in that they provide a comprehensive and unbiased analysis and synthesis of the literature in the area under study. They are undertaken primarily to bring together the state of knowledge and understanding in a given area as a basis for identifying what is well known and less well known. They provide a valid basis for evaluating the quality and efficacy of evidence in an area of research or practice. Traditionally, systematic reviews originated in the medical sciences and thus have a quantitative origin. The need to pull together the evidence for the impact of a given intervention, such as a new treatment, is fundamental to decisions about the wider application of those interventions and treatments. Although systematic reviews are now an important part of testing evidence in qualitative research, their use is not as extensive as it is in quantitative research dimensions.

There are multiple definitions of systematic reviews in the literature, which reflect varying emphases and focuses. However, there seems to be general agreement that systematic reviews collate empirical evidence that fits specified eligibility criteria in pursuit of answers to pre-specified research questions (Petticrew and Roberts, 2008). Three critical elements appear to be important in the conceptualisation of systematic reviews. The first is the aspect of drawing evidence from empirical research, not just from random practice guides and sources of good practice. Secondly, systematic reviews are based on eligible evidence. This has to be determined by the reviewers and specifically defined to provide the parameters within which the evidence is collated. The third element of systematic reviews is that they provide evidence for pre-specified questions. It is broadly agreed that systematic reviews are developed around the following assumptions and purposes:

A systematic review:
Answers a focused research question
Employs a comprehensive, reproducible search strategy
Identifies all relevant studies (both published and unpublished)
Assesses all results for inclusion/exclusion and quality
Presents an unbiased, balanced summary of findings.

Types of systematic reviews

There is a wide variety of systematic reviews, which sometimes makes this area a rather difficult one to understand. To simplify matters, the multiplicity of systematic review types can be described meaningfully in two broad ways: by the models through which they are conducted and by the functions they serve.

Three broad models representing the three extensive research world views are recognised: quantitative, qualitative and mixed methods models.

Quantitative systematic reviews bring together evidence about a specific topic based on research in the quantitative paradigm. However, just like other broad world views, the quantitative domain is not a monolithic entity, as it shelters several varieties of numerically driven statistical data of a strict measurement type, using valid and reliable measurement tools (Stern et al., 2018). Examples of quantitative research include experimental, quasi-experimental, surveys, amongst others. For instance, a researcher working in the area of educational wastage might wish to determine the most important causes of school dropout in a specific district based on studies that utilised the questionnaire survey approach to yield quantitative data.

Qualitative systematic reviews pull evidence from more constructivist research (Seber and Lee, 2012) based on observations, interviews, focus group discussions, amongst others. Here the data is open to interpretation and the researcher and the researched are integral to the new knowledge production process and outcome. For example, using the same example of educational wastage, a researcher interested in determining the causes, impact and effects of school dropout interventions might wish to review all research that used in-depth interviews with high school learners to investigate the phenomenon over a stipulated period. Review papers might then be sampled from the pool of qualitative research that sought to explore the three interrelated dimensions.

Mixed methods systematic reviews utilise evidence from research based on combinations of qualitative and quantitative models of data gathering and analysis. Again, using educational wastage as an example, researchers may seek to draw on evidence from studies that utilised surveys and interviews with learners in school. Such studies usually privilege the notion of triangulation as a quality assurance mechanism. Evidence from different research traditions on the same topic is brought together to inform decisions about policy and practice.

Systematic reviews: Approaches and purposes

Within the three models mentioned, three quite distinct approaches are deployed commonly to serve equally distinct purposes. The first approach refers to scoping reviews. These are normally used, as the name suggests, to develop an idea of the nature, types and approaches to researching phenomena, especially in an emerging area. Often, the starting point is that not enough is known about the nature and efficacy of the evidence, how the research was done, who the researchers were, their aims and other unknowns. The major purposes of scoping reviews are to: understand what aspects of a phenomenon seem to be generating interest and why; what methodological approaches seem to characterise the research in the field of interest; what seem to be the convergences and divergences in the evidence; and the identification of what still needs to be done (gaps) and developed in the area (Munn et al., 2018).

The second approach is a meta-review, also known as an integrative review. These tend to be conducted in well-established research areas awash with a wealth of evidence available in peer-reviewed journals. Also, such areas usually have a strong tradition of systematic reviews. In such cases, meta-reviews tend to build on already available evidence to see if, cumulatively, the evidence can be built into theory. Meta-reviews tend to deploy analytic techniques that include the integration of statistical modelling to summarise the results of several studies

(Deeks et al., 2001). Although meta-reviews are more common in quantitative analyses, they are increasingly being used in qualitative research especially for purposes of gathering or integrating evidence from previous systematic reviews in each area (Muka et al., 2020).

The third approach is a diagnostic test accuracy systematic review. As the name implies, these reviews pull evidence from published research based on test measurements of specified phenomena. For example, learner performance in a given subject could be measured through multiple-choice tests, open-ended tests, practical activities and oral presentations, amongst others. The question for educators might have been to determine the most reliable test to verify learner performance and to make decisions about certification and progression. The reviewer might then analyse the reliability and validity of a variety of test regimes to determine which of these score highest in predicting future performance, progression and quality of learning.

We finally examine the major methodological steps in conducting a systematic review.

Key steps in conducting a systematic review

There are a significant number of review publications especially under the ambit of major systematic review organisations such as the Cochrane, the Joanna Briggs Institute for healthcare research, the Campbell Collaboration for social sciences and the impact of social interventions, and PROSPERO, an umbrella organisation for many systematic review entities. Conducting a systematic review is considered a four-step process, although the procedure has been expanded into longer lists in various systematic review protocols. The following is a condensed protocol that is extensively detailed in various places (see for example Higgins et al., 2019; Boland et al., 2014).

1. **Putting together a team for the review**

A minimum of two or three people is often recommended for a systematic review. This provides an opportunity for cross-checking the findings and collating decisions to enhance the efficacy of the evidence.

2. **Defining the question/s for the review**

This requires an initial scoping of the literature to determine gaps in the field of interest based on which the question/s can be formulated.

3. **Identifying the research or studies to be included in the review**

This requires clarity on inclusion and exclusion criteria for admitting studies in the review. Inclusion and exclusion criteria might include when the studies were published, the research models used such as all research conducted using questionnaire surveys, whether gender participation is important, amongst others.

The exclusion and inclusion criteria should reflect gaps in the literature and the research questions set out for exploration.

4. Careful reading of the admitted articles to determine answers to the research questions followed by analysis and conclusions

We now turn to the context of education in South Africa.

The context of education under apartheid

It is important to briefly frame the context by going back to where it all began. Both structurally and legislatively, apartheid was an extremely vicious institution under which the black majority was exposed to the most degrading and excruciating circumstances. The system exerted various forms of violence on local populations, as briefly outlined in the following sub-sections.

Intellectual violence

The primary aim of education under apartheid was to produce a cadre of unambitious and feeble-minded learners who saw themselves only as subservient to the needs of their white masters (Ndlovu-Gatsheni, 2015). Under apartheid, education for blacks was the starkest symbol of separate and unequal development. Government subsidies for education were administered according to race, for example, favouring white schools with educational subsidies that were close to 30 times better than those for black schools (Ndlovu-Gatsheni, 2015).

The purpose of this policy was to develop a vast pool of unskilled labour within the black population whose mental capacities were carefully honed for a life of unquestioning service to the white masters (Ndlovu-Gatsheni, 2015). The virtues and ambitions of education as a desirable pursuit were flagrantly ignored. At no time did the ambitions for educating children of the black majority reflect the intentions of the enlightenment period under which settler regimes were operating. On the contrary, despite the avowed mission of emancipating the 'dark continent', the children of the majority black population were never to be educated to the same levels as their white counterparts. This sustained epistemic violence left a legacy of underdevelopment of the victims of apartheid, and more broadly, of colonialism in South Africa.

Cultural violence

A strategy for capturing the local people's minds was to make sure that blacks viewed their culture as being inferior to that of whites (Galtung, 1990). A sustained campaign through the media, learning materials and books, religion and language policies in schools ensured the decimation of indigenous cultures in favour of white culture (Galtung, 1990). Using local languages in black schools was punishable. For example, black children, despite learning in separate schools from white children, were prevented from using local languages, even for informal communication on the school grounds. As language is a cornerstone of any people's culture, denying people the use of their mother tongue is a clear act of violence against their cultural being. In some places in South Africa, there were notices which read 'Dogs and Africans not allowed beyond this point'. This was a clear indication of the lack of value attached to blacks as people and as cultural beings.

The idea that 'white is good' while 'black is bad' was subtly communicated in multiple ways. Skin lightening creams were heavily marketed to influence people to despise their original skin colours in favour of lighter skin colours. For example, a skin lightening product named Ambi was an acronym translated by blacks to mean 'Africans May Be Improved'. In films, black people were always presented as backward and uneducated. In Tsodzo (1981), a textbook that was used in black schools, Zuze was delivering bread from the bakery to a company in the city when he decided to eat one of the loaves because he was hungry. The company wrote back to the bakery indicating that the delivery was one loaf short. Zuze was puzzled as to how a simple letter (that could not 'speak') could land him in so much trouble. He then beat up the invoice with a long stick, blaming it for reporting him. That is how backward – to the point of retardation – blacks were depicted in some books.

Religious violence
To a large extent, African traditional practices, including their religious beliefs, were the subject of immense violation during apartheid. While local people had a strong belief in God, one aspect tried Christianity tried to eliminate from black people's belief systems was the role of spirit mediums in connecting with the Lord (Matheba, 2001). For whites and Christianity in particular, black spirit mediums could not be depicted as conduits of God's purpose for mankind. Instead, the view was that such mediation is possible only through a white representation of Jesus, who would have had blood lineage closer to Africans than to Europeans (Coetzee and Roux, 2003). Until recently, practices such as traditional African weddings were considered as religiously (and even legislatively) invalid, as only a 'white wedding' would be satisfying to the Lord.

Social violence
Apartheid had the effect of disrupting the social organisation of indigenous lives. Due to urbanisation, men, and to a lesser extent women, were drawn to the urban centres, and mining or farming areas to do menial tasks as labourers or domestic workers (Osman and Petersen, 2010). The sophisticated organisation of local people's social lives, which they lived communally, respectfully and with dignity, was replaced by more individualistic lifestyles, based not so much on social cohesion, but on a monetised system of competitive and exploited existence. The entire social fabric of black societies, where entire villages (not only families) had the responsibility of raising children, was fractured as new patterns of settlement grew and new forms of labour developed. In education, such fracturing of the social

fabric continued, as evidenced by the emphasis on individual learning approaches, high stakes assessments and learning content that had little or no relevance to people's everyday experiences.

In short, apartheid sought to destroy the entire essence and value system of local indigenous people, through an orchestrated, epistemicidal process (Grosfoguel, 2007). Schools taught new values, new knowledge and new belief systems while wiping out existing ones that were considered as subhuman, barbaric and underdeveloped.

Table 1.1 summarises the nature, form, purpose and impact of apartheid education on blacks and whites in South Africa. The summary portrays a highly differentiated, divided and unequal education system based on a deliberate racialisation of society, through which advantages and privileges were apportioned along racial lines. This racialisation of privilege became the cornerstone of the apartheid regime, the lens through which the regime sought to be understood and justified.

Table 1.1 *Comparing the racial bases of apartheid education in South Africa (own summary)*

Dimension of education	White system and learners	Black system and learners
Philosophy and purpose	To develop leaders of industry and society	To develop cheap labour for menial tasks
Nature of curriculum	Leadership and critical thinking skills Emphasised STEM subjects	Conformity focusing on basic functional competencies Emphasised liberal arts
Teacher capacity	Highly qualified and well paid	Poorly qualified and poorly paid
Subsidy	30 times more than blacks	30 times less than whites
Teacher-student ratio	Small 1:15 (private)	Large 1:45 (public)
Progression routes	Majority proceeded to university and other tertiary institutions	Majority did not succeed and became absorbed in low-paying jobs
Leadership	Well qualified, graduate principals	Poorly trained, non-graduate principals
Educational throughput	Highly efficient	High wastage and poor learning outcomes

Post-apartheid educational reform: Successes and failures

In this section of the chapter, we briefly, but critically review the post-democracy interventions in the basic education sector in South Africa. We refer to the work of Badat (1997), Christie (1996), Fataar (2008), Fleisch (2008), Spaull and Jansen (2019) and Kallaway et al., (1997) to support the argument that while much has been achieved to promote physical access to schools, plenty remains to be done to achieve epistemological access across the basic education system in South Africa.

At first, at the dawn of democracy in 1994, there were almost a million black children out of school (Kallaway et al., 1997), so the new government was expected to urgently address the matter. Education became democratised, in that access to schools was no longer based on race. Successive colonial and apartheid governments had excluded black, and to a lesser extent, coloured and Indian children from white schools, in line with the principle of separate and unequal development based on race. Almost overnight, by 1995-6, all school-age children had earned their right to be in school, although often in crowded conditions and sometimes under trees. Today, evidence shows that South Africa has achieved almost 100% participation for school-age children (Government of Education, 2020), accommodated in schools throughout the country. However, legacies of apartheid are still evident, and five legacies are discussed in the following sections.

Basic education in South Africa is a paragon of inequality. The South African basic education system, despite being the most well-funded on the African continent, including being a product of more than 20 years of development following the collapse of apartheid in 1994, is one of the most unequal systems of education in the world. Basic education provision in the country continues to trace the contours of poverty, deprivation and social status. For example, Fleisch (2008) discusses two systems of basic education in South Africa. One is for the rich and serves the needs of approximately 10% of the richest people in the country, most of whom are whites. This system operates in state schools with abundant and modern infrastructure, facilities and resources, including the best teachers in the country. The majority of the children who attend these schools proceed to universities in the country and elsewhere. The remaining 90% of the children in South Africa learn in poorly resourced schools, with poor infrastructure (such as pit toilets, no running water and inadequately trained teachers) and without adequate books and other learning materials. The majority of learners in these schools contribute to the phenomenon of wastage, to which we now turn.

Secondly, basic education in South Africa is blighted by high wastage. Wastage in education is a symptom of an ailing system, manifesting in several ways: schools in South Africa experience some of the highest rates of dropout, failure, repeating and non-completion. In aggregate terms, basic education in South Africa loses approximately 35% of children who do not complete the full 12-year cycle. For example, about 1.2 million children started school in 2007 and only 800 000 registered to write the final matric (NSC) examination in 2019. This means only 67% of learners completed the full 12-year cycle, while close to 35% were unaccounted for. The majority of learners appear to dropout in year 3, when the initial excitement about going to school seems to wane, and in Grade 10, when the schools actively cull out struggling learners from schools, to allow only those with proven capability to proceed to the final two years of basic education. Evidence for this was found in a large-scale study in 2 000 schools in Mpumalanga in South Africa (Maringe, 2017). In primary schools (Grades 1 to 7), more boys dropout than girls, while, in secondary schools (Grades 8 to 12), more girls dropout than boys. Teenage pregnancies tend to account for the majority of girl child dropouts at secondary level. The majority of boys who drop out tend to do so for academic reasons. In the Mpumalanga study, close to 60% of boys dropped out of secondary school on academic grounds, largely based on the inability to read and write. The Maringe (2017) study also found evidence of over-age learners in many schools. They represented a small, but significant 11% and were mainly the result of poor achievement and the requirement for schools to achieve minimum learner outcomes and targets before they could be progressed to higher levels of learning. The basic school system is a wasteful system.

Thirdly, the basic education system delivers poor literacy and numeracy outcomes. Many studies in South Africa show that learners are generally two to three classes below their expected reading levels. For example, by the time learners leave primary school at the end of Grade 7, close to 60% have reading levels equivalent to those expected of children in Grade 5 (Van der Berg, 2008). Almost 75% of learners in Grade 7 cannot perform basic mathematical operations, such as addition, subtraction, division and multiplication (Spaull and Kotze, 2015). Inadequacies in these two areas are due to a wide range of factors including weaknesses in teachers who are not skilled in teaching reading and writing and lack of resources, especially in schools located in areas of multiple deprivation.

Fourthly, the basic education system does not deliver strong outcomes in the STEM subjects, which have stronger relevance to economic development. Both in relation to participation and performance, learners involved with STEM subject learning are significantly fewer and exhibit weaker performances, compared to participation and performance in other subjects of the school curricula (Spaull, 2013). In 2019, the lowest pass rates in Grade 12 were recorded for mathematics, physical sciences and accounting. Fewer students also registered to write examinations in these subjects (Mlachila and Moeletsi, 2019). Further, the evidence suggests that female students tend to shy away from studying these subjects. This perpetuates the gendered nature of careers, where, for example, more males become engineers, while more females tend to join the caring professions in nursing or early grade teaching.

Finally, the basic education school system is led by principals with no formal leadership background. School principals in South Africa are recruited in schools not so much because of their leadership abilities, but because of the length of experience and service as teachers in schools. This delivers several weaknesses to the system. For example, school leadership is wrongly linked to people's length of service as teachers, rather than as a function of people's leadership capabilities

(Mestry and Singh, 2007). In the end, school principals become simple purveyors of other people's bright ideas, as they resort to uncritically replicating what they have learnt from those who led schools before them. They tend to be passive implementers of tacit knowledge exhibiting normative, rather than critical, understanding of ideas and the context of school leadership. Without a theoretical understanding of school leadership, many school principals in South Africa tend to impose solutions that have little or no relevance to the specific contexts of their schools. For example, imposing rules about arriving early at school before dealing with the issue of reliable transport systems in the area constitutes the application of the right solution to the wrong problem. There is a limit to which school leaders in South Africa can be expected to drive meaningful school change and improvement. While a significant amount of research in education is published by South African scholars, compared to scholars in other parts of the continent, the evidence continues to exist in disparate spaces, which are not always accessible to those who work in the school systems. Also, much of the evidence that gets reported in South African peer-reviewed journals tends to be based on small scale research and interventions deemed to be inadequate evidence to support new practices and interventions on their own. This book has been written with the hope of pulling together disparate sets of evidence and assessing the extent to which we could make generalisations to influence teacher action and interventions and to drive school improvement in the country.

This book, thus, aims to identify weaknesses and strengths of the basic education system in South Africa and to become a useful basis upon which meaningful change and transformation can be conceptualised and developed. For a country perpetually languishing at the bottom of performance league tables and which persistently is outperformed by countries that spend much less on education with poor resources, the book will provide a solid base for understanding what works and what does not work in South African schools.

The above scenario paints a picture of a school system with good intentions and with a record of achieving high levels of physical access, but with a shockingly poor record of epistemological access, poor leadership, poor results in STEM subjects, poor numeracy and literacy outcomes, high wastage and inequality. In the following section we explore the literature on school effectiveness and improvement.

The need for education improvement

Much research highlights the need for improving education as a prelude and stimulus for development (Gibbs et al., 2001). Five interlocking elements are closely linked to school improvement research (Gates et al., 2019; Hoachlander et al., 2003). The elements are human capacity development (that includes improving teachers' pedagogical competencies), improving the leadership and management of schools, deployment and utilisation of educational resources and infrastructure, improving and enhancing the quality of learner-learning time and improving school infrastructure (especially learning and teaching technologies). Amongst the most promising evidence of what works in fostering school improvement, by helping to raise learner outcomes, are the following:

1. Focusing on learner achievement all the times
2. Increasing learner engagement and motivation
3. Providing sustained professional development
4. Focusing strongly on the management of learning
5. Building links between schools and parents, other equally ambitious and interested schools and private organisations
6. Establishing a culture of strong assessment for learning to support learning outcomes
7. Promoting effective school leadership practices that enable school improvement

A key purpose in this work is to evaluate the extent to which the material covered in this book provides further evidence to support the above framework of school improvement recommendations. In the context of South Africa, we need to identify the gaps in school practices in light of the evidence from research. In particular, in this context, many of the current gaps and challenges originated during the apartheid era. Education is considered to be a significant tool in developing countries. The next two sections discuss the role and contribution of the education sector to development.

The role of education in development

The need to improve education has always been at the forefront of all nations' developmental aspirations (Altbach, 2015). This is even more applicable to countries such as South Africa that existed under repressive regimes for many years, where education was used not as an instrument for developing people, but as a strategy for subjugating the majority of the local population into positions of servitude, servanthood and disadvantage (Ndlovu-Gatsheni, 2015). During the apartheid era, education for the black majority was a pale shadow compared to that provided for their white counterparts. Education for black children was delivered separately and it was poorly resourced, financially, materially and in terms of the quality of its teachers. No other factor is more important than education in the development trajectories and ambitions of a country, since the education sector provides the basis for development in any country. To appreciate this notion, we briefly outline some of the key contributions of a solid and effective education sector to the development of nations.

Chapter 1

Contribution of the education sector to development

Classical economic theory propounded by Smith (1960), Schultz (1961) and Dennison (1962), amongst others, clearly identifies three facilitators of economic production, namely human capital, financial capital and the land. Education is at the centre of economic and social growth through the development of knowledge, skills and attitudes as fundamental elements of human capital development. Through education, sometimes referred to as schooling or training, albeit with both nuanced and fundamental differences, societies prepare their citizens to participate more broadly in development. Financial capital is best understood from the observation that challenges are not simply resolved if we allocate great amounts of money to them. Financial prudence, namely the judicious allocation and use of monetary capital, occurs only through people who are specially trained for that purpose. Therein lies the central importance of human capital developed through our education systems. The third element, land, is a repository and producer of minerals and agricultural produce, as well as a sanctuary for flora and fauna. Without knowledgeable human capital, land on its own does not provide the added value needed for development, food security and environmental sustainability.

Although (as we shall see below) South Africa allocates and spends extensive sums of money on its education systems, such large-scale investment does not seem to yield commensurate dividends. For example, according to Cohen (2017), in relative terms, South Africa allocates a higher proportion of its budget toward education than do the United States, United Kingdom and Germany. Yet in terms of outputs and performance, measured via several international instruments such as the Programme for International Student Assessment (PISA), South Africa performs poorly compared to the rest of the world, including countries with a lower GDP and those whose education budgets are a fraction of that it is in South Africa (Mlachila and Moeletsi, 2019). An OECD (The Organisation for Economic Co-operation and Development) report, for example, shows that South Africa's school children are ranked 75th out of 76 countries in the world in maths and science, better only than Ghana (Keeley, 2015). Relatively poor countries outperform South Africa, such as Kazakhstan (ranked 49), Tunisia (ranked 64), Botswana (ranked 70), and Morocco (ranked 73). Even though the amount spent on education can be viewed as a criterion of educational performance, based on the assumption of a link between resources and outcomes (Fourie, 2006), the inverse relationship between education financing and performance in South Africa provides a hard-to-explain case and calls for serious review.

Hierarchies of knowledge from research

To begin with, there is widespread belief that quantitative research provides better and more robust evidence. For us, this is an over-generalisation, which should be treated with caution. Research evidence is only as good as the questions it seeks to answer. If the question is about the comparison of performance in different treatment groups, then we will be the first to admit that a quantitative approach to the comparisons would be the best way to handle this question. However, one may be interested in knowing stories told and the feelings that people have about a new intervention, how they have experienced it and what they think needs to be done for better impact. Thus a qualitative design would be best suited to the purpose of finding the answers. We are the least likely to be persuaded by the idea of hierarchies of knowledge, as we know them, except to say that there remains a strong view that quantitative research provides more efficacious answers to research questions (Table 1.2).

Table 1.2 *Hierarchies of knowledge from research*

The most highly valued knowledge form	Systematic reviews	Most highly valued knowledge, as it represents the best knowledge in any area for a given time	Select best research from both traditions to estimate the state of knowledge in needed areas
Quantitative knowledge approaches that are highly valued	Randomised control experiments	Designed to test whether treatment effects differ significantly from control effects	Often utilised for high-stake decisions, such as when people want to know if a newly a discovered treatment is effective
	Quasi-experimental	Designed to conduct experiments with no control effects	Used in situations where, for ethical and social justice reasons, groups cannot be separated
	Surveys	Administered via questionnaires, anonymously and in confidence	Capacity to reach out to large populations and, therefore, the potential for high representativeness
Qualitative knowledge approaches that are highly valued	In-depth interviews	One-on-one encounters	Valued for their in-depth nature, rather than for generalisability of findings
	Narratives/biographies	Stories told by participants	Valued for the interpretive nature of the data and the personally meaningful accounts
	Focus group interviews	Small groups that share understandings and opinions about broad social issues	Valued for their social constructivist potential to knowledge generation
	Ethnographic studies	Observing people in their natural environments over time, involves living with the research participants	Valued for its socio-cultural embeddedness

Knowledge obtained through quantitative approaches is valued for its:
- Predictive value
- Generalisability
- Representativeness across relevant segments of society
- Relative ease and ability to be turned into visually meaningful representations

On the other hand, knowledge obtained from qualitative approaches is valued for its:
- Specificity and in-depth nature
- Ability to present opportunities for unsolicited knowledge to emerge
- Value in being context-specific rather than in being generalisable
- Capacity to be turned into stories, as they comprise of people's views and perceptions

The Quantitative/Qualitative debate

There is no question that quantitative knowledge has exerted dominance and significance over qualitative evidence for the reasons listed above. There is a general belief that numbers do not lie, whereas words can mean anything. Quantitative knowledge is thus associated with universal truths, which can be generalised and applied more broadly, while qualitative knowledge is of more specific and particularistic relevance (Bryman et al., 2008).

Despite the obvious advantages associated with each, the approaches to evidence gathering have their weaknesses too. Quantitative research depends on the possibilities of gathering representative samples, from which the relevant generalisations are made (Polit and Beck, 2010). Establishing truly representative samples is notoriously difficult at the best of times. Individual's responses to questions can be influenced by environmental conditions. For example, if a company wanted to launch a new drink, participants tasting the drink in hot and cold climates may react differently to the question of how refreshing the drink is. Even if the responses are consistent within the different groups, the decisions could very well be skewed by the influence of an external environmental issue. Further, the statistical modelling required tends to frighten people who have minimal mathematical skills. So, quantitative knowledge has the potential to be inaccessible to the majority of the population and because of that, it can be considered as exclusionary and/or exclusive or elitist. Because of the large size of audiences and participants, quantitative research can be quite resource-intensive and expensive to conduct. This also contributes to its exclusiveness, where only the financially privileged can utilise these knowledge systems.

On the other hand, while qualitative knowledge brings depth to our understanding of issues, it cannot be generalised to the population in the same way quantitative evidence can be (Rahman, 2017). Equally, qualitative research generally utilises small samples, which may not always be truly representative of the population under study. There is also a great deal of investment needed to develop a personal relationship with the participants, since the extended and repeat interviews have to be negotiated on trust. It is also notoriously difficult to judge the quality and authenticity of data from qualitative interviews.

Kuhn's paradigm wars have highlighted the debates and controversies surrounding quantitative and qualitative research. However, emerging from these debates is a third way of looking at research from a mixed-method perspective. Although the term 'mixed-method perspective' seems easy to grasp, it has become a broad church of ideas, which seek integration, rather than isolation and exclusion; pluriversality, rather than universality; and a preoccupation with a holistic understanding of phenomena, rather than understanding driven by single perspectives (Fetters et al., 2013). Several designs have been developed to represent mixed-method approaches. These include iterative mixed-method designs, which are based on the dynamic interplay of quantitative and qualitative approaches in a spiral way, aimed at creating interpretive value to the research; and embedded, or nested, mixed-method designs, in which some methods are located or interlocked within other approaches. For example, one may seek to determine the number of times an issue is raised by different interviewees in a quantitative way. Such approaches value complementarity of knowledge designs. Holistic designs utilise independent research approaches to explore single phenomena to bring a better understanding of complex phenomena.

The authors were invited to a launch meeting, where these ideas about systematic reviews and basic education were explored first. In particular, the meeting required participants to go away with a carefully crafted question around agreed themes in basic education in South Africa. The following section gives a synopsis of the chapters of the book.

A synopsis of chapters in the book

Chapter 2 is titled *Interventions to improve learner achievements in South Africa: A systematic meta-analysis*. Besharati, Fleisch and Tsotsotso argue that non-achievement of learners is one of the significant concerns in basic education. Some literature indicates that 90% of the learners in South Africa underperform because they learn in poorly resourced schools, with poor infrastructure and without adequate books and other reading materials (Spaull, 2013). As discussed previously in this chapter and elsewhere, all the international comparative education performance measurements indicate that overall, South Africa's education system performs relatively poorly, particularly in science and mathematics, and reading and comprehension tests, compared to similar education systems in the world (Fleisch, 2010 Spaull, 2013). Thus, this chapter conducted by Besharati, Fleisch and Tsotsotso is very necessary. They completed a review of 165 effects of 37 education interventions implemented in South Africa post-1994. The review appraises 35 impact evaluations and conducts a comparative meta-analysis of rigorous experimental and quasi-experimental studies implemented in South African schools. The chapter aims to explore the various contextual factors and internal design features that influence the magnitude of the effects reported in various impact studies. It provides a synthesis of 20 years of empirical evidence from post-apartheid South Africa. Through the use of multiple treatment meta-analysis, the study analysed the impact of some of the major interventions implemented in public schools over the past twenty years. The South African education system continues to suffer from a weak public school system. In comparison with regional and international learner assessments, South Africa's underperformance is well documented and despite the numerous interventions, the challenges remain apparent.

Chapter 3 is titled *The impact of poverty on basic education in South Africa: A systematic review of literature*. Authors Chikoko and Mthembu examine how poverty has impacted on basic education in South Africa, even long after the apartheid regime. As discussed earlier and elsewhere, there is an enduring phenomenon of poverty that afflicts the majority of schools in the country and that is an indictment of a systemic paralysis of unprecedented proportions in the sector. This phenomenon is exacerbated by the unabated widening of school and educational inequalities and deepening poverty differentials between schools that serve different racial and socio-economic groups in South Africa. While there is a substantial body of research on the impact of poverty in education, there remains a dearth of evidence that evaluates the impact of post-democracy interventions introduced to circumvent the effects of poverty on schooling. This chapter therefore reviews the literature on how poverty has impacted basic education in post-apartheid South Africa. The authors have established the gap that, although some necessary steps to eradicate poverty are evident in the extant literature, the impact thereof is not sufficiently evident. The methodology involved a three-stage systematic literature review process to select work for review and subsequent inclusion in the chapter. The three stages involved a search of a wide variety of literature through Google Scholar, EBSCOhost, Sabinet and ERIC. From the wide choice in stage one, the authors selected peer-reviewed journals in stage two and working papers presented by academics in stage three, to use for the systematic review, which covered ten years, from 2009 to 2019.

Chapter 4 is titled *School effectiveness and improvement: Review and evaluation studies in South Africa: A systematic and critical appraisal*. There is a real need to review the literature on school effectiveness and improvement because despite several studies that inform school improvement, there is a far more resilient legacy from the past that is the low quality of education within the formerly disadvantaged parts of the school system (Taylor, 2007). De Clercq and Shalem critically analyse eight reviews and evaluation studies of school effectiveness and improvement interventions conducted in South Africa from 2000 up to recent. The chapter aims to explore and understand what exists in the extant literature about learner improvement and theories of change. This is achieved by answering the following questions: What do these studies tell us about school effectiveness and school improvement factors associated with better learner performance? How and why may these factors improve school effectiveness? The chapter argues that current studies on review and evaluation do not engage with any theories of change. It further argues that they largely bracket out how chronic poverty, in which most learners in South Africa live, affects knowledge acquisition.

Chapter 5 is titled *Leadership research on basic education in South Africa: A systematic review*. Leadership is acknowledged to be critical for school improvement and success. However, it seems that school leadership in South Africa remains devoid of training for incumbents. Thus, this research conducted by Bush and Glover is crucial. The authors explore the policy background to school leadership from 1996 to 2007. The chapter argues that this was a period of radical change and it consequently aimed to ascertain how policy and practice are reflected in existing research outputs. The chapter performs a systematic literature review and also builds on the authors' previous research and writing on school leadership in South Africa. Through general search engines, 473 references were considered, but the fine-grained selection identified 138 sources. The chapter acknowledges the growing body of empirical evidence, but also notes that data is still uneven and research remains underdeveloped in some areas. Moreover, the available literature takes a normative stance, which often has weak empirical underpinnings.

Chapter 6 is titled *A Systematic review of trends in teaching and learning research*. Teaching and learning are significant ways that move societies out of poverty, yet we lack substantive research that examines it. Dison and Kearney report on the findings of a systematic review of studies on teaching and learning in Basic Education and Training (BET) and Further Education and Training (FET) in South Africa over the past twenty-five years, to discern and expand the existing knowledge base. This chapter also aims to provide a conceptual framework for critiquing the assumptions and criteria used by researchers to select their sources of evidence. The authors were prompted by a lack of extensive research that examines teaching and learning in the classroom. In the systematic literature review, the gathering of literature was done using various search engines and identified 38 articles that met the eligibility criteria. These were determined using the analytical tool developed by the authors.

Chapter 7 is titled *Science teacher professional development in post-apartheid South Africa: A systematic review of the literature on basic education*. Learners from historically disadvantaged communities perform poorly in science subjects that contribute more to the development of the country. Vhurumuku conducts a systematic review that involves analysing and synthesising existing research on science teacher professional development, from 1994 to 2019. Twenty articles were identified and selected, using various search engines. The purpose of this chapter is to identify the models that had a positive impact on science teachers, hence the potential to improve teacher effectiveness.

Chapter 8 is titled *Dealing with differences: A scoping review of disability in education in South Africa*. Authors McKenzie, Watermeyer and Meyerson utilise the inclusive education policy framework to examine access and participation of children with disabilities in basic education in South Africa. The purpose of the chapter is to explore the effects of the implementation of the inclusive education policy, as expressed in EWP6, in relation to the right to education and reasonable accommodation of children with disabilities, rights mandated in the Constitution and the United Nations Convention on the Rights of Persons with Disabilities (Republic of South Africa, 1996; Mégret, 2008). The literature, which was systematically reviewed specifically using the scoping review, has shown that these children's needs are largely subsumed within inclusive education research. Using various search engines, the chapter identified a total number of 1 281 records and 47 articles that were selected and included in the analysis. The chapter has indicated that there is very little research on the role or effectiveness of special schools in attaining desired outcomes.

Chapter 9 is titled *Research on mathematics teacher knowledge in Southern Africa: A 2010-2018 systematic review*. Despite the interventions, learners still perform badly in mathematics. Makonye conducted a systematic review, using Ball et al.'s (2008) research theme of mathematics knowledge for teaching (MKT). The purpose is to explain how pedagogical content knowledge (PCK) can be extended to the teaching of mathematics. The articles reviewed are from between 2010 and 2018 and the MKT framework was used to code articles. The literature reviewed showed that knowledge for content and student (KC & S) and knowledge of content and teaching (KC & T) are well-researched areas, but there is very little research on specialised content knowledge (SCK) and common content knowledge (CCK).

Chapter 10 is titled *A Systematic literature review of literacy and reading in South Africa* and reports on a critical literature review of scholarship in literacy and reading in South Africa from 2010 to 2020 that draws on critical discourse analysis. Key issues, trends and criticisms in the field are discussed. A three-staged methodology was used, which starts with searching educational databases to locate literature focused on literacy and reading scholarship. Each article and data were categorised. Motilal examines literacy-focused empirical studies and theoretical papers in scholarly journals to reveal trends in the questions that researchers find interesting enough to pursue, the theories they find useful and the kinds of interactions that capture their attention.

Chapter 11 is a conclusion chapter titled *Imperatives for educational improvement in South Africa's basic education system.* Maringe and Chiramba conclude that there is still a crisis in the South African education system, despite the post-apartheid interventions. We highlight the complexity of the education process and its numerous interacting influences, the limitations and potential strength of research and the particular research challenges experienced when seeking evidence to guide educational decisions in South Africa.

Furthermore, we attempt to synthesise the evidence for what needs to be done to enhance the quality of several aspects of basic education in South Africa. We deduced and summarised some significant factors emanating from evidence from critical reviews in this book and propose interventions using insights from the evidence and conclude by highlighting ideas for policy review and further research.

References

Altbach, P. G. (2015). What counts for academic productivity in research universities?. *International Higher Education*, 79, 6-7. https://doi.org/10.6017/ihe.2015.79.5837

Badat, S. (1997). Harold Wolpe: Reminiscences and reflections. *Keynote address at the launch of the Harold Wolpe Memorial Trust, Spier Auditorium, Stellenbosch, 31.*

Ball, D. L., Thames, M. H., & Phelps, G. (2008). Content knowledge for teaching: What makes it special? *Journal of Teacher Education*, 59(5), 389-407. https://doi.org/10.1177/0022487108324554

Boland, A., Cherry, M. G., & Dickson, R. (Eds.). (2014). *Doing a Systematic Review: A Student's Guide*. London: Sage

Bryman, A., Becker, S., & Sempik, J. (2008). Quality criteria for quantitative, qualitative and mixed methods research: A view from social policy. *International Journal of Social Research Methodology*, 11(4), 261-276. https://doi.org/10.1080/13645570701401644

Christie, P. (1996). Globalisation and the curriculum: Proposals for the integration of education and training in South Africa. *International Journal of Educational Development*, 16(4), 407-416. https://doi.org/10.1016/S0738-0593(96)00061-2

Coetzee, P. H., & Roux, A. P. J. (Eds.). (2003). *The African philosophy reader*. Abingdon: Routledge. https://doi.org/10.4324/9780203493229

Cohen, B. J. (Ed.). (2017). *International political economy*. Routledge. https://doi.org/10.4324/9781315251950

Deeks, J. J., Altman, D. G., Bradburn, M. J. (2001). *Statistical methods for examining heterogeneity and combining results from several studies in meta-analysis*. In: Egger, M., Smith, G. D., Altman, D.G. (Eds.). *Systematic reviews in health care: meta-analysis in context*. 2nd Ed. London: BMJ Publication Group.

Dennison, J. M. (1962). Graphical aids for determining reliability of sample means and an adequate sample size. *Journal of Sedimentary Research*, 32(4), 743-750. https://doi.org/10.1306/74D70D58-2B21-11D7-8648000102C1865D

Fataar, A. (2008). Education policy reform in postapartheid South Africa: Constraints and possibilities. In: *The Education of Diverse Student Populations* (pp. 97-109). Dordrecht: Springer. https://doi.org/10.1007/978-1-4020-8204-7_6

Fetters, M. D., Curry, L. A., & Creswell, J. W. (2013). Achieving integration in mixed methods designs—Principles and practices. *Health Services Research*, 48(6pt2), 2134-2156. https://doi.org/10.1111/1475-6773.12117

Fleisch, B. (2008). *Primary education in crisis: Why South African school children underachieve in reading and mathematics*. Cape Town: Juta.

Fleisch, B. (2010). The politics of the governed: South African Democratic Teachers' Union Soweto Strike, June 2009. *Southern African Review of Education with Education with Production*, 16(2), 117-131.

Fleisch, B., & Schöer, V. (2014). Large-scale instructional reform in the Global South: insights from the mid-point evaluation of the Gauteng Primary Language and Mathematics Strategy. *South African Journal of Education*, 34(3), Article # 933. https://doi.org/10.15700/201409161040

Fourie, J. (2006). Economic infrastructure: a review of definitions, theory and empirics. *South African Journal of Economics*, 74(3), 530-556. https://doi.org/10.1111/j.1813-6982.2006.00086.x

Galtung, J. (1990). Cultural violence. *Journal of Peace Research*, 27(3), 291-305. https://doi.org/10.1177/0022343390027003005

Gates, S. M., Baird, M. D., Master, B. K., & Chavez-Herrerias, E. R. (2019). *Principal pipelines: A feasible, affordable, and effective way for districts to improve schools*. California: RAND Corporation. https://doi.org/10.7249/RR2666

Gibbs, D. C., Jonas, A. E. G., Reimer, S., & Spooner, D. J. (2001). Governance, institutional capacity and partnerships in local economic development: theoretical issues and empirical evidence from the Humber Sub-region. *Transactions of the Institute of British Geographers*, 26(1), 103-119. https://doi.org/10.1111/1475-5661.00008

Government of South Africa. (2020). Minister Angie Motshekga on Basic Education Sector Plans to support learners during Coronavirus COVID-19 lockdown. Accessed 08/04/2020, available from https://www.gov.za/speeches/minister-angie-motshekga-basic-educationsector-plans-support-learners-during-covid-19

Grosfoguel, R. (2007). The epistemic decolonial turn: Beyond political-economy paradigms. *Cultural Studies*, 21(2-3), 211-223. https://doi.org/10.1080/09502380601162514

Higgins, J. P.T., Thomas, J., Chandler, J., Cumpston, M., Li, T., Page, M. J., & Welch, V. A. (Eds.). (2019). *Cochrane handbook for systematic reviews of interventions*. Chichester: John Wiley & Sons. https://doi.org/10.1002/9781119536604

Hoachlander, G., Alt, M. l., & Beltranena, R. (2001). Leading school improvement: What research says. Atlanta, GA: Southern Regional Education Board.

Kallaway, P., Kruss, G., Fataar, A., & Donn, G. (Eds.). (1997). Education after apartheid. South African education in transition. Cape Town, South Africa: University of Cape Town Press.

Keeley, B. (2015). *Income inequality. The gap between rich and poor: The gap between rich and poor, OECD Insights.* Paris: OECD Publishing. https://doi.org/10.1787/9789264246010-en

Maringe, F. (2017). Creating opportunities for a socially just pedagogy: The imperatives of transformation in post-colonial HE spaces. In: Osman, R., Hornsby, D. (Eds.). *Transforming Teaching and Learning in Higher Education* (pp. 59-78). Cham: Palgrave Macmillan. https://doi.org/10.1007/978-3-319-46176-2_4

Matheba, G. (2001). Religion and political violence in apartheid South Africa. *Journal of Cultural Studies*, 3(1), 108-123. https://doi.org/10.4314/jcs.v3i1.6218

Mégret, F. (2008). The disabilities convention: Human rights of persons with disabilities or disability rights? *Human Rights Quarterly*, 30(2), 494-516. https://doi.org/10.1353/hrq.0.0000

Mestry, R., & Singh, P. (2007). Continuing professional development for principals: A South African perspective. *South African Journal of Education*, 27(3), 477-490.

Mlachila, M., & Moeletsi, T. (2019). Struggling to make the grade: A review of the causes and consequences of the weak outcomes of South Africa's education system. *International Monetary Fund Working Papers*. Working paper No. 19-47. https://doi.org/10.5089/9781498301374.001

Moher, D., Shamseer, L., Clarke, M., Ghersi, D., Liberati, A., Petticrew, M., et al. (2015). Preferred reporting items for systematic review and meta-analysis protocols (PRISMA-P) 2015 statement. *Systematic Reviews*, 4(1), Article number 1. https://doi.org/10.1186/2046-4053-4-1

Muka, T., Glisic, M., Milic, J., Verhoog, S., Bohlius, J., Bramer, W., et al. (2020). A 24-step guide on how to design, conduct, and successfully publish a systematic review and meta-analysis in medical research. *European Journal of Epidemiology*, 35(1), 49-60. https://doi.org/10.1007/s10654-019-00576-5

Munn, Z., Peters, M. D. J., Stern, C., Tufanaru, C., McArthur, A., & Aromataris, E. (2018). Systematic review or scoping review? Guidance for authors when choosing between a systematic or scoping review approach. *BMC Medical Research Methodology*, 18(1), Article number 143. https://doi.org/10.1186/s12874-018-0611-x

Ndlovu-Gatsheni, S. J. (2015). Decoloniality in Africa: A continuing search for a new world order. The *Australasian Review of African Studies*, 36(2), 22-50.

Osman, R., & Petersen, N. (2010). Students' engagement with engagement: the case of teacher education students in higher education in South Africa. *British Journal of Educational Studies*, 58(4), 407-419. https://doi.org/10.1080/00071005.2010.527665

Petticrew, M., & Roberts, H. (2008). *Systematic reviews in the social sciences: A practical guide*. New Jersey: John Wiley & Sons.

Polit, D. F., & Beck, C. T. (2010). Generalization in quantitative and qualitative research: Myths and strategies. *International Journal of Nursing Studies*, 47(11), 1451-1458. https://doi.org/10.1016/j.ijnurstu.2010.06.004

Rahman, S. (2017). The advantages and disadvantages of using qualitative and quantitative approaches and methods in language "testing and assessment" research: a literature review. Journal of Education and Learning, 6(1), 102-112. https://doi.org/10.5539/jel.v6n1p102

Republic of South Africa. (1996). *Constitution of the Republic of South Africa, 1996*. South Africa: Government Printer.

Schultz, T. W. (1961). Investment in human capital. *The American Economic Review*, 51(1), 1-17.

Seber, G. A. F., & Lee, A. J. (2012). *Linear regression analysis* (Vol. 329). New Jersey: John Wiley & Sons.

Smith, A. (1960). An inquiry into the nature and causes of the wealth of nations. In: Campbell, R. H., & Skinner, A. S. (Eds.). *The Glasgow edition of the works and correspondence of Adam Smith*. Vol. 2a and 2b. Oxford: Oxford University Press.

Spaull, N. (2013). South Africa's education crisis: The quality of education in South Africa 1994-2011. *Johannesburg: Centre for Development and Enterprise*, 1-65.

Spaull, N., & Jansen, J. D. (2019). *South African Schooling: The Enigma of Inequality*. Cham: Springer. https://doi.org/10.1007/978-3-030-18811-5. https://doi.org/10.1007/978-3-030-18811-5

Spaull, N., & Kotze, J. (2015). Starting behind and staying behind in South Africa: The case of insurmountable learning deficits in mathematics. *International Journal of Educational Development*, 41, 13-24. https://doi.org/10.1016/j.ijedudev.2015.01.002

Stern, C., Munn, Z., Porritt, K., Lockwood, C., Peters, M. D. J., Bellman, S., et al. (2018). An international educational training course for conducting systematic reviews in health care: The Joanna Briggs Institute's comprehensive systematic review training program. *Worldviews on Evidence-Based Nursing*, 15(5), 401-408. https://doi.org/10.1111/wvn.12314

Taylor, E. W. (2007). An update of transformative learning theory: A critical review of the empirical research (1999–2005). *International Journal of Lifelong Education*, 26(2), 173-191. https://doi.org/10.1080/02601370701219475

Tsodzo, T. K. (1981). *Rurimi Rwaamai. Bhuku 4*. Zimbabwe: Scholastic Books.

Van der Berg, S. (2008). How effective are poor schools? Poverty and educational outcomes in South Africa. *Studies in Educational Evaluation*, 34(3), 145-154. https://doi.org/10.1016/j.stueduc.2008.07.005

CHAPTER 2

Interventions to improve learner achievement in South Africa: A systematic meta-analysis

Neissan Alessandro Besharati[1], Brahm Fleisch and Khotso Tsotsotso

Abstract

The paper summarises a systematic review of 165 effects of 37 education interventions implemented in South Africa post-1994, by public and private education agencies. The review appraises 35 impact evaluations and conducts a comparative meta-analysis of rigorous experimental and quasi-experimental studies implemented in South Africa's schooling sector. The meta-analysis reveals many locally-produced studies, which had not been captured in previous international reviews, and highlights some of the programmes and policies that had the most impact on language, mathematics and science learning in South African public schools. It also explores the various contextual factors and internal design features that influence the magnitude of the effects reported in various impact studies. The paper provides researchers, funders, governments and education managers with a synthesis of 20 years of empirical evidence from South Africa that can inform programming and policies for improved learning outcomes in developing countries.

Keywords: South Africa, Education, Meta-Analysis, Systematic Review, Impact Evaluations, Effect Size

Introduction

Though a middle-income emerging economy, South Africa is a country that suffers from an extremely weak public school system. This exacerbates other national development challenges, such as unemployment, poverty and inequality and racial divides. Both international and regional learner assessments consistently show South Africa's underperformance, not only in comparison to the rest of the world, but also to lower-income countries on the African continent (Fleisch, 2008; Spaull, 2013).

The historical legacy from the apartheid era was racially segregated schooling systems, designed to privilege the white minority and limit the aspirations and potentials of the black majority. With the ushering in of the democratic dispensation in 1994, the government had the arduous task of undoing decades of structural inequality and amalgamating the previously "white", "Indian",

---

[1] This review is based on a chapter of Besharati's (2016) PhD thesis at the University of the Witwatersrand

"Coloured" and "black" schools within one schooling system. Numerous reforms were introduced, such as the South African Schools Act (1996), Integrated Quality Monitoring System (IQMS), the national school feeding scheme and a National Qualifications. Framework. The national curriculum was revamped several times (1997, 2002, 2008) with little impact on the bimodal pattern of achievement (Fleisch, 2008; Spaull, 2013).

The results from the national public external examination provide an important signal about learner knowledge and ability to enter further education and the work force (Kanjee, 2007). In an effort to assess learning at earlier points in the school system, the Department of Basic Education initially introduced the Systematic Evaluations (SEs) and later the Annual National Assessments (ANAs). Some provinces, such as the Western Cape, have also been implementing their own systematic learner assessments in the schools. It was assumed that these assessment processes would contribute to education improvement through a combination of external and internal accountability (Elmore, 2008).

Notwithstanding twenty years of education reforms, the international and national assessments consistently showed that the majority of learners in previously black schools continued to perform significantly lower than learners in previously white schools (Bloch, 2009; Spaull, 2013). At secondary level, the learning gaps are particularly wide in the subject areas of mathematics and sciences.

Numerous studies (Besharati, 2014; Botes & Mji, 2010; Taylor & Prinsloo, 2005; Simkins, 2010) have highlighted how language has been a serious obstacle to the learning of more complex mathematical and scientific concepts. The issue becomes more complicated when 83% of South African learners' home language is one of the nine African languages, but would switch to English or Afrikaans as their medium of instruction from Grade 4 onward. Linked to this is the findings (Van der Berg, 2008; Gustafsson, 2007; NPC, 2011; Taylor, 2011) that social-economic status (SES), such as household poverty, race, location, parents' educational background and other community factors, are also very highly correlated to learner performance.

Aside from the broader social-economic factors, constraints within the education system contribute to unequal learning outcomes. Many schools, especially in the rural and poor parts of the country, lack adequate infrastructure, facilities, materials and resources to facilitate effective teaching and learning. Schools attended by children from poor and working-class families are more likely to be staffed with unmotivated and ineffective teachers (Christie, Butler & Potterton, 2007; Deacon & Simkins, 2011; Taylor, 2011). Although the majority of South African educators have been trained under the post-1994 dispensation (CDE, 2011), there is evidence that suggests that many have poor content knowledge and weak pedagogical skills (Spaull, 2011; Taylor, 2009). Absenteeism, accountability, productivity and professionalism are serious concerns in the South African schooling system

(Chisholm, Hoadley, & Kivilu, 2005; NPC, 2011; Taylor, 2011) that extend from teachers and school managers all the way to the educational authorities at district and provincial level.

Notwithstanding the grim picture illustrated above, education has always been a high priority in South Africa's national development planning processes (NPC, 2012), as this is closely linked to other social and economic problems affecting the country. South Africa contributes 5-6% of its GDP every year to the education sector (OECD, 2008). The majority of financing has been undertaken by the government, which utilises around 20% of national budget and 30-50% of provincial budgets every year on education spending (National Treasury, 2015). Education remains a high priority in the Government's 2030 National Development Plan, as well as the Department of Basic Education Strategic Action Plans.

The private sector has also played a very prominent role in South Africa's education sector. Acknowledging the importance of a well-educated and capable young workforce for the success of businesses, the domestic corporate sector invests the largest portion of its social investments (around R3-5 billion a year) in education (Trialogue, 2015). Corporate social investments in South Africa's education sector are ten time larger than the aid provided by the traditional donors, such as DFID, GIZ, UN, and World Bank (Besharati, 2015). Numerous public-private partnerships, such as the Joint Education Trust (JET), the Business Trust, the National Business Initiative (NBI) and the latest National Education Collaboration Trust (NECT), have also been established to coordinate stakeholders in addressing the education challenges of the country.

Over the past two decades, national and provincial governments, foreign donors, private companies, foundations, NGOs and universities, have piloted and implemented a range of diverse initiatives to improve the situation of South Africa's education sector. Where resources have been limited, interventions have been typically narrower and more focused. Government and bigger donors, on the other hand, have often recognised the complexity and the multi-layered deficiencies in the education system; thus they have often taken on more comprehensive whole school development (WSD) programmes. These, however, have been fairly expensive initiatives and viewed by some as "scattered gun shot" (Bloch, 2009).

There is a growing body of research internationally that provides insights into what works to improve education (Conn, 2017; Glewwe et al., Hattie, 2009, 2014; Krishnaratne, White, & Carpenter, 2013; McEwan, 2015; Kim et al. 2019). What this literature shows is that there are numerous types of education interventions aimed at achieving a variety of outcomes. Some, like school feeding, might achieve a number of simultaneous objectives, such as incentivising enrolment/retention and improving nutrition – thus cognitive abilities of learners (i.e., Conn, 2017). While this literature is useful as a starting point, given the unique history and challenges of South African education, we need to build on evidence of what works to improve learning outcomes in South African schools.

The focus of the following meta-analysis, is the interventions specifically aimed at improving learning outcomes and achievement (Table 1). Eight categories of interventions have been defined for the purpose of conducting a systematic review of South Africa's education sector. These categories include interventions targeted directly at learners; teachers' development and incentives for teachers; the provision of educational materials; management and governance; school infrastructure; change in policies; interventions that attempt to provide integrated school reform. The typology is inevitably limiting, subjective and reductionist as these divisions are not as clear-cut as they appear to be, as most education programmes and policies operate in a complex manner and are often the combination of different interventions and approaches, and the interplay between them. The classification of interventions used in studies like this, can greatly affect the final results and conclusions of systematic reviews, as was found also by Evans and Popova (2015).

Table 2.1 *Categories of education interventions*

Learner-targeted support	Typically implemented by the private sector and civil society groups for a small group of selected learners, they consist of supplementary enrichment classes or tutoring by specialised teachers, often done after school hours, on weekends or during the school holidays. Another category of learner-focused interventions can be scholarships, bursaries and support to disadvantaged-but-promising learners to be placed in high-end schools or special courses.
Teacher development initiatives	Interventions implemented to address teacher quantity, quality and performance. This can include the provision of additional teachers and assistants for a short or long period of time. Teacher development is usually divided into pre-service (PRESET) training and in-service training (INSET). The latter consists of upgrading of qualifications, knowledge or skill-sets through different models of training implemented over weekends/evenings, school holidays or several months of block-release college/university programmes. Many teacher development programmes often also have a component of classroom visits, coaching, monitoring and experience sharing between participants.
Learning & teaching study material (LTSM)	Materials, technology and other resources provided to schools to enhance teaching and learning experience. Examples of such can be textbooks, workbooks, study guides, lesson plans, science-kits, computers, multi-media accessories, educational toys, reading books, etc.
Management & governance	Interventions aimed at strengthening school management and leadership, often done in the form of training and coaching of principals and school management teams (SMTs). These are often geared to putting new systems in place to improve school functionality and to promote accountability, efficiency and good governance. These can include the introduction of specific incentives and prizes for achievement and performance.
Infrastructure & facilities	The classical *hardware* investments, such as building, upgrading, expanding and refurbishing schools, classrooms, administration blocks, toilets, science labs, sporting facilities and libraries. Although not always as obvious as some of the above interventions, the atmosphere, cleanliness, size, lighting, order and other environmental aspects of a school can have an impact on the learning processes.

Structural reforms, policies & incentives	These are interventions aimed at improving the broader education systems that support the schools. These can include programmes for district development, introduction of specific language policy, systematisation of learner assessments, performance rewards, decentralisation of functions and other structural changes to improve management and accountability. These are normally interventions done by, or with, the government's Department of Education at national and sub-national level.
Community & family involvement	These acknowledge the important role parents and community play in the learning process inside and outside the formal schooling process. Such initiatives extend programme components to other non-school stakeholders and broader community actors. These include interventions aimed at strengthening school governing boards (SGBs), which often include parents and other local authorities.
Integrated School Development	These are complex multi-layered programmes that combine three or more of the above interventions into a holistic strategy to improve school functionality and, ultimately, learning results. These are usually organised in the form of whole school improvement models that are built on prior research and specific theoretical frameworks, piloted in a few areas and then scaled to many schools, with large injections of funding and cooperation of various partners.

Challenges in evaluating education interventions

In the past two decades, there has been an abundance of projects and initiatives implemented by different institutions to improve learning results in South African schools. Each of these interventions may have been evaluated with different methods and approaches, and with different degrees of rigour – thus successes or the failures of each programme have been reported in a very heterogeneous manner.

A number of evaluations undertaken in South Africa's education sector have utilised the case study approach (Mouton et al., 2013), often due to the limitations with data, methodological expertise, budget, time and context in which they were implemented. Although, in many cases, such studies were the only option, these still carried value and contributed knowledge to the field. Nonetheless, the bulk of South Africa's education evaluations relies heavily on qualitative approaches which, on one hand, provide depth, context and texture, but on the other hand, by nature, are more subjective and susceptible to bias and personal experiences of the evaluator, the client and the respondents (Bamberger, 2009). This poses questions with regard to the independence and scientific validity of many of the agency-commissioned evaluations (Roche & Kelly, 2005). Many of the education evaluations commissioned by funding agencies and corporate social investors (Trialogue, 2015), focus on the reporting of inputs (how much was spent), activities (what was done) and, occasionally, outputs of a programme (i.e. number of beneficiaries). Few evaluations are done looking at the impact of initiatives at the level of outcomes, such as real changes (behavioural, institutional, social-economic) in the recipient population. Evaluations capturing no or negative results of interventions often go unpublished or are concealed from public debate, while positive evaluations are used by donor and implementing agencies as marketing material. Because of their methodological heterogeneity, qualitative studies are also more difficult to compare between each other and assess against a common scale.

The quantitative education evaluations have utilised statistical indicators to empirically measure and compare change in outcome of interest, most commonly *learner achievement* (Schollar, 2015). This is traditionally measured through the indicators of *test scores* or *pass rates*. In South Africa, most learning assessments are designed and implemented by experienced evaluation and research organisations, such as the Human Sciences Research Council, JET Education Services and Eric Schollar and Associates. Some researchers, however, prefer to use state-run standardised universal learner assessments, such as National Senior Certificate examination results and Annual National Assessment (ANA) results (for 2011 to 2014).

Like much of the developing world, most education evaluations in South Africa have been non-experimental. Many studies, popularly referred to as impact evaluations, are actually case studies, where beneficiary outcomes are observed only after the intervention. More advanced evaluations conduct baselines and are able to measure change before and after intervention, but these are relatively rare (Bamberger, Rao, & Woolcock, 2010). Some studies have gone to the extent of creating a comparison group and, in best-case scenarios, have measured pre- and post-results of both programme and control group. A range of literature also exists in South Africa (i.e., Fleisch, 2006; Gustafsson, 2007; Hunt et al., 2010; Simkins & Paterson, 2005; Van der Berg, 2008) that utilises more complex econometric models to control for different variables and estimate effects of interventions, school and community factors on learning outcomes.

In the past decade, there has been a rise in the use of experimental approaches for the evaluation of education interventions in developing countries (Duflo, Glennerster & Kremer, 2008; McEwan, 2014) and also in South Africa (i.e. Fleisch et al., 2011; Louw, Muller & Tredoux, 2008; Schollar, 2015; Taylor & Watson, 2013). However, randomised control trials (RCTs) often face ethical, political and practical constraints, as they need to be built in at the design stage in the beginning of an intervention. Impact evaluations of South African government policies have been difficult to conduct as interventions have often been rolled out in all schools of the country, leaving no space for a counterfactual. This challenge was encountered, for instance, by Coetzee and Van der Berg (2012), as they attempted to evaluate the impact of South Africa's school nutrition programme.

Because of the above constraints, what has dominated much of the impact evaluations in South Africa's education sector has been the use of descriptive and quasi-experimental approaches. By and large, the most common counterfactual evaluations used in South Africa's education sector have been the combination of Difference-In-Difference (DID) designs, with some form of matching techniques – including Propensity Score Matching (PSM; Besharati, 2014; Hobden & Hobden,

2009).[2] Other South African researchers have tried to emulate RCTs, by using other evaluation approaches, such as natural experiments (Gustafsson & Taylor, 2013) or cut-off point design (Fleisch & Schoer, 2014; Fleisch et al., 2016).

In South Africa, government agencies, private philanthropies and academia have tried to address the deficiencies in the education sector by reviewing the evidence emerging from the numerous policies and programmes implemented over the years. The JET Education Services, a not-for-profit education agency established in the early 1990s, has been one of the forerunners in the use of research and evaluation to inform education programming in South Africa. Zenex Foundation, a prominent education grant-maker committed to evidence-based programming, commissioned education evaluators (Roberts & Schollar, 2006) to conduct a meta-evaluation on the interventions aimed at improving language, mathematics and science learning outcomes in South Africa. A similar follow-up review on the Zenex-funded school programmes was conducted again by the same authors in 2011. Building on some of their previous scholarly work, Taylor, Fleisch and Schindler (2008) conducted a review for the Presidency on the changes in South Africa's education system since 1994. In the same year, the Organisation for Economic Cooperation and Development (OECD) conducted a large review of national education policies implemented in South Africa (OECD, 2008).

In more recent years, Sayed, Kanjee and Nkomo (2013) published a review of some of the most prominent programmes to improve the quality of education in South Africa, compiling lessons learnt from the Education Quality Improvement Partnership (EQUIP), the District Development Support Programme (DDSP), IMBEWU I and II, Quality Learning Programme (QLP), Learning for Living (LfL), the Integrated Education Programme (IEP) and the Khanyisa School Development Programme.

One of the most comprehensive review efforts in South Africa's education literature was conducted by Mouton et al. (2013) in order to inform the Zenex Foundation of the next phase of school development programming. The review synthesised evidence from hundreds of evaluation reports, journal articles, books and previous meta-evaluations that looked at the effectiveness of education development programmes. The report provided the Foundation with a framework to analyse the literature and make evidence-based decisions on their future school development programme. As part of the review, Mouton et al. (2013) provided an evaluation framework which illustrated the range of studies that spanned from experimental, theory-based evaluations (TBE) to case studies. Although containing

---

[2] DID is a design technique that approximates an experimental design by measuring the differential effects of a treatment between two groups but in a natural experiment. PSM is a technique that allows a researcher to calculate an effect of an intervention by comparing two groups, one having received the intervention compared with one that did not by matching the groups on key variables.

many elements of systematic reviews, Mouton et al.'s review (2013) did not strictly follow the systematic review protocols outlined by the Campbell Collaboration, or by the PRISMA (www.prisma-statement.org) for systematic reviews. Mouton's review included quality appraisal of the primary studies, identifying these as "credible" and "moderately credible" to draw out evidence and lessons to inform future programming. The approach Mouton used could best be characterised as a narrative review, as it provided qualitative analysis, depth, texture, context and elaboration on the *mechanisms of change* of school development in South Africa. Mouton et al.'s review did not, however, provide an empirical comparator between impact results (i.e., effect sizes) from the different evaluation studies, therefore making it more difficult for policy-makers and investors to assess the most cost-effective among the competing options. In order to take Mouton et al.'s (2013) review a step further, the following chapter presents a systematic meta-analysis of the major education interventions implemented in South Africa from 1994 to 2017, integrating statistical analysis of effect sizes with qualitative analysis of the interventions and the evaluations conducted on them.

Method

Multiple Treatment Meta-Analysis
In the following review, aimed at comparing effectiveness of different types of education programmes implemented in South Africa, a specific type of methodological approach multiple treatment meta-analysis (MTMA) was used. MTMA has been elaborated upon by statisticians such as Caldwell (2005), Lu and Ades (2006) and Salanti (2012), and applied also in other meta-analyses of education interventions in developing countries (Conn, 2017; McEwan, 2015).

In contrast to standard meta-analysis, multi-treatment meta-analysis assesses and compares different types of interventions aimed at achieving the same outcome (i.e. improved learner results). This method helps to answer policy questions and assists decision-makers when there are multiple options on what investments to make and which type of interventions to favour. In MTMA, heterogeneity is expected, therefore a random effects model that excludes the calculation of the average pooled effect size, is used (Figure 2.2).

Individual impact evaluations of different interventions are tested against different populations, which can be more or less responsive to the treatment (Cranney et al., 2002), depending on context, time and other factors. One key feature of MTMA is that it tries to emulate a large multi-treatment experiment by utilising a common control group. Comparisons are made through observational means, by assessing one intervention in relationship to another intervention, or a null situation. This model is based on the assumption that the comparator used to assess the effectiveness of the various interventions is somewhat similar and consistent. In our particular case the common control group is South African public schools running business as usual and affected by the same social, economic, political and environmental factors present in the country. Although the various experimental evaluations have occurred in the same country's educational system, it needs to be acknowledged that the contexts do vary, based on the provincial/local characteristics and the historical period in which the intervention and the evaluation occurred. Figure 2.1 presents a graphic illustration of the MTMA that was conducted in this study.

In line with standard practice (Campbell, 2015; http://www.prisma-statement .org), the following MTMA of South Africa's education sector was conducted by multiple reviewers, following all the key steps of standard systematic reviews and meta-analyses. It is elaborated upon in more detail in the succeeding sections.

Systematic review protocol

Inclusion criteria. The studies that were included in the following systematic review met these specifications:

- **Study designs.** Rigorously performed experimental and quasi-experimental impact evaluations, ideally with pre- and post-measures for both treatment and control groups. Sample sizes were relatively large to allow for enough statistical power of the results.
- **Participants.** Only studies conducted in South Africa's schooling sector, both primary and secondary phases (grades 1 to 12), post-1994. Both programme and control groups consisted of learners or schools from South Africa. This was to ensure a certain level of consistency with regard to context, social, economic, political, and systematic confounders.
- **Interventions.** Any type of interventions aimed at improving learning outcomes. These ranged from teachers-based, learner-focused materials and resources, management- or system-oriented, whole school development. See Table 2.1.
- **Outcomes.** Learner achievement, measured through test-scores or pass-rates. Particular focus was given to the domains of language, mathematics and science, but other learning results were also included.

Identification strategy

As with any systematic review, the study endeavoured to uncover all the published and unpublished materials in order to reveal studies that would meet the above requirements. These included academic papers, journal articles and research and evaluation reports from government, corporations, NGOs and consultants – and any other grey literature or papers hidden in "file drawers".

Search terms and key words utilised included: *impact, *evaluation, *South Africa, *education, *effects, *learning, *achievement, *mathematics, *science, *language, *programme, *outcome, *projects, *school, *teacher, *numeracy, *literacy – or a combination of these.

In the literature search the following sources[3] were consulted:

- databases and libraries of specialised agencies;
- academic databases and journals;
- collegial networks and informal communication with prominent evaluators and researchers in South Africa's education sector;
- other South African reviews, meta-evaluations, primary studies and edited books; and
- previous international reviews and meta-analyses on education in developing countries.

Appraising quality and bias in the studies

Once all the studies that met the inclusion criteria had been identified and short-listed from the literature, one of the most complex tasks was to decide on their quality. The subsequent exercise was the screening of individual evaluations on methodological rigour and design quality, to decide whether they should be included, or not, in the meta-analysis. The tension always lies between not leaving out any useful and important piece of evidence, while also making sure that a few bad studies do not negatively influence the overall findings of the meta-analysis (Hombrados & Waddington, 2012). In deciding which studies are methodologically sound, careful assessments needed to be made about internal and external validity, construct measures and statistical errors.

In the medical field, meta-analyses restrict themselves almost entirely to rigorously implemented RCTs. In the social sciences and in education policy, however, as discussed earlier, the field is dominated by quasi-experiments, which can present numerous different threats to validity and risk of biases. These can be mitigated if treatment/control allocation rules are clear (Hansen et al., 2011), selection bias has been appropriately addressed and programme implementation and causality are carefully controlled. Whether big or small, any bias, assumptions, errors or problems in a particular study need to be carefully examined and reported, so that these can be taken into account in the meta-analysis and used as controls in the subsequent sensitivity and moderator analysis.

More than 50 different threats to validity exist in both experimental and quasi-experimental studies, but, in the current meta-analysis on the interventions in South Africa's education sector, the following aspects have been given special attention in the evaluation quality appraisal process:

---

[3] For a detailed list of sources, refer to Bisharati (2017).

- **Selection bias.** If the counterfactual is not strong, or if programme and control group are practically and significantly different. The experiment therefore becomes compromised from the start.
- **Implementation bias.** If the programme was not implemented correctly according to plan, or if the two groups received essentially different treatments from different service providers. Implementation bias can also include spillover between treatment and control group and contamination of the samples by other interventions.
- **Data and testing bias.** If a large portion of the data is unreliable, inaccurate or missing. Large amount of attrition occurring, or no-show of participants between pre- and post-tests. This can also include the presence of ceiling effects or floor effect in the data-gathering process.
- **Evaluator bias.** If the authors of the evaluation had a conflict of interest (political or financial), were directly involved in the implementation of the programme and might have had a vested interest in the results of the study. This compromises the independence of the study.
- **Motivational bias.** If there is a strong presence of Hawthorne or John Henry effect, where the participants of either the treatment or control group behave differently, as they are conscious of being observed and have a vested interest in the results of the evaluation.

In education evaluation there is often a tension between trying to avoid selection biases and contamination biases. To allow for similar characteristics in programme and control groups, schools and learners are often matched based on proximity of location; however, this can also increase the likelihood of control participants taking advantage of the intervention when they are not supposed to. These challenges have also been illustrated by Schollar (2015) in his RCT of the Primary Math Research Project (PMRP) in Limpopo Province. These highlight again the many practical and ethical complications of conducting experimental evaluations in real-life scenarios, such as in the education policy field.

Many tools and instruments, developed by many organisations conducting systematic reviews, exist to assess risk of bias; however, rating studies are generally very controversial, subjective and discouraged as a source of reliable quality assessment (Conn, 2017; Wilson et al., 2011). Assessing the quality of studies ultimately remains a judgement call based on the expertise of the reviewer, both in statistics and the content matter. Having acknowledged all the limitations, this systematic review used an adapted version of the Cochrane risk of bias tool (Higgins et al, 2011). After a careful assessment by the review team, each study was rated against the five major bias areas discussed above. A score, from 1 (minimum) to 5 (critical), was assigned to each study, signalling the degree of bias and problems detected.

Most of the studies that were included in this meta-analysis had pre- and post-scores for both treatment and control groups, allowing them all to integrate the DID method in the evaluation design. The consistent use of the double difference method reduced some of the biases by combining the time variable (before and after) with the counterfactual variable (participants and non-participants). Any inherent differences between programme and control groups, because of observed or unobserved differences, was significantly reduced, assuming that these differences remained constant over time (Blum, Krishnan, & Legovini, 2010). This is the case with most studies and interventions included in this meta-analysis, as the learner population was affected by the same systemic and external influences in the same country during the same period of time.

Data extraction and follow-up. The effect size, which was used in this meta-analysis, is Hedge's g, which is an enhanced version of the *standardised mean difference (SMD)* and *Cohen's d*. To compute this effect size, what is essentially required is mean scores, standard deviations and the sample sizes for both treatment and control groups in both pre- and post-tests (as most of our primary studies were DIDs). These statistics also allow for the calculation of the confidence intervals and standard errors for each effect size.

In many studies, the sample sizes of the participants would not be the same in the pre- and post-tests, because of learner attrition, thus posing a threat to validity in the implementation of the experiment. Other times, pre- and post-tests were not done with the same cohort of participants, but rather longitudinally with the same grade level. In such cases, the reviewers decided either to use the average sample sizes, or to use only the values from the individuals that appeared in both pre- and post-tests. These situations are explained when discussing the merits of each individual evaluation design (see Besharati, 2016). When experimental studies were conducted using cluster sampling techniques (i.e. randomising at school or class level), standard errors and confidence intervals of effect sizes were adjusted, taking into account the clusters, to ensure more precision and fair estimates of results in the comparative meta-analysis.

The required statistics were reported in their entirety in only some of the studies that were reviewed. In most of the cases, the standard deviations were not reported, therefore the reviewers had to contact the original authors to request the missing data. At other times, standard deviations would be re-calculated manually, by going through the raw data provided by the author of the primary study. Following up with the original authors also provided the reviewers with an opportunity to seek further clarification on the evaluations, the interventions and other important details of the studies. Except for the Dinaledi evaluation, which was conducted by World Bank economists based in Washington DC, following up with the original authors on clarifications and data requests was relatively easy, as they were all based in South Africa and easily accessible through informal e-mail, telephone communication and face-to-face discussion.

The data collection and data cleaning; the risk of bias rating; and the coding of the various studies was conducted by a team of reviewers (the primary researcher and two research assistants) to allow for double-checking of the accuracy of all the data throughout the process. In some complex situations, the reviewers had to debate how to handle a particular case and take decisions on which data to use. Once the required statistics were checked and extracted from all the studies, effect sizes and confidence intervals were calculated utilising Comprehensive Meta-Analysis (CMA) statistical software package.

For a couple of studies, numerous attempts were made to contact the original authors of the papers to seek the missing statistics. However, no response was received and these studies unfortunately had to be excluded from the meta-analysis.

Results

Qualitative overview of studies and interventions

At the end of the systematic literature search, the eligibility screening and data extraction phases, the review yielded a grand total of 35 studies, 37 interventions and 165 effect sizes (Table S1 online only), based on impact measured against different learning outcomes (language, mathematics, science, etc.), or within different sub-groups (i.e. classes, cohorts, years, locations, testing instruments, intervention combination and dosage). Similar to McEwan's (2014) and Conn's (2017) reviews of education interventions, many experimental evaluations included in this meta-analysis had multiple treatment arms. Each primary study, in fact, reported anything from 1 to 21 effect sizes. If an intervention had more than one effect size due to different learning outcomes or sub-groups being assessed, these were each calculated separately and the cases would be identified: for instance as Plus-Time A, Plus-Time B, Plus-Time C, and so forth. Some studies assessed more than one intervention (i.e., Baumgartner et al., 2012; Besharati, 2014; Taylor et al., 2017) and a number of studies were also found for the same intervention.

It is interesting to note that, of the 301 impact studies on education interventions in low- and middle-income countries captured in the six international reviews discussed by Evans and Popova (2015), only one of the South African studies listed above (Louw et al., 2008) was found in only two of the international reviews (Conn, 2017; Glewwe & al., 2014). This points to a serious publication bias present in most international systematic reviews, that gives more prominence to academic studies conducted by Northern scholars (Conn, 2017). The international education reviews, conducted between 2013 and 2016, appear to have overlooked a large portion of the knowledge produced locally in South Africa, which is often published as evaluation reports by governmental, research and private education agencies active in the sector.

For analytical purposes, all the interventions included in this review have been grouped into (a) government programmes and policies; (b) private sector projects; and (c) academic experiments. The full report of the systematic review (Besharati, 2016) contains a detailed narrative section discussing the various South African education programmes and policies. It also includes a commentary on the quality, strength, weaknesses and limitations of the studies that were conducted for each of the interventions. For each of the primary studies, the potential biases and threats to validity are discussed and the methodological quality of the evaluation is rated, based on the risk of bias scale discussed earlier.

Some of the studies had substantial risk of bias and other methodological problems that precluded them from being included in the subsequent quantitative meta-analysis. A further screening of the above studies was conducted to exclude any evaluation that had high (4) or critical risk of bias (5). This left only the well-implemented RCTs and strong quasi-experimental studies, such as the ones using RDD, PSM or other techniques that took care of selection bias. Evaluations with credible results were normally conducted with large samples and therefore had low standard errors and small confidence intervals.

The screening process now left the meta-analysis with *26 credible studies of 28 different interventions*, which covered overall *110 different effect sizes*, as the main cases and units of analysis. This allowed for a legitimate comparison of results that had a certain level of reliability, and of studies and interventions that were placed on the same level plane, with similar contexts and evaluation parameters.

The funnel plot (Figure 2.1) illustrates the effect sizes against the sampling errors in all the studies in the meta-analysis, once the ones with high risk of bias had been removed. From the funnel plot, we can see that most studies are at the top, therefore the majority of the results reported are statistically significant, although some studies, with a standard error below 0,1, provide slightly less reliable results than the evaluations done with larger sample sizes.

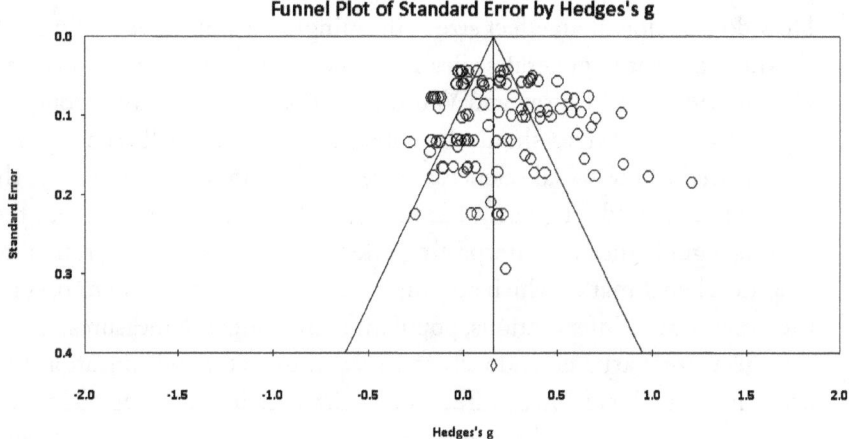

Figure 2.1 *Funnel plot SA education meta-analysis*

Funnel plots normally help in assessing the degree of publication bias. However, we can also see that there is a similar number of South African studies that show positive, as well as negative, effects on both sides of the zero effect line. The symmetrical nature of the funnel plot highlights that both studies reporting negative results, as well as positive results, were captured in this meta-analysis and thus there is a fairly limited presence of publication bias. There are, however, a number of major outliers at the right hand side of the plot, which indicate extremely and unusually high effect sizes. Most of these cases emerge from Schollar's evaluations (2002, 2005, 2014, 2015), therefore results from these studies need to be assessed with more caution.

Interpreting the effect sizes

Once all the studies included in the review were systematically screened for quality and appropriately short-listed, the statistical meta-analysis could begin through the aid of CMA software. The results of meta-analyses are normally represented through forest plots that illustrate effect sizes of the various treatments, together with their respective confidence intervals, which is reflective of their standard error. The statistical results of the South African education meta-analysis produced a grand total of 110 effects sizes, ranging from interventions with a lowest (negative) Hedge's g of *-0,28* to a highest of *+1,21*.

While researchers are concerned with statistical significance, policy-makers are interested in educational significance and with the magnitude of the impact. The effect sizes give an indication to non-academic readers, policy-makers, investors and the general public as to whether the interventions have a substantial and practical impact on real-life population outcomes. The question is whether the effect of an education intervention is large enough to warrant replication, transferability to public policy, extension and scale to the rest of the district, province or country. How do we know if an effect size is meaningful or not for education policy?

There are some general scales introduced by meta-analysis experts, such as Cohen (1988) and Lipsey and Wilson (2001), which provide a rough indication of whether effect sizes should be considered big or small. These guidelines are widely used in the social sciences; however, they are merely a 'rule of thumb' and should not be used religiously. Bloom et al. (2008) argue, in fact, that there are no universal guidelines for interpreting effect sizes. They suggest, rather, to develop empirical benchmarks, which are contextualised in relationship to past research on the same type of interventions, population and outcome measures.

Effect sizes vary tremendously from sector to sector and education programmes are known to have lower effect sizes than in other fields (McEwan, 2014). Different education analysts argue that interventions need to be taken seriously in the policy space, once they demonstrate effect sizes over 0,25 (Coe, 2002), 0,4 (Hattie, 2009) and 0,59 (Marzano, 2003). What has also become clear is that different magnitudes of effect can be expected from different types of education interventions, with learner-targeted one-to-one tutoring, for example, producing much bigger effect sizes than whole school development programmes (Slavin & Smith, 2009).

The way evaluations are conducted and the methodologies that are used also matter greatly in meta-analysis. Lipsey et al. (2012) have, for example, discovered that impact studies using researcher self-developed testing instruments tend to yield higher effect sizes than evaluations which use broad standardised state-run assessments (such as the South African NSC exams). Whether RCTs or other quasi-experimental techniques are used could also have an influence on the results achieved during an impact evaluation.

When conducting experiments in the education sector, Bloom et al. (2008) have also highlighted that effect magnitude may vary depending on the school levels in which the programmes have been implemented. The education and child developmental literature (Bloom et al., 2008) shows that, even in the absence of an intervention, a child is expected to improve his or her learning abilities year after year as a natural course of life.

Although these effect sizes may change in different countries and social contexts – and with different subject outcomes being assessed, the trajectory of learning is clearly the same, where larger gains occur at lower grades and at younger ages while less learning occurs at older ages and at the end of the formal schooling process. This also highlights, again, the importance of using appropriate control groups and good counterfactual evaluation when assessing the impact of interventions in the education sector, in order not to be misled by large learning gains occurring anyway in early grades of the schooling system (i.e., Fleisch et al., 2015).

Context, population, and learning outcomes all play a major role in affecting the results of impact studies and meta-analyses. The vast majority of field experiments and systematic reviews in the education sector are still conducted in the United States and in the industrialised world. Thus, one of the best ways to benchmark the results from the South African impact evaluations is to assess the results against one another, as these were all implemented under similar circumstances and population contexts.

Clemens, Radelet and Bhavnani (2004) also explain that the time at which the impact of the intervention is measured can make a significant difference in the magnitude of the effect. Most interventions measure large effect sizes, during and shortly after they are implemented, due to the excitement and attention given to the beneficiaries during the project life-span (Schollar, 2013). But, several years after the project has finished, a natural process of *decay* or *compound* is expected to occur (Harris, 2009), therefore impact can look very different if measured in the short-term (right after the intervention), medium-term or long-term (several years later). Almost all the effect sizes included in this meta-analysis have been measured at the end of the final year the intervention was administered. The only exception was in Schollar (2015), where the effect size of the PMRP workbooks was measured also three years later (in 2010), with effects of the programme still high, though lower than when measured right after the treatment was provided in 2007.

From the preliminary results of this South African education meta-analysis, we can see that the same intervention (PMRP workbooks) evaluated with the same technique (RCT) in two different studies yield strikingly opposite results, where the *Back to the Basics Workbooks* feature in the same meta-analysis (see forest plot above) as the top most impactful intervention, as well as the third least effective among the 110 effect sizes reviewed. This specific case will be discussed in more detail later in the paper, but overall this goes to further prove that evaluation design and context does matter a lot and effect sizes within a meta-analysis can be confounded by many other factors beyond the simple treatment intervention.

Exploring heterogeneity through moderator analysis

Having acknowledged that effect size is highly contingent on population and study design, it may not be appropriate to accept the results of the meta-analysis at face value. What would possibly be more useful is to explore, in more depth, the heterogeneity within these effects, so as to better understand which interventions seem to be most impactful within specific contexts and circumstances.

In the early stages of the review, all studies that met the inclusion criteria were subsequently coded one-by-one: on the characteristics of the interventions of the population, on the outcome measures and on the evaluation design. Each of these elements would potentially become *predictor variables*, or what is known in meta-analysis as *moderators*, which would be used to analyse heterogeneity in results. The various moderators would be statistically analysed to see if they had any influence on the effect sizes (as well as the standard errors) emerging from the studies.

To the extent possible, the reviewers tried to code as many moderators as possible in numerical format to allow for regression analysis. Some binary categorical variables could be converted into dummy variables, but others had to remain in categorical format and better analysed through ANOVA and sub-group analysis. Data was entered, checked and organised – first in Microsoft Excel and later into SPSS and CMA – for more complex analyses. The variables coded as part of the review are illustrated in Table S2 (online only), with the right column of the table providing an example from the Besharati (2014) study.

Once all the outcome, intervention, context and evaluation variables were appropriately coded for each study in the meta-analysis, meta-regression, meta-ANOVA and sub-group analysis were used in order to conduct a more in-depth moderator analysis. The next sections will present and discuss the results of this exploration.

Meta-regression and meta-ANOVA

The first step in the moderator analysis was to conduct a meta-regression to observe which of the many studies, interventions and contextual variables (listed in Table 2.4) had a strong influence on the meta-analysis results. Previous education systematic reviews by Conn (2017) and McEwan (2014), which conducted meta-regression as part of moderator analysis, have also highlighted that effect sizes may vary significantly once you control for other factors (simultaneous treatments, intervention features, context, methodology).

When conducting a meta-regression, all the same assumptions, checks and rules which apply to a normal multivariate regression also need to be taken into consideration: large samples, linearity, normality, multi-collinearity, independence of cases, homoscedasticity. As explained previously, the meta-analysis contained 110 valid cases of effect sizes extracted from 26 high-quality studies of 28 interventions. If the meta-regression was conducted using the interventions or studies as the unit of analysis, these would possibly be too small a sample to yield enough statistical power to infer conclusions. Also, the various effect sizes reported in each study were referring to different outcome measures and, therefore, would not be appropriate to collapse under one average effect size per study.

On the other hand, if the meta-regression is conducted at the level of effect sizes (n=110), there would be more statistical power; however, a lot of key assumptions of regression analysis could be violated. In our South African meta-analysis, one study cluster may yield anything from 1 to 21 effect sizes. This means that the effect sizes are actually *nested* within the studies and therefore may suffer from the same standard errors, sampling, biases, quality concerns and variations caused by context and methodological design. The individual cases used in the regression model are therefore not independent, but, in fact, strongly correlated with other cases from the same study cluster.

Considering this challenge, a separate meta-regression was conducted using both effect sizes and studies as units of analysis. If results were consistent across the two levels, one could safely deduce that a certain moderator had a strong influence on the results of the meta-analysis. Considering the rule of thumb that the relationship between cases and variables in a regression should be roughly 1 to 10, the reviewers decided to test only 1 or 2 moderators at a time to explore if there was a significant and substantive correlation of the variable to the effect sizes. Meta-regression functions were available in Comprehensive Meta-Analysis version 3 (CMA3), which facilitated the exploration.

When doing the analysis with the 110 *non-independent* effect sizes, the study variables named 'test instrument', 'units of analysis', 'matched cohorts', 'counterfactual IE method' and 'statistical significance' link to Hedge's g. This, however, would not be clear when the analysis was conducted at the level of studies (possibly due to low statistical power). The only variable that yielded statistically significant correlation to the effect size in both levels of analysis was 'grade of assessment'. The results were almost identical in both models. Table S3 (online only) presents the results from the regression conducted on the 110 effect sizes using 'grade of assessment' as the predictor variable.

From the regression results, we can observe that the grade in which the learning assessments are conducted has a clear negative correlation with the effect size and this is also statistically significant. This explains at least some of the variances between the studies. This is also clearly illustrated in the scatter plot of Hedge's g by grade of assessment (Figure 2.3), which shows that all studies regress along the same slope (black line) and are all contained within the same prediction interval (blue lines). The only outliers are the effect sizes from the Schollar (2015) study, which had previously been flagged to produce exceptionally high results.

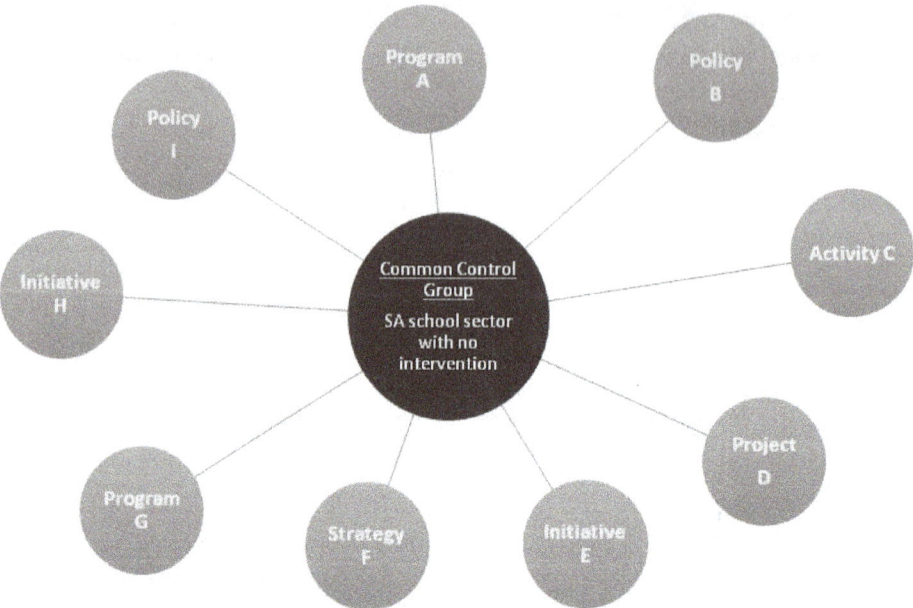

Figure 2.2 *Graphical illustration of SA education Multi-Treatment Meta-analysis (MTMA)*

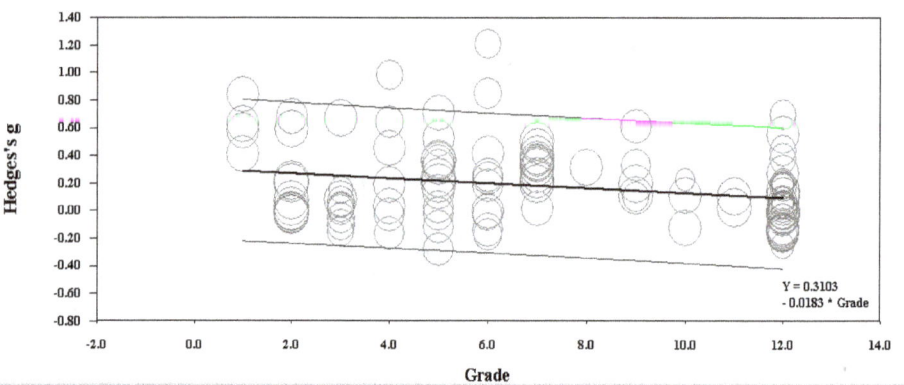

Figure 2.3 *Regression of effect size on school grade*

The finding from our meta-regression gives further evidence to the general education theories and the meta-analytical consideration, raised by Bloom et al. (2008), that the higher the school grades in which the intervention occurs (and thus also where the learning assessments are conducted), the lower the effect sizes are to be expected. For the education policy debates, these findings further strengthen the call for more interventions to be conducted in the earlier years of schooling for more impact to be expected on learner achievement.

The meta-regression technique was useful to assess the correlation of continuous numerical variables on the outcome variable of effect size. However, there are also some moderators which are dichotomous or categorical, which are worth exploring using other techniques analogous to the analysis of variance (ANOVA). This is commonly conducted in meta-analysis as part of the analysis of heterogeneity.

We have seen earlier that certain parameters from the evaluation design could have potentially played a role in influencing the magnitude of the impact. The researcher decided, therefore, to test if there is a significant difference in the effect sizes of the various studies, depending on the methodological framework that was used in the evaluation. As discussed earlier, there was an indication that 'counterfactual IE method', 'assessment instrument', 'units of analysis' and 'matched cohorts' could have influenced the magnitude of the impact results. A variance test was conducted of the methodological parameters used throughout the various studies. In a similar way to an ANOVA test, a heterogeneity test was performed using Q-value statistics to analyse variance of different sub-groups of studies within the meta-analysis.

What is evident from Table 2.3 is that all of the moderators of methodology (impact evaluation technique, units of analysis, test instrument, the use of pre- and post-matched cohorts), produced significantly different results within the meta-analysis, therefore a portion of the heterogeneity in the effect sizes is derived by the above variables and not just by the intervention itself. These results further confirm some of the findings of Lipsey et al. (2012): that impact studies generally report larger effects when researcher-developed test instruments (versus state assessments) are used to measure outcomes and analysis is conducted at learner level, rather than school level. As expected, larger effect sizes were also linked to statistical significance, though this was often dependent on the standard error and sampling process. To further reduce the amount of effect sizes under observation, the reviewers decided to focus only on the *55 statistically significant results* in the meta-analysis, where the confidence intervals of Hedge's g didn't include zero.

As demonstrated before in the meta-regression, the grade in which the learning assessments are conducted has a substantial and significant influence on the effect size. With the same logic, interventions conducted in lower phases of the South African school system should also report a larger impact than those occurring at the later stages of school grades. This assumption was tested again using the same ANOVA-like heterogeneity test on the 55 statistically significant Hedge's g, with the results illustrated in Table 2.4.

Just as before, with regression on grade of assessment, the pattern is unmistakable. The lower the phases of the school system in which interventions occur, the higher the impact observed on learning outcomes. Even with a limited number of studies and effect sizes, the analysis above proves that the school phase is statistically and substantially significant in predicting the impact of the interventions.

As much as these meta-regressions provide some useful indications about the various factors that influence effect size, the results above need to be interpreted with caution, as they are based on a fairly limited number of cases which violate some of the key regression assumptions. As discussed earlier, the 110 effect sizes under analysis are not completely independent, as they are correlated with one another within each study group. Nonetheless, it is clear that grade and school level in which the evaluation is conducted does clearly have an effect on the results of education impact studies. From the coefficient estimate, one can also see that there is a negative correlation – as the school phase increases the Hedge's g reported in the impact study tends to decrease.

Sub-group analysis

Having established that heterogeneity in effect sizes, the second phase involved a sub-group analysis. Rather than asking which is the most effective intervention to improve learning outcomes in South African schools, it is more appropriate to continue the investigation asking when, where and how are education interventions effective?

The forest plots (Figures 2.4-2.5) break down the results of the meta-analysis according to the different learning areas, intervention types and implementing agencies. This provides useful insights for policy-makers and investors who need to make decisions about which interventions to design, invest and support in different contexts of South Africa's education sector.[4]

From the subject sub-group analysis (Figures 2.4-2.5), one can observe that literacy and numeracy interventions have a greater impact on learner achievement when implemented in earlier grades in primary schools, such as in the case of Back to the Basics (B2B), COUNT, Gauteng Primary Language and Maths Strategy (GPLMS), Integrated Education Program (IEP), and sJsK Literacy Project. Learning interventions on sciences and other subjects taught at higher stages of the schooling system register a much lower impact than learning occurring in language and mathematics in lower grades. The Dinaledi (Figure 2.6) and the Epoch & Optima Programme (Figure 2.5), however, emerge as exceptional cases in which interventions at high school level produce substantial effects on science and maths learning - even when utilising grade 12 NSC assessments, which are known to normally yield relatively small effect sizes.

What seems to have a significant impact on high school pass rates and test scores is the introduction of additional teachers, assistants and human resources in order to improve educator-learner ratios, reduce class sizes, offer extra remedial

---

[4] Depending on the range of effects registered in each sub-group, forest plot scales have been adjusted from *(-1/+1)* to *(-2/+2)* accordingly, for example, with the inclusion of the Schollar (2015) results which include effect sizes above *+1,0*. As seen earlier, grade and school phase are very prominent factors influencing effect size; therefore from this point forward they will be included among the descriptive identifiers in the next sub-group analyses.

Intervention	Study	Learning Outcome	Gr. Phase	Hedges's g	Standard error
GPLMS A	Fleisch & Schoer (2014)	English	03 - Prim	0.669	0.076
Learning for Living A	Schollar (2005)	English - Read	05 - Prim	0.371	0.051
Learning for Living G Ch 3-7	Schollar (2005)	English - Read	07 - Prim	0.362	0.056
Learning for Living B	Schollar (2005)	English - Write	05 - Prim	0.360	0.054
Learning for Living D	Schollar (2005)	English - Read	07 - Prim	0.348	0.057
EQUIP C Ch 5-7	Schollar (2002)	English	07 - Prim	0.334	0.101
Plus Time A	Prinsloo (2009)	English FAL	09 - Sec	0.329	0.150
EQUIP E	Schollar (2002)	English	05 - Prim	0.316	0.101
Learning for Living E	Schollar (2005)	English - Write	07 - Prim	0.229	0.060
Learning for Living H Ch 3-7	Schollar (2005)	English - Write	07 - Prim	0.196	0.058
RCUP A	Fleisch, Taylor S, et al (2015)	Literacy - ANA	04 - Prim	0.189	0.095
Quality Learning Project A	Prinsloo & Kanjee (2005)	English	09 - Sec	0.112	0.062

Figure 2.4 *Impact of interventions to improve language abilities*

classes and generally provide more time for, and attention to, the individual learners, as illustrated by the findings emerging from the Besharati (2014) study on secondary school interventions in North West and Limpopo provinces, as well as from the evaluations of the Dinaledi schools (Blum et al., 2010), Plus Time (Prinsloo, 2009) and the Epoch & Optima Trusts Maths Challenge Programme (Schollar & Mouton, 2014).

Forest plots, in Figures 2.7-2.8, analyse the effect sizes of some of the most popular types of interventions frequently implemented in South Africa, such as the provision of LTSMs, teacher-development programmes and integrated school development. It needs to be noted that most programmes of LTSM provision in South Africa (i.e. READ, GPLMS, B2B, EGRS) are structured pedagogic programmes (Snilstveit et al., 2016), with multiple components – including teacher training and coaching.

The most striking finding from the forest plot on LTSMs (Figure 2.7) is that Back to the Basics (B2B) workbooks appear as the most effective, as well as one of the least effective, educational support materials for grade 6 pupils in South Africa. Two well-performed RCTs by two different authors (Fleisch et al., 2010; Schollar, 2015) evaluating the same intervention, which supposedly was implemented in a similar manner, led one study to conclude that the workbooks have a phenomenal effect size of *+1,21* and the other to report a disappointing effect size of *-0,17*. At first, a reader will interpret this drastic difference in the results as possibly caused by the different provincial contexts (rural Limpopo versus urban Gauteng), but

Intervention	Study	Learning Outcome	Gr. Phase	Hedges's g	Standard error
B2B Workbooks D (high dose)	Scholar (2013)	Math	06 - Prim	1.210	0.185
B2B Workbooks C (high dose)	Scholar (2013)	Math	04 - Prim	0.982	0.177
B2B Workbooks B	Scholar (2013)	Math	06 - Prim	0.849	0.161
EQUIP F	Scholar (2002)	Math	05 - Prim	0.705	0.103
E&O Math Challenge A	Scholar & Mouton (2014)	Math 30%	12 - Sec	0.698	0.176
COUNT Family Math A	SAIDE (2007)	Math	02 - Prim	0.688	0.115
B2B Workbooks A	Scholar (2013)	Math	04 - Prim	0.645	0.155
Plus Time C	Prinsloo (2009)	Math	09 - Sec	0.610	0.124
EQUIP D Ch 5-7	Scholar (2002)	Math	07 - Prim	0.468	0.102
E&O Math Challenge B	Scholar & Mouton (2014)	Math 50%	12 - Sec	0.436	0.173
EQUIP B Ch 4-6	Scholar (2002)	Math	06 - Prim	0.412	0.103
E&O Math Challenge D	Scholar & Mouton (2014)	Math Score Average	12 - Sec	0.378	0.172
B2B Workbooks E Ch 4-7	Scholar (2013)	Math	07 - Prim	0.361	0.155
Numeric CAL	Bohmer (2014)	Math	08 - Sec	0.313	0.092
Learning for Living F	Scholar (2005)	Math	07 - Prim	0.311	0.058
MPSI INSET F	Scholar (1999)	Math	06 - Prim	0.257	0.131
EQUIP H	Scholar (2002)	Math	07 - Prim	0.257	0.100
Language Comparison	Bates & Mji (2010)	Math	05 - Prim	0.239	0.041
Learning for Living C	Scholar (2005)	Math	05 - Prim	0.199	0.051
Quality Learning Project C	Prinsloo & Kanjee (2005)	Math	09 - Sec	0.196	0.056
Quality Learning Project D	Prinsloo & Kanjee (2005)	Math	11 - Sec	0.104	0.057
Mine Proximity B	Besharati (2014)	Math SG	12 - Sec	-0.144	0.078
B2B Workbooks G (high dose)	Fleisch, Taylor N et al (2011)	Math	06 - Prim	-0.173	0.146
MPSI INSET D	Scholar (1999)	Math	05 - Prim	-0.288	0.134

Figure 2.5 *Impact of interventions to improve mathematics abilities*

Intervention	Study	Learning Outcome	Gr. Phase	Hedges's g	Standard error
Dinaledi C	World Bank DIME (2010)	Science SG	12 - Sec	0.550	0.077
Dinaledi D	World Bank DIME (2010)	Science HG	12 - Sec	0.269	0.076
MTG Study Guides G	Taylor & Watson (2015)	Geography	12 - Sec	0.141	0.060
MTG Study Guides D	Taylor & Watson (2015)	Science - Life	12 - Sec	0.106	0.060
Mine Proximity E	Besharati (2014)	Science SG	12 - Sec	-0.154	0.078
Mine Proximity H	Besharati (2014)	NSC Batchelor	12 - Sec	-0.160	0.078
Mine Proximity G	Besharati (2014)	NSC Pass	12 - Sec	-0.168	0.078

Figure 2.6 *Impact of interventions to improve science and other FET subjects*

Intervention	Study	Learning Outcome	Gr. Phase	Hedges's g	Standard error	Hedges's g and 95% CI
B2B Workbooks D (high dose)	Schollar (2013)	Math	06 - Prim	1.210	0.185	
B2B Workbooks C (high dose)	Schollar (2013)	Math	04 - Prim	0.982	0.177	
B2B Workbooks B	Schollar (2013)	Math	06 - Prim	0.849	0.161	
B2B Workbooks A	Schollar (2013)	Math	04 - Prim	0.645	0.155	
B2B Workbooks E CH4-7	Schollar (2013)	Math	07 - Prim	0.361	0.155	
Numeric CAL	Bohmer (2014)	Math	08 - Sec	0.313	0.092	
Language Companion	Botes & Mji (2010)	Math	05 - Prim	0.239	0.041	
MTG Study Guides G	Taylor & Watson (2015)	Geography	12 - Sec	0.141	0.060	
MTG Study Guides D	Taylor & Watson (2015)	Science - Life	12 - Sec	0.106	0.060	
B2B Workbooks G (high dose)	Fleisch, Taylor N et al (2011)	Math	06 - Prim	-0.173	0.146	
				0.426	0.090	

-2.00 -1.00 0.00 1.00 2.00

Figure 2.7 *Impact of LTSM provision*

a closer analysis of the two studies will highlight that the variation lies in the methodological approach used in implementing the two experiments. Schollar used this as his counterfactual 'null intervention', while Fleisch and Taylor utilised an alternative textbook (*enhanced standardised practice*), which arguably could also have contained some of the pedagogical elements of the B2B workbook. Eric Schollar and Associates (ESA) were very involved in the design and delivery of the B2B workbooks and thus had a different set of interest and passion for the intervention than possibly the JET and Wits University researchers in the 2010 evaluation, who also ended up using a different set of testing instruments from ESA.

Another interesting insight emerging from the forest plots is that contrary to some of the education impact evaluation literature (Glewwe et al., 2004; Hanushek & Woessmann, 2012; Kremer, Brannen & Glennerster, 2013), but of support to other international reviews (Conn, 2017; Krishnaratne et al., 2013; McEwan, 2014), evidence from South Africa shows that simple provision of effective learning and teaching material (i.e., Botes & Mji, 2010; Schollar, 2015; Taylor & Watson, 2015) can yield a similar impact on learning outcomes as more complex and expensive whole school development programmes – shotgun approach (Bloch, 2009; Mouton et al., 2014). It needs to be highlighted, however, that different intervention modalities are not necessarily mutually exclusive. Often the impact of

Intervention	Study	Learning Outcome	Gr. Phase	Hedges's g	Standard error
EQUIP F	Schollar (2002)	Math	05 - Prim	0.705	0.103
EQUIP D Ch 5-7	Schollar (2002)	Math	07 - Prim	0.468	0.102
EQUIP B Ch 4-6	Schollar (2002)	Math	06 - Prim	0.412	0.103
Learning for Living A	Schollar (2005)	English - Read	05 - Prim	0.371	0.051
Learning for Living G Ch 3-7	Schollar (2005)	English - Read	07 - Prim	0.362	0.056
Learning for Living B	Schollar (2005)	English - Write	05 - Prim	0.360	0.054
Learning for Living D	Schollar (2005)	English - Read	07 - Prim	0.348	0.057
EQUIP C Ch 5-7	Schollar (2002)	English	07 - Prim	0.334	0.101
EQUIP E	Schollar (2002)	English	05 - Prim	0.316	0.101
Learning for Living F	Schollar (2005)	Math	07 - Prim	0.311	0.058
EQUIP H	Schollar (2002)	Math	07 - Prim	0.257	0.100
Learning for Living E	Schollar (2005)	English - Write	07 - Prim	0.229	0.060
Learning for Living C	Schollar (2005)	Math	05 - Prim	0.199	0.051
Quality Learning Project C	Prinsloo & Kanjee (2005)	Math	09 - Sec	0.196	0.056
Learning for Living H Ch 3-7	Schollar (2005)	English - Write	07 - Prim	0.196	0.058
Quality Learning Project A	Prinsloo & Kanjee (2005)	English	09 - Sec	0.112	0.062
Quality Learning Project D	Prinsloo & Kanjee (2005)	Math	11 - Sec	0.104	0.057
Mine Proximity B	Besharati (2014)	Math SG	12 - Sec	-0.144	0.078
Mine Proximity E	Besharati (2014)	Science SG	12 - Sec	-0.154	0.078
Mine Proximity H	Besharati (2014)	NSC Batchelor	12 - Sec	-0.160	0.078
Mine Proximity G	Besharati (2014)	NSC Pass	12 - Sec	-0.168	0.078
				0.218	0.043

Figure 2.8 *Impact of whole school development programmes*

one intervention is confounded by the effects of other treatment components (Bold et al., 2013; Friedman et al., 2011). For instance, many of the LTSMs provided by educational agencies (workbooks, lesson plans, science equipment, etc.) are often accompanied by systemic training of teachers and management on how to use them. The provision of extra teachers is also often linked to class and school restructuring.

The last forest plot analyses the difference in effect sizes among the education interventions developed by government agencies and academic researchers (Figure 2.9). Even from an eye-ball glance, it is clear (and somewhat expected) that interventions designed and implemented by academics in a semi-controlled environment, for the purpose of research, experimentation and piloting, yield bigger effect sizes and more precise estimates than the on-going education policies and programmes run in large-scale policy environments by government or major private-public partnerships.

Although various studies conducted in South Africa's education sector (i.e., Blum et al., 2010; Fleisch & Schoer, 2014; Gustaffson & Taylor, 2013; Van

Group by Lead Agency	Intervention	Study	Learning Outcome	Gr. Phase	Hedges's g	Standard error	Hedges's g and 95% CI
academic	B2B Workbooks D (high dose)	Scholar (2013)	Math	06 - Prim	1.210	0.185	
academic	B2B Workbooks C (high dose)	Scholar (2013)	Math	04 - Prim	0.982	0.177	
academic	B2B Workbooks B	Scholar (2013)	Math	06 - Prim	0.849	0.161	
academic	B2B Workbooks A	Scholar (2013)	Math	04 - Prim	0.645	0.155	
academic	B2B Workbooks E CH 4-7	Scholar (2013)	Math	07 - Prim	0.361	0.155	
academic	Numeric CAL	Bohmer (2014)	Math	08 - Sec	0.313	0.092	
academic	Language Companion	Botes & Mji (2010)	Math	05 - Prim	0.239	0.041	
academic					0.629	0.133	
government	GPLMS A	Fleisch & Schoer (2014)	English	03 - Prim	0.669	0.076	
government	Plus Time C	Prinsloo (2009)	Math	09 - Sec	0.610	0.124	
government	Onaled C	World Bank DIME (2010)	Science SG	12 - Sec	0.550	0.077	
government	Onaled D	World Bank DIME (2010)	Science HG	12 - Sec	0.269	0.076	
government	MPSI INSET F	Scholar (1999)	Math	06 - Prim	0.257	0.131	
government	MTG Study Guides G	Taylor & Watson (2015)	Geography	12 - Sec	0.141	0.060	
government	MTG Study Guides D	Taylor & Watson (2015)	Science - Life	12 - Sec	0.106	0.060	
government	MPSI INSET D	Scholar (1999)	Math	05 - Prim	-0.283	0.134	
government					0.295	0.097	

-2.00 -1.00 0.00 1.00 2.00

Figure 2.9 *Impact of government programmes versus academic experiments*

der Berg, 2008) suggest that programmes have a different impact in different geographic areas and socio-economic contexts, the results from the above meta-analysis illustrate that geographic locations within South Africa provide relatively little heterogeneity, with regard to the effect sizes of interventions, compared to other influencing factors, such as education phase and evaluation design. Though the original review (2016) provided a geographic sub-group analysis for the provincial education authorities and private investors working in the specific regions of the country, the forest plots on the effects of interventions conducted in the six provinces of South Africa have been omitted from this paper, as this is less relevant for an international audience.

Discussion

Despite twenty-five years of reform efforts, South Africa continues to face serious weakness in the education system. Government, non-profit organisations and the private sector have tried to compensate for these weaknesses through large investments, innovative education models, complex school development programmes, bold education policies and numerous other initiatives implemented by a diversity of agencies. Notwithstanding the financial, technical and political resources invested in the education sector, this study has confirmed that very few interventions have had a substantial impact on learning outcomes in South Africa's public school system (Bloch, 2009; Fleisch, 2008; Sayed et al., 2013; Taylor et al., 2003). This meta-analysis does not take a formal position with regard to the merits of any particular pedagogical approach, school development programme or learning theory. It rather introduces empirical and systematic methods of evaluation and comparative analysis to the field of education programming.

This meta-analysis is a contribution to evidence-based education research and policy in South Africa. It has captured many of the South African impact studies that international reviews had not previously picked up (Evans & Popova, 2015) and has advanced the work of Mouton et al. (2014) by providing the first quantitative meta-analysis of interventions to improve learning outcomes in South Africa's schooling sector. Numerous impact evaluations have been conducted on education programmes in South Africa, with different methods, degrees of quality and scientific rigour. A number of reviews have also been undertaken (Mouton et al., 2014; Roberts & Schollar, 2011; Sayed et al., 2013) to reflect on the experiences and the learning that have emerged in South Africa's education sector post-1994. Nonetheless, education policy-makers and investors require standardised impact measures to allow for more robust empirical comparison of the effectiveness of different options available to them.

This review has presented the application of a methodological framework for the comparison of intervention effectiveness within the education policy arena of South Africa. Through the use of multiple treatment meta-analysis, the study has analysed the impact of some of the major interventions implemented in public schools over the past twenty years. It has identified some of the programmes that have been most successful in improving learning outcomes and the context and circumstances in which these effects have occurred. While not being conclusive on what are the best education programmes, it has shed some light on when, where, how and why some interventions have shown a significant impact on learner achievement.

What has emerged strongly is that context, methodology and study design have a substantial influence on the effect sizes that are reported in education impact evaluation. Assessment tools, evaluation methods, units of analysis and other methodological choices all appear to influence the type of results that emerge from these impact studies. The focus of the intervention (Slavin & Smith, 2009), the timing in which evaluations are conducted (Clemens et al., 2004; Harris, 2008) and potential Hawthorne effects (Schollar, 2015) are all factors that influence impact evaluations. The findings from this South African meta-analysis resonate with similar findings emerging from the education meta-analysis conducted by Lipsey et al. (2012). It also confirms several of the findings by Conn (2017) and Evans and Popova (2015), where diverging results of different reviews are dependent on the sample of studies included and the intervention categorisation utilised by the different reviewers. The South African meta-analysis has also shown how results of impact evaluations cannot be taken at face value, as context and study design have a significant influence on the effect sizes reported in the various programme evaluations.

A vivid illustration of the main story emerging out of the South African meta-analysis is the case of the evaluation of the Back to the Basics (B2) workbooks, where the methodological approach undertaken by two different evaluators (Fleisch et al., 2011; Schollar, 2015) led to diametrically opposite results, though they both implemented rigorous RCTs of the same intervention on the same grade level of learners in different provinces of South Africa. Both experiments, though well implemented, had methodological problems and limitations. A third RCT of the B2B workbooks by a different researcher in a new context would definitely be a project worth pursuing in order to reach more definitive conclusions on the impact of guided workbooks in South African primary schools.

The strongest predictors of effect size in this systematic review have been the schooling phase and grade in which the interventions were implemented, school subjects and the implementation of multi-component models that combine resources and professional development. Programmes implemented at lower levels of the school system and in core subjects, such as literacy and numeracy, (i.e., Fleisch & Schoer, 2014) report much larger learning impact than programmes implemented in higher grades (i.e., Taylor & Watson, 2015). This is also consistent with the general child development literature and some of the international meta-analytical work done in the field of education (Bloom et al., 2008; Lipsey et al., 2012). Several evaluations of high school interventions in South Africa (Besharati, 2014; Blum et al., 2010; Schollar & Mouton, 2014) have discovered that major learning gains occur when there is an injection of additional human resources and teachers into the schools, that help reduce class size and teacher-learner ratios. Numerous studies conducted in primary schools have highlighted the importance of interventions in the area of language (i.e., Early Grade Reading Study, Learning for Living, READ, Reading Catch Up Programme, sJsK Literacy Project), which produce important gains not only on language outcomes, but also on other learning areas (Bohmer, 2014; Fleisch et al., 2015; Schollar, 2005; Taylor et al., 2017). While not included in this systematic review, the very latest studies (Cilliers et al., 2019; Kotze et al., 2018) largely confirm these findings. Finally, well-designed and comprehensively-delivered learning and teaching resources (LTSMs) appear impactful, as well as cost-effective, in improving learning outcomes relatively quickly – compared to more complex and expensive integrated school development programmes (Taylor & Watson, 2015).

The only two exceptions to the above finding have been the Epoch & Optima programme and the Dinaledi initiative, which have both produced remarkable results on mathematics and science learning outcomes in the FET band (senior high school), which is an education phase traditionally known to report very small gains in learner achievement. Schollar and Mouton's (2014) evaluation of the Epoch & Optima programme, however, suffered from potential selection bias and the World Bank (Blum et al., 2010) evaluation of Dinaledi had some serious data limitation. A follow-up replication of the Dinaledi study is well warranted, as the government flagship programme has meanwhile evolved and the Department of Education data has also significantly improved.

This meta-analysis has also shown that experimental evaluations conducted by researchers in carefully controlled environments, such as the testing of innovative teaching approaches or special learning aids (Bohmer, 2014; Hattingh, 2003; Louw et al., 2008; Padayachee et al., 2011), produce high effect sizes. However, there is no guarantee that the same impact results are to be expected when the interventions are transferred to the broader policy environment, where beneficiaries often receive partial or incorrect exposure to the treatment. High effect sizes in academic studies can also be due to to publication bias towards studies with positive results and to some degree to Hawthorne effects.

Finally, this review has underlined the need for more empirical evidence in South Africa's education sector and the use of rigorous counterfactual evaluations, such as RCTs and strong quasi-experimental designs, which address selection bias and allow for rigorous analysis of causality. Attention needs to be given to sampling processes to provide more power and confidence in the results of education impact studies (Fleisch et al., 2015; McEwan, 2014; Taylor et al., 2017). It is hoped that this meta-analysis inspires both public and private agencies to improve the quality of their evaluations and to utilise the best available scientific methods to systematically plan future programmes, make smarter investments and improve their on-going efforts in South Africa's education sector.

References

References marked with an asterisk (*) indicate studies included in this meta-analysis.

Bamberger, M. (2009). Strengthening the evaluation of program effectiveness through reconstructing baseline data. *Journal of Development Effectiveness* 1(1), 37-59. https://doi.org/10.1080/19439340902727610

Bamberger, M., Rao, V., & Woolcock, M. (2010). Using mixed methods in monitoring and evaluation: experiences from international development evaluation. In A. Tashakkori, & C. Teddlie (Eds.), *SAGE handbook of mixed methods in social and behavioral research* (2nd ed., pp. 613-641). Thousand Oaks, CA: Sage Publications. https://doi.org/10.4135/9781506335193.n24

*Baumgartner, J., Smuts, C., Malan, L., Kvalsvig, J., Van Stuijvenberg, M., Hurrell, R., Zimmermann, M. (2012). Effects of iron and n3 fatty acid supplementation, alone and in combination, on cognition in school children: a randomized, double-blind, placebo-controlled intervention in South Africa. *American Journal of Clinical Nutrition*, 96, 1327-38. https://doi.org/10.3945/ajcn.112.041004

*Besharati, N. (2014). *Platinum & passes: the impact of mining investments on education outcomes in South Africa* (Research Report No. 16). Johannesburg: SAIIA & Wits School of Governance.

Besharati, N. (2015). *Private sector investment in South Africa's education sector: nature, extent and incentives* (Research Brief, 2015). Johannesburg: Jet Education Services.

Besharati, N.A. (2016). *Evaluating development effectiveness assessing and comparing the impact of education intervention in South Africa* (University of the Witwatersrand, Johannesburg. Doctoral Dissertation).

Bloch, G. (2009). *The toxic mix: what's wrong with South Africa's schools and how to fix it*. Cape Town: Tafelberg.

Bloom, H., Hill, C., Black, A.R., & Lipsey, M. (2008), Performance trajectories and performance gaps as achievement effect-size benchmarks for education interventions. *Journal of Research on Educational Effectiveness*, 1, 289-328. https://doi.org/10.1080/19345740802400072

Blum, J., Krishnan, N., & Legovini, A. (2010). *Expanding opportunities for South African youth through math & science: the impact of the Dinaledi program*. Washington DC: World Bank Development Impact Evaluation Initiative (DIME).

Bohmer, B. (2014). *Testing Numeric: Evidence from a randomized controlled trial of a computer based mathematics intervention in Cape Town High Schools*. Unpublished Masters Thesis. University of Cape Town.

Bold, T., Kimenyi, M., Mwabu, G., Ng'ang'a, A., & Sandefur, J. (2013). *Scaling up what works: experimental evidence on external validity in Kenyan education.* Working Paper, (321). Washington DC: Center for Global Development. https://doi.org/10.2139/ssrn.2241240

Botes, H., & Mji, A. (2010). Language diversity in the mathematics classroom: does a learner companion make a difference? *South African Journal of Education*, 30(1), 123–138. https://doi.org/10.15700/saje.v30n1a318

Caldwell, D.M. (2005). Simultaneous comparison of multiple treatments: combining direct and indirect evidence. *British Medical Journal*, 7521, 897. https://doi.org/10.1136/bmj.331.7521.897

Campbell Collaboration (2015). *Campbell Collaboration systematic reviews: policies and guidelines* (Monograph Series, Supplement 1). Oslo: Campbell Collaboration.

Cilliers, J., Fleisch, B., Prinsloo, C., & Taylor, S. (2019). How to improve teaching practice? An experimental comparison of centralized training and in-classroom coaching. *Journal of Human Resources*, 0618-9538R1. https://doi.org/10.35489/BSG-RISE-WP_2018/024

Centre for Development and Enterprise (CDE, 2011). *Schooling Reform is Possible: Lessons for South Africa from International Experience.* (Round Table No. 18). Johannesburg: Centre for Development Enterprise.

Chisholm, L., Volmink, J., Ndhlovu, T., Potenza, E., Mahomed, H., Muller, J., & Malan, B. (2005). *A South African curriculum for the twenty first century.* Report of the Review Committee on Curriculum. Pretoria: Human Science Research Council.

Christie, P., Butler, D., & Potterton, M. (2007). *Schools that work* (Report to the Minister of Education). Pretoria: Department of Education, Republic of South Africa.

Clemens, M.A., Radelet, S., & Bhavnani, R.R. (2004). *Counting chickens when they hatch: the short term effect of aid on growth* (Center for Global Development Working Paper No. 44). Washington DC: Center for Global Development. https://doi.org/10.2139/ssrn.567241

Coe, R. (2002). *It's the effect size, stupid: what effect size is and why it is important.* Retrieved from http://www.leeds.ac.uk/educol/documents/00002182.htm

Coetzee, M., & Van der Berg, S. (2012). *Report on a scoping study to evaluate the feasability of undertaking an impact evaluation of the national school feeding programme and Grade R, based on existing data sources.* Study for the Department of Basic Education and the Department of Policy Evaluation and Monitoring in the Presidency. Stellenbosch: Stellenbosch University.

Cohen, J. (1988). *Statistical power analysis for the behavioral sciences* (2nd edition). Hillsdale: Lawrence Eribaum.

Conn, K.M. (2017). Identifying Effective Education Interventions in Sub-Saharan Africa: A Meta-Analysis of Impact Evaluations. *Review of Educational Research*, DOI: 10.3102/0034654317712025. https://doi.org/10.3102/0034654317712025

Cranney, A., Guyatt, G., Griffith, L., Wells, G., Tugwell, P., Rosen, C., et al. (2002). Summary of meta-analyses of therapies for post-menopausal osteoporosis. *Endocrine Review*, 23, 570. https://doi.org/10.1210/er.2001-9002

De Chaisemartin, T. (2010). *Evaluation of the Cape teaching and leadership institute.* Johannesburg: JET Education Services.

Deacon R., & Simkins, C. (2011). *Value in the classroom: The quantity and quality of South Africa's teachers.* Johannesburg: Centre for Development and Enterprise (CDE).

Duflo, E., Glennerster, R., & Kremer, M. (2008). Using randomization in development economics research: A toolkit. In T. Schultz & J. Strauss (Eds.), *Handbook of Development Economics*, Vol. 4. Amsterdam and New York: North Holland. https://doi.org/10.1016/S1573-4471(07)04061-2

Elmore, R. (2008). Leadership as the practice of improvement. *Improving School Leadership*, 2, 40-41. https://doi.org/10.1787/9789264039551-4-en

Evans, D., & Popova, A. (2015). *What really works to improve learning in developing countries? An analysis of divergent findings in systematic reviews.* (February 26, 2015). World Bank Policy Research Working Paper, (7203). Washington, DC: World Bank. https://doi.org/10.1596/1813-9450-7203

Fleisch, B. (2006). Bureaucratic accountability in the education action zones of South Africa. *South African Journal of Education*, 26(3), 369-382.

Fleisch, B. (2008). *Primary education in crisis: Why South African school children underachieve in reading and mathematics.* Johannesburg: Juta & Co. Ltd.

*Fleisch, B., Taylor, N., Herholdt, R., & Sapire, I. (2011). Evaluation of the Back to Basics Mathematics Workbooks: A randomized Controlled Trial of the primary mathematics research project. *South African Journal of Education*, 31(4), 488-501. https://doi.org/10.15700/saje.v31n4a466

*Fleisch, B., & Schöer, V. (2014). Large-scale instructional reform in the Global South: insights from the mid-point evaluation of the Gauteng Primary Language and Mathematics Strategy. *South African Journal of Education*, 34(3), 01-12. https://doi.org/10.15700/201409161040

*Fleisch, B., Taylor, S., Schöer, V., & Mabogoane, T. (2015). *Assessing the impact of the RCUP: The findings of the impact evaluation of the Reading Catch-Up Programme*. Report, Johannesburg.

Fleisch, B., Schöer, V., Roberts, G., & Thornton, A. (2016). System-wide improvement of early-grade mathematics: New evidence from the Gauteng Primary Language and Mathematics Strategy. *International Journal of Educational Development*, 49, 157-174. https://doi.org/10.1016/j.ijedudev.2016.02.006

Fleisch, B., Taylor, S., Schöer, V., & Mabogoane, T. (2017). Failing to catch up in reading in the middle years: The findings of the impact evaluation of the Reading Catch-Up Programme in South Africa. *International Journal of Educational Development*, 53, 36-47. https://doi.org/10.1016/j.ijedudev.2016.11.008

Fleisch, B. (2018). *The Education Triple Cocktail: System-wide Instructional Reform in South Africa*. UCT Press/Juta and Company (Pty) Ltd.

Friedman, W., Kremer, M., Miguel, E., & Thornton, R. (2011). *Education as liberation?* (NBER Working Paper No. 16939). Cambridge, MA: NBER (National Bureau of Economic Research). https://doi.org/10.3386/w16939

Glewwe, P., Kremer, M., Moulin, S., & Zitzewitz, E. (2004). Retrospective vs. prospective analyses of school inputs: The case of flip charts in Kenya. *Journal of Development Economics*, 74(1), 251-268. https://doi.org/10.1016/j.jdeveco.2003.12.010

Glewwe, P.W., Hanushek, E.A., Humpage, S.D., & Ravina, R. (2014). School resources and educational outcomes in developing countries: A review of the literature from 1990 to 2010 in *Education Policy in Developing Countries*, Ed. P. Glewwe, Chicago and London: University of Chicago Press.

Gustafsson, M. (2007). Using the hierarchical linear model to understand school production in South Africa. *South African Journal of Economics*, 75(1), 84-98. https://doi.org/10.1111/j.1813-6982.2007.00107.x

Gustafsson, M., & Taylor, S. (2013). *Treating schools to a new administration. The impact of South Africa's 2005 provincial boundary changes on school performance*. Stellenbosch: Stellenbosch University.

Hansen, L.O., Young, R.S., Hinami, K., Leung, A., & Williams, M.V. (2011). Interventions to reduce 30-day rehospitalization: a systematic review. *Annals of Internal Medicine*, 155(8), 520-528. https://doi.org/10.7326/0003-4819-155-8-201110180-00008

Hanushek, E., & Woessmann, L. (2012). Do better schools lead to more growth? Cognitive skills, economic outcomes, and causation. *Journal of Economic Growth*, 17(4), 267-321. https://doi.org/10.1007/s10887-012-9081-x

Harris, D. (2009). Toward policy-relevant benchmarks for interpreting effect sizes combining effects with costs. *Educational Evaluation and Policy Analysis*, 31(1), 3-29. https://doi.org/10.3102/0162373708327524

*Harvey, J., & Prinsloo, C. (2015). *Hope for rebuilding language foundations: part 2 – replication in a second cohort*. Evaluation Report. Pretoria: Human Science Research Council.

Hattie, J. (2009). *Visible learning: A synthesis of 800+ meta-analyses on achievement*. Abingdon: Routledge.

Hattingh, A. (2003). Examining learning achievement and experiences of science learners in a problem-based learning environment. *South African Journal of Education*, 23(1), 52.

Hobden, P., & Hobden, S. (2009). *RUMEP Project Summative Evaluation*. Johannesburg: Zenex Foundation.

Hombrados, J.G., & Waddington, H. (2012). *Internal validity in social experiments and quasi-experiments: An assessment tool for reviewers*. Mimeo, London: International Initiative for Impact Evaluation (3ie).

Hunt, K., Schoer, V., Ntuli, M., Rankin, N., & Sebastiao, C. (2011). A blurred signal? Comparability of NSC mathematics scores and former SC mathematics scores: how consistent is the signal across time? *Education as Change*, 15(1), 3-16. https://doi.org/10.1080/16823206.2011.574097

Joint Education Trust (JET, 2006). *READ mother tongue literacy programme*. Evaluation Report. Johannesburg: Zenex Foundation.

Joint Education Trust (JET, 2007). *Towards optimal usage of mindset resources in South African Schools: Five Case Studies in Western Cape and Gauteng*. Johannesburg: JET Education Services.

Kanjee A. (2007). *Large-scale assessments in South Africa: supporting formative assessments in schools*. Paper presented at the 33rd International Association for Educational Assessment Conference, Baku, Azerbaijan, 16 to 21 September.

Kim, Y.S.G., Lee, H., & Zuilkowski, S.S. (2019). Impact of Literacy Interventions on Reading Skills in Low-and Middle-Income Countries: A Meta-Analysis. *Child Development*. https://doi.org/10.1111/cdev.13204

Kotze, J., Fleisch, B., & Taylor, S. (2018). Alternative forms of early grade instructional coaching: Emerging evidence from field experiments in South Africa. *International Journal of Educational Development*. https://doi.org/10.1016/j.ijedudev.2018.09.004

Kremer, M., Brannen, C., & Glennerster, R. (2013). The challenge of education and learning in the developing world. *Science*, 340(6130), 297-300. https://doi.org/10.1126/science.1235350

Krishnaratne, S., White, H., & Carpenter, E. (2013). *Quality education for all children? What works in education in developing countries?* Working Paper (20). New Delhi: International Initiative for Impact Evaluation (3ie) https://doi.org/10.23846/WP0020

Lipsey, M.W., & Wilson, D.B. (2001). *Practical meta-analysis.* Thousand Oaks, CA: Sage Publications, Inc.

Lipsey, M.W., Puzio, K., Yun, C., Hebert, M.A., Steinka-Fry, K., Cole, M.W., & Busick, M.D. (2012). *Translating the Statistical Representation of the Effects of Education Interventions into More Readily Interpretable Forms.* (No. ED-IES-09-C-0021). Washington DC.

Louw, J., Muller, J., & Tredoux, M. (2008). Time-on-task, technology and mathematics achievement, *Evaluation and Program Planning*, 31(1), 41-50. https://doi.org/10.1016/j.evalprogplan.2007.11.001

Lu, G., & Ades, A.E. (2006). Assessing evidence inconsistency in mixed treatment comparisons. *Journal of the American Statistical Association*, 101 (474), 447-459. https://doi.org/10.1198/016214505000001302 Marzano, R.J. (2003). *What works in schools: Translating research into action.* ASCD.

McEwan, P.J. (2015). Improving learning in primary schools of developing countries: a meta-analysis of randomized experiments. *Review of Educational Research*, 85(3), 353-394. https://doi.org/10.3102/0034654314553127

Motala, S., Morrow, S., & Sayed, Y. (2014). Gauteng Department of Education: A policy review In F. Maringe & M. Prew (Eds.), *Twenty years of education transformation in Gauteng 1994 to 2014: an independent review* (Chapter 2). Johannesburg: Gauteng Department of Education.

Mouton, J., Wildschut, L., Richter, T., & Pocock, R. (2013). *Zenex Review Project* (Final Revised Report). Johannesburg: Evaluation Research Agency (ERA).

National Planning Commission (NPC, 2012). *National development plan vision 2030.* Pretoria: Presidency.

National Planning Commission (NPC, 2011). *Diagnostic overview.* Pretoria: Presidency.

Organisation for Economic Co-operation and Development (OECD, 2008). *Review of national policies for education: South Africa.* Paris: OECD.

Padayachee, P., Boshoff, H., Olivier, W., & Harding, A. (2011). A blended learning Grade 12 intervention using DVD technology to enhance the teaching and learning of mathematics: original research. *Pythagoras*, 32(1), 1-8. https://doi.org/10.4102/pythagoras.v32i1.24

Piper, B. (2009). *Integrated education program: Impact study of SMRS using early grade reading assessment in three provinces in South Africa*. Park, NC: RTI International, Research Triangle.

Prinsloo, C., & Kanjee, A. (2005). *Improving learning in South African schools: the Quality Learning Project (QLP) summative evaluation (2000-2004)*. Pretoria: Human Sciences Research Council.

Prinsloo, C.H. (2009). *Extra classes, extra marks? Report on the Plus Time Project*, Pretoria: Human Science Research Council.

Research Institute for Education Planning (RIEP) (2008). *Report on the impact study in the Eastern Cape and KwaZulu-Natal on literacy and numeracy grade 4*. Bloemfontein: University of Free State.

Roberts, J. (2006). Evaluation of the numeracy programme operated by COUNT in Uitenhage schools. Final Report. Johannesburg: Zennex Foundation.

Roberts, J., & Schollar, E. (2006). Meta-evaluation of interventions in math, science and language 1998-2006. Johannesburg: ESA.

Roberts, J., & Schollar, E. (2011). Meta-Evaluation of programmes and projects supported by the Zenex Foundation 2006-2011. Johannesburg: ESA.

Roche, C., & Kelly, L. (2005). Evaluating the performance of development agencies. In G. Pitman, O. Feinstein, & G. Ingram, Vol. 7. *Evaluating development effectiveness. World Bank Series on Evaluation and Development*. Edison, NJ: Transaction Publishers.

*Sailors, M., Hoffman, J.V., Pearson, P.D., Beretvas, S.N., & Matthee, B. (2010). The effects of first- and second-language instruction in rural South African schools. Bilingual Research Journal, 33(1), 21-41. https://doi.org/10.1080/15235881003733241

Salanti, G. (2012). Indirect and mixed-treatment comparison, network, or multiple-treatments meta-analysis: many names, many benefits, many concerns for the next generation evidence synthesis tool. *Research Synthesis Methods*, 3(2), 80-97. https://doi.org/10.1002/jrsm.1037

Sayed, Y., Kanjee, A., & Nkomo, M. (2013). *The search for quality education in post-apartheid South Africa: Interventions to improve learning and teaching*. Cape Town: HSRC Press.

Schollar, E. (1999). *Final Report of the Evaluation of the Impact of the INSET Component of the Mpumalanga Primary Schools Initiative (MPSI)*. Pretoria: DFID.

Schollar, E. (2001). A Review of Two Evaluations of the application of The READ Primary Schools Programme in the Eastern Cape province of South Africa. *The International Journal of Educational Research (IJER)*, 35(2). https://doi.org/10.1016/S0883-0355(01)00017-9

Schollar, E. (2002). *The Evaluation of the Pilot EQUIP project of the National Business Initiative* (Final Report). Johannesburg: ESA.

Schollar, E. (2005). *The evaluation of the Learning for Living Project*. Johannesburg: Eric Schollar and Associates.

Schollar, E. (2008). *The Primary Mathematics Research Project 2004-2007: towards evidence-based educational development in South Africa* (Final Report). Johannesburg: Eric Schollar & Associates.

Schollar, E. (2013). The Learning for Living Project: a book-based approach to learning of language in South African primary schools. In Y. Sayed, A. Kanjee, & M. Nkomo (Eds.), *The search for quality education in post-apartheid South Africa* (pp. 237-256). Cape Town, South Africa: HSRC Press.

Schollar, E. (2015). *The Primary Mathematics Research Project: 2004-2012. An evidence based programme of research into understanding and improving the outcomes of mathematical education in South African primary schools.* PhD Thesis. Cape Town: University of Cape Town.

Schollar, E., & Mouton, J. (2014). *Epoch and Optima: Public Schools Math Challenge Programme. An impact evaluation* (Final Report). Johannesburg: ESA & ERA.

Simkins, C. (2010). *The maths and science performance of South Africa's public schools: some lessons from the past decade* (Executive Summary No. 1). Johannesburg: Centre for Development Enterprise.

Simkins, C., & Paterson, A. (2005). *Learner performance in South Africa: social and economic determinants of success in language and mathematics*. Pretoria: HSRC Press.

Slavin, R., & Smith, D. (2009). The relationship between sample sizes and effect sizes in systematic reviews in education. *Educational Evaluation and Policy Analysis*, 31(4), 500-506. https://doi.org/10.3102/0162373709352369

Snilstveit, B., Stevenson, J., Menon, R., Phillips, D., Gallagher, E., Geleen, M., ... & Jimenez, E. (2016). The impact of education programmes on learning and school participation in low- and middle-income countries. https://doi.org/10.23846/SRS007

South African Institute for Distance Education (SAIDE, 2007). *Evaluation of COUNT Family Math School Pilot Project*. Main Report. Johannesburg: SAIDE.

South African Schools Act (SASA), 1996 (Act No. 84 of 1996). Retrieved from http://www.acts.co.za/south-african-schools-act-1996/index.html

Spaull, N. (2011). *A preliminary analysis of SACMEQ III South Africa* (Stellenbosch Economic Working Papers 11/11). Stellenbosch: University of Stellenbosch.

Spaull, N. (2013). *South Africa's education crisis: the quality of education in South Africa 1994-2011* (CDE Report). Johannesburg: Centre for Development and Enterprise.

*Summers, H.C. (2008). *Maths Centre/Zenex Foundation Project: upgrading of Teacher Qualifications at Foundation Phase KwaZulu-Natal and the Eastern Cape (2005-2008)*. Summative Evaluation Report. Johannesburg: Zenex Foundation.

Taylor, N., Fleisch, B., & Shindler, J. (2008). *Changes in education since 1994*. Pretoria: South Africa Presidency.

Taylor, N. (2009). Standards-based accountability in South Africa. *School Effectiveness and School Improvement*, 20(3), 341-356. https://doi.org/10.1080/09243450902916704

Taylor N., (2011) *A five-year plan for South African schooling: a report commissioned by the National Planning Commission*. Johannesburg: JET Education Services.

Taylor, N., Muller, J., & Vinjevold, P. (2003). *Getting schools working*. Cape Town: Pearson Education South Africa.

Taylor, S., & Watson, P. (2015). *The impact of study guides on matric performance: evidence from a randomised experiment*. Stellenbosch Economic Working Paper. University of Stellenbosch.

Taylor, S., Fleisch, B., Cilliers, J., Prinsloo, C., & Reddy, V. (2017). *Early Grade Reading Study Summary Report: Results of Year 2 Impact Evaluation*. Pretoria: Department of Basic Education.

Trialogue. (2015). *The Trialogue 2015 CSI handbook*. Cape Town: Trialogue.

Van der Berg, S. (2008). How effective are poor schools? Poverty and educational outcomes in South Africa. *Studies in Educational Evaluation*, 34(3), 145-154. https://doi.org/10.1016/j.stueduc.2008.07.005

Van Stuijvenberg, M.E., Kvalsvig, J.D., Faber, M., Kruger, M., Kenoyer, D.G., & Benadé, A.S. (1999). Effect of iron-, iodine-, and β-carotene-fortified biscuits on the micronutrient status of primary school children: a randomized controlled trial. *The American Journal of Clinical Nutrition*, 69(3), 497-503. https://doi.org/10.1093/ajcn/69.3.497

Wilson, S.J., Tanner-Smith, E.E., Lipsey, M.W., Steinka-Fry, & Morrison, J. (2011). Dropout prevention and intervention programs: Effects on school completion and dropout among school-aged children and youth. *Campbell Systematic Reviews* 2011 (8). https://doi.org/10.4073/csr.2011.8

Analysis of heterogeneity by evaluation design parameters

Group	Num. Studies	Point estimate	Stand. error	Lower limit	Upper limit	Z-value	P-value	Q-value	df Q	P-value
Counterfactual Method										
PSM	20	0,00	0,06	-0,10	0,11	0,08	0,94			
RCT	35	0,11	0,03	0,05	0,16	3,60	0,00			
RDD	2	0,37	0,30	-0,21	0,95	1,26	0,21			
Simple match	53	0,28	0,03	0,22	0,34	9,60	0,00			
Total between								28,40	3	0,000
Overall	110	0,17	0,02	0,13	0,21	8,85	0,00			
Assessment Instrument										
Own	71	0,22	0,03	0,17	0,27	8,15	0,00			
State	39	0,12	0,04	0,04	0,20	2,96	0,00			
Total between								4,38	1	0,036
Overall	110	0,19	0,02	0,14	0,23	8,42	0,00			
Units of Analysis										
Learners	84	0,21	0,02	0,16	0,26	8,59	0,00			
Schools	26	0,10	0,06	-0,02	0,21	1,63	0,10			
Total between								2,95	1	0,086
Overall	110	0,19	0,02	0,15	0,24	8,58	0,00			
Matched Cohorts										
No	50	0,12	0,03	0,06	0,19	3,66	0,00			
Yes	60	0,23	0,03	0,17	0,29	7,66	0,00			
Total between								6,16	1	0,013
Overall	110	0,18	0,02	0,14	0,23	8,12	0,00			
Statistical significance										
Yes	55	0,34	0,03	0,28	0,40	11,17	0,00			
No	55	0,00	0,01	-0,02	0,02	0,02	0,98			
Total between								109,7	1	0,000
Overall	110	0,04	0,01	0,02	0,06	3,89	0,00			

Analysis of heterogeneity by school phase

Group	Effect size and 95% confidence interval					Test of null (2-Tail)		Heterogeneity		
	Num. Studies	Point estimate	Stand. error	Lower limit	Upper limit	Z-value	P-value	Q-value	df Q	P-value
Prim - 1 Foun.	9	0,53	0,08	0,36	0,69	6,34	0,00			
Prim - 2 Inter.	27	0,36	0,04	0,29	0,43	10,19	0,00			
Sec - 3 Senior	7	0,34	0,07	0,21	0,47	5,10	0,00			
Sec - 4 FET	12	0,14	0,07	0,00	0,28	2,02	0,04			
Total between								12,84	3	0,00
Overall	55	0,34	0,03	0,29	0,40	12,70	0,00			

CHAPTER 3

The impact of poverty on basic education in South Africa: A systematic review of literature
Vitallis Chikoko and Pinkie Mthembu
University of KwaZulu-Natal

Abstract

In this chapter, we examine how poverty has impacted upon basic education in post-apartheid South Africa. Our position is that without rooting out poverty, South Africa's very noble transformation agenda for society in general and education in particular, may not come to fruition. After all, education is the major instrument of such transformation. Education has great potential to drastically reduce or even eradicate poverty, but poverty can drastically reduce one's success in education. The knowledge gap we saw was that while post-apartheid South Africa has made tremendous strides in fighting poverty in education, the impact thereof is not sufficiently evident. Through a three-stage systematic literature review process, we settled for and discussed seven themes: poverty and reading achievement, poverty and school dropout, poverty and returns to schooling, poverty and the post-apartheid education policy landscape, poverty as a categoriser of schools, poverty and the implementation of inclusive education, and lastly, poverty as a trigger for self-emancipation. We conclude that poverty remains a great enemy to South Africa's educational aspirations. While reading literacy is the backbone of all learning, sadly, due to poverty, many learners are unable to achieve such foundation. Some of the country's otherwise well-meaning landmark education policies are difficult to implement fully in poor contexts. Thus, poverty has rendered the same previously disadvantaged communities to be at risk. In the latter communities, education is inevitably of low quality. Low-quality education has a negative ripple effect on the employability of students therefrom. We recommend that the struggle should be two-pronged: fighting poverty on one hand, and crafting and implementing ways to improve the quality of education on the other. In that struggle, schools and communities need to drastically shift from deficit to asset-based thinking and doing.

Introduction

South Africa's National Development Plan (NDP) 2030 identifies poverty as one of the country's greatest enemies which must be fought and defeated. According to its Foreword, the NDP is a plan for the country to eliminate poverty and inequality by 2030. Goal 1 of the United Nations' (UN) 2030 Agenda for Sustainable

Development is to eradicate extreme poverty for all people everywhere by 2030. Jim Yong Kim (2015), President of the World Bank Group, had the following to say about poverty:

> To end poverty, boost shared prosperity, and achieve the Sustainable Development Goals, we must use development financing and technical expertise to effect radical change. We must work together to ensure that all children have access to quality education and learning opportunities throughout their lives regardless of where they are born, their gender, or their family's income (Education 2030, Incheon Declaration, p. 12).

Tarabini (2010) rightly argues that reducing poverty remains a matter of concern in the world because the number of poor people continues to rise. Without disrupting poverty, it is not possible to achieve the UN's Sustainable Development Goal (SDG) 4: 'Ensure inclusive and equitable quality education and promote lifelong learning opportunities for all', or any other SDG for that matter. There is therefore a strong relationship between education and poverty.

In this chapter, we seek to address this question: How has poverty impacted upon basic education in post-apartheid South Africa? The knowledge gap we see is that while post-apartheid South Africa has made tremendous strides in fighting against poverty in education, there seems to be not enough evidence regarding the impact thereof. As Salisbury (2016, p. 43) rightly puts it, '…South Africa continues to have one of the most unequal distributions of income and wealth in the world'. We thus couch the chapter against the backdrop that in all its efforts to transform society the post-apartheid South African government has had and continues to fight poverty in its various forms without which fight there may be no meaningful and sustainable transformation to talk about. Because education is a major instrument for transforming any society, it is befitting that we scrutinise how poverty is impacting upon education. As we attempt to address the said question, we shall also seek to draw implications for educational policy.

We commence the chapter through three preliminary issues. First, we attempt to explain the concept of poverty in the context of the chapter. Second, we briefly explore the interface between education and poverty. Third, we highlight the systematic review methods we adopted and justifications thereof. From there we cast the literature review evidence through seven themes namely: poverty and reading achievement, poverty and school dropout, poverty and returns to schooling, poverty and the post-apartheid education policy landscape, poverty as a categoriser of schools, poverty and the implementation of inclusive education, and lastly, poverty as a trigger for self-emancipation. In response to the research evidence from the seven themes, we then discuss briefly what we learn therefrom regarding the impact of poverty on education after which we close the chapter with concluding remarks.

We wish to identify one limitation of the chapter. It was our plan to discuss every theme drawing from more than one piece of research evidence. However, we did not always find such evidence in large quantities. In cases where we use single studies, this was after we were satisfied that such work was topical enough to represent the theme in question.

Methods

Search strategy and sources of information

For this systematic literature review we adopted Khan, Kunz, Kleignen and Antes' (2003) five steps. These steps include framing the review question(s), identifying relevant work, assessing the quality of studies, summarising the evidence and interpreting the findings. We cast our net as wide as possible. This enabled us to read a wide variety of literature written in English published between 2009 and 2019 in Google Scholar, Ebscohost, Sabinet, JSTOR and ERIC databases. Key search phrases included 'poverty and education', 'impact of poverty in education', 'effects of poverty in South African schools', 'effects of poverty in learning', 'poverty and academic performance for children in South Africa', 'poverty in deprived communities in South Africa', 'vulnerable children impact on education', 'inequality in education', and 'socio-economic status and education'. The searches yielded works including reports, policy analyses, journal articles, working papers, book chapters, research reviews, books, unpublished theses, position papers, and national and international conference presentations. Not only did we realise that it would not be possible to harness all such works, we also became convinced that among these many types of literature, peer-reviewed journal articles would constitute some of the strongest and most reliable sources of evidence. Thus, the chapter is based on evidence from peer-reviewed journal articles. We resolved to settle for a ten-year period. We felt that most works older than 2009 were not likely to adequately represent the current state of affairs, particularly given the many interventions the Government of South Africa and other agencies have implemented to transform education.

We originally collected 1 090 articles, and subsequently added to this from references of some of the articles we read, giving a total of 1 127.

Study selection process

We followed a two-stage process. We firstly read abstracts and summaries on the basis of which we rejected 803 articles using the following exclusion criteria: (i) not focusing on poverty and inequality (121); (ii) not education focused (192); (iii) not focusing on South African schooling (223); (iv); only had abstract (113); and (v) published prior to 2009 (154).

In the second stage, we evaluated eligibility of the remaining 324 articles. We individually conducted readings and applied the following criteria for inclusion: i) a paper had to be about post-apartheid basic education (primary and secondary schooling) in South Africa, ii) a paper should have been about poverty or inequality in education or related issues, and iii) a paper had to have been published within the period 2009-2019. After a series of iterative discussions between the two of us, we decided to settle for 21 articles on two criteria: they were the most relevant; and the quantity was manageable.

Data analysis

In line with our research question, we independently used an inductive content analysis approach to analyse the impact of poverty on basic education in South Africa. We then generated data categories through developing common understanding between the two of us. Finally, we organised the data into themes on which basis we wrote the chapter.

Understanding the term 'poverty'

Quoting Barrientos (2010), Mokomane (2011) reports that in developed countries, social participation and inclusion policies view poverty as the inability of certain people to minimally take part in their communities' social life. In developing countries the 'resourcist' perspective dominates, where poverty is defined as an individual's or family's inability to command resources to sufficiently satisfy basic needs. Looking at these two, Mokomane rightly argues that all in all poverty is an inability by an individual, household, family or entire community to sustain a minimum and socially acceptable standard of living. Currently, extreme poverty is measured as people living on less than US$1.25 a day (The 2030 Agenda for Sustainable Development, Goal 1, item 1.1).

While income and material deprivation go a long way in defining poverty, scholars generally agree that the concept is more nuanced than that – it is multidimensional. In this connection, the UN, as quoted by Mokomane (2011, p. 3), offers the following definition:

> A denial of choices and opportunities, a violation of human dignity. It means lack of basic capacity to participate effectively in society. It means not having enough to feed and clothe a family, not having a school or clinic to go to, not having the land on which to grow one's food or a job to earn one's living, not having access to credit. It means insecurity, powerlessness and exclusion of individuals, households and communities. It means susceptibility to violence, and it often implies living in marginal or fragile environments, without access to clean water or sanitation.

We see therefore a number of manifestations over and above lack of income and productive resources, including but still not limited to, ill health, limited or lack of access to education and other basics, inadequate housing or even homelessness, and lack of participation in social and civic decisions.

Drawing from Noble et al. (2007) and Townsend (1987), Maringe and Moletsane (2015) identify what they found to be the most widely used notions of poverty, which are quite consistent with the notions expressed in the preceding paragraphs. One is income poverty, a situation of low or no income. While South Africa is quite a wealthy country compared to other countries in its 'league' of development, a large proportion of its population suffers severe income poverty. This explains why there is currently debate about the possibility of introducing a minimum wage of R3 500 per month (Chikoko, 2018). The fact that about 14 million South Africans (about a quarter of the total population) rely on government social grants for their upkeep is typical evidence of income poverty. With a Gini co-efficient ranging from 0.660 to 0.696 (Bhorat, Online), South Africa is one of the most consistently unequal countries in the world. Those in the population positioned at the wrong end of the continuum suffer excruciating income poverty.

Material poverty is another. This includes such infrastructure as buildings, transport, water, power supplies, and roads. In schools this may include classrooms, staffrooms, libraries, laboratories and other specialist rooms, and toilets with running water (Maringe & Moletsane, 2015). In South Africa's township settings (high population density settlements in urban settings) for example, most schools therein suffer material poverty because of extremely large enrolments. Classrooms overflow, teacher-learner ratios are big, making teaching and learning largely ineffective. In those and other school contexts such as rural settings, specialised buildings may either be in short supply or ill-equipped. Regarding transport, in the latter contexts, while some schools along main roads may enjoy government-sponsored learner transport and are therefore very accessible, others off the main roads do not have such facility, and therefore suffer such material poverty. In some such contexts, when it rains heavily, teachers reportedly leave their cars some distance away from their schools and walk to work. In some South African schools, material poverty is suffered as a result of vandalism and other forms of unruly behaviour that sees property such as doors, windows, water pipes and other infrastructure either broken or stolen.

Capability poverty is a third type. This refers to inability to accomplish a given task due to lack of requisite knowledge and skills. For example, schools require qualified and competent teachers, among other things, to be able to achieve successful teaching and learning. The apartheid system left a legacy of poor education among black South Africans especially. It is therefore not surprising that the teaching competence of some teachers today is questionable. This is arguably a major factor contributing to the poor performance of the majority of public schools in the National School Certificate examinations year after year. Not only are teachers' capabilities questionable in some cases, school managers' leadership and management capabilities to run their institutions are equally suspect. Thus, we argue that many a school in South Africa suffers capability poverty.

Health poverty is yet another. This relates to a high prevalence of diseases in a given context. It may also entail the prevalence of poor infrastructure where people therein have to travel long distances to health facilities. South Africa has a high prevalence of HIV and AIDS. In such context, those suffering other forms of poverty are likely to be most affected by HIV/AIDS. The most vulnerable are usually people living in remote areas and those in high population density settlements. In South Africa, like in other countries, particularly in the developing world, the HIV/AIDS pandemic has devastated many families, robbing them of parents and breadwinners, resulting in child-headed families and in some cases homelessness.

Nutritional poverty is the last in this series. This is not only to do with a shortage of basic food, it also entails situations of low levels of knowledge about basic nutrition on the part of families and communities. After recognising the prevalence of nutritional poverty among the vulnerable population in the country, South Africa has rolled out a feeding scheme in all needy schools. However, this scheme can only go some distance in addressing the nutritional challenge but cannot totally end such poverty.

Highlights of the education–poverty interface

Emphasising the importance of investing in education as a strategy towards reducing poverty, Tarabini (2010, p. 204) had the following to say:

> International bodies, northern and southern governments and even non-governmental organisations agree on emphasising the virtues of educational investment as a key strategy in the fight against poverty and achieving development.

Drawing from Green (2007), Tarabini further reports that globalisation has involved both winners and losers in terms of how different regions of the world have fared in the global market. The net effect has been the widening of the gap between the richest and poorest nations. Economic growth alone has proved to be insufficient as the dominant solution for achieving development and ending poverty and inequality. Education has attained international legitimacy as a workable strategy in the fight against poverty. This knowledge-based world economy places education at the centre of both national development and competitiveness (Tarabini, 2010).

Similarly, emphasising the crucial role of education in development, the South African National Development Plan 2030 (p. 296) has the following to say:

> South Africa has set itself the goals of eradicating poverty, reducing inequality, growing the economy by an average of 5.4 percent and cutting the unemployment rate to 6 percent by 2030. Education, training and innovation are critical to the attainment of these goals.

According to UNESCO's Global Education Monitoring Report (2017, p. 9), 'Many studies have shown a strong association between poverty and education regarding both school attendance and learning outcomes'. This report indicates that the rates of out-of-school primary and secondary school learners are highest in poor countries. The report shows that the primary out-of-school rate is 19% in low-income countries and 3% in high-income countries. In lower secondary it is 38% and 2% respectively. In upper secondary school it is 62% and 7% respectively.

In the preceding paragraphs we have attempted to show evidence that there seems to be global agreement that education is pivotal towards stimulating development and reducing poverty. Tarabini (2010, p. 210) puts it well that there '… is no doubt that poor people would be in a worse position if they had no access to education'. However, this same author hints that there are limits to education as a priority strategy in fighting poverty. In the author's words:

> If more and better education is not parallel to more and better jobs, if poor people have no options to take advantage of the educational investment, if only access to school for poor pupils is guaranteed, without substantially altering the school and social conditions under which the schooling process takes place, there is a risk of obtaining a better-educated population but that is still as poor as before. A population highly disappointed by the impossibility to fulfil the 'educational promise' (p. 210).

In the section on poverty and returns to schooling, we pursue this matter in greater depth. But to sum up this section on the link between poverty and education, we argue that education is a commodity that must be purchased. Even where a nation has declared free education, the nation in question must purchase education on behalf of its people, the beneficiaries. Where this happens, especially in developing countries, due to other demands competing for resources, governments can only go some way and would expect parents, communities and other stakeholders to play some role towards purchasing education. Inside schools and classrooms, learners from poor families are often vulnerable because they are not likely to have all the learning materials required. Such vulnerability is likely to negatively impact on their attention levels. Such learners' school attendance may be irregular. Such irregularity is likely to lead to school dropout. This explains why as UNESCO's Global Monitoring Report above shows, the rates of out-of-school primary and secondary school learners are highest in poorer countries. Therefore the poorer a community is, the weaker the quality of education it is likely to be able to provide to its people. Turning to the other side of this debate, through developing in the learner, knowledge, skills and positive attitudes, thus increasing chances of one finding employment and therefore sustaining one's own and one's family's livelihoods, education is an instrument for fighting poverty. Therefore, education has great potential to drastically reduce or even eradicate poverty, but poverty can drastically reduce one's success in education. What does the literature say about whether or not basic education is reducing poverty in South Africa? How has education been impacted upon by poverty? These two questions constitute the knowledge gap this chapter seeks to contribute some insights towards.

The impact of poverty on reading literacy achievement

Drawing on evidence from preProgress in International Reading Literacy Study (prePIRLS) 2011, Van Staden and Bosker (2014) studied factors that affect South African reading literacy achievement among Grade 4 learners. They used selected items from the prePIRLS 2011 learner, parent and teacher questionnaires in a two-level model '… to determine the effect of learner aptitude, opportunity to learn and quality of instructional events on reading literacy achievement' (p. 1). These authors rightly argue that reading literacy is one of the most crucial abilities learners should acquire as they progress through their early school years. They further position reading literacy as a foundation for learning across all subjects. Such literacy is not only at the centre of learning in school contexts, it is also required for one to participate more meaningfully and extensively in one's community and society (Van Staden & Bosker, 2014). The latter authors say reading literacy refers to the ability to understand and use appropriate written language forms, to construct meaning from a variety of texts, and to read to learn as well as to read for enjoyment. Reading literacy is particularly important to South African education as the country seeks to transform its national education system from the traditional rote learning approach towards a constructivist school of thought and practice where learning is to be an active process of sense making.

In their own words, Van Staden and Bosker (2014, p. 1) have the following to say regarding the results of this study, among others:

> The results point to the statistical significance of engaged reading and cultivating motivation for reading among learners from an early age, specifically through parental involvement in introducing early literacy activities as foundation of reading literacy by school-going age.

These authors report that the results of their study are consistent with those of other previous studies. For example, they cite Geske and Ozola (2008b) who established that higher reading literacy is likely to occur in cases where children come from families where reading is valued. They further cite Senechal and

Young (2008) who found parental involvement to be crucial in children's literacy development, with more dividends accruing when parents tutored their children. They also cite Becker and Luthar (2002) who found

> ...evidence of the achievement gap that still pervade[s] patterns of achievement among disadvantaged learners and others, despite concentrated efforts to improve inferior academic outcomes in countries across the globe (p. 7).

Currently, it is not contestable that the majority of South African public schools are located in poor communities largely in rural and township contexts. The South African government's landmark decision to quintile schools according to levels of poverty in their surrounding communities, and to fund schools accordingly, is testimony to the gravity of poverty among many South Africans, particularly amongst the formerly oppressed black majority. Poor schools constitute the majority in the country. The majority of the latter schools is still under-performing in terms of learner performance in the National Senior Certificate examinations as well as in learner retention throughout the 12 years of formal schooling. Given the crucial role of learners' reading literacy ability in their academic achievement levels, given the poverty among the majority of parents in South Africa, and given the crucial role parents play towards their children's reading literacy achievement levels, it is not surprising that the majority of South African public schools underperform. Thus, we argue that parental poverty has had and continues to impact negatively on the academic performance of the majority of learners in South Africa.

How poverty is impacting on school dropout

In South Africa, Grades 1-9 comprise a band of compulsory schooling. Section 3(1) of the South African Schools Act of 1996 stipulates that all children must attend school from the first day of the academic year in which a learner reaches seven years until the last day in which one reaches fifteen years or the ninth grade whichever comes first. Within the latter band, South Africa has a very high rate (over 95%) of learner participation (Hartnack, 2017). 'Most school dropout in South Africa occurs in grades 10 and 11, resulting in 50% of learners in any one cohort dropping out before reaching grade 12' (Hatnack, 2017, p. 1 quoting Spaull, 2015). Interestingly, research evidence shows that poorer provinces such as Limpopo, Mpumalanga and the Free State record a higher proportion of Grade 1-9 learners in school than wealthier ones such as Gauteng, Northern Cape and Western Cape. The tendency is that more learners drop out in cities than in rural contexts with the exception of rural farming areas of the Western Cape where the opposite is true (Fleisch et al., 2009). One possible explanation for this apparent contradiction is that schools in very poor communities provide food to learners. If this explanation is anything to go by, we can argue that something bad has reared something good. Poverty reared a response by government to provide food which, in turn, has apparently kept learners in school at least up to the end of the compulsory band. However, if learners stay in school more for the sake of food than learning, such children are not likely to adequately benefit from the education system. Communities in question are seemingly trapped in continued dependence on government handouts.

Due to social, spatial and economic policies of apartheid which continue to be exclusionary and unjust, thus causing severe inequality (Moses et al., 2017 in Hatnack, 2017), levels of learner dropout markedly differ by race. The results of the 2011 General Household Survey show that only 44% of Black and Coloured youth between ages 23-24 had attained a Senior School Certificate compared to 83% of Indian and 88% of White youth (Spaull, 2015). How learners experience poverty in school and in their daily lives will impact upon their decision to drop out or stay in school. Learners who feel unequal to their counterparts are likely to absent themselves more frequently and eventually drop out. Spaull (2015) reports that teenage pregnancy among many black South Africans living in poverty serves as a strong risk factor for dropping out of school. Branson, Hofmeyr and Lam (2014), also report that a number of researchers (Gustafsson, 2011; Grant & Hallman, 2006; and Strassburg et al., 2010), indicate that pregnancy is a common reason female students give for dropping out. While Government policy says such learners must not be excluded, other attendant problems, such as the phenomenon being a stigma among one's peers, may still cause dropout.

Hartnack (2017), drawing from De Witte et al. (2013) reports that repeating a Grade or Grades is one of the most, if not the strongest predictor of school dropout. Being older than one's classmates comes with stigma. Older girls are more prone to pregnancy. Older boys and girls, particularly those from poor families, are likely to face the need to work. Other factors such as learning disabilities aside, learners from poor families are more likely to repeat Grades than those from affluent ones. As Spaull (2015, p. 37) rightly reports, over 75% of South African learners are from low socio-economic status families. They attend poorly performing schools that offer them poor-quality education. Because these learners attend struggling schools, many of them become struggling learners. Struggling learners in equally struggling schools are at higher risk of dropping out than those in better performing schools (Branson et al., 2013, in Hartnack, 2017).

Schools in poor communities are often under-resourced (De Witte et al., 2013). This includes such challenges as inadequate desks and chairs, shortage of text books, limited or no libraries and other resources, shortage of specialist teachers or even teachers in general, and so on. Such schools often endure large class sizes. They are also likely to have weak leadership. Overall, such schools' social and economic capitals are low. All these challenges impact negatively on teaching. The net effect is likely to be what De Witte et al. (2013) call 'a troubled learner'. Such learner is more likely to drop out of school than stay.

Drawing from Gustafsson (2011), Hartnack (2017) rightly argues that the South African curriculum's focus on maths and science skills at the expense of other subjects makes school difficult for those learners whose aptitudes are aligned elsewhere. While vocational subjects are part of the national 'menu', due to shortage of teachers, they may not always be readily available in the schools that need these subjects most. This may cause learners to lose faith in the school system the result of which may be dropping out of the system.

Lambani (2011) investigated the cause of teenage pregnancy in Thulamela Municipality in the Limpopo province of South Africa. She randomly selected and interviewed ten young mothers of an average age of 18 years all of whom had children on their backs, having come to a shopping complex to receive the child support grant (CSG). All these young mothers were reportedly school dropouts. On why they had fallen pregnant at an early age, Lambani reports that the participants said it was largely due to pressure from friends who enticed them with the prospect of receiving the CSG. The friends impressed upon them that through the CSG they enjoyed financial freedom to buy clothes and groceries of their choice, as opposed to depending upon their parents.

The down-stream effects of falling pregnant at such an early age obviously outweigh the benefits of accessing a child support grant. However, what we learn here is that in a context of poverty, such logic may not prevail. In this case, poverty conquered these young women's minds to the extent of abandoning the schooling project and all its attendant prospects. We know it is government policy that girls are free to return to school after giving birth, but it seems this is a matter easier said than done. Ranchhod et al. (2011) found that childbearing had a direct effect on the mother's decision to drop out.

Branson et al. (2014) found that not keeping pace at school is a major determinant of who drops out. They also found that in South Africa, falling behind at school was strongly related to one's socio-economic status as well as school quality. They conclude that better quality schools can partially cushion struggling learners from dropping out, thus suggesting that improving school quality could play a role in reducing dropout.

The evidence suggests that learners in poverty-stricken school contexts are more likely to fall behind in school than those in better-resourced environments. Thus they are more likely to drop out than those not falling behind. Worse still, the former schools are ill-equipped to help their learners move out of the falling behind bracket. Therefore poverty is implicated in learner dropout in a big way.

Inglis and Lewis (2013) studied adolescents at risk of dropping out in a high-risk community secondary school in Western Cape Province. Through a qualitative, case study research approach, they sought to understand the subjective experiences of adolescent learners in that regard. They define 'at risk' as situations where certain dynamics may cause learners to drop out of school. In the context they studied, such dynamics included dysfunctional families, poor schools, substance abuse and negative social interactions. Findings reveal that the adolescents experienced several barriers to learning embedded within interconnected contexts, which placed them at high risk of dropping out of school. These included single-parent families, conflict in families, little or no parental support, substance abuse and emotional challenges. These barriers encapsulate all the types of poverty we identified earlier in this chapter. To illustrate, we can associate conflict with capability poverty. Drug abuse relates to health poverty. All the barriers boil down to material, income and capability poverty.

Therefore we can safely argue that poverty puts communities, schools and learners at risk. Learners at risk are likely to drop out of school. Communities and schools at risk are likely to be suffering capability poverty to be able to turn around the dire situations in which they find themselves.

Poverty and returns to schooling in post-apartheid South Africa
During the apartheid era in South Africa, there existed a yawning economic gap between whites and the rest of the population. In the initial post-apartheid years, there was hope that with increased levels of education among all population groups of the country, there would be fairer labour market practices and greater labour mobility, which would see a significant reduction in the large gaps in earnings between white South Africans and other racial groups.

In a study on education and inequality in South Africa, Salisbury (2016) utilised a newer data set than those used in previous studies from the 1990s, to calculate both the social and private returns to schooling. Specifically, Salisbury examined whether the returns for African and Coloured nationals have improved since the initial 1990s post-apartheid era. Salisbury reports that during the latter era, returns for Africans and Coloureds were higher than in previous decades. However, the overall picture still favoured whites. To illustrate, Salisbury (2016) reports that as of 2008, remuneration outcomes for Africans and Coloureds continued to lag behind those of white South Africans by more than 20 percent. Salisbury's 2016 study is important in that although the gap in economic outcomes between races as reported above is no longer an institutionalised feature of the South African society, but despite massive increases in the past two decades, in average educational attainment by the formerly oppressed population groups of the country, racial differences persist.

Out of the study, Salisbury concluded that on average, white South Africans earn 369 and 355 percent more than Africans and Coloureds respectively. When this is translated into returns per additional year of schooling, whites earn 23 percent more compared to 16 and 19 percent for Africans and Coloureds respectively. Salisbury argues that if this discrepancy persists, the macro inequality situation in South Africa's economy will get worse over time. This author reports that one of the major barriers against progress towards equality is to do with the undervaluing of the productive characteristics of Africans and Coloureds compared to whites. As we indicated earlier, average education levels among African and Coloured groups continue to rise. However, Salisbury rightly argues that this achievement will not reduce economic disparities so long as those years are valued less than those for whites. Although there may still exist salient racial discrimination, Salisbury raises an important point that the situation may be a reflection of lower quality of education obtained by Africans and Coloureds during their school years particularly regarding the productive skills employers reward. Therefore, additional schooling on its own will not necessarily translate into additional earning power and, by implication, better life.

Low-quality education is a function of a number of forms of poverty including income, material and capability poverty. Poor parents and communities will suffer income poverty, preventing them from adequately providing for their children's educational needs. Schools in poor communities will suffer material poverty, thus negatively impacting on the effectiveness of their services. Teachers in resource-scarce schools may not be the best professionals available as they may suffer capability poverty, thus making their teaching ineffective. The net result is low-quality education.

Poverty and the new educational policy landscape in post-apartheid South Africa

We have also detected the impact of poverty on education through an analysis of post-apartheid educational policies and implications for attempting to implement them. In this regard, we draw from a journal article by Christie (2010). Christie reports that because apartheid educational policies were structured along unequal racial lines, the post-1994 government had to shoulder a two-pronged responsibility: to dismantle the old structure and design and implement a new system. The author cites specific landmark policies in this regard. The National Education Policy Act of 1996 set decision-making structures. The South African Schools Act of 1996 established governance frameworks. The Education Labour Relations Act of 1995 set the framework regarding teachers' conditions of service, codes of conduct as well as duties and responsibilities. These and other policies, Christie (2010, p. 702) argues, were designed to end apartheid and establish a new dispensation in education. They constitute '…an elegant cartography but one not necessarily suited to the complex and uneven terrain that required change'.

Christie (ibid) cites the area of school governance as one of those characterised by such complexity and unevenness. A school's School Governing Body (SGB), comprising of the principal (*ex officio*), elected parents, teachers, non-teaching staff, and in secondary schools, students, is given extensive powers. These include determining the school's admissions policies, deciding the school's language policy, determining school fees, determining choice of subject options, recommending the appointment of staff, acquiring and controlling school assets and opening and maintaining a school account, among others. Christie (2010, p. 702) rightly argues that while this rich list of powers requires considerable amounts of time and expertise for a school to implement, '…it goes without saying that South African schools are vastly unequal in terms of the human and financial resources they are able to draw on in implementing policies at school level'. She further argues that while parent bodies of the well- functioning schools (former white and Indian schools) have leveraged their resources and social capital to their schools' advantage, including being able to hire additional teachers and therefore offering broad and rich curricula, the majority of schools (former black) find themselves serving communities too poor to pay basic fees, have their teachers working in difficult conditions, and governing bodies therein are often unskilled. Therefore, although both the rich and the poor schools operate within the same governance structure, the terrain is grossly uneven. Thus it goes without saying that the quality of the governance outcomes will differ markedly. This is how poverty is impacting upon the otherwise very noble school governance policy.

The second area Christie identifies is that of Labour Relations. She reports that a new dispensation to regulate teachers' conditions of work had to be put in place, largely to replace the hitherto conflictual one where schools and the entire education system were sites of political contestation. The powerful South African Democratic Teachers' Union (SADTU) is a product of the teacher militancy then. Today, what we see on the ground is that SADTU is represented most in the majority of schools serving former black communities and therefore the historically generally poorer population of the country. Schools in the latter communities often experience teacher strikes some of which stretch for weeks of no teaching and learning. While this happens, schools in more affluent communities (largely former white and to some degree Indian) will be in full scale teaching and learning. In our experience as educationists in South Africa, we know that teachers, like most professionals, tend to send their children to the more affluent schools in search of a better quality education which of course is more expensive and out of reach of poorer families. What it means therefore, is that while a teacher from the former school context is on strike, their own children will continue to learn in the latter school context. This state of affairs shows that children of poorer families are likely to suffer less teaching-learning time, let alone the quality thereof, compared to their counterparts in contexts where strikes are almost non-existent.

The third and last area Christie identifies is performance management. This is to do with ensuring accountability, in this case on the part of all civil servants. Christie reports that after the breakdown of apartheid, and because of continuing disparities between schools, a number of accountability systems were agreed upon. In education, these included Developmental Appraisal in 1998, Whole School Evaluation in 2001 and Performance Management in 2003 (Christie, 2010). The three were integrated in 2003 to form the integrated quality management system (IQMS). This performance management system, as Christie (p. 706) rightly puts it, '…requires a complex system of paperwork and a time-consuming monitoring system'.

The complexity and time-consuming nature of the performance management system are to be expected. After all, education is a complex affair involving a multiplicity of stakeholders, among many other factors. However, we borrow the main argument from Christie that schools in South Africa do not function equally. Many schools remain dysfunctional. Well-functioning schools can successfully implement the complex performance management system, but the same is unachievable in dysfunctional schools which are often characterised by such misconduct as teacher and learner absenteeism, late coming and early knocking off, weak grasp of content by the teachers and of course subsequent poor learner performance in both national and international tests and examinations. These ills are rife in the poorer communities of South Africa. We can therefore safely argue that poverty is implicated in the unevenness of the terrain in different schools and communities of the country. Christie (2010, p. 708) succinctly sums up the impact of the new educational policy landscape as follows:

> It is by now a well-established criticism of South Africa's policies that they are more suited to the well-functioning parts of the education system and have unintentionally widened inequalities.

Poverty as a categoriser of some schools

Maringe, Masinire and Nkambule (2015) studied the specific challenges that schools in multiple deprived communities in South Africa face. They conducted the study in three selected schools against the backdrop that in South Africa, even decades after the dismantling of apartheid, '…the "two-nation" metaphor continues to rear its ugly head in the education sector, as it does in other spheres' (p. 364). In other words, the hitherto poor and marginalised communities have largely remained in that state. The authors view multiple deprivation as the combined impact of a multiplicity of indicators of poverty negatively impacting on the quality of people's livelihoods. Drawing from international and local census data, and as we reported earlier on in this chapter, these researchers identify multiple deprivation indices including income, material, education, employment, living environment and health deprivation (Nobel, et al., 2009, in Maringe, Masinire & Nkambule, 2015).

They identified what they refer to as distinctive features of schools in multiple deprived communities. First, a shared framework of community poverty. The schools are situated within a 10 km radius. They are trapped in a context of low-paid jobs in mines, farms, a game park, self-employment, high levels of unemployment, high adult illiteracy and HIV/AIDS. Second, a culture of underperformance. Because of this, learners often fail to qualify for further and higher education, employment and training. The schools also fail to attract a critical mass of new learners. Morale among teachers and school managers decreases, and so does communities' confidence in the school as well as their commitment thereto. Third, a shared context of inadequate teaching-learning resources. These include learning spaces such as classrooms and books. Fourth, staff instability. These arose due to factors such as conflict and fluctuating teacher-pupil ratios resulting in some teachers being redeployed. Those teachers redeployed to these multiple deprived schools are often the troublesome and not-so-competent ones who have not much choice. Fifth and last, physical but not epistemological access. While the South African government has made tremendous strides to provide access to schooling for every child, the plethora of challenges we identified in the other distinctive features above collectively militate against quality teaching and learning in the schools in question.

Poverty and the implementation of inclusive education
Inclusive education is about providing for equity and social justice. This is particularly important in post-apartheid South Africa, as a strategy to cater for the previously severely marginalised learners with special learning needs. Stofile et al. (2011) studied teachers' experiences on how poverty affected the implementation of inclusive education in one district of the Eastern Cape Province. They indicate that the province is one of the poorest provinces in South Africa. Through focus group discussions with teachers as well as individual interviews with school principals, these researchers concluded that poverty was a major barrier to education participation by both learners and their parents.

Participants reported that hunger and poor nutrition among learners was one barrier. As a result, some learners reportedly experienced attention and concentration difficulties, leading to dropout or non-completion. In some cases, learners lacked basic reading and writing materials. This resulted in only a few being able to read and do homework after school. Also, basic infrastructure such as washrooms was often below standard. Learners consumed considerable amounts of time away from classes to attend to hygiene matters. Parents or guardians were largely unable to provide the needed support. This placed enormous pressure on the teachers who often found themselves altering their main roles to attend to learners. This took a toll on the teachers' wellbeing. Teachers reported that they were effectively unpaid social workers over and above their conventional role as classroom practitioners. Because parental participation was either very low or non-existent, teachers were denied parental perspectives and inputs regarding their children. The participants were of the view that the situation should not be interpreted as a lack of interest on the part of parents in their children's education but an indication of the extant poverty that they suffer.

Poverty as a trigger for self-emancipation

While many schools in South Africa, as the bulk of the evidence we presented in the preceding section testifies, have severely suffered from the effects of poverty, research shows that a few have refused to remain in that state of victimhood and mourn unendingly. Instead, such schools have developed and are implementing largely home-grown approaches towards successful teaching and learning.

Chikoko, Naicker and Mthiyane (2015) studied school leadership practices that work in contexts of multiple deprivation in South Africa. This study was triggered by a realisation that the hitherto two main categorisations of schools namely, previously and still advantaged, very functional schools on one hand, and previously disadvantaged, and still so, dysfunctional schools on the other, were no longer portraying the full picture. A middle-of-the-continuum type of schools had emerged, ones that succeeded in severely deprived contexts. In that connection, the researchers sought to understand the nature of leadership in such schools. They found that such schools tended to adopt inside-out development approaches, driven by a conviction that they were and had to be masters of their own destiny; therefore solutions had to be crafted from within. Some of their own assets they brought to bear included time, commitment, and accountability on the part of every 'player'. The schools used their small successes as platforms for bigger, stronger synergies with the local and broader communities. These researchers conclude that the greatest instrument for emancipation in those schools was leadership that shifts minds from notions of helplessness or deficit thinking, towards asset-based thinking.

Similarly, Mbokazi (2015) studied dimensions of successful leadership in selected township secondary schools (townships are a typical example of largely deprived contexts) and came up with four such dimensions. First, the strategic dimension. The school principals were found to have successfully articulated the vision and values of their schools. They created positive climates for achievement. They also invested in capacity-building of stakeholders. Second, the pedagogic dimension. In this regard, the schools focused on managing teaching and learning. Teachers not only worked hard but did so in co-operative ways. Third, the regulatory dimension. The schools had clear disciplinary practices in place. They acted decisively on matters such as late-coming, absenteeism and substance abuse. The schools were also very efficient in managing time. Lastly, the compensatory dimension. The schools invested in building strong links between school and community in general and school and home in particular. This entailed not just fluent communication between the two but also involvement in the affairs of both school and community on the part of both the school staff and parents and other members of the community.

In a conceptual paper, Maringe and Moletsane (2015) report that studies on successful principals in schools facing severe deprivation (which is essentially what we are calling poor schools in this chapter), develop strong and sustainable ties with their communities, they are philanthropic in approach, they are generous with their time as they engage with stakeholders, work hard to alleviate poverty among learners, and focus strongly on ensuring high-quality teaching and learning.

In a study in KwaZulu-Natal province on the nature of school leadership in a school in a poor context, Bayeni (2018) reports that in order to tackle the school's many challenges, the school principal, working together with both the staff and the local community, transformed the school into both a home and a school for the learners. So a school-based policy was formulated. Because learners' homes were not conducive for them to do homework and further study, all the work would now be done at the school. At the end of the normal school day at 14:30 hrs, learners would be released for an hour to spend at home and required to be back at school thereafter until 18:00 hrs. The school organised both lunch and dinner for the learners out of donations from local businesses. They also provided transport for them to travel back home in the evening. During the extra hours at the school, learners would do homework, receive extra tuition, and do personal study. By the time they got back home, all school work would have been done. This programme entailed the buy-in of teachers and the total commitment of the school management, both of whom had to put in extra hours to supervise and manage the programme.

What we learn here is that the state of poverty can and has awakened otherwise dormant energy where people adopt a 'we can do it' approach. Had such communities not suffered poverty, perhaps the 'we can do it' factor may not have been that strong.

Sound leadership has emerged as one of, if not the most influential factor to explain such success.

Learning from the evidence

Poverty has dealt a severe blow to the foundation for learning. Evidence shows that despite efforts to improve educational achievement for all learners, generally, there remains an achievement gap between learners from disadvantaged backgrounds compared to those from well-provided ones. Reading literacy, which is the foundation of all learning, is better achieved among learners growing up in the latter contexts than those from the former. This emphasises the importance of a child's home in building this learning foundation. However, we contend that in South Africa, many families and communities remain materially constrained to the extent that the situation is not likely to drastically change in the near future. It therefore seems to us that there is a need to build capacity in schools to enable them to go the extra mile in building learning foundations for the disadvantaged child.

Poverty is a major determinant of learner dropout. Due to material and other forms of poverty, learners from poor backgrounds often feel a sense of inadequacy in classroom and school contexts. They feel a sense of inequality and therefore become learners at risk. Such learners often absent themselves, thus worsening their capability regarding coping with school work, eventually leading to dropout. Thus, poverty seems to have a negative impact on a learner's self-efficacy.

The evidence also shows that poverty is a major determinant of girls falling pregnant. The certainty of one receiving a child social grant from the government after the baby is born and the false financial independence it brings, have reportedly motivated girls to fall pregnant. Once pregnant, most girls drop out of school. What emerges here is that poverty seems to negatively impact on the mind-sets of those affected.

Poverty has a negative impact on the quality of education a school can offer. Due to financial constraints, schools in poverty-stricken contexts are likely to offer only the most basic of curricula. They cannot afford to hire extra teachers. They cannot attract teachers with special, rare skills and expertise. They are ill-equipped to offer broad curricula. But we know that the broader a school curriculum is, the greater the chances that learners of different capabilities and interests may find learning meaningful to them. We can therefore safely argue that the quality of education in poverty-stricken school contexts is largely lower than the one in more affluent communities. The evidence shows that this reality has a direct link with the subsequent social and private returns of education in that, rightly or wrongly, employers tend to undervalue the potential productivity of one who would have studied in poor education contexts. The net effect is that poverty is a big catalyst to continued huge inequalities in the South African society. In complete contrast to the United Nations' 2030 Agenda for Sustainable Development's adage that no one shall be left behind, poverty is leaving the affected communities, including learners therein, behind.

Poverty is challenging the efficacy of the post-apartheid one-size-fits-all notion of the implementation of some education policies. To illustrate, the broad-based powers given to the School Governing Bodies remain un-exercisable in poor school contexts where the majority office bearers are not only unskilled but also incapable of leveraging society for the betterment of the school. Similarly, the complexity and protracted nature of the performance management system is such that the less knowledgeable and lowly skilled poor school communities are unlikely to be able to implement it effectively. The otherwise noble and democratic policy framework to give voice to labour through unions such as SADTU has had to contend with loss of teaching-learning time mostly in disadvantaged communities due to protracted teacher strikes. Thus, the government is caught between a rock and a hard place to either craft differential policies and run the risk of retrogressing, or seek to develop capacity among stakeholders who implement these policies, which resources it does not have in abundance.

Poverty has, by default, impacted positively in some schools and their communities by awakening agency in themselves as their own 'liberators' in terms of generating solutions towards improving school performance. This has entailed a shift from deficit thinking to asset-based approaches. Such a shift is quite consistent with the notion of sustainable development.

Conclusion

The evidence we have presented in this chapter is consistent with South Africa's National Development Plan 2030's position that poverty in the country is a great enemy that must be fiercely fought. Reading literacy is the backbone of all learning but sadly, due to poverty, many learners are unable to achieve such foundation. It is not enough for South Africa to have put in place landmark education policies because despite them being well-meaning, they are difficult to implement fully in poor contexts. Thus, poverty has rendered the same previously disadvantaged communities to be at risk. In the latter communities, education is inevitably of low quality. This has a negative ripple effect on the employability of students therefrom as their education is largely under-valued. Therefore the struggle should be two-pronged: fighting poverty on the one hand, and crafting and implementing ways to improve the quality of education on the other. In that struggle, schools and communities need to drastically shift from deficit- to asset-based thinking and doing.

References

Bayeni, S. (2018). School Leaders Leading and Managing in Deprived School Contexts: A Policy Perspective, In V. Chikoko (Ed.), *Leadership that Works in Deprived School Contexts of South Africa*, pp. 227-246, New York: Nova Science Publishers.

Bhorat, H. (Online), FactCheck: is South Africa the most unequal Society in the World? https://theconversation.com/factcheck-is-south-africa-the-most-unequal-society-in-the-world-48334. Accessed on 04 November 2019.

Branson, N., Hofmeyr, C., & Lam, D. (2014). Progress through school and the determinants of school dropout in South Africa. *Development Southern Africa*, 31(1), 106-126. https://doi.org/10.1080/0376835X.2013.853610

Chikoko, V. (2018). The Nature of the Deprived School Context, In V. Chikoko (Ed.). *Leadership that works in deprived school contexts of South Africa*. New York: Nova Publishers.

Chikoko, V., Naicker, I., & Mthiyane, S. (2015). School leadership practices that work in areas of multiple deprivation in South Africa. *Emal*, 43(3), 453-467. https://doi.org/10.1177/1741143215570186

Christie, P. (2010). Landscapes of Leadership in South African Schools: Mapping the Changes. *Educational Management, Administration & Leadership* 38(6), 694-711. https://doi.org/10.1177/1741143210379062

Christie, P., Butler, D., & Potterton, M. (2007). *Schools that Work*. Report of the Ministerial Committee. Pretoria: Government Printer.

De Witte, K., Cabus, S., Thyssen, G., Groot, W., & Van den Brink, H.M. (2013). A Critical Review of the Literature on School Dropout. *Tier Working Paper Series:* Tier WP 14/14. https://doi.org/10.1016/j.edurev.2013.05.002

Hartnack, A. (2017). Background document and review of key South African and international literature on school dropout. *Sustainable Livelihoods Foundation*, July 2017.

Inglis, D., & Lewis, A. (2013). Adolescents at risk of dropping out in a high-risk community secondary school. *Child Abuse Research: A South African Journal*, 14(1), 46-54.

Khan, K.S., Kunz, R., Kleijnen, J., & Antes, G. (2003). Five steps to conducting a systematic review. *Journal of the Royal Society of Medicine*, 96(3), 118–121. https://doi.org/10.1258/jrsm.96.3.118

Lambani, M.N. (2015). Poverty the cause of teenage pregnancy in Thulamela Municipality. *Journal of Sociology and Social Anthropology*, 6(2), 171-176. https://doi.org/10.1080/09766634.2015.11885656

Maringe, F., & Moletsane, R. (2015). Leading schools in circumstances of multiple deprivation in South Africa: Mapping some conceptual, contextual and research dimensions. *Educational management, administration & leadership,* 43(3), 347-362. https://doi.org/10.1177/1741143215575533

Maringe, F., Masnire, A., & Nkambule, T. (2015). Distinctive features of schools in multiple deprived communities in South Africa: Implications for policy and leadership. *EMAL,* 43(3), 363-385. https://doi.org/10.1177/1741143215570303

Mbokazi, Z. (2015). Dimensions of successful leadership in Soweto township secondary schools. *EMAL,* 43(3), 468-482. https://doi.org/10.1177/1741143215570304

Mokomane, Z. (2011). *Anti-Poverty Family-Focused Policies in Developing Countries.* Background paper presented to the Secretariat of the United Nations.

Prew, M. (2007). Successful principals: why some principals succeed and others struggle when faced with innovation and transformation. *South African Journal of Education* 27(3), 447-462.

Ranchhod, V., Branson, N., Lam, D., & Marteleto, L. (2011). *Estimating the effect of adolescent childbearing on educational attainment in Cape Town using a propensity score weighted regression.* SALDRU Working Paper No 59, University of Cape Town, Cape Town.

Salisbury, T. (2016). Education and inequality in South Africa: Returns to schooling in the post-apartheid era. *International Journal of Educational Development,* 46 (2016), 43-52. https://doi.org/10.1016/j.ijedudev.2015.07.004

Spaull, N. (2015). Schooling in South Africa: How Low-quality Education Becomes a Poverty Trap. *South African Child Gauge 2015.*

Tarabini, A. (2010). Education and poverty in the global development agenda: Emergence, evolution and consolidation. *International Journal of Educational Development,* 30, 204-212. https://doi.org/10.1016/j.ijedudev.2009.04.009

United Nations, (2015). Transforming Our World: The 2030 Agenda for Sustainable Development. New York: *United Nations, A/RES/70/1.*

Van Staden, S., & Bosker, R. (2014). Factors that affect South African Reading Literacy Achievement: evidence from prePIRLS 2011. *South African Journal of Education,* 34(3), 1-9. https://doi.org/10.15700/201409161059

CHAPTER 4

Review and evaluation studies of school effectiveness and improvement in South Africa: A systematic and critical appraisal
Francine de Clercq and Yael Shalem

Abstract

This chapter provides a scoping review of recent research and evaluation studies of various South African school improvement interventions. The aim is to present the findings of the studies as well as their strengths and weaknesses in terms of what they say about factors associated with improved learners' results and the kind of support and pressure mechanisms needed for effective school change. While all studies focus on school-based factors, and some acknowledge factors outside of the formal education system that undermine learners' results, none of the studies provides a reasonable explanation of how and why certain factors work better to improve and change schools. It therefore argues that reviews and evaluation studies need to rely on theories of education in society and theories of teaching and learning in examining improvement interventions. It is only then that scholars will contribute to knowledge about effective intervention programmes or policies that can reduce educational inequalities.

Introduction

In the last 25 years, South African education departments have struggled to improve the performance of disadvantaged black schools through various school improvement projects and interventions. More recently, education departments and NGOs have worked in partnership towards more large-scale improvement programmes. Scholars and evaluators have studied these different improvement interventions with the view to improving the knowledge base for effective South African school improvement models.

This chapter conducts an overview of eight qualitative research and evaluation studies of South African school improvement interventions. The focus of these studies, based on secondary data, is to identify the key effectiveness and improvement factors associated with improved learner performance as well as the support and pressure mechanisms needed for effective school improvement and change interventions. This overview takes the form of a qualitative scoping review that asks the following question: what do these studies tell us and do not tell us and how can a broader perspective add to the study of school improvement.

A qualitative scoping review is a relatively new approach that aims to provide an overview of the available research evidence and findings in a research area. Scholars mention that scoping reviews examine the extent, range, and nature of research activity in a topic area, determine the value and potential scope and identify research gaps in the existing literature (Arksey & O'Malley, 2005). Daudt et al. explain that scoping reviews "map the literature on a particular topic or research area and provide an opportunity to identify key concepts; gaps in the research [which] inform practice, policy-making and research" (Daudt et al., 2013, p. 8).

To select the eight review and evaluation studies of South African improvement interventions, we used three criteria. First, the studies had to be available to the public in the recent period. We went on the net and benefited from the assistance of expert consultants studying or evaluating improvement interventions. The eight studies we cover in the review were published in the period 2006-2016 as reports, chapters in books and one is part of a PhD. Second, the studies had to synthesize or assess recent South African improvement interventions targeting a large number of schools. The eight improvement interventions studied or evaluated occurred in the period 2000–2014 and involved many schools (and sometimes districts). Third, the studies had to cover interventions that rely on a diversity of improvement models with underlying theories of change. Many of the eight studies concluded with the need to change the focus of improvement interventions while others proposed a new model from which to assess school improvement interventions. Two studies argued for the need for large-scale systemic improvement interventions (interventions that happened subsequently, and two of which are analyzed at the end of this chapter), while one or two studies advised that review and evaluation studies should focus on the design and implementation of school interventions. The inclusion of these criteria proved productive as it enabled us to develop a broad perspective 'from above' of various South African school effectiveness and improvement factors as well as of drivers for pressure and support towards districts, schools and teachers.

In examining the eight research and evaluation studies of South African school improvement interventions (henceforth 'the studies'), this review first clarifies the concepts of effectiveness and improvement factors as well as change tools of pressure and support. It shows that the studies provide evidence and findings about the 'what' of school improvement and change interventions. However, this review argue that they leave important knowledge gaps by not conceptualizing the 'how' and 'why' of improvement and change factors associated with better school performance. This review concludes that the only way to advance our understanding of SA school improvement models is by unpacking and further developing the theories of schooling and learning as these inform (often implicitly) the design of school improvement interventions and their review and evaluation studies. Critical insights from the political economy field will also improve school improvement research.

In section one, we outline the international debates around school effectiveness and improvement research. Section two traces recent developments in the school effectiveness and improvement research in South Africa to give a background against which section three explores the findings, strengths and weaknesses of the South African studies in a chronological order. It then compares their similarities and differences in terms of the factors targeted and the kind of pressure and support used for effective school improvement and change interventions. This section ends with a critical appraisal of these studies. In section four, we draw on a study of schooling (Taylor et al., 2003) to explain the institutional complexity involved in changing teacher practices and demonstrate the importance of theorizing learning and change. We argue that a reliance on theories of schooling, of teaching and learning as well as of change is essential to explain under what conditions and why certain school improvement interventions are likely to have more or less impact. This theoretical dimension is illustrated in our critical appraisal of two promising large-scale systemic interventions and informs our suggestions for effective school improvement research. We conclude on the powerful explanatory power of the field of political economy.

International lens on school effectiveness and improvement research

The question of why some students from within and across countries perform better than others led researchers, such as Coleman (1968) and Bowles and Gintis (1976), to investigate the impact of schooling on the socio-economically and racially stratified US society. They found that students' achievements were more influenced by their socio-economic and family background than by school input effects. With the increasing availability, from the 1970s onwards, of large data sets on the education system, its throughput and outcomes, researchers continued to study the impact of different non-school and school inputs and practices on students' academic achievements (Jenks, Smith, et al., 1972; Teddlie & Reynolds, 2000). These statistical research studies became known as school production function studies and a basis for the School Effectiveness Research (SER).

In identifying the factors mostly associated with students' achievements, these researchers relied on quantitative regression analyses and multi-modelling techniques to correlate quantifiable school input and practices [independent variables] with students' achievements or results [dependent variable]. Being policy-driven, they hoped to identify causal links between policy variables and educational outcomes, or between socio-economic contexts and educational inputs and educational outcomes. SE researchers were influenced by, and rooted in, the dominant theories of the time, which, in the 1970s, were the liberal functionalist sociological theory of education, the liberal human capital theory and/or the neoclassical theory of economic growth. Unlike social reproduction theorists influenced by Marxism, who saw schooling as a tool for the reproduction of class (and other social) inequalities, these theories argued that education matters and is beneficial to all in society because of its contribution to the skills needed by the country's socio-economic development and the promotion of social upward mobility.

Within liberal sociological theory, researchers in the field of school reform investigated processes of school improvement (Hopkins, Ainscow, & West, 1994; Slavin, 1998). Their interest was not in a snapshot of effective and non-effective schools but rather in what it takes for different schools to improve. School improvement research (SIR) developed swiftly during the 1980s and 1990s, at a time when international policy called to decentralise greater powers to schools because schools were then perceived to be the best level at which to take decisions to improve school performance. The SI researchers argue that school improvement strategies differ and have to be tailored to the state and context of each school. Following Fullan's emphasis (1982) on pressure and support as the two main drivers or mechanisms of change, Elmore (2005) theorises a version of this idea in his study on reciprocal accountability, where he argues that: "for every unit of change performance that is required, an equivalent unit of support and capacity building is expected to be invested".

Historical lens on school effectiveness and improvement research in South Africa

During the 1980s and 1990s, educational research was focused on how apartheid and capitalism worked together to produce two radical unequal systems of education, serving the interests of whites for racial oppression and class exploitation (Christie & Collins, 1982; Kallaway, 1984; Nkomo, 1990). The first evaluation study based on empirical investigations in schools was *Getting Learning Right* (Taylor & Vinjevold, 1999), and this was followed with an empirical and conceptual analysis of schooling: *Getting Schools Working: Research and Systematic Reform in South Africa* (Taylor et al., 2003).

Arguably, one of the more influential school effectiveness studies which sparked other production function analyses was *No magic bullets, just tracer bullets* (Crouch & Mabogoane, 2001). This was one of the first SE studies post-1994 liberation that established the claim that poverty should not be seen as the main binding constraint in school effectiveness. These researchers argue that, taking into account various measures of poverty and school resources, some 30% of the performance of schools remains 'unexplained' and should be based on in-school differences. *Schools as (Dis) organisations* (Christie, 1998) turned to psychoanalytical organisational theorists to argue that poor organisational capacity is compounded by negativity and apathy and so school reform needs more than efficiency. It needs an understanding of the unconscious group activity which, under poor organisational conditions and poverty, gives rise to conflicts and contestations (1998, p. 293). School reform, she argues (drawing one from Zaleznik), needs to engage with the 'psycho-politics' of school members. In *Schools that work*, a Ministerial committee report (Christie, Butler, &

Potterton, 2007) on poor schools in poor contexts which succeeded despite their circumstances, it is argued that these schools focus on their central task of teaching, learning, and management. The schools display a sense of responsibility, purpose and commitment, and their organisational culture emphasises work ethic, achievement and success. These schools became known as resilient schools.

Initially, the post-1994 national department of education (NDoE) introduced many school-based policy reforms (such as SASA, Curriculum Policy Framework, National Policy Framework for TED – or NPFTED). These reforms tend to focus on structural issues, such as democratic governance and school management, or systemic issues such as curriculum framework, the NPFTED and public sector capacity building. Yet, as many scholars warned, policies are blunt instruments that cannot easily affect the core business of schools, namely teaching and learning or the 'instructional core'. This understanding, combined with the fact that many school issues (such as school culture, teaching practices) were beyond bureaucratic reach, explains where NGOs saw a gap to fill. In the 1990s, various NGOs initiated school improvement interventions, in particular for some disadvantaged schools. While some of them specialised in more effective and conducive school leadership and governance relationships, school culture and schools as learning organisations, others focused on school-based teacher training. Soon, the NGOs working with a whole school development approach saw the need to add or privilege the important target of professional development of teachers for better practices (e.g., Education Quality Improvement Partnership Programme (EQUIP), Imbewu). Noteworthy is that many NGO interventions acknowledged the negative role of poverty but they themselves did not to work with very poorly performing schools for the reason that they did not have any formal authority over these schools to achieve the basic level of functionality needed for their interventions.

In 2007, when SACMEQ II pointed to very poor school results, the Minister of Education (Naledi Pandor) in her budget speech argued that resources could no longer be considered as a legitimate reason for lack of improvement. Aware of the lack of sustainability of the school-by-school reform approach and informed by a systems theory approach (Gallie in Sayed, Kanjee & Nkomo, 2013), many NGOs moved away from school projects towards large-scale programmes in partnership with provincial departments of education or districts (such as the District Development Support Programme (DDSP) and the Khanyisa School programme), using pressure and support as the framework for intervention. This led to the incorporation of district capacity building because this level was perceived as vital to improve teaching and learning through better school support and monitoring and this for all schools including the seriously poorly performing schools. This improvement approach, which Soudien (in Sayed et al., 2013, p. 104) call combined "outside in" [state through a top-down approach] and "inside out" [NGOs through a bottom-up approach], was also known as a system-wide approach.

Eight review and evaluation studies: What do they tell us about school effectiveness and improvement factors, accountability and support?

In this section, we briefly summarise eight review and evaluation studies published between 2007 and 2016. The studies we chose are published either as separate reports, part of a PhD or as chapters in a book. We used two selection criteria for choosing the eight studies. First, they synthesise and assess all the main interventions that targeted a large number of South African schools (and sometimes districts) during the period of 2000 to 2014. In this specific period, South Africa had tried large-scale interventions for the first time in its history of school reform. Second, these interventions relied on a diversity of improvement models and underlying theories of change. Some pointed towards the school improvement model most dominant to date, at the centre of which is the idea of improving children's reading and writing. Two of the studies went as far as proposing a framework of school improvement interventions focused on design and implementation. There are no other review and evaluation studies on large-scale reform in basic education in South Africa. The inclusion of these two criteria proved to be productive as it enabled us to develop a view from above of the school effectiveness factors and the drivers for pressure on and support of districts, schools and teachers, respectively. We provide a critical appraisal of these studies and propose a more appropriate alternative improvement model.

History of school effectiveness and improvement movements in Africa (Fleisch, 2007)

Fleisch reviews the literature of school effectiveness and school improvement studies in Africa, during the 1990s, which, at the time of his writing, was dominated by the World Bank and other donor organisations as well as by American and European scholars who were not working or living on the continent (2007, p. 344). The central question he borrows from this literature is, "Do the same list of effective factors apply across contexts for all students?" (Riddle in Fleisch, 2007, p. 345). Alongside his analysis of the slow start of what he calls 'home grown movement' of school improvement, Fleisch emphasises the need to acknowledge the different political and organisational contextual factors that contribute to different levels of learners' achievements in developed and developing countries. He recommends that more attention be paid to contextual factors (geographic isolation), cultural teaching factors (mode of teaching and authority relations) and curriculum relevance.

Equity, efficiency and the development of South African schools (Taylor, 2007)

Taylor synthesises school effectiveness and improvement studies with the view to understanding whether they promote greater educational equity and efficiency. His review puts emphasis on systemic school reforms, showing the value and the limitation of school-based interventions (mainly NGO-led). He classifies interventions conducted between 1994 and 2003 (for example, Education Action Zones, the Quality Learning Project and Dinaledi I) and after 2003 (Dinaledi II and a variety of production function studies). His study identifies the main effectiveness and improvement factors as poverty, language, home background, school management (instructional leadership) and cognitive resources. He also mentions teaching practices with appropriate pacing, evaluation and expectations from learners, better curriculum coverage as well as multi-support for instructional core. Taylor draws a distinction between top, moderately and poorly performing schools and argues that the accountability approach has not proven successful in the poorly performing schools and requires strong and well-functioning state organs to intervene.

Fleisch and Taylor attempted to refocus school reform from school-based intervention to systemic form, even if at the same time they recognised the weak organisational capacity (sometimes dysfunctionality) of many districts and provincial departments, as well as the importance of contextual differences.

Meta-analysis of programmes and projects supported by the Zenex Foundation between 2006 and 2011 (Roberts & Schollar, 2011)
Roberts and Schollar conduct a qualitative 'meta-evaluation' of 17 projects reports for the donor, Zenex Foundation. They use the project logic model which they developed for the purpose of "describing and analysing the development assumptions that underpin the different projects initiated and funded by the Foundation" (2011, p. 4). The different interventions include in their meta-analysis targeted learners, teachers, schools and supportive materials. Their analytical model is aimed at understanding the services (e.g. training) and material assistance (e.g. learning support materials) offered in the respective projects and the target group (learners, teachers, schools, etc.) as well as the intended change process outcomes (changes in practice or behaviours, access to materials). Their specific contribution lies in identifying key factors which affect a successful implementation. They argue that interventions should target only functional schools and require a multi-pronged approach such as support programmes, integration of aspects of teacher/administration and learner development, provision of materials, the enhancement of organisational effectiveness and rigorous monitoring and evaluation.

Creating effective schools (Taylor, Van der Berg, & Mabogoane, 2013)
This review begins with a summary of previous studies and lists key explanatory factors that undermine school performance including poverty; the lack of departmental bureaucratic capacity; the lack of teacher subject knowledge; effective classroom practices and accountability; and the lack of instructional leadership and systemic accountability (especially before the 2010 ANA results).

It then analyses the quantitative studies and the evolution of School Effectiveness (SE) versus what the authors call Economics of Education (EE) research studies. They also engage with some qualitative studies to explain the reproduction of social inequalities through educational inequalities. To understand how to optimise disadvantaged learners' learning, they draw on multilevel modelling techniques in identifying variables with different effectiveness impact and their interactional effects.

The search for quality education in post-apartheid South Africa: Interventions to improve learning and teaching (Sayed et al., 2013)

This book asks insiders to seven different improvement interventions (EQUIP, Imbewu Project, DDSP, Quality Learning Project, Learning For Living, Integrated Education Programme, Khanyisa School Programme) to comment on their interventions and relatively low impact on students' achievements. Gallie (in Sayed et al., 2013) provides a critical appraisal of these interventions. He argues that the lessons learnt from the evaluation of these interventions are that student achievements "can be associated with the social settings, institutional structures and organizational capacity" (in Sayed et al., 2013, p. 321). Notwithstanding, the interventions do not identify the priority needs of these educational institutions nor their theory of teaching and learning, within a context of sustainability and replicability. Gallie argues for the importance of an appropriate conceptualisation of the problem(s) and design of intervention in a specific context. He concludes that these studies lack an engagement with 'the how of change' (or an underlying theory of change).

In concluding the book, Kanjee and Sayed argue that interventions to improve school quality are informed by school improvement rationale, but analyses of the interventions do not make clear "the key issues to effect education changes" (in Sayed et al., 2013, p. 365). This is particularly worrying because the overall learners' performance still "falls well short of the acceptable norm for a specific grade level" (2013, p. 369). Like many other reviewers, Kanjee and Sayed assert that the priority interventions needed are those close to the instructional core, such as improving numeracy and literacy in primary and secondary schooling. They foreground enhancing teacher performance and management/district practices; back-to-basics pedagogical approach; effective teacher supervision and monitoring and teachers as agents of change. Other necessary enabling conditions noted are: stable and effective provincial and district as well as governance structures; stable policy environment; community mobilisation, consent, legitimacy and mutual trust.

Review project: Final revised report (Mouton, Wildschut, Richter, & Pocock, 2013)

These researchers conducted a systematic review of 57 "intervention evaluation articles" of school improvement published between 2005 and 2012. The uniqueness of this review is that it develops "an intervention design framework" (2013, p. 68) which is offered as a heuristic device to both organise the findings and results from the "intervention evaluation articles" and serve as a decision-making framework to inform future designs of school interventions and their evaluations. The framework combines three key aspects: identification of effectiveness factors, conceptualisation of the modes of intervention and their underlying theory of change, and implementation context and obstacles.

Like other reviewers, Mouton et al. argue that interventions should deal with changes at the classroom, school and systemic levels while targeting school management, teachers, learners and parents and that they should be institutionalised. In particular, interventions should focus on early grade acquisition of literacy, language and reading skills; improvement of teacher knowledge for better coverage, pacing and sequencing and curriculum management; and school leadership. Their analysis calls for interventions to also aim at mitigating the negative influence of contextual societal forces affecting poor learner performance, such as HIV, violence and increased social inequalities.

They conclude that most interventions and their studies don't make their theory of change explicit. Mouton et al. reinforce Roberts and Schollar's contribution that, as much as effectiveness and improvement factors are important, implementation planning and implementation obstacles are also key to take into account because they influence the intervention impact. The main implementation issues, they note, are the quality of the implementing agencies and their quality assurance and monitoring. How long does the intervention last? How much is provided and how often? Do all the stakeholders around this intervention support and/or own this intervention programme? What is the temporal and socio-political context at the time? What is the unions' stance on the intervention, what are the teachers' attitudes and morale or political interests, stakeholder pressure, or other significant historical events that could assist or derail the implementation?

Identifying binding constraints in education (Van der Berg, Cloete, Wills, Gustafsson, & Kotze, 2016)

Van der Berg et al. summarise research literature and develop an evidence-based hierarchy of problems in need of being addressed. They identify four binding constraints that influence school outcomes and which perpetuate the cycle of poor educational outcomes, further entrenching students' poverty and weak labour market outcomes: (1) Weak institutional functionality. (2) Weak teacher content knowledge and pedagogical skills. (3) Undue union influence, especially in appointing/promoting officials and school management. (4) Wasted learning time and insufficient opportunity to learn rooted in both poor teacher capacity and lack of accountability. They recommend stabilisation of early childhood development by increasing funding for training programmes, norms and standards for post-provisioning, correct utilisation of DBE Workbooks for curriculum coverage and better calibre of school principals (Van der Berg et al., 2016, p. 11).

It is important to emphasise that, by the time they had done their analysis, a few provincial education departments had introduced a new kind of system-wide interventions which focused (to various degrees) on reading and writing at the Foundation Phase. Some of these large-scale system-wide primary school interventions seemed to produce better results than previous interventions, even though some did not seem to have been sustained.

Comparative meta-analysis of interventions to improve learners' achievement in South African schools (Besharati, 2016)

In a chapter (5) of his PhD, Besharati conducts a comparative meta-analysis of 18 credible studies of 19 different interventions, which covered 82 different effect sizes. These interventions, implemented throughout South Africa in the past two decades, were grouped in five categories, which include teacher-based, learner-focused, materials and resources, management- or system-oriented, whole school development. He notes that the positive impact of these interventions (even if the initial results had a very low base) is correlated with the study design, population sample, specific context/ circumstances, geographic areas and socio-economic contexts. He also warns that there is no guarantee of a similar impact from these structured pedagogic interventions if these are transferred to a broader policy environment.

His findings confirm that the greatest impact on learner achievement comes from early grade interventions in the form of literacy and numeracy programmes. These interventions refer to structured pedagogic programmes with multiple components, such as Learning and Teaching Support Materials and teacher training/coaching on how to use these resources. At high school level, additional teachers, assistants and human resources are the interventions with most benefits (e.g. Dinaledi).

Being mainly concerned with a quantitative meta-evaluation study, Besharati does not explain the 'why' of these interventions nor the implicit theory of change nor the implementation issues to be considered.

To summarise the studies, we created the Table 4.1 below in which we frame the variety of factors, ideas and proposals for improvement found in the studies around three sets of ideas:

- School effectiveness factors
- Accountability/pressure as a lever for change and improvement
- Capacity building/support as a lever for change and improvement[5]

By using these three categories at the different levels of the education system in this table, we can see the similarities in the eight school improvement studies as

---

[5] We refer to the author/s of studies only if the particular item in the table is specific to that study.

Table 4.1 *Our own compilation of a summary of effectiveness factors, pressure and support coming from different levels of the education system*

Education systems levels	School effectiveness factors	Accountability/ pressure as a lever for change and improvement	Capacity building/ support as a lever for change and improvement
Outside school factors	Poverty, parents' education, family settlement & structure, home language, reading and writing practices at home	Ensure minimum negative outside influence from unions (Van der Berg et al.); School/Community	Decision on appropriate LoLT, (Taylor et al., 2003); Positive school-community relations (Roberts and Schollar)
District (monitoring)	Minimum level of district infrastructure and organisational capacity to support and monitor schools and their staff; District management and leadership for effective institutional structures; Stable district and policy environment (Sayed et al.)	Effective district monitoring of curriculum coverage; Monitoring and evaluation of schools with mutual trust, consent and legitimacy (Sayed et al.)	Effective district administration of resource distribution; Effective district support of schools and curriculum delivery through meaningful school visits and training (Taylor et al., 2013)
School (management)	Functional schools; Minimum level of school infrastructure and capacity; School organisational effectiveness; School leadership and management with instructional focus; Good relationship between school staff and management of different districts	Effective monitoring and administration of teachers' work; Rigorous school monitoring of time on task and of teacher plans & assessment practices; Monitoring and evaluation of teachers with mutual trust and legitimacy (Sayed et al.)	Support from school management and instructional leadership re: teacher work, textbooks, time and time-on-task (Taylor, 2007); School organisational capacity and effectiveness (Sayed et al.)
School (classroom: appropriate use of cognitive resources)	Teacher qualification, teacher subject knowledge; Numeracy and literacy focus, back to basics curriculum pacing and sequence, pedagogy and evaluation, opportunity to learn, time-on-task	Monitoring of time on task, curriculum coverage, homework and learner achievement; Monitoring of teacher planning and assessment records; Reading frequency and quantity and quality of learners' writing in workbooks; Grade learner achievement test; teacher supervision (Sayed et al.)	Support for higher teacher expectations, for teaching reading and writing; time management and time on task (Taylor, 2007); Teacher training in LoLT; subject matter and pedagogical knowledge (Roberts and Schollar); Teacher training (Sayed et al.) back to basics (Mouton et al., Taylor et al., 2013)
Conditions increasing the chance of success	Functioning district and schools, young teachers, student resilience and ability to adapt and keen interest to improve, partnership (Mouton et al. and Sayed et al.); Interventions imply a *change process* which require an understanding of how effectiveness and improvement factors [in need of improvements] start changing, and so a theory of change or action is needed; Interventions need a theory of change to identify exactly the priority needs of educational institutions within a context of sustainability and replicability, drawing explicitly on a theory of learning and teaching.		

far as the factors targeted and the kind of pressure and support used as well as the conducive conditions for such improvement interventions.

Critical appraisal of these eight studies

The studies refer to school effectiveness factors such as the learners' home background, classroom and school processes and district management in order to test, through various sophisticated models of production functions and multi-level modelling, their correlations with learners' achievements. Yet, we identify five problematic issues. First, the predictor factors are not straightforward factors: they are often not easy to find proxies for and measure, and they may hide or obstruct other factors. The input and process factors all relate to, and influence, one another in a specific way, as they exist in a nest of complex relationships and contexts (Carrim & Shalem, 1999; Creemers & Kyriakides, 2006).

Second, the reviews do not provide a theoretical explanation of how such input and process factors relate to, and work with one another, nor how these factors affect learners' learning. Input and process predictor factors such as poverty, management practices, teacher practices or reading practices are rather complex because they are relational and socially constructed and have contradictory and even biased impact on different officials, teachers or learners.

Third, many SI researchers have long warned of the importance of context differentiation. The argument here is that teachers may need differentiated forms of training and professional accountability, and learners may require different pedagogies, assessments and socio-psychological support. It is therefore problematic to talk about teachers' competences or learners' achievements as monolithic categories. For example, curriculum pacing and district monitoring of curriculum coverage are unlikely to improve *all* teachers' teaching and *all* learners' learning as well as the promotion of greater opportunities for all teachers and learners to learn. We contend that these preferred changes will leave behind the more disadvantaged/struggling teachers or learners, with the possible effect of deepening already unequal educational opportunities.

Fourth, the only studies that engage explicitly with how schools and teachers start changing their behaviours, practices and performances are Sayed et al. and Mouton et al. The other studies work with the idea that pressure and support can change behaviour (see Table 4.1 above). The challenge is to ensure pressure and support are context-specific, well-calibrated, sequenced and aligned to each other.

Fifth, although the studies point to poverty as a factor in school improvement, none of the studies deals with the specific challenges of the very poorly performing schools. In fact, some studies (Taylor; Roberts and Schollar; Mouton et al.) suggest that interventions should target functioning schools only, which leave the poorest schools to the responsibility of the state.

The questions that are crucial to engage with are: What forms of teacher or principal training for what kind of teachers and principals? What comes first: accountability for development or development for accountability? What is the school and district capacity to monitor and support curriculum delivery, coverage, time on task and school readiness? Is there a school and district commitment and a will to do what is necessary?

In the next section, we draw on the conceptual work offered by *Getting Schools Working* (Taylor et al., 2003) in order to highlight both the complexity involved in changing teacher practice and to offer some insights into the institutional coordination which underpins large-scale interventions.

In search of a theory: Importance and role of theories of schooling and learning

Looking back at the reviews of improvement studies and their evaluations, it is clear that the majority is not concerned to provide a theorisation of schooling and learning in order to explain why, how and under what conditions the selected improvement factors are associated with students' improved learning. A theory of schooling could explain under what conditions and how schools' contexts matter; how and under what conditions teachers or learners sustain what they have learned. Beyond explaining more clearly why and how the key school factors affect different learners' achievements, such a theorisation could also guide the search for specific data on identified factors. They could specify which factors are to be privileged because they constitute vital entry points to improve schooling and learning.

In chapter 5 of *Getting Schools Working* Taylor, Muller and Vinjevold (2003) developed a theory of schooling with a view to analysing the relations between the factors and forces that shape the transmission and acquisition of school knowledge. Their primary interest is to understand how the many factors that constitute the phenomenon of schooling, and more specifically learning and achievement, "fit together and produce effects" (2003, p. 68). The conceptual syntax their theory develops is defended both conceptually (largely drawing on Basil Bernstein's work) and empirically (by reference to empirical data). Although their work is not a meta-analysis of school improvement, their analysis of schooling offers critical insights into the models of school improvement currently operating in schools in South Africa. They also state clearly that their analysis of schooling is intended to show "how to improve its processes and outcomes" (2003, p. 85).

The first claim in their theory prioritises one of the following three sets of what they call "categories of variables" which affect learning (2003, pp. 68-69). Their argument is that it is in the third set of factors that the school can add value to poor learners, despite their socio-economic disadvantages, as expressed in the first two sets of factors.

- *Contextual factors* or the socio-economic status of the child's family. This set consists of factors external to the school with influence on learning experience and achievement. They refer to the relation between poverty levels of the family, education levels of the parents AND literate forms used at the home. In broad terms, this set of factors refers to the parents' capability to act as a second site of acquisition.
- *Resource factors* or the material and cognitive resource factors internal to the school (pupil-teacher ratio, teacher education level, libraries and IT resources). More often than not, this set of factors mirrors 'the socio-economic status of the catchment of the school'.
- *Educational process factors*: "Management and leadership factors at school, district and higher levels, and classroom instructional factors can make a critical difference to pupil and school performance. These factors offer opportunities for education officials, principals and teachers to make more or less effective use of available resources, thereby facilitating or inhibiting the progress of children through the school system."

Most of the studies acknowledge that the first and second sets of factors mirror the socio-economic contexts of the school and therefore *'more resources' is a necessary condition for poor schools' improvement*. However, the studies also emphasise that *the form in which material and cognitive resources are managed by school leaders and by teachers, makes those resources sufficient or not* (Crouch & Mabogoane, 2001; Spaull, 2013, 2015).

The third set of factors, which is dominant in South Africa up to today, indicates that opportunity to learn can add value to poor learners if structured properly:

> ...after the socio-economic origin, *pedagogic practices* – reflected in the orchestration of classroom activities and the management of the institutions – collectively constitute *the most important set of factors which structure the educational opportunity of children*. Furthermore, the quality of pedagogic practice is the key mechanism for overcoming the influence of social origin (Taylor et al., 2003, p. 82).

The second claim in the theory of *Getting Schools Working* is based on Bernstein's theory of language code acquisition, which explains the extra difficulties poor learners experience in acquiring formal knowledge. Following this proposition, the authors' analysis prioritises learning of reading and writing, arguing that these are fundamental to the acquisition of school knowledge (which is radically different from everyday knowledge). Programmes, material and monitoring process have to be developed at three systemic levels (national, provincial/district, school/classroom) to maximise learning language proficiency. Since several studies (Howie et al., 2017; Spaull, 2015) have documented the poor *reading, writing and numeracy levels of early graders* in poor schools in South Africa, the more recent interventions increasingly focus on improving reading and writing practices in the classroom. As our summaries above have shown, prioritising primary over secondary education is also dominant.

The third claim in their theory is that school improvement should target teachers' knowledge and/or practice – *how they teach and how they work.* Taylor et al. argue that teachers' better curriculum pacing and strongly framed evaluation practices are likely to provide levers of change and impact on the quality of schooling and the achievements of learners from poor social classes. This claim is at the heart of the complexity involved in school improvement: the practice of teaching is nested in other substantive practices (curriculum, pedagogy, evaluation and school management). At every level of the system (classroom, school, district), there is some function or process which affects what and how teachers teach whatever they teach, and how they work. The question of school improvement therefore cannot be: which level to choose to improve but *what kind of intervention will bring the other levels into productive relations.*

From his study of a specific NY district, Elmore (1997) concludes that only a coherent conceptualisation of whole intervention programmes, that have strongly aligned components at different levels, have a chance of working. Districts need a comprehensive strategy to mobilise their knowledge and resources into alignment "in the service of professional development for system-wide instructional improvement" (1997, p. 3). This vision, purpose and rationale for the district and its schools, he qualifies, have to become "a joint, collegial responsibility of everyone in the system, working together in a variety of ways across all schools. Only then, a long enough commitment can be expected from people to actually internalize the change required" (1997, p. 9). Hence, the challenge is to put together and mobilise various factors at the different levels into a comprehensive, coherent and aligned strategy.

The idea that teaching is nested in other substantive practices, spread over different levels of schooling, presents a complicated challenge in school reform. The more dimensions or levels are incorporated in intervention programmes, the more partners are needed to be brought in to offer their expertise, and the focus on improvement of teaching and learning is in greater danger of becoming diluted, non-aligned or not coherent. Some of the studies show that too often partners work in silos to improve or build the capacity and accountability of the school effectiveness and improvement factors they are in charge of, whether at the level of the classroom, school and/or district. Gallie (in Sayed et al., 2013) goes as far as suggesting to appoint a single service provider to develop the material and capacitate trainers to use the material results in greater reliability and effectiveness of delivering aligned services. What is at stake in school improvement is the need for some or other form of relation between *coordination of activities* and *regulation of agents at different levels of schooling*. Any intervention needs to filter through levels and different categories of agents with their specific needs and interests.

By *coordination* we refer to standardisation of the main functions of schooling, making sure that learners in all the different schools are exposed to the same curriculum and the pedagogical forms used by teachers to cover the curriculum provide learners with similar enough meaningful opportunities to learn. Education systems embody social values and their management brings about the question of power relations between management and teachers. *Vertical regulation* of agents refers to the regulation of the movement of management and curriculum knowledge from its centre of production to its application (at different points of the educational division of labour and in the classroom, respectively). Overall, this is about regulation of the social relations between knowledge experts and trainers, district officials, school management, teachers and learners.

In *Getting Schools Working*, the authors advocate a productive relation between opposites – *hierarchal coordination and regulation of cognitive resources, on the one hand, and open interaction between agents around learning and acquisition of knowledge, on the other*. The idea here is that 'what is to be taught, when and at what pace' is stipulated by the national curriculum and curriculum specification of different forms (such as scripted lesson plans, curriculum trackers). What counts as appropriate performance is specified by assessment standards and evaluative criteria transmitted through the curriculum (such as cyclical tests and national standardised assessment), with some discretion for teachers in view of their learners' needs and contexts. Also, rules of behaviour are regulated by monitoring teachers' punctuality and attendance, curriculum coverage and time-on-task.

The social relation around learning should on the other hand be open and personal, particularly when giving feedback on performance. Taylor et al. argue that learners' understanding of evaluative criteria can be transmitted centrally by various means of assessment. There is, however, a personal dimension in the relation between learners and teachers that has to be nurtured: "evidence shows that the teacher's response is more likely to achieve its desired social and cognitive effects, if it is done through a personal mode of communication, as opposed to the one that foregrounds the hierarchical role of the teacher" (2003, p. 83). Openness is argued to be effective in teachers' learning ("providing advice to teachers by management") (Taylor, 2007, p. 534) and teachers' discretion in learners' learning ("pupils perform better in maths when the teacher is responsive to the stage of development of individual children, gives explicit feedback in response to pupil knowledge")(2007, p. 535).

Taylor (2007) classifies the school system into three types (top, moderately and poorly performing schools). His analysis of moderately functioning schools foregrounds the hierarchical model of coordination of tasks and regulation of behaviour at district, school and classroom levels, with some discretion for teachers on adjusting pace to learners' ability. He also emphasises time regulation of teachers' attendance, coordinating and monitoring of teachers' plans for curriculum coverage, and management of classroom assessment.

Equipped with this theoretical explanation of schooling, and in particular using the concepts of coordination and regulation, we are now ready to provide a critical appraisal of two promising recent large-scale improvement interventions, which have the potential of becoming system-wide sustained and institutionalised school reforms.

Two large-scale multi-dimensional improvement interventions

As more data sets became available indicating the poor performance of schooling in all provincial departments, the DBE developed an Action Plan (Department of Basic Education, 2015) to put pressure on provincial departments to attend to the poorly performing schools. Many introduced a system-wide strategy for instructional improvement to improve their average learners' results by focusing on early grade literacy and numeracy classes in underperforming schools. Informed by the claim that calibration consists of hierarchical coordination and regulation of cognitive resources, on the one hand, and open interaction between agents around learning, on the other, we now move on to examining the two largest system-wide improvement interventions.

In Gauteng, the 2010 Gauteng Primary Literacy and Mathematics Strategy (GPLMS) introduced in schools a triple cocktail intervention combining scripted lesson plans, learner materials and quality teaching capacity building (Fleisch, 2018). This instructional improvement intervention focused on learners' learning by a hierarchical coordination of teachers' activities through the introduction of scripted lesson plans. The introduction of coaches created (in most cases) a space for open relations around teacher learning and teacher discretion around pacing (Shalem, Steinberg, Koornhof, & De Clercq, 2016). This intervention produced some positive results with the learners of the 1 000 primary schools targeted (See Besharati, 2016), but it did not survive beyond 2013. This explains why the GPLMS remained limited to a system-wide classroom intervention, and did not involve many HoDs, let alone school principals, parents and district curriculum advisers. In actual fact, the strategy had planned to start with instructional improvement and subsequently involve parents and community as well as target the management of teaching and learning through stronger school management teams and better district support systems.

In 2015, this triple cocktail model of school reform intervention was reproduced in a slightly different form as quasi-experimental research interventions, also known as the Early Grade Reading Studies (EGRS) which were supported by the Department of Basic Education and implemented in selected provincial education departments (North West and Mpumalanga) during the period 2015–

2019. Using RCTs in around 200 provincial schools at a time (some targeted primary schools and others constituting a control group for comparison), the leading researchers tested the relative effectiveness of components within the triple cocktail treatment, while adding a few new components (e.g. provision of teacher tablets; classroom libraries) which were perceived as potential vital entry points to improve Foundation Phase performance. What is emerging so far is that, in addition to lesson plans and learners' quality materials, coaches seem to be a more effective component than teacher training (Cilliers et al., 2018) and that the recent experiment with classroom libraries appears encouraging. The only component that has not been tested is the quality and appropriateness of the lesson plans for all primary schools. Some qualitative studies have pointed to serious limitations of lesson plans in improving teacher learning of quite a variety of new and complex teaching practices (Hoadley, 2018; Shalem, 2018; Shalem et al., 2018; Shalem et al., 2016).

The findings suggest the importance of achieving calibration between context-specific support in the form of openness around teacher learning (coaches) and hierarchal coordination and regulation of the cognitive resource selected for this intervention. Yet, without a systematic study of the lesson plans and the way they are enacted in the classroom, the quality of teacher learning cannot be established.

While this GPLMS/EGRS large-scale system-wide instructional interventions never became full systemic interventions involving all the different levels of the system, another intervention in KwaZulu-Natal, managed by the Programme to Improve Learning Outcomes (PILO), was set up in two pilot districts from 2015 to 2017 and rolled out to other KZN districts from 2018 to 2021 (Christie & Monyokolo, 2018). PILO targets, right from the beginning, all stakeholders: the KZN department, the district, the trade unions, the school management and HoDs and, in that sense, became the only large-scale *systemic* improvement programme, with a sustainability and institutionalised aim (De Clercq & Shalem, 2019). PILO, however, does not target classroom instruction directly because its aim is to empower the HoDs and school principals to create a professional conducive environment for professional dialogues with their staff, with the view to improving their practices. PILO also targets the district and its circuits because of the belief in the link between effective districts and improved learner performance. The aim is to change "the working practices of CM [Circuit Managers], regular school visits, conversations based on evidence, improved reporting, sharing and reflection… System interventions that introduce new routines must be embedded to shift practices and create new support dynamics" (Mc Lennan, Muller, Orkin, & Robertson, 2018, p. 231). Practices of coordination included HoD toolkits which regulated the supervision and monitoring expected of them; curriculum planners and trackers (and scripted lesson plans only for Foundation Phase teachers), weekly reflections and professional conversations to regulate teachers' work. This model appears more horizontal in terms of authority structure and by far more multi-levelled. The emphasis on professional conversations (openness around teacher learning) is strong but with weaker guidance on teacher practice. The emphasis of monitoring of curriculum coverage can be in conflict with the aim of building teachers' confidence to reflect on their weaknesses (Shalem & De Clercq, 2019).

Conclusion: Towards new theories?

Many scholars argue that the quality of school and non-school factors, which affect learning, are distributed differentially to the unequal socio-economic groups of society, with the consequence that socio-economic inequalities are reproduced and enhanced by educational inequalities. Indeed, more than often, school policies or improvement interventions benefit the better-off schools, teachers or learners rather than the underperforming schools (Jansen & Spaull, 2019; Sayed et al., 2013; Soudien, Reddy, & Woolard, 2019). This could be illustrated not by tracing the national changes in average learners' results but by analysing the changing composition of the breakdown of learners' results according to social classes (Van der Berg et al., 2016; Van der Berg & Gustafsson, 2019).

One main shortcoming of these review and evaluation studies of school reforms in South Africa is that they largely bracket out the ways in which chronic poverty, in which most learners in South Africa live, affect knowledge acquisition. Associated with this is Carnoy's argument (2019) that SE and SI researchers cannot easily explain the reasons behind sudden improvements or declines of students' results. He contends that the answer lies most likely outside of the formal education system and changes in the students' socio-economic status. He suggests that it is influenced by a broader set of socio-political factors which he calls 'social capital' (the degree of social consensus or level of trust vs violence in society, not unlike Sayed et al. suggest (2013). It is also influenced by the power politics, which have contradictory effects on why and how some learners engage [or not] with the knowledge acquisition process.

Last but not least, learning is significantly conditioned by psychological processes of cognitive development and of wellbeing. Most review studies do not deal with the question of how different teachers or learners learn. Interesting research is now available from cognitive neuroscience, or what others prefer to call the bio-psychosocial emotional approach to learning (Maté, 2019). Increasingly, evidence shows how the core cognitive capacities (such as Sustained Attention, Response Inhibition, Speed of Information Processing, Cognitive Flexibility and Control, Multiple Simultaneous Attention, Working Memory, Category Formation and Pattern Recognition) can be negatively influenced by the inter-relationship between poverty, ill-health, stress and adversity/trauma. Researchers (Darling-Hammond, Flook, Cook-Harvey, Barron, & Osher, 2019, p. 1) argue that, according to insights from the science of learning, the "development of the brain is an experience-dependent process" and further "children's development and learning are shaped by interactions among the environmental factors, relationships and learning opportunities, both in and out of school, along with physical, psychological, cognitive, social, and emotional processes that influence one another – both biologically and functionally – as they enable or undermine learning". Some South African researchers dealing with poor learners (Fleisch, 2008; Harber & Muthukrishna, 2000; Richter, Mathews, Kagura, & Nonterah, 2018) have mentioned the difficult, traumatic and stressing environment that dominates the lives of many learners from poor and disadvantaged schools. These new theoretical and empirical insights have to be incorporated in research work on factors which affect learning.

One of the conclusions that this contention raises is that it is unlikely that all teachers need and will benefit from the same support and monitoring, and all learners need and will benefit from the same pedagogic and assessment practice and support.

From our theoretical perspective, PILO is the only large-scale intervention which is explicitly intending to slowly build a professional collegial set of practices, which allow learners' differentiated needs to influence the system. Yet, placing curriculum coverage at the centre of its institutional vision seems to have resulted in HoDs and teachers focusing on the monitoring of, and accountability for, more curriculum coverage and much less on improvements in teachers' understanding of the strengths and weaknesses of certain choices they make when they teach a topic and how different learners learn the topic or the raison d'être hidden behind the failure of particular learners to grasp an aspect of the topic (De Clercq & Shalem, 2019).

References

Besharati, N.A. (2016). *Evaluating development effectiveness assessing and comparing the impact of education intervention in South Africa* (Doctoral Dissertation). University of the Witwatersrand, Johannesburg.

Bowles, S., & Gintis, H. (1976). *Schooling in Capitalist America: Educational Reform and the Contradictions of Economic Life*. New York: Basic Books.

Carnoy, M. (2019). *Transforming Comparative Education: Fifty Years of Theory Building at Stanford*. California: Stanford University Press. https://doi.org/10.1515/9781503608825

Carrim, N., & Shalem, Y. (1999). School effectiveness in South Africa. *International Journal of Qualitative Studies in Education*, 12(1), 59-83. https://doi.org/10.1080/095183999236330

Christie, P. (1998). Schools as (Dis)Organisations: The 'breakdown of the culture of learning and teaching' in South African schools. *Cambridge Journal of Education*, 28(3), 283-300. https://doi.org/10.1080/0305764980280303

Christie, P., Butler, D., & Potterton, M. (2007). *Schools that work* [Report of ministerial committee].

Christie, P., & Collins, C. (1982). Bantu Education: Apartheid ideology or labour reproduction. *Comparative Education*, 18(1), 59-75. https://doi.org/10.1080/0305006820180107

Christie, P., & Monyokolo, M. (Eds.). (2018). *Learning About Sustainable Change in Education in South Africa: The Jika iMfundo campaign 2015-2017*. Johannesburg: SAIDE.

Coleman, J.S. (1968). Equality of educational opportunity. *Equity & Excellence in Education*, 6(5), 19-28. https://doi.org/10.1080/0020486680060504

Creemers, B., & Kyriakides, L. (2006). Critical analysis of the current approaches to modelling educational effectiveness: The importance of establishing a dynamic model. *School Effectiveness and School Improvement*, 17, 347-366. https://doi.org/10.1080/09243450600697242

Crouch, L., & Mabogoane, T. (2001). No magic bullets, just tracer bullets: The role of learning resources, social advantage, and education management in improving the performance of South African schools. *Social Dynamics*, 27(1), 60-78. https://doi.org/10.1080/02533950108458704

Darling-Hammond, L., Flook, L., Cook-Harvey, C., Barron, B., & Osher, D. (2019). Implications for educational practice of the science of learning and development. *Applied Developmental Science*, 1-44. https://doi.org/10.1080/10888691.2018.1537791

De Clercq, F., & Shalem, Y. (2019). Large-scale improvement interventions in the education system: PILO's contribution to the theory of change in education. *Southern African Review of Education*, 25(2).

Department of Basic Education. (2015). *Action Plan to 2019: Towards the realisation of schooling 2030*. Pretoria.

Elmore, R. (1997). *Investing in teacher learning: Staff development and instructional improvement in community school districts #2, New York City*. New York City: New York.: National Commission on Teaching and America's Future and the Consortium for Policy Research in Education.

Elmore, R. (2005). Agency, Reciprocity, and Accountability in Democratic Education. In S. Fuhrman & M. Lazerson (Eds.), *The Institutions of American Democracy: The Public Schools* (pp. 277-301). Oxford: Oxford University Press.

Fleisch, B. (2007). History of the School Effectiveness and Improvement Movements in Africa. In T. Townsend, *International Handbook on School Effectiveness and Improvement* (pp. 341-350). Dordrecht: Springer. https://doi.org/10.1007/978-1-4020-5747-2_18

Fleisch, B. (2008). *Primary education in crisis: Why South African schoolchildren underachieve in reading and mathematics*. Juta and Company Ltd.

Fleisch, B. (2018). *The Education Triple Cocktail: System-wide instructional reform in South Africa*. Cape Town: Juta and Company Ltd.

Fullan, M. (1982). *The new meaning of educational change*. London: Cassell.

Harber, C., & Muthukrishna, N. (2000). School Effectiveness and School Improvement in Context: The Case of South Africa. *School Effectiveness and School Improvement*, 11(4), 421-434. https://doi.org/10.1076/sesi.11.4.421.3559

Hoadley, U. (2018). *Pedagogy in poverty: Lessons from twenty years of curriculum reform in South Africa*. Routledge. https://doi.org/10.4324/9781315680927

Hopkins, D., Ainscow, M., & West, M. (1994). *School improvement in an era of change*. New York: Cassell.

Howie, S., Combrinck, C., Roux, K., Tshele, M., Mokoena, G., & McLeod Palane, N. (2017). *PIRLS Literacy 2016: South African Children's Reading Literacy Achievement*. Pretoria: Centre for Evaluation and Assessment.

Jansen, J., & Spaull, N. (Eds.). (2019). *South African Schooling: The Enigma of Inequality: A Study of The Present Situation and Future Possibilities*. Springer. https://doi.org/10.1007/978-3-030-18811-5

Jenks, C., Smith, M., Ackland, H., Bane, M.J., Cohen, D., Gintis, H., & Michelson, S. (1972). *Inequality, a reassessment of the effects of family and schooling in America*. New York: Basic Books.

Kallaway, P. (Ed.). (1984). *Apartheid and education: The education of black South Africans.* Johannesburg: Ravan.

Maté, G. (2019). *Scattered Minds: The Origins and Healing of Attention Deficit Disorder.* New York: Random House.

Mc Lennan, A., Muller, M., Orkin, M., & Robertson, H. (2018). District support for curriculum management change in schools. In P. Christie & M. Monyokolo (Eds.), *Learning About Sustainable Change in Education in South Africa: The Jika iMfundo campaign 2015-2017.* Johannesburg: SAIDE.

Mouton, J., Wildschut, L., Richter, T., & Pocock, R. (2013). *Review Project Final Revise Report.* Evaluation Research agency.

Nkomo, M. (1990). *Pedagogy of domination: Toward a democratic education in South Africa.* Africa World Press.

Richter, L.M., Mathews, S., Kagura, J., & Nonterah, E. (2018). A longitudinal perspective on violence in the lives of South African children from the Birth to Twenty Plus cohort study in Johannesburg-Soweto. *South African Medical Journal*, 108(3), 181. https://doi.org/10.7196/SAMJ.2018.v108i3.12661

Roberts, J., & Schollar, E. (2011). *Meta-analysis of programmes and projects supported by the Zenex Foundation between 2006 and 2011.* Johannesburg: Xenex Foundation.

Sayed, Y., Kanjee, A., & Nkomo, M. (Eds.). (2013). *The search for quality education in post-apartheid South Africa.* Cape Town: HSRC press.

Shalem, Y. (2018). Scripted lesson plans — What is visible and invisible in visible pedagogy? In B. Barrett, U. Hoadley, & J. Morgan (Eds.), *Knowledge, Curriculum and Equity: Social realist perspectives.* London: Routledge. https://doi.org/10.4324/9781315111360-12

Shalem, Y., & De Clercq, F. (2019). Teacher development and inequality in South Africa: Do we now have a theory of change? In J. Jansen, & N. Spaull (Eds.), *South African Schooling: The Enigma of Inequality: A Study of The Present Situation and Future Possibilities.* Springer. https://doi.org/10.1007/978-3-030-18811-5_13

Shalem, Y., De Clercq, F., Steinberg, C., & Koornhof, H. (2018). Teacher autonomy in times of standardised lesson plans: The case of a Primary School Language and Mathematics Intervention in South Africa. *Journal of Educational Change.* https://doi.org/10.1007/s10833-018-9318-3

Shalem, Y., Steinberg, C., Koornhof, H., & De Clercq, F. (2016). The what and how in scripted lesson plans: The case of the Gauteng Primary Language and Mathematics Strategy. *Journal of Education*, 66, 1-24. https://doi.org/10.17159/2520-9868/i66a01

Slavin, R.E. (1998). Sand, Bricks, and Seeds: School Change Strategies and Readiness for Reform. In A. Hargreaves, A. Lieberman, M. Fullan, & D. Hopkins (Eds.), *International Handbook of Educational Change* (pp. 1299–1313). Dordrecht: Springer Netherlands. https://doi.org/10.1007/978-94-011-4944-0_62

Soudien, C., Reddy, V., & Woolard, I. (Eds.). (2019). *The state of the nation: Poverty & inequality: Diagnosis, prognosis and responses.* Cape Town: HSRC.

Spaull, N. (2013). *South Africa's education crisis: The quality of education in South Africa 1994-2011.* Johannesburg: Centre for Development and Enterprise.

Spaull, N. (2015). Accountability and capacity in South African education. *Education as Change*, 19(3), 113-142. https://doi.org/10.1080/16823206.2015.1056199

Taylor, N. (2007). Equity, efficiency the development of South African Schools. In T. Townsend (Ed.), *International handbook of school effectiveness and school improvement.* Dordrecht: Springer.

Taylor, N., Muller, J., & Vinjevold, P. (2003). *Getting schools working: Research and systematic school reform in South Africa.* Cape Town: Maskew Miller Longman.

Taylor, N., Van der Berg, S., & Mabogoane, T. (2013). *Creating effective schools.* Cape Town: Pearson Education.

Taylor, N., & Vinjevold, P. (Eds.). (1999). *Getting learning right: Report of the President's Education Initiative Research Project.* Johannesburg: Joint Education Trust.

Teddlie, C., & Reybolds, D. (Eds.). (2000). *International handbook of school effectiveness research.* London: Falmer Press.

Van der Berg, S., Cloete, N., Wills, G., Gustafsson, M., & Kotze, J. (2016). *Identifying Binding Constraints in Education.* Research on Socio-Economic Policy, Department of Economics, University of Stellenbosch. https://doi.org/10.2139/ssrn.2906945

Van der Berg, S., & Gustafsson, M. (2019). Educational outcomes in post-apartheid SA: signs of progress despite great inequality. In J. Jansen & N. Spaull (Eds.), *South African Schooling: The Enigma of Inequality: A Study of The Present Situation and Future Possibilities.* Springer. https://doi.org/10.1007/978-3-030-18811-5_2

CHAPTER 5

Research on school leadership in South Africa: A systematic review
Tony Bush and Derek Glover

Introduction

This chapter explains the policy background to school leadership in South Africa, beginning with the Task Team report in 1996, the 1998 stated intention to establish a national leadership centre, the establishment of the Matthew Goniwe School of Leadership and Governance (MGSLG) in 2003, and the development of the national Advanced Certificate of Education (School Leadership) programme, piloted from 2007. The purpose of the chapter is to review the literature on school leadership during this period of radical change, to ascertain the ways in which policy and practice are reflected in published research outputs.

The chapter is based on a systematic literature review and builds on the authors' previous research and writing on school leadership in South Africa. This literature research was conducted using electronic database searching, hand searching of key journals, searching of specialist websites, and using general search engines on the internet such as "Google" and "Google scholar". The databases included the University of Nottingham's NUSearch, Swetsnet, Eric, British Educational Index, JStor and *South African Journal of Education* archives, and the South African university dissertation lists. A total of 473 references were considered by reading the abstracts and selecting sources that might contribute to a comprehensive analysis of literature, predominantly that published between 2007 and 2019. Fine-grained selection identified 138 sources, which were considered in greater detail and form the basis of this review. The criteria for inclusion were that the papers focused centrally on leadership or management in the South African schools' context. Filtering took place to identify and use those sources which offer findings from empirical research on the major aspects of school leadership.

The literature search was informed by consideration of the following sub-themes, which provide the structure for this chapter:
- Policy on school leadership
- Leadership styles and models
- Leadership roles, including principals, deputy principals, and heads of departments.
- School management teams
- Curriculum management and instructional leadership

- Management of finance and resources
- School governance
- Leadership and management of people
- Leadership and diversity, to include gender, race and ethnicity
- Leadership culture and structures
- Leadership and student outcomes
- Leadership preparation and development

In addressing these themes, we take account of contextual variables, such as rural/urban differences, gender, socio-economic factors, and school type: ex Model C, township, rural and farm schools. Where appropriate, we also examine relationships between school leaders and key stakeholders, including district and provincial officials, and teacher unions.

Policy on school leadership

The newly democratic government gave high priority to school leadership by setting up a task team as early as 1996. The mandates set out by the Minister of Education included:

1. To make practical strategic proposals for improving education management capacity in South Africa.
2. To make specific proposals for establishing a national institute for education management development in South Africa.

The task team report (Department of Education 1996) proposed the establishment of an Education Management Development Institute to lead and coordinate management development initiatives:

> 'The institute would operate as a node in a national network of institutions with strong linkages to the provincial education management development initiatives, and would provide a locus for intellectual leadership and new ideas and policies, for research and development in the arena' (ibid: 57).

However, despite this clear recommendation, and a ministerial mandate, the Institute has never been established, although provincial units, notably Gauteng's Matthew Goniwe School of Leadership and Governance, have been set up.

The next major national initiative was the development of the national ACE: School Leadership programme, piloted in five provinces from 2007 to 2009. The evaluation of the programme (Bush, Kiggundu & Moorosi, 2011) concluded that:

The national programme [should] become an entry-level qualification for new principals as soon as there are sufficient qualified candidates . . . to meet the demand for new principals (ibid: 41).

Although both the pilot programme, and the evaluation, were instigated by the National Department, this recommendation has never been implemented. In 2011, the Council of Education Ministers stated that all new principals should complete the ACE within three years of appointment but this stipulation has also not been implemented. Such policy discontinuities bedevil school leadership development in South Africa, more than 20 years after the Task Team report.

Leadership styles and models

There are numerous leadership models (Bush & Glover, 2014). This section briefly reviews the literature on the major models applied to education in South Africa.

Transformational leadership

Transformational leaders succeed in gaining the commitment of educators through building school vision, establishing school goals, modelling best practices, and demonstrating high performance expectations (Bush, 2011; Leithwood, 1994; Steyn, 2013). In South Africa, there is extensive use of transformational language in the post-apartheid policy discourse but only limited evidence of its impact in schools (Bush & Glover, 2016).

Singh and Lokotsch (2005, p. 286), drawing on interviews with educators in two urban primary schools, discuss the understanding and reality of transformational leadership in South Africa, and comment that 'the transformational approach must respond to needs amongst followers and must look for motives, extrinsic and intrinsic, to satisfy those needs by enhancing opportunities, empowering people, giving more freedom, performance evaluation and the full support of the leader'.

Distributed leadership

Distributed leadership is increasingly popular in Western literature but evidence of its efficacy is mixed (Bush & Glover, 2014). Consideration of this model in South Africa needs to take account of the deeply embedded managerial culture. Grant (2017) comments that distributed leadership is gaining prominence, due to its normative and representational appeal. However, she expresses concern that the concept has become a catch-all phrase to describe any form of devolved or shared leadership and is being espoused as 'the answer' to the country's educational leadership woes. She argues for a theoretically robust form of distributed leadership conceptualised as socio-cultural practice and framed as a product of the joint interactions of school leaders, followers and aspects of their situation (p. 457).

Hoadley et al. (2009, p. 377) are cautious about the applicability of distributed leadership in a culture where hierarchical structures have predominated, a point also made by Singh and Lokotsch (2005). Naicker and Mestry (2011), drawing on interviews and observation in three Soweto primary schools, and subsequently with 100 teachers from a range of schools (2014), make a similar point about how autocracy inhibits distributed leadership:

> This study indicates that leadership in the three Soweto primary schools is rooted in classical leadership practices and that a shift from autocratic styles of leadership, hierarchical structures and non-participative decision-making is needed if distributive leadership is to develop (Naicker & Mestry, 2011, pp. 12-13).

Williams (2011) and Mafora (2013) also argue that distributed leadership is difficult to implement in traditional hierarchical contexts and point to the dysfunctional and unintended consequences of the transformational agenda:

> The majority of South African schools function in contexts which are generally not conducive to distributed leadership. The transformation of the South African education system since 1994 has resulted in what one school principal referred to as "policy overload". In an effort to deal with the transformational initiative, educators have generally become strained and spent, and increasingly unmotivated and frustrated (Williams, 2011, p. 190).

In contrast to the arguments summarised above, Botha and Triegaardt (2015) claim that shared or distributed leadership is vital in a system of school-based management, to enable classroom teachers to play an important role in improving teaching and learning. Their qualitative study in KwaZulu-Natal province suggests that distributed leadership contributes to improved teaching and learning in effective schools. This leaves open the question of whether it would be a helpful approach in less effective contexts.

Teacher leadership

Teacher leadership is one manifestation of distributed leadership (Bush, 2011) but it is also growing in significance as a model in its own right. Grant (2006, p. 511) reports on a study in five KZN schools and notes that "few teachers appear to be embracing a teacher leadership role". She also echoes the negative impact of bureaucratic structures:

> The main barriers to teacher leadership that emerged in this initiative included hierarchical school organization controlled by autocratic principals, an understanding of leadership as linked to a formal position, as well as teachers who are initially resistant to change because of their lack of understanding of the complexity of the change process. These barriers are real and must be taken seriously in the quest for teacher leadership (Grant, 2006, p. 529).

Grant et al.'s (2010, p. 416) subsequent survey of 81 schools in KwaZulu-Natal led her to confirm her earlier view of the restricted nature of teacher leadership in many KwaZulu-Natal schools. Grant (2006, p. 529) adds that "developing a culture of teacher leadership must be seen as an evolutionary process, underpinned by a new understanding of leadership […]. Principals need to be supported as they learn to delegate authority and teachers need to be supported as they take up their leadership role."

The discussion of transformational, distributed and teacher leadership shows that the introduction of these approaches to leadership is inhibited by entrenched managerial leadership. Academic discourse is changing but there is little evidence that these emerging models are widely practised in South African schools.

Leadership roles in South African basic education

The formal leadership roles prescribed for South African schools are those of principal, deputy principal, and head of department. These leaders collectively comprise the school management team.

The role of the school principal

The changing context for leadership (see above) has been accompanied by changes in the roles of school principals. This is manifested partly through professionalising the principalship (Van der Westhuizen & Van Vuuren, 2007) and partly by an emphasis on developing a shared vision (Ngcobo & Tikly, 2010). The principal's role also includes ensuring the best possible resource achievement, allocation and evaluation, and the security of the site and property. Xaba (2012) adds that such processes are required to ensure that teaching and learning are of high quality, whatever the context. This links to the growing attention to instructional leadership, and the effective use of all educators through distributed leadership (Bush & Glover, 2016).

Naidoo (2019) argues that the poor educational outcomes in public schools are partly attributable to the poor leadership displayed by many principals. The author explored the perceptions of teachers and school management team (SMT) members of the leadership qualities exhibited by principals who acquired the Advanced Certificate in Education: School Leadership and Management (ACESLM). The findings show that leadership development for principals is crucial for school improvement because it enhances teaching and learning. Where there is high leadership capacity, instructional leadership develops into sound leadership practices (Naidoo, 2019).

Mestry (2017) claims that school principals are faced with more new demands, complex decisions and additional responsibilities than ever before. Their day is usually filled with diverse administrative and management functions such as procuring resources, managing learner discipline, resolving conflicts with parents and dealing with unexpected teacher and learner crises. Drawing on open-ended questionnaires and personal interviews with eight school principals, the author shows that many school principals repudiated claims that their primary function was to manage teaching and learning. He concludes that those school principals who place a high priority on curricular matters undoubtedly influence teacher and learner performance positively.

Mohale (2014) examined the role of the principal as an instructional leader in the Motupa Circuit primary schools of Limpopo Province. The findings revealed that principals are beset with a number of contextual factors such as inadequate provision of teaching and learning resources and infrastructure needs, lack of monitoring and support of curriculum implementation, inadequate support from the Department of Basic Education, and lack of parental involvement in the education of their children. The author recommended that principals should conduct regular class visits and also ensure that strategies are developed to involve parents of learners in the education of their children.

Deputy Principals and Heads of Departments (HoDs)

There are few major studies of the role of deputy principals in South Africa, a clear research gap. One exception is Bipath's (2015) survey (n=228) of deputy principals and departmental heads, focused on instructional leadership (see below). Research on HoDs is also limited but Ali and Botha's (2006) important research with 100 secondary school HoDs in Gauteng provides some valuable insights. They stress the need for HoDs to focus their time on managing teaching and learning. This should include systematic analysis of results, planning for improvement, and monitoring classroom practice, using observation and target setting.

School management teams

Bush et al. (2010) found several examples of dysfunctional school management teams (SMT) in their small-scale study in Limpopo and Mpumalanga. However, Bush and Glover's (2013) survey of 180 Mpumalanga SMT members showed that the framework for greater team effectiveness was in place in many schools with almost a third meeting weekly and the great majority (88 per cent) meeting at least monthly. There was also an enhanced focus on instructional leadership, with more than half of respondents including curriculum management, and monitoring teaching and learning, among their top two priorities. However, Hoadley et al.'s (2009) research in the Eastern and Western Capes found that the priority role of the principal is that of school administration, thus minimising the leadership function of SMTs.

Phalane's (2016) mixed methods study, with a survey and six case studies, focused on the leadership strategies employed by secondary school management teams (SMT) in managing teamwork in Tshwane North District schools. The participants' perceptions of leadership strategies are generally favourable. The author recommends that strategies and systems need to be in place, implemented, monitored and reviewed on a regular basis to check if they are yielding required outcomes. SMT should also be aware of the importance of communicating those strategies to all staff members, and to seek comments and opinions before implementation, to avoid staff resistance.

Curriculum management and instructional leadership

Bush and Heystek (2006) note the low priority given to this activity by Gauteng principals but there has been some change in attitudes since then, partly prompted by the inclusion of Managing Teaching and Learning (MTL) as a core module in the national ACE: School Leadership programme. In this section, we review the research on different aspects of MTL.

Curriculum management

Most of the research on this theme relates to the macro level of curriculum management, rather than to classroom practice. Hoadley et al. (2009) show how curriculum management in 200 schools was affected by the social context of the school, the nature of school culture, so that it is "learning centred", relationships between schools and homes, good use of resources, and the extent of leadership dispersal within the school. The findings point to the importance of parental support and engagement as well as the instructional focus of the school in achieving student gains over time. They add that the school curriculum should be fully covered, with a well worked out plan to improve student results, and making the fullest use of the day for maximum learning. This requires a stress on learning, a positive culture, positive home-school relationships, good resource management, and effective distributed leadership as well as an instructional focus (Bush & Glover, 2016).

Lumadi (2012) argues that the SMT is responsible for planning, and directing the work of a group of teachers and students, monitoring their work, and taking corrective action where necessary. They have the authority to change the work assignments of team members. The leadership of secondary schools in Mpumalanga involves the evolution of a shared vision through effective strategies that allow that vision to be realised. This involves putting all available resources to work in the most effective way to ensure that the best standard of education for all students is provided. Lumadi (2012, p. 121) adds that this is a topic "driving the school management team frantic" in Mpumalanga.

Instructional leadership

There is increasing recognition that instructional leadership may be an appropriate approach to school improvement in South Africa. However, Bush (2013) adds that little attention has been given to the processes by which improvement can be achieved, including the need for modelling, monitoring and professional dialogue. These may be manifested through high-quality observation of classrooms, discussion of practice within learning areas or phases, and the achievement of consistency in expectations of behaviour and practice for both learners and educators.

Middle managers are also responsible for instructional leadership and Ali and Botha (2006), in the first major study of HoDs in South Africa, focused on 100 secondary school HoDs in Gauteng. They note that, if teaching and learning are to improve significantly, "HoDs will have to spend much more time in supervising the teaching and learning activities that occur daily in their subject or learning area" (p. 17). Significantly, 79 per cent of their respondents refer to "monitoring the teaching and learning standards of educators and learners" as one of their major contributions to school improvement (p. 80), but the authors question whether the HoDs are really carrying out this task. They also suggest that middle managers should develop a routine of analysis of results, planning for improvement, monitoring classroom practice, using observation and target setting.

These points are similar to the recommendations made by Bush et al. (2010) in their study of MTL in the Limpopo and Mpumalanga provinces. Their suggestions are that HoDs should:

- hold regular meetings of the educator team to plan teaching and to discuss problems;
- model good practice by taking lessons while educators observe;
- observe educators regularly and provide structured and constructive feedback to enhance teaching and learning;
- evaluate learner outcomes and design strategies to improve classroom practice; and
- monitor the work of educators through scrutiny of work plans and learner outcomes.

Hoadley et al.'s (2009, p. 385) research showed that curriculum management is more effectively managed where it is seen as a whole school responsibility and where instructional leadership is used. However, they note that the great disparity of leadership style, resourcing and management, and the delegation of curriculum matters to subject leaders, is hampering improvement.

Naidoo and Petersen (2015) argue that robust training and development in instructional leadership practices are necessary to support school leaders. Their study of five principals, who have completed the ACESLM programme, indicate that some principals are not fully conversant with their roles and responsibilities as instructional leaders. They mainly interpret their functions to be purely managerial and to be leaders and administrators of schools.

Bipath's (2015) survey (n=228) of deputy principals and departmental heads showed that instructional leadership was composed of four sub-dimensions, which could be used to identify areas for possible improvement. The findings show that the sub-dimension of "Monitoring and providing feedback on the teaching and learning process" was the best predictor of instructional leadership. The self-confidence of the principal, knowledge of current developments in the curriculum regarding instructional leadership, attending and participating in curriculum-related workshops, and communicating curriculum goals to teachers, were considered crucial to ensure that principals become instructional leaders.

Management of finance and resources

Physical and financial resources provide much of the support required to implement the management of teaching and learning in South Africa (Bush & Heystek, 2006). Their survey of Gauteng principals showed that they regarded financial management as their main development need. Mestry and Hlongwane (2009, p. 341) add that principals feel that financial management is more complex when involving SGB members, as required by the legal framework.

Hoadley et al. (2009, p. 374) stress the importance of the resource base for educational improvement, and the significance of the local context. Their evidence demonstrates the continuing disparity in resources available to schools in different contexts:

> New funding arrangements allowed for fees to be levied, introducing a quasi-market into schooling, and at the same time provision was made for a measure of funding redistribution in favour of poor schools [...] The new policies, designed to change the system from top to bottom, [...] did not speak to the conditions of the majority of schools, or adequately address the deep historical inequalities and uneven quality that existed within and across the country's schools.

There is limited research about the way in which individual schools make use of financial planning, resource management, and the monitoring and evaluation of funds. However, Mestry (2004, p. 127), following focus group interviews and observations with SGB members and educators in four schools south of Johannesburg, concludes that there were four main problems at that time. First, in some schools, the principal and the school governing bodies did not work collaboratively with each other in managing the school's finances. Second, the SGBs were not trained effectively to manage the school's finances. Third, some of the principals objected to the cascading model of training and found the content of the workshops to be too theoretical. Fourth, the Department of Education had no mechanisms in place to support schools on financial issues and problems.

These findings are similar to those of Mestry and Hlongwane (2009, p. 333), who investigated the perceptions of 20 secondary school governors in Gauteng and noted that problems arose from the lack of financial resources, the imperfections of cascading training, variations in the frequency and attendance at training sessions, the quality of training on offer, and a general apathy amongst SGB members. Lekalakala (2009) found similar problems with either lack of training opportunities, or lack of quality provision, in the Ramotse area of Tshwane, Gauteng. Thenga's (2012) study of practice in Gauteng township schools shows a lack of SGB training, inconsistent training, lack of accounting skills, and differing practice by local district education officials (Bush & Glover, 2016).

Basson and Mestry (2019) report that many SGB members lack the necessary knowledge and financial skills to manage school finance effectively. This has resulted in more financial responsibilities being assigned to principals, who in turn solicit the assistance of other members of school management teams (SMTs). However, their findings revealed that collaboration between members of the SGBs and SMTs on school finances is very limited. Dibete's (2015) study of the role of SGBs in managing finances in no-fee schools in Limpopo produced some similar findings. The author shows that many of their participants lacked the knowledge and skills required to manage their school funds effectively, mainly due to low literacy levels and lack of training.

School governance

The introduction of school governing bodies from 1997 was widely regarded as an important aspect of grassroots democracy in the new South Africa. However, Xaba's (2011, p. 210) research shows the problems inherent in establishing effective governance:

> It is clear from the participants' responses that there are difficulties in understanding governance, mainly because governors perceive their roles differently, which detracts from their main responsibility – promoting the best interests of the school. This, combined with less than adequate capacity-building, as required by the Schools Act, adds to the ineffective execution of functions.

Mestry and Khumalo (2012) examine governor involvement in relation to learner discipline, regarded as one of the most contentious issues, and stress the importance of developing a code of conduct for learners. They add that, despite the problems of illiteracy and lack of confidence, and the associated lack of knowledge of legislation, some schools are moving forward to develop, monitor and evaluate policies.

Mncube (2009, p. 102) conducted research with governors in four schools, leading to a survey of 430 parents in ten different schools, supplemented by observation of two SGB meetings. He concludes that, with the complexity of the legal framework, and the nature of the relationship between stakeholders, it is not surprising that the democratic voice of parents is barely heard in some schools:

> While representation and debate are theoretically open and fair, structural and behavioural factors still inhibit the extent to which SGBs operate; the authoritarianism of school leadership and governance, characteristic of the apartheid era, have disappeared, yet issues concerning values, behaviour, attitudes and skills necessary for full democratic participation remain.

Mbokodi and Singh (2011) report on parental partnerships in the governance of ten schools in townships close to Port Elizabeth where, although legal requirements are being met, parental involvement is ineffective because of problems arising from the poor education of those involved. Brown and Duku (2008), drawing on interviews with 48 parents in rural parts of the Eastern Cape, note the poor conceptions of governance and management in all component groups and report extensive use of micro-political groupings within the SGBs, the silencing of minority (usually female or younger male) members, and the gender related conflicts and tensions, where "traditional" views of women are upheld by dominant males.

Clase et al. (2007, p. 253) examined tensions between the SGB, and district or provincial authorities, based on surveys and interviews with 63 officials and 40 SGB groups in Afrikaans Free State schools. They argue that these tensions arise from different interpretations of the concepts of management and control, uncertainty regarding the purpose and responsibilities of the SGB, mutual mistrust and weak relationships.

Mabovula (2009, p. 219) notes that learner participation in school governance is guaranteed in the National Department of Education's guidelines for Representative Councils of Learners, as part of democratic governance. He concludes that the "potential, limitations, constraints, consequences, and challenges facing learners in the school governance structure need to be revealed and debated". Mathebula (2005, p. 190) comments that the role of the representative councils is hampered by the minimal democracy evident in many schools. As noted above, Mncube (2008) also concluded that there is very limited involvement of learners in school governance, despite the national framework for their involvement.

> To secure changes to increase learner participation will require modification of both principal and educator attitudes, especially in those areas where the culture is still "elder" dominated, and where challenge in debate is seen as disrespectful.

Smit and Oosthuizen (2011, p. 64), drawing on a survey of 456 principals, SGB chairs and district officials, and on workshop discussions, also stress the importance of all stakeholders understanding the difference between participative democracy and political democracy and show that these concepts are frequently confused. They point out that the development of democratic principles in action may be inhibited by the political activity of educators, notably through teacher union activity.

Levy and Shumane (2017) explore governance dynamics in four case study schools in low-income communities in the Eastern Cape. The case studies uncovered both vicious circles of capture and virtuous spirals – with the latter characterised by shared developmental commitment among school leaders, teachers, parents and the community. The findings offer encouragement that non-hierarchical entry points for improving educational outcomes may lead to gains.

Levy, Cameron and Hoadley (2016) synthesise the findings of research on the politics and governance in South Africa, undertaken at multiple levels, and using multiple methods. While policy-making, the regulatory framework, and resourcing, are uniform nationally, responsibility for implementation is delegated to the country's nine provinces, which differ substantially from one another, both politically and institutionally. School-level case studies detail how, in the Western Cape, a combination of strong bureaucracy and weak horizontal governance can result in unstable patterns of internal governance, and sometimes a low-level equilibrium of mediocrity. In the Eastern Cape, pro-active engagement by communities and parents can support school-level performance even where the broader governance environment is dysfunctional.

Leadership and management of people

Leading and managing people are central aspects of school leadership in all contexts (Bush & Middlewood, 2013). Two aspects, in particular, are reported in the South African literature (Bush & Glover, 2016).

Staff development and mentoring

The emerging research on staff development is concerned with teacher perceptions of the context within which they work and leadership plays a large part in determining this context. Bantwini (2012. p. 517) explains how this affects teacher quality through professional development in primary schools in the Eastern Cape:

> Teachers had negative perceptions that led to the belief that they were not receiving the support and tools they needed for professional development from their district. The impact of their perceptions was evident in the slow or non-implementation of the district's newly launched curriculum reforms [...] Failure to address teachers' perceptions is likely to result in teachers not benefiting from their professional development programs.

Luneta's (2012, p. 377) literature review on teacher attitudes to further training also concludes that educator involvement in planning activities assists a more positive attitude. Moorosi (2012, p. 501) draws upon the data sets from two investigations to consider the impact of mentoring as a means of leadership development. She differentiates between the groups of people providing the mentoring and the context within which the process takes place. She links mentoring to several aspects of diversity within South Africa:

> Although the majority of mentors were male and protégés were female, gender alone does not appear to have jeopardized these mentoring relationships. Instead, more protégés benefited from cross-gendered relationships. However, the racial composition of mentors seems to have had some influence on mentoring. Same-race relationships appear to have worked better than cross-race ones and more disadvantage was experienced where there were two or more levels of diversity.

Mestry et al. (2009, p. 480) stress the links between effective professional development and teacher motivation: "For professional development to be effective, motivation should be intrinsic rather than extrinsic."

Performance management

The under-performance of South African schools (see above) has led to attempts to manage the performance of educators. The most prominent, and enduring, model is the Integrated Quality Management system (IQMS). De Clercq (2008, p. 9) comments on the IQMS approach and its impact on teacher development:

> IQMS makes problematic assumptions about educator quality and improvement in South African schools. It is not aligned with the status and work of most educators, and over-estimates the implementation readiness of the majority of schools as well as the appraisal and support capacity of senior school and district management. The challenge is to make educators behave and be treated as professionals, as well as to manage the inevitable tensions of appraisal systems.

De Clercq (2008) concludes that a systemic approach to teacher monitoring and development is not sufficient because it also requires changes in the beliefs and attitudes of educators and appraisers. For appraisal to be effective it is necessary to develop support systems to foster development.

Queen-Mary and Mtapuri (2014) conducted open-ended interviews with various stakeholders and conclude that the IQMS was implemented too readily. They posit an alternative, bottom-up model, focused on educator development informed by participation and empowerment. Mosoge and Pilane (2014), drawing on interviews with 15 participants, also claim that development has been neglected within IQMS, in favour of appraisal linked to incentives.

Leadership and diversity

South Africa offers a distinctive example of the importance of inter-sectionality in understanding school leadership and diversity. The statutory separation of learners, educators and leaders under the apartheid regime provides clear evidence of a racist approach to society, including education. Meanwhile, patriarchy was, and arguably continues to be, a pervasive element of South African education. Social class is a significant predictor of educational opportunity and life chances, and is still largely stratified by race, despite the emergence of a black middle class. This section draws on research on various aspects of diversity.

Heystek (2009) discusses teacher appointments in ethnically diverse schools. The government's policy of centralising decisions about appointments can, therefore, be understood as a part of the policy of redress and equal opportunity in reaction to apartheid. In the current context, the opposite of forced separation is applied in the appointment of teachers at schools. The provincial departments of education, who are the official employers of teachers, want to appoint black teachers in formerly white schools. Although it may be politically correct to do so as part of emphasising equal opportunity in the work place, it ignores a sociological approach to diversity and the identity preference indicated by the teachers in the research project. Social identity theory explains that individuals – and therefore also groups – will identify with other individuals and groups in accordance with their preferences. This may provide an option during the appointment of teachers. Thus governing body members could appoint teachers according to the local community's needs and criteria, as long as the governing body does not discriminate unfairly against any individual (p. 21).

Bush and Moloi (2007) offer a different perspective on the deployment of teachers and leaders in post-apartheid South Africa. Their study of 'cross-boundary' leadership in Gauteng showed that educators overwhelmingly (more than 90%) continue to practise in schools previously reserved for their own racial groups. The researchers interviewed 46 school leaders who crossed these racial boundaries and found some disturbing evidence:

> The experience of these 'cross-boundary' leaders differs significantly along racial lines. White, Indian and 'Coloured' leaders are generally welcomed in the former Black schools but [black leaders] often face discrimination and even hostility in the previously white schools (p. 45).

This evidence links to the ingrained belief that white people were 'superior' to those of other groups, a direct consequence of the apartheid philosophy. One of the black participants in this study comments that 'black educators believe that white is good and clever' (ibid, p. 47). Despite the legislation promoting equal opportunities for all racial groups, it will take some time for such attitudes to change.

Sayed (2016) also examines the unintended class differentiated and inequality reproducing effects of post-apartheid educational legislation. He argues that such policies have had the unintended consequence of creating an unequal two-tier education structure in South Africa. While formally de-racialising schooling, and aiming to make it more equitable, the policies have not fundamentally eradicated the class and race bifurcation of the education system. A relatively well-functioning, well-resourced semi-private education for the middle class, stands in stark contrast to a largely dysfunctional poorly resourced system for the disadvantaged poorer majority. Policy has thus permitted the middle class to secure control of the historically white school sector, facilitating a 'new deracialised middle class' who have 'opted out' of the public system of schooling in favour of semi-privatised schooling. The introduction of 'no fee' schools to address concerns of educational affordability and access in poor communities also fails to address the underlying structural issue of inequality.

Maringe, Masinire and Nkambule (2015) show how multiple deprivation affects a large proportion of schools in South Africa. The authors argue that a broad-brush policy application fails to recognise the contextualised challenges faced in specific schools. The central purpose of the research was to discover the specific challenges and leadership issues that schools in multiple deprived communities face, and to identify ways in which such schools dealt with these challenges. The research was conducted through a case study approach of three schools in one of the most impoverished provinces of the country. The authors found that, while the three schools shared many similar conditions of poverty that drove the poor to marginal performance, stories of success tended to be strongly related to four key factors. These are, first, leadership that went beyond an ordinary focus on instruction; second, staff stability; third, flexible scheduling that allowed parental involvement; and, fourth, a focus on a school-wide project that acted as a rallying point and a source of pride for the entire school.

Moorosi (2010, p. 560), drawing from her research in KZN, argues that transformation should include changes in community attitudes to women:

> The interplay between the social and organizational levels becomes stark where the social norms and beliefs appear to be informing what happens in the school context. This perpetuates the reproduction of a continued male domination in the management of a field occupied mostly by women.

Similarly, Naidoo and Perumal (2014, p. 822) claim that 'more still needs to be done in order to redress gender equality in school leadership'. Their research shows that female principals in disadvantaged school communities rely on their own spiritual, ethical, moral and maternal values to help them in their role as leaders. The key finding that emerged from the study is that social expectations of women need to change. Women should be appraised by what they can do, not by their gender, and should not be pressurised into choosing between work and home.

Leadership culture and structures

The transformation of the policy context, and the changing demography of learners and educators, has profound implications for school culture (Zulu, 2004; Villiers and Pretorius, 2011). Nieman and Kotze's (2006, p. 614) survey of 30 school staff in the Free State led them to conclude that school culture is characterised by sociability (friendship and morale) and solidarity (collective will and mutual interest). They also note the links between culture and leadership:

> Organisational culture [is] cultivated by management and, therefore, it would be a true asset to a school if a suitable principal could be appointed: a principal who leads in such a way that a culture, in which teaching and learning could thrive, is established (p. 622).

Barnes et al. (2012, p. 73) undertook a similar investigation in the Eastern Cape. Their findings show a clear link between enhanced school culture and climate, and lower levels of violence. Understanding this relationship made it possible for school leaders to institute positive action to recognise culture and climate as a means of securing safer schools.

Vos et al. (2012, 2013) consider the way in which culture is reflected in educators' attitudes to their working environment in primary schools in North-West province. Their findings, based on a survey of 904 teachers in 68 schools, indicate that educators are not only determinants of culture but are affected by it.

The role of the principal in developing a culture of teaching and learning is discussed by Bush (2013, p. 14), who comments that:

> Changing school culture has to be a deliberate process, intended to achieve specific results, such as enhanced learner outcomes. Culture is usually deeply embedded and is difficult to shift particularly if, as in most South African schools, most educators have substantial experience in the same school and are used to working in a certain way. It often takes an external stimulus or threat to produce new patterns of working.

Weeks (2012, p. 9), following an extensive literature review, argues that the dysfunctionality of so many schools in South Africa requires a "quest for learning", involving both learners and educators, and building upon their cultural heritage to establish a learning community within the classroom.

Christie et al. (2007) carried out a literature review, and also conducted an enquiry with 18 middle-ranking schools. Their research showed that all these schools had organisational cultures or mindsets that 'supported a work ethic, expected achievement, and acknowledged success, leading to a sense of purpose, commitment, achievement, acknowledged success, and an enabling work ethic' (Christie et al., 2007, p. 5).

Leadership and student outcomes

Heystek (2015) argues that it is a 'formidable challenge' for most school leaders to improve academic results in state schools. In terms of their contracts, principals are accountable for the academic results as reflected in examination and test results for their schools. The Department of Basic Education has made attempts to implement a performance agreement with principals and deputy principals, which would hold them directly and specifically accountable for the examination results. However, research with principals and deputy principals indicates that a performance agreement of this kind is potentially demotivating because they do not feel they would be able to achieve the goals it sets (p. 1).

Moorosi and Bantwini (2016) examine whether and how leadership styles in Eastern Cape school districts support school improvement, through questionnaires and semi-structured interviews with school principals. Their findings reveal the prevalence of more authoritarian top-down leadership styles, which tend to have negative effects on school improvement.

Role of parents

Gwija (2016) examines the role of parents in their children's education and notes that parents play a significant role in improving a school's academic results. The investigation focused on two secondary schools in the Western Cape and the findings revealed that participants overlooked the role of parents. Although they involve parents in some school activities, there is a need for training on how the school principals should optimally involve parents in school activities.

Leadership preparation and development

Since the introduction of the ACE: School Leadership programme there has been growing awareness that the functions of leadership should be exercised by a wider range of people within schools. In their review of the programme, Bush et al. (2011, p. 39) conclude that:

> The flexibility and initiative required to lead and manage schools in periods of rapid change suggest that preparation should go beyond training principals to implement the requirements of the hierarchy to developing rounded and confident leaders who are able to engage all school stakeholders in the process of school improvement for the benefit of learners and their communities.

Leadership development is fundamental to change but R. Botha (2011) is critical of the leadership style of authoritarian principals, as a limiting factor in leadership development, and notes the overwhelming need for enhanced professionalism for principals. E. Botha (2012, p. 406) suggests than one approach might be to create professional learning communities which consider change through talking, asking relevant questions, and making decisions together.

Mentoring for leadership development has been investigated by Msila (2011, p. 51) who, following in-depth observation of 12 mentors and their mentees, notes that:

> The mentors and their mentees had a huge role to play in the process; the personalities of the individuals involved were very crucial in their relationship [...] Change agents for both mentors and mentees learn easily and are open to ideas different from their own. In a mentoring relationship, this proves very important because one listens and understands because they have embraced change.

Msila (2011) also points to the need for mentors to be effective in all aspects of their leadership practice and that the development of this approach is dependent upon the availability of trained and respected mentors.

Mestry (2017) shows that the Department of Basic Education has made numerous attempts to raise the professional standards and competencies of school principals by formulating the South African National Professional Qualification for Principalship (DoE, 2004) and, subsequently, the South African Standards for Principalship (SASP). The DBE recognises the current lack of a co-ordinated system to meet these identified needs, and is therefore seeking to develop and implement a system of career pathing for education leaders and managers, and a framework of leadership and management development processes and programmes. It is envisaged that these will be built upon agreed understanding of the core purposes of the leadership roles, the key functions within these, the values which underpin them, and the personal and professional attributes required to carry out the role (p. 8).

Research gaps

This review of research shows a considerable body of evidence about the nature of school leadership in South Africa. However, the data are uneven and some areas of research remain under-developed. For example, a great deal of research focuses on the role of the principal with much less attention to other leadership roles, including deputy principals, heads of departments (HoDs), and school management teams. Similarly, research on functional aspects of leadership and management, such as curriculum, finance, physical resources, and managing people, offers only limited evidence about how these functions are enacted in schools. A feature of much literature on school leadership in South Africa is a normative stance, often connected to a social justice agenda, but with weak empirical underpinning. There are also geographical variations in the availability of research data, with more evidence from Gauteng and the Western Cape, for example, and fewer papers from other South African contexts, especially from rural areas. Finally, while there are pockets of excellence, there are few major centres for school leadership research, with a critical mass of senior and emerging academics. Given the widely-accepted links between leadership and school improvement, a focused research agenda is required to produce robust evidence to inform policy and practice.

Implications and conclusion

The building blocks for the field of school leadership are policy, theory, research and practice. This review of research in the field draws on theory and offers insights into policy and practice. Recognition of the importance of school leadership is a continuing feature of the policy discourse, beginning with the Task Team report (Department of Education 1996), and continuing with the development and piloting of the national ACE: School Leadership programme, from 2007. However, discontinuities in this strand of policy-making are also evident. For example, in 2011, the Council of Education Ministers announced that the ACE: SL would become a requirement for new principals but this stipulation has not been acted upon. The subsequent intention to replace the ACE with an Advanced Diploma has not advanced beyond the planning stage.

This chapter shows that, while empirical evidence has been growing, it remains inadequate to draw firm conclusions about many aspects of school leadership and management in South Africa. As noted above, some topics still have limited research. In other areas, for example on the role of the principal, and on school governance, there is more relevant literature but some of this is normative and even empirical sources are often based on small-scale projects, for example from a very limited number of case studies. More substantial research is required on many topics, notably leadership preparation, the roles of senior and middle leaders, resource management, and stakeholder participation. New research should include larger-scale projects, comparative cross-cultural studies, and observational studies of leadership practice. In particular, as Bush and Glover (2016) argue, more evidence is required to answer the key research question: Why do most South African schools continue to under-perform?

References

Ali, F., & Botha, N. (2006). *Evaluating the Role, Importance and Effectiveness of Heads of Department in Contributing to School Improvement in Public Secondary Schools in Gauteng.* Johannesburg, MGSLG.

Bantwini, B.D. (2010). How teachers perceive the new curriculum reform: Lessons from a school district in the Eastern Cape Province, South Africa. *International Journal of Educational Development,* 30(1), 83. https://doi.org/10.1016/j.ijedudev.2009.06.002

Barnes, K., Brynard, S., & De Wet, C. (2012). The influence of school culture and school climate on violence in schools of the Eastern Cape Province. *South African Journal of Education,* 32(1), 69-82. https://doi.org/10.15700/saje.v32n1a495

Basson, P., & Mestry, R.. (2019). Collaboration between school management teams and governing bodies in effectively managing public primary school finances. *South African Journal of Education,* 39(2), 1-9. https://doi.org/10.15700/saje.v39n2a1688

Bipath, K. (2015) .Predictors of instructional leadership practices: lessons learnt from Bushbuckridge, South Africa. *Journal of Educational Studies* 1, 163-180.

Botha, E.M. (2012). Turning the tide: creating professional learning communities (PLC) to improve teaching practice and learning in South African public schools. *Africa Education Review,* 9(2), 395-411. https://doi.org/10.1080/18146627.2012.722405

Botha, R.J. (2011). The managerial role of the principal in promoting teacher professionalism in selected Eastern Cape schools. *Africa Education Review,* 8(3), 397-415. https://doi.org/10.1080/18146627.2011.618620

Botha, R.J, & Triegaardt, P.K. (2016).The Perceptions of South African Classroom Teachers with Regard to the Role of Distributed Leadership in School Improvement. *International Journal of Educational Sciences,* 14(3). https://doi.org/10.1080/09751122.2016.11890498

Brown, B.A., & Duku, N. (2008). Negotiated identities: dynamics in parents' participation in school governance in rural Eastern Cape schools and implications for school leadership. *South African Journal of Education,* 28(3), 431-450. https://doi.org/10.15700/saje.v28n3a122

Bush, T. (2007). Educational leadership and management: Theory, policy and practice. *South African Journal of Education,* 27(3), 391-406.

Bush, T. (2011). *Theories of Educational Leadership and Management: Fourth Edition*, London, Sage.

Bush, T. (2013). Instructional leadership and leadership for learning. *Education as Change*, 17(S1), 5-20. https://doi.org/10.1080/16823206.2014.865986

Bush, T., & Glover, D. (2009). *Managing Teaching and Learning: A Concept Paper.* Johannesburg, MGSLG.

Bush, T., & Glover, D. (2012). Leadership development and learner outcomes: Evidence from South Africa, *Journal of Educational Leadership, Policy and Practice*, 27(2), 3-15.

Bush, T., & Glover, D. (2013). School management teams in South Africa: A survey of school leaders in the Mpumalanga province. *International Studies in Educational Administration*, 41(1), 21-40.

Bush, T., & Glover, D. (2016). School leadership and management in South Africa: findings from a systematic literature review. *International Journal of Educational Management*, 30(2), 166-176. https://doi.org/10.1108/IJEM-07-2014-0101

Bush, T., & Heystek, J. (2006). School leadership and management in South Africa: Principals' perceptions. *International Studies in Educational Administration*, 34(3), 63-76. https://doi.org/10.1177/1741143206068212

Bush, T., Kiggundu, E., & Moorosi, P. (2011). Preparing new principals in South Africa: The ACE: School Leadership programme. *South African Journal of Education*, 31(1), 31-43. https://doi.org/10.15700/saje.v31n1a356

Bush, T., & Moloi, K. (2007). Race, racism and discrimination in school leadership: Evidence from England and South Africa. *International Studies in Educational Administration*, 35(1), 41-59.

Christie, P., Butler, D., & Potterton, M. (2007). *Schools that Work: Report of Ministerial Committee.* Pretoria, Government Printer.

Clase, P., Kok, J. & Van der Merwe, M. (2007). Tension between school governing bodies and education authorities in South Africa and proposed resolutions thereof. *South African Journal of Education*, 27(2).

De Clercq, F. (2008). Teacher quality, appraisal and development: The flaws in the IQMS. *Perspectives in Education*, 26(1), 9-13.

Department of Education. (1996). *Changing Management to Manage Change in Education: Report of the Task Team on Education Management Development.* Pretoria, Department of Education.

Dibete, K.J. (2015). The role of the school governing bodies in managing finances in no-fee schools in the Maraba circuit of Limpopo Province (Thesis). University of South Africa, Pretoria, http://hdl.handle.net/10500/19901

Grant, C. (2006). Emerging voices on teacher leadership: Some South African views. *Educational Management, Administration and Leadership*, 34(4), 511-532. https://doi.org/10.1177/1741143206068215

Grant, C. (2017). Distributed leadership in South Africa: yet another passing fad or a robust theoretical tool for investigating school leadership practice? *School Leadership & Management*, 37(5),457-475. https://doi.org/10.1080/13632434.2017.1360856

Grant C., Gardner K., Kajee F., Moodley R., & Somaroo, S. (2010). Teacher leadership: a survey analysis of KwaZulu-Natal teachers' perceptions. *South African Journal of Education*, 30(3), 401-419. https://doi.org/10.15700/saje.v30n3a362

Gwija, M. (2016). The role of parents in enhancing academic performance in secondary schools in the Metro-Central Education District, Western Cape. University of South Africa, Pretoria.

Heystek, J. (2009). Teacher appointment in ethnic diverse schools. Paper presented at the British Educational Research Association Annual Conference, University of Manchester, 2-5 September 2009.

Heystek, J. (2015). Principals' perceptions of the motivation potential of performance agreements in underperforming schools. *South African Journal of Education*, 35(2), 1-10. https://doi.org/10.15700/saje.v35n2a986

Hoadley, U., Christie, P., & Ward, C.L. (2009). Managing to learn: instructional leadership in South African secondary schools. *School Leadership and Management*, 29(4), 373-389. https://doi.org/10.1080/13632430903152054

Leithwood, K. (1994). Leadership for school restructuring. *Educational Administration Quarterly*, 30(4), 498-518. https://doi.org/10.1177/0013161X94030004006

Lekalakala, M.T. (2009). Problems Encountered by School Governing Bodies in Executing their Financial Tasks. Unpublished thesis, UNISA.

Levy, B., Cameron, R., & Hoadley, U. (2016). *The Politics and Governance of Basic Education: A Tale of Two South African Provinces*. ESID Working Paper No 67. Manchester: Effective States and Inclusive Development Research Centre, The University of Manchester. https://doi.org/10.2139/ssrn.2887441

Levy, B., & Shumane, L. (2017). *School Governance in a Fragmented Political and Bureaucratic Environment: Case Studies from South Africa's Eastern Cape Province*. ESID Working Paper No. 84. Manchester: Effective States and Inclusive Development Research Centre, The University of Manchester. https://doi.org/10.2139/ssrn.2956313

Lumadi, M.W. (2012). Curriculum management: 'driving the school management team frantic'. *Africa Education Review,* 9(1), 121-135. https://doi.org/10.1080/18146627.2012.755282

Luneta, K. (2012). Designing continuous professional development programmes for teachers: A literature review. *Africa Education Review,* 9(2), 360-379. https://doi.org/10.1080/18146627.2012.722395

Mabovula, N. (2009). Giving voice to the voiceless through deliberative democratic school governance, *South African Journal of Education,* 29(2), 219-233. https://doi.org/10.15700/saje.v29n2a162

Mafora, P. (2013). Learners' and teachers' perceptions of principals' leadership in Soweto secondary schools: a social justice analysis. *South African Journal of Education,* 33(3), 1-18. https://doi.org/10.15700/201503070742

Maringe, F., Masinire, A., & Nkambule, T. (2015) Distinctive features of schools in multiple deprived communities in South Africa: Implications for policy and leadership. *Educational Management Administration & Leadership,* 43(3), 363-385. https://doi.org/10.1177/1741143215570303

Mathebula, T. (2005). The role of Representative Councils for Learners in South African Schools: Maximal or minimal participation? *Africa Education Review,* 2(2), 189-204. https://doi.org/10.1080/18146620508566300

Mbokodi, S.M., & Singh, P. (2011). Parental partnerships in the governance of schools in the Black townships of Port Elizabeth. *South African Journal of Education,* 29(4).

Mestry R. (2004). Financial accountability: The principal or school governing body? *South African Journal of Education,* 26(1), 27-38.

Mestry, R. (2017). Principals' perspectives and experiences of their instructional leadership functions to enhance learner achievement in public schools. *Journal of Education,* 69, 257-275.

Mestry, R, Hendricks, I, & Bisschoff, T. (2009). Perceptions of teachers on the benefits of teacher development programmes. *South African Journal of Education,* 29(4), 475-490. https://doi.org/10.15700/saje.v29n4a292

Mestry, R., & Hlongwane, S. (2009). Perspectives on the training of school governing bodies: towards an effective and efficient financial management system. *Africa Education Review,* 6(2), 324- 342. https://doi.org/10.1080/18146620903274654

Mestry, R., & Khumalo, J. (2012), Governing bodies and learner discipline: managing rural schools in South Africa through a code of conduct. *South African Journal of Education,* 32(1), 97-110. https://doi.org/10.15700/saje.v32n1a402

Mncube, V. (2008). Democratisation and education in South Africa. *South African Journal of Education*, 28(1), 77-90.

Mncube, V. (2009). The perceptions of parents of their role in the democratic governance of schools in South Africa: Are they on board? *South African Journal of Education*, 29(1), 83-103. https://doi.org/10.15700/saje.v29n1a231

Mohale, A.B. (2014). The role of the principal as an instructional leader: a case study of three schools in the Motupa Circuit, Limpopo, University of South Africa, Pretoria, <http://hdl.handle.net/10500/18675

Moorosi P. (2010). South African females' career paths: understanding the gender gap in secondary school management. *Educational Management, Administration and Leadership*, 38(5), 547-562. https://doi.org/10.1177/1741143210373741

Moorosi, P. (2012). Mentoring for school leadership in South Africa. *Professional Development in Education*, 38(3), 487-503. https://doi.org/10.1080/19415257.2011.637430

Moorosi, P., & Bantwini, B.D. (2016). School district leadership styles and school improvement: evidence from selected school principals in the Eastern Cape Province. *South African Journal of Education*, 36(4). Msila, V. (2011). School management and the struggle for effective schools. *Africa Education Review*, 8(3), 434-449. https://doi.org/10.15700/saje.v36n4a1341

Naicker, S.R., & Mestry, R. (2011). Distributive leadership in public schools: Experiences and perceptions of teachers in the Soweto region. *Perspectives in Education*, 29(4).

Naidoo, P. (2019). Perceptions of teachers and school management teams of the leadership roles of public school principals. *South African Journal of Education*, 39(2). https://doi.org/10.15700/saje.v39n2a1534

Naidoo, P., & Perumal, J. (2014). Female principals leading at disadvantaged schools in Johannesburg, South Africa. *Educational Management Administration & Leadership*, 42(6), 808-24. https://doi.org/10.1177/1741143214543202

Naidoo, P., & Petersen, N. (2015). Towards a leadership programme for primary school principals as instructional leaders. *South African Journal of Childhood Education*, 5(3). https://doi.org/10.4102/sajce.v5i3.371

Ngcobo, T., & Tikly, L.P. (2010), Key dimensions of effective leadership for change: A focus on township and rural schools in South Africa. *Educational Management, Administration and Leadership*, 38(2), 202-228. https://doi.org/10.1177/1741143209356359

Nieman, R., & Kotze, T. (2006). The relationship between leadership practices and organisational culture: an education management perspective. *South African Journal of Education*, 26(4), 609-624.

Phalane, M.M. (2016) Leadership strategies employed by secondary school management teams in managing teamwork in Tshwane North District schools. University of South Africa, Pretoria.

Queen-Mary, T.N., & Mtapuri, O. (2014), Teachers' perceptions of the Integrated Quality Management System: lessons from Mpumalanga, South Africa. *South African Journal of Education*, 34(1), Art. #719, 14 pages. https://doi.org/10.15700/201412120945

Sayed, Y. (2016). The governance of public schooling in South Africa and the middle class: social solidarity for the public good versus class interest. *Critical Perspectives on Southern Africa*, 91, 84-105. https://doi.org/10.1353/trn.2016.0019

Singh, P., & Lokotsch, K. (2005). Effects of transformational leadership on human resource management in primary schools. *South African Journal of Education*, 25(2), 279-286.

Smit, M., & Oosthuizen, I. (2011). Improving school governance through participative democracy and the law. *South African Journal of Education*, 31(1), 55-73. https://doi.org/10.15700/saje.v31n1a415

Steyn , T. (2013). Professional and organisational socialisation during leadership succession of a school principal: a narrative inquiry using visual ethnography. *South African Journal of Education*, 33(2), 1-17. https://doi.org/10.15700/saje.v33n2a702

Thenga, C.M. (2012). *Managing School Funds in selected secondary schools in Gauteng province.* Unpublished thesis, UNISA.

Van der Westhuizen, P., & Van Vuuren, H. (2007). Professionalising principalship in South Africa. *South African Journal of Education*, 27(3), 431-445.

Villiers, E., & Pretorius, S.G. (2011). Democracy in schools: are educators ready for teacher leadership? *South African Journal of Education*, 31(4), 574-589. https://doi.org/10.15700/saje.v31n4a453

Vos, D., Van der Westhuizen, P.C., Mentz, P.J., and Ellis, S.M. (2012). Educators and the quality of their work environment: an analysis of the organisational climate in primary schools. *South African Journal of Education*, 32(1), 56-68. https://doi.org/10.15700/saje.v32n1a520

Weeks, F., (2012). The quest for a culture of learning: a South African schools perspective. *South African Journal of Education*, 32(1), 1-14. https://doi.org/10.15700/saje.v32n1a565

Williams, C.G. (2011). Distributed leadership in South African schools: possibilities and constraints. *South African Journal of Education*, 31(2), 190-200. https://doi.org/10.15700/saje.v31n2a421

Xaba, M. (2011). The possible cause of school governance challenges in South Africa. *South African Journal of Education*, 31(2), 201-211. https://doi.org/10.15700/saje.v31n2a479

Xaba, M. (2012). A qualitative analysis of facilities maintenance – a school governance function in South Africa. *South African Journal of Education*, 32(2), 215-226. https://doi.org/10.15700/saje.v32n2a548

Zulu, S., (2004). *The instructional role of school principals*, Unpublished Ph.D. thesis, UNISA.

Chapter 6

A Systematic review of trends in teaching and learning research in South African schools

Dr Laura Dison and Dr Alison Kearney
Curriculum Division, Wits School of Education

Abstract

Despite the persistence of poor learner performance in an inequitable schooling system in South Africa, there is a surprising lack of extensive research that examines teaching and learning practices in the classroom. Hoadley (2012), in a presentation to a Carnegie conference, based on a review of South African primary schools, highlighted the strengths and limitations of teaching and learning studies in terms of their methodologies and consistency of findings. This chapter builds on these insights by reporting on the findings of a systematic review of studies on teaching and learning in Basic Education and Training (BET) and Further Education and Training (FET) in South Africa over the past twenty-five years in order to discern and expand the existing knowledge base. This systematic review aims to contribute to an understanding of what we know about learning and teaching in South African schools as well as provide a conceptual framework for critiquing the assumptions and criteria used by researchers to select their sources of evidence. Drawing out emergent themes, the review identifies the key aspects of learning that are most researched as well as gaps in the nature of student engagement and participation in pedagogical processes. The purpose of this systematic review is to gain an understanding of what research on learning has been conducted at the BET and FET levels in South Africa in the past twenty years. Drawing out emergent themes, the systematic review identifies the key aspects of learning that are most researched and highlights important gaps in the research. This will contribute to a more nuanced and complex understanding of what is known about learning in South African schools.

Keywords: classroom pedagogies, classroom studies, learner-centred, learner success, learning strategies, student learning, teaching approaches.

Introduction

This chapter reviews two decades of research specifically addressing teaching and learning practices in South African primary and high school classrooms. It synthesises the current corpus of empirical and conceptual studies and reveals the manner in which research on learning focuses on the influence of curriculum policies, teacher activities and socio-cultural and environmental conditions of learning more than on teaching and learning activities, or the processes of learning.

Through the process of engaging in a systematic review of teaching and learning studies, we wished to make explicit the research design and methods used to generate relevant data in the field of teaching and learning. The chapter reveals differences and tensions that emerged between the studies that focus on broad characterisations of teaching (e.g. teacher-centred or learner-centred) and those that focus on the significance of teaching practices in enhancing learning and epistemological access to knowledge in the classroom. It provides an account of the search strategies and the search engines used to identify relevant South African sources. Studies selected for the systematic review include small-scale classroom studies (based on classroom observations and interviews), school effectiveness and improvement studies, language and literacy studies and studies focusing on the impact of teaching approaches and styles. The analysis highlights some of the limitations of these studies such as the sample sizes and methods of analysis, and the extent to which the research questions address pertinent issues and debates within the discourse community.

The overarching goal of the systematic review was to gain an understanding of **what research** on learning has been conducted at the (BET) and (FET) levels in South Africa over the past twenty-five years and on **how** this research has been conducted at different levels of schooling in different learning contexts. A range of themes have emerged from the analysis which indicate the key aspects of learning that are most researched. The intention is to contribute to an understanding of what we know about learning and teaching in South African schools by providing a critical perspective of these studies and by making suggestions for further research to address the gaps.

Methodology

In order to understand what research has been done on teaching and learning in South Africa over the past twenty-five years, we conducted a systematic review of journal articles, published in the past twenty-five years, that focused on learner-centred teaching in South African schools. A systematic review is one which aims to establish what research has been conducted and what literature has been published, and reports on the outcome of a comprehensive data search. For this systematic review South African education journals, Google scholar, ERIC and EBSCOHOST were searched for studies on South African Basic Education and Training (BET) and Further Education and Training (FET), that focused on learner-centred teaching, as well as classroom-based studies of learner activities and teaching approaches. We chose to focus on SA schooling studies conducted in the past twenty-five years since this time frame marks the emergence of democracy in South Africa, after which curricula, teaching and research became more inclusive of the whole South African population. The keywords used for the literature search included learner-centered teaching, teaching and learning in South Africa, learner achievement, factors that influence learning, teaching approaches in South Africa and classroom practices in Basic Education and Training (BET) and Further Education and Training (FET). We also looked for studies on the effects of teaching styles on learning, relationships between teaching and learning, epistemological access, teaching to promote learner achievement, as well as constraints on learning and factors that influence learners' underachievement and success.

We were mindful that this systematic review exists in a book alongside chapters on education leadership and policy development, language learning, teacher professional development and the effects of information and computer technologies (ICT) on teaching and learning. In order to avoid repetition, we therefore excluded papers that focused on managing teaching and learning, teacher training, teacher's professional identity and articles on the use of and effects of ICT in the classroom unless they had a direct bearing on teaching and learning practices. We chose to focus on accredited, published journal articles since these are peer reviewed. After the initial search, 38 articles were identified. We divided the articles between the two authors, and used the analytic tool we developed to assist with reading the articles with a critical lens. This tool consisted of a table of questions that each reviewer applied to the articles under review. The questions were focused on the following central aspects in each reviewed study:

- Level of schooling
- The discipline upon which the study was focused
- The purpose of the research in response to the research problem that was identified
- The conceptual framing of the research
- The methods of research the researchers used
- The nature of the research problems to be investigated
- The findings or results
- Possible gaps identified and areas for future research

We peer reviewed each other's analysis to ensure that the analytic tool was applied consistently. Our peer review enabled us to refine our themes and validate the main findings across all 38 articles. Our priority was to conduct a critical appraisal of the studies. In this chapter we synthesise and report our findings by discussing the themes that emerged from our in-depth analysis.

Emergent themes

In what follows, the emergent themes are explored in order to create a snapshot of the kinds of research that have taken place over the past 25 years on teaching and learning, and to identify the key findings of the research. What has become clear from this systematic review is that many of the research papers we reviewed do not address the issue of student learning directly, but do so as part of their quest to analyse other aspects of teaching and learning such as the factors that influence learner achievement, teaching practices, the effects of the use of ICT on learning, teaching and learning cultures in schools and so on. We have structured the discussion in this chapter around the five main themes that have emerged, namely, socio-economic conditions affecting learning, school cultures, the effects of curriculum change, teacher activities and learner-centred approaches to teaching. Most of the studies used small-scale qualitative methods based on interviews, questionnaires and classroom observations and have a range in focus from pre-school to high school.

Socio-economic conditions affecting learning and teaching

In this category, several studies have documented the material, social and cultural factors that impact negatively on learning and teaching in schools. In one such study, Nic Spaull (2013) reported on the findings of econometric modelling using the SACMEQ[6] III dataset. The study found that when building models to measure or monitor student performance separately for the wealthiest 25% of schools compared to the poorest 75% of schools, there were striking differences in the factors influencing student performance. Only five of the 27 factors were shared between the two models for mathematics, and 11 of the 30 factors for reading. Spaull (2013) acknowledges this contrast by pointing out the impact of elements such as 'ill-discipline, inefficient management, and low cognitive demand – all legacies of apartheid'. Emerging from the study, Spaull (2013) suggested that researchers and policy-makers understand that South Africa has two education sub-systems when trying to interpret educational data and develop educational policy.

Similar findings had emerged from a study conducted by Smith (2011) two years previously which explored the extent to which learners' socio-economic status (SES) was associated with differences in their reading and mathematics attainment towards the end of primary schooling. These findings indicated that material and social conditions such as unstable home environment, poor nutrition, fewer home resources/amenities (e.g. books, electricity) and teaching pedagogies were key factors in the learners' performance. Pupils placed in the poorest social group

---

[6] Southern Africa Consortium for Monitoring Educational Quality

attained the lowest test scores and the study found that targeted funding did not improve the low throughput rates and high drop-out rates. The study found that these learners did not reach their full potential regardless of school interventions compared to learners in better resourced community schools with lower teacher-pupil ratios, writing materials, textbooks and access to video equipment, TVs and computers.

Findings about the importance of resources emerged from a study by Nassimbeni and Desmond (2011) who investigated the availability of books as a factor in promoting reading and learning in twenty disadvantaged primary schools. The intervention was a direct result of a donation of books to these schools, and researchers attributed the positive changes that they documented to the training that supported the implementation. The researchers concluded with what they described as "an important learning for those involved in policy and planning for the improvement of literacy skills in our primary schools – that you cannot expect the teachers to work confidently with materials at their disposal without providing specialised training in their use." (102).

In an earlier study of the relationship between primary school learners' proficiency in English and their achievement in mathematics, Howie (2003) reviewed studies that focused on factors that influence learners' achievement. Some of the factors that influenced leaners' achievement identified by Howie, like those pointed out by Smith (2011), included: socio-economic status, availability of books in the home, influence of parents, including their education, occupation, relationships with their children, parental pressure, parents' self-concept, pupils' attitudes to mathematics, family size, and jobs in the home. Howie (2003) also found that learners' personal attributes, such as their aspirations, peer group attitudes, pupils' self concept, self expectations, pupils' anxiety, enjoyment of mathematics, attitudes towards mathematics, reading ability, gender, age, attitudes towards teachers and time spent on homework affected their achievement in mathematics and English.

In the same time period, a study that examined specific ways in which socio-economic factors affect learners' school performance, was a mixed methods research study which examined the factors influencing Grade 12 performance conducted by Legotlo, Maaga and Sebego (2002). The study was carried out with 4 secondary schools from each of the 12 districts in North West province: one good, one average and 2 poorly performing schools. Legotlo et al. (2002, 117) found that "inadequate physical and human resources, lack of discipline and commitment, ineffective and unclear policies, and failure to develop effective strategies to address the unanticipated consequences of implementing changes in the school system" were the major causes of learners' poor performance. The role of resources was identified as a critical factor for addressing teaching and learning challenges and for boosting the "morale of educators" (117). The factors that contributed to learners' poor performance in Grade 12 were not only complex in nature but were also intertwined with teacher morale, as it was found that even in impoverished circumstances learners thrived with teachers with high job satisfaction, who were committed and invested in their work.

A newer study by Carrim (2011) drew on empirical data to highlight "the significant impact of social conditions on children's participation in pedagogical spaces and their schooling more generally". The author analysed the discourses of participation in the classroom as compared to official constructions of participation. He argued that legislation and policy provide a generalised view of the 'learner' and disregard socio-cultural issues of race, class, gender and family circumstances. The aspect of the paper relevant to this systematic review refers to the contradiction between the construction of learners in official documentation in terms of their critical thinking and problem-solving capacities, and their limited opportunities for participation in classroom situations. Carrim (2011, p.78) pointed out that while children can be active participants in 'pedagogical encounters in the classroom', they are not given opportunities to participate in schooling governing processes.

A later study that also focused on the relationship between poor performance of learners and teacher motivation in selected high schools in the Western Cape in South Africa, by Chux, Saphetha, Henrie, and Robertson (2013), found that lack of resources and work overload negatively impacted on teachers' motivation, which, in turn, affected learners' performance. In this study, a survey questionnaire of closed and open-ended questions regarding job satisfaction and morale was administered to a random sample of 279 educators drawn from the database of the poorly performing high schools in the Western Cape. The results suggest that there is a correlation between teachers' motivation and their learners' achievement. Chux et al. (2013, p. 849) found that "highly motivated educators experience job satisfaction; and also perform better than their poorly motivated counterparts". The researchers found that a mix of intrinsic and extrinsic factors tend to exert influence on the educators' motivation. Extrinsic factors included working conditions, job security, and perceived growth opportunities. The lack of resources, work overload and lack of recognition were noted as obstacles that the teachers faced in their daily lives.

Culture of teaching and learning in schools

Empirical research on teaching and learning has frequently documented issues related to the culture of learning in South African classrooms and the nature of dysfunctional schools (Christie, 1998; Christie et al. 2007). Weeks (2012) extended the investigation by Christie (1998) into the poor functioning of a large number of previously black schools (which they commonly termed 'the breakdown of the culture of teaching and learning') traced back to apartheid education. He proposed an alternative approach to analysing and restoring the 'culture of teaching and learning' by pointing out that "a golden thread that emerges from the literature is that context, social interaction within this context, and the cultural attributes that emerge from this interaction are instrumental in either engendering a culture that facilitates or inhibits learning within the classroom" (Weeks, 2012, 4). Weeks (2012) raised issues around the culture of violence that has become 'endemic' in many South African schools and argued that traditional culture-management approaches advocated in the literature he reviewed may not be all that effective in practice. He drew on a range of literature and studies to critique a more 'mechanistic approach' for addressing issues in dysfunctional schools. Articles which explore the organisational dimensions of school failure make some suggestions for remedying the situation at a macro-level of school management. How these issues affect teaching and learning per se is not the object of enquiry.

A number of studies have found that levels of school violence contribute significantly to the culture of learning and teaching in South African schools. In their investigation into school violence among a sample of learners in 16 high schools in KwaZulu-Natal. Zulu, Urbani, Van der Merwe and Van der Walt (2004), found that school violence continued to impact negatively on the culture of teaching and learning. The researchers drew on literature to explore the relationship between school violence and the climate of teaching and learning which included the dispositions and attitudes of both the teachers and the learners. They argued that teacher and learner morale and relationships were compromised by physical and emotional violence, especially in poor socio-economic contexts with adverse material and psychological factors in addition to high failure and drop-out rates. A number of findings from the questionnaires of 288 learners pointed to the enormity of the learning obstacles. Some of these were over-age learners, overcrowding and unconducive living and learning conditions at home, lack of parental supervision or support for learning and a vicious cycle of aggressive and abusive learner-learner and learner-teacher relationships. Zulu et al. (2004, p. 173) emphasised that the increasing "presence of violence and other forms of anti-social behaviour" counteracted possibilities for a productive and respectful spirit of commitment and dedication in these schools. The conclusion was that there was no evidence of a culture of learning in all the schools based on the perceptions of the respondents.

From a different perspective, Christie, Butler and Potterton (2007, p. 6) conducted a study to investigate the lessons that could be learnt from South African "schools that work" and to determine whether the lessons could be applied to other schools on a wider and more general basis. This study revealed that all of the participating 'schools that worked' were focused on their "central tasks of teaching, learning, and management with a sense of responsibility, purpose and commitment"(Christie et al., 2007, p. 83). Important for our systematic review of teaching and learning is their finding that student achievement emanated "from the quality of learning in interactions" between teachers and learners (Christie et al., 2007, p. 84). The study highlighted the nature of the relationship between teachers and learners and the importance of a culture of care and support.

An additional aspect of the culture of teaching and learning worth mentioning involves environmental factors such as number of learners in the classroom and noise levels in the school. In one study on the impact of environmental factors on learning in Grade 1, Naude et al. (2019, p.1) found that "noise, as a result of the large number of learners in the class, as well as noise from the outdoor environment, contributes to the overload of learners' working memory, which ultimately impacts negatively on learning".

Effects of curriculum change

The standard way of thinking about research into teaching and learning is to locate it within research on broader educational policies and curriculum transitions and trends. Building on Hoadley (2012), this section shows how the substantial number of phases of curriculum reform in South Africa's history before and after apartheid have shaped classroom pedagogies, for example, in the development of social constructivist and learner-centred approaches or more traditional, direct pedagogies. Our review revealed the manner in which the curriculum reform impacted on educational research, since it was found that a number of studies were conducted that either examined the effect of curriculum reform, or advocated for particular approaches to teaching in response to curriculum reform. Emerging from classroom studies in the 1990s, Taylor and Vinjevold (1999) described how teachers' poor conceptual knowledge led to minimal learning in classrooms despite the rhetoric of learner-centredness. In the literature review conducted by Hoadley (2012), learner under-achievement was attributed to constructivist theories of learning. She suggested that Bernsteinian frameworks for analysing classroom pedagogy achieved more of a balanced 'mixed model of pedagogy' that supported both teacher and learner-centred approaches. Reeves (2005) also foregrounded the importance of focusing on 'curriculum coverage' arguing that curricular concerns far outweighed the effects of teacher-centred or learner-centred pedagogies.

It was common in the early 2000s to analyse the profound effect of curriculum shifts in a South African context on teachers' pedagogical practice, especially those aligned with learner-centredness. Both Nykiel-Herbert (2004) and Gouws (2007) formulated theoretical arguments for particular approaches to teaching in response to the needs of Outcomes Based Education (OBE). Nykiel-Herbert (2004) explored the role of learner-centred pedagogies within the context of curriculum reform in South Africa and Gouws (2007) conducted a conceptual study to understand multiple intelligences theory and its application in OBE classrooms. Gouws (2007) posited that multiple intelligences theory could be used in OBE classrooms to help learners, specifically those who were previously disadvantaged, to achieve their full potential, because this approach to teaching provided varied opportunities for learners to learn and showed evidence of their learning. Studies such as these are useful for building a theoretical framework to understand practice; however, they remain speculative, since there is no empirical research backing up their claims. Furthermore, Gouws' (2007) paper is limited to the authors' interpretation of theory and lacks critical engagement with OBE and multiple intelligences theory.

In their critique of OBE as an effective approach to curriculum in South Africa, Todd and Mason (2005, p. 228) explored "whether there are strategies for enhancing learning that are more effective and that might be more easily and successfully implemented than an outcomes-based education". They argued that most structural innovations aimed at improving learning, such as financial resources, the quality of facilities, school policies, and streaming according to ability groups, did not have a sizeable effect on student learning. It appears that once distal factors (such as students' socio-economic background) are taken into account, and a certain minimum level of quality (in the provision of schools, classrooms, textbooks, qualified teachers) is realised by the provision of sufficient state funds for education, we are more likely to see the impact of proximal factors such as feedback, goal-setting, and the quality of teaching. The point is that satisfaction of these distal factors makes it more likely that the proximal factors can have an impact on learning; and, inversely, as long as these distal factors remain unrealised or at a sub-critical level, the probability of the realisation of circumstances conducive to the operation of these key proximal factors will remain low.

One study extending the work by earlier researchers on the influence of OBE (Aldridge, Rüdiger C. Laugksch, Mampone, Seopa & Fraser, 2006), focused on developing and validating instruments to investigate learners' perceptions of their learning environments. The goals of the study were 'to assist teachers, teacher educators, and researchers to monitor and guide changes towards outcome-based classroom learning environments' (Aldridge, et al., 2006, p. 46). They developed and validated an instrument that could elicit learners' perceptions of their learning environments. This study included a complex research design, consisting of two phases. In the first phase, data collected from 2 638 Grade 8 science students from 50 classes in 50 schools in the Limpopo Province of South Africa were analysed to provide evidence about the reliability and validity of the new instrument. In the second phase, two case studies were used to investigate whether profiles of class mean scores on the new instrument could provide an accurate and 'trustworthy' description of the learning environment of individual science classes. This project stands out in its attempts to validate theories put forward. The findings point to the importance of feedback from learners. Aldridge et al. (2006, p. 64) point out:

'A critical evaluation of the perceptions of students' actual and preferred outcomes-based classroom learning environments could show the degree of capability, as well as the level of success, of teachers in the Limpopo Province in implementing outcomes-based education in their classrooms.'

There were only a few studies that focused on the implications of aspects of curriculum change for teaching specific subjects despite Hoadley's (2012) emphasis on the importance of subject-specific knowledge in considerations of classroom-based research. An example of an exploration into the nature of learning in disciplines and how this affects pedagogical processes is that of Nompula (2012) who conducted an inquiry into an 'integrated learning experience and instruction in the teaching of creative art subjects'. The researcher used a qualitative methodology to find out teachers' perspectives on the 'realities of arts experiences in South African schools and to strategise new teaching approaches for the successful implementation of the arts programme' (Nompula, 2012, p. 293). All 36 participating teachers discouraged the use of teacher-centred methods such as what one participant described as the 'telling' method where the teacher appears dominant and favoured the 'discovery method' which used educational DVDs, excursions and computer-assisted learning to facilitate 'learning by discovery' (Nompula, 2012, p. 298). A strong focus that emerged from the data was the preference for practical work for all art subjects and a call for more of an integration between theory and practice through focusing on learners' 'creative outputs'. Despite the teachers' stated preferences, Nompula (2012) found that challenging teaching conditions resulted in teachers falling back on theory and neglecting practical work.

An interesting inter-disciplinary study was conducted by Muthivhi and Kriger (2019) who interrogated how conceptual skills in one subject discipline might benefit the learning and development of related conceptual skills in a different but related subject discipline. Specifically, they were interested in whether participation in school music instruction might benefit primary school learners' development of early reading abilities. Data were obtained from two groups of 16 Foundation Phase learners from a boys' school in Cape Town, that were differentiated by participation and non-participation in the school's music instruction curriculum. The research group participated in music lessons, while the comparative group did not participate in the school's music curriculum. Both groups participated in the reading instruction curriculum, and their performance scores in reading were compared to establish possible comparative performance levels between the music learners and non-music learners. By comparing the learners' reading results, the study found that participation in school music instruction had the potential to enhance primary school learners' development of early reading abilities "when instructional activities are purposefully structured to benefit cognate conceptual skills" (Muthivhi et al., 2019, p. 544).

A further discipline-based study traced the history of religious education in South Africa and the processes involved in arriving at the new curriculum proposals (Chidester, 2003). This was a conceptual study that aimed to understand the ways in which curriculum reform impacts on approaches to subject teaching, and concluded by making an argument for the relevance of "advancing education in human rights, citizenship, social justice, and diversity by paying attention to religion and religions, not as a religious activity, but as an educational priority in teaching and learning about our world" (Chidester, 2003, p. 277).

Teacher activities

A number of studies we reviewed examined aspects related to 'what the teacher does' to explore teaching and learning in South African classrooms. These studies point to a variety of factors that affect teachers' capacity to enhance student learning. At the classroom level, factors found in the literature were the learning environment, teachers' characteristics (including gender) teachers' personality, competence, confidence, education background, qualifications and methods as well as class size, time on task, disruptions in class, the use of computers and calculators, content coverage, and assessment. Teacher training, and a teacher's qualifications were identified as an over-arching factor impacting on learning.

According to Todd and Mason (2005, p. 234), in-service teacher training plays a significant role in preparing teachers to "set appropriate, challenging, and specific learning goals for their students, provide lots of feedback that is appropriate to students' current levels of understanding, and offer plenty of reinforcement to motivate their students to achieve their learning goals". In their critique of the effectiveness of OBE, discussed above, Todd et al. (2005) emphasised teachers' knowledge of their disciplinary curriculum, their skills in assessing students' current levels of understanding, their skills of classroom management, their pedagogical skills of actual teaching, and their sense of self-efficacy, enthusiasm and motivation.

A similar position was posited by Nykiel-Herbert (2004, p. 262) who suggested that "learner-centred pedagogy can become a destructive weapon if practised by teachers lacking the necessary conceptual knowledge and practical skills". The author conducted a case study drawing on document analyses and a twelve-year-long involvement, through work with non-governmental organisations (NGOs) and publishing in the South African education system during the 1990s and early 2000s. The central argument was that a severe shortage of the necessary expertise within the existing school system, specifically, extremely poor mastery of the content area, and low levels of language skills and pedagogical know-how on the part of South African teachers turned the intended recipe for educational success into a new variety of educational malpractice, producing yet another generation of illiterate, innumerate South Africans. The Global Monitoring Report (2008) showed that despite the importance of 'well-educated and trained teachers', many poor countries in sub-Saharan Africa faced many challenges such as a chronic shortage of teachers and a predominance of large numbers of unqualified and under-qualified teachers. The report argued for a 'three-way' relationship between learner, teacher and materials like textbooks lying 'at the heart of the education quality'.

While such research has provided important information about the absence of teachers' expert knowledge and skills, other studies have investigated the benefits of professional development for teachers. Botha (2012) investigated the impact of Professional Learning Communities (PLC) on teaching and practices to promote higher levels of learning amongst students. She found that these communities enhanced the overall learning in schools and that teachers became more learner-centred as a result of this form of support. Although some of the literature shows that there are challenges in the implementation of PLC if there is a poor understanding of their purposes and shared cultural beliefs, Botha (2012) found that active engagement with PLC had a positive impact on her participants' teaching.

Along similar lines, a study was conducted in Limpopo by Aldridge, Fraser, & Sebela (2004) to assist South African teachers to become reflective practitioners in their daily mathematics classroom teaching. The study used journals as a means of encouraging teachers to reflect on teaching strategies and improve their learning environments. In the first phase of the study the researchers used the Constructivist Learning Environment Survey (CLES) to assess learners' perceptions of the emphasis on constructivist teaching using a quantitative survey. In the second phase of the research, on the basis of the survey results, teachers were assisted to develop strategies to improve the constructivist orientation of their classroom learning environments. Teachers maintained a daily journal as a means of reflecting on their teaching practices and the survey was re-administered to assess improvements. The study found that the use of journals helped the teachers to think about possible solutions to problems and plan more effectively and there were sizeable pre-post changes in CLES scores.

More recently, Ramnarain (2014) investigated the perceptions of 660 physical science and chemistry teachers from a range of urban, suburban, township and rural schools on the implementation of inquiry-based learning in schools in the north-eastern province of Gauteng. Quantitative data were generated through structured questionnaires. The findings showed that teachers at all locations of school had a positive perception of inquiry-based learning, and identified benefits for learners such as the development of experimental skills and making science more enjoyable. However, despite the perceived benefits of inquiry-based learning, the study found that in most schools "the implementation of open-ended inquiry [was] being constrained by classroom realities, and the prioritisation of the mastery of subject matter knowledge" (Ramnarain, 2014, p. 69). Corroborating findings by Spaull (2012), Ramnarain claimed that the empirical evidence from this study revealed how "the diversity of schools contribute to the disjuncture between curriculum policy and classroom practice" (p. 72). The findings pointed to a need for further research to be conducted to establish the extent to which teachers understand the nature of inquiry-based learning, since it is a method of teaching and learning with the potential to be adopted in poorly resourced schools if teachers have expertise in using the method. Furthermore, given that the conclusions drawn were based on teachers' perceptions of an approach to teaching and learning, this points to a need to critically evaluate the usefulness of studies based entirely on 'teachers' perceptions'.

In a science teaching context, Paul Webb (2009, p. 313) conducted a study on what he referred to as "integrated learning" in which participating teachers experimented with different teaching styles in order to address the lack of science literacy that was evident in the poor Science results at FET level. The research design followed a mixed methods approach, in which the researcher conducted research on what pedagogies would work for promoting science literacy, followed by the development and testing of an integrated learning approach to teaching Science. The study included 12 grade seven teachers and their pupils in 4 semi-urban schools in the Western Cape. There was a mixture of control and experiment classes to enable comparison and establish whether the proposed new pedagogies made any difference. It was found that "the integrated strategies approach to scientific literacy that was developed clearly identifies the role of language in learning science and promotes writing, talking, reading, discussion and arguing" (Webb, 2009, p. 331). It is noteworthy that while the study did not directly discuss the South African curriculum reforms, it mentioned these as a contributing factor to the poor performance of learners because of the effect of constant curriculum reforms on teachers. This study stands out as one that focused on approaches to teaching in order to make a difference to the quality of learning. It contrasts with studies focusing on teacher activities, and teacher-driven decisions rather than on the learning affordances of teaching and the specific processes of learner actions.

A few studies in the systematic review focused on more practical concerns of teaching and learning. For example, with regards to the issue of pacing, Hoadley (2012) highlighted several small-scale studies that reported on the poor use of instructional time in classrooms. She stressed the significance of using time productively, given that learners coming from poor homes with less support for learning rely on time allocated for learning at schools. She drew on studies by Ensor et al. (2009) and Chisholm et al. (2005) that found a slow pace of learning detrimental to the learning needs of diverse learners and how this compromised the quality of the teaching time.

Learner-centred approaches to teaching and learning

The studies reviewed in this section focus predominantly on the nature of learner-centred pedagogies in a range of learning contexts and schools. In her overview, Hoadley (2012) pointed out that recent research had produced interesting findings on teaching and learning in primary schools beyond conceptions of teacher and learner-centredness. She countered the critiques of these small-scale studies on the grounds of the absence of methodological and theoretical rigour and identified key factors emerging from these studies that impacted on student learning. The Khanyisa Education Support Programme (Taylor & Moyana, 2004), for example, produced findings from a baseline study which suggested low levels of cognitive demand, minimal reading and writing in the classroom and weak forms of assessment.

In a comprehensive study on learner-centred education (LCE) in the global South, Schweisfurth (2011, p. 426) conducted a review of 72 studies in the *International Journal of Educational Development* (IJED), "comprising a weighty body of evidence concerning the nature and implementation of LCE". The majority of studies explored the problems of implementation of LCE-based programmes in particular settings. The researcher identified a number of issues and challenges emerging from these investigations in relation to socio-economic factors, cultural and policy issues, and questions of 'power and agency'. She analysed the implications of these studies for future implementation and questioned why not much theoretical and pragmatic progress had been made in the field of LCE. She made the point that the concentration of South African articles (10) indicated the significance of this area of research post-apartheid and the development of educational research capacity. The South African case studies in Schweisfurth's systematic review of LCE, explored the influence of national educational reform policies on teaching and learning practices. What emerged from her review is that although LCE was generally viewed as a solution to intractable constraints and challenges and requires changes to professional development, gaps in attaining LCE goals were a result of the slow pace in implementation and lack of understanding of policies such as OBE. Inadequate teacher education and teaching not seen as a first choice are seen as big factors in teacher preparation for LSE. Other factors emerging from these studies were the influence of authoritarian, non-questioning classroom cultures (Chisholm & Leyendecker, 2008) and LSE approaches being perceived of as 'Western'. The author acknowledged some positive outcomes of LSE in certain learning contexts but raised questions about its feasibility and desirability in a South African context given the range of obstacles.

Prior to Schweisfurth's systematic review, a South African study by Nkhoma (2002) examined factors that contributed to black South African students' mathematics success rates using the lens of learner-centred teaching practices. The author unpacked the meaning of learner-centredness in the context of OBE that was introduced after 1994 in South Africa. He described the nature of learner-centred activities in mathematics classes driven by students working individually or in small groups. The study analysed data from questionnaires and interviews from successful mathematics students in two tertiary institutions to elicit reasons for their success. The study highlighted two key factors for success: firstly, extra classes provided students with an opportunity to discuss solutions to complex mathematics problems both with each other and with their teachers; secondly, students' active participation in class, for example volunteering to go up to the board and demonstrate their mathematical thinking to teachers and their peers. The study pointed out that "teaching from the front" had positive affordances for learning and success if accompanied with consistent practice (111). The author concluded that a combination of teacher-centred and learner-centred approaches promoted mathematical competence, and that the government at the time did not have the capacity to implement the system of OBE to promote optimal learning.

A further South African study on the theme of learner-centred practices (Brodie, Lelliot & Davis, 2002) used observations and interviews to investigate teaching in the mathematcs classrooms of teachers registered for an in-service teacher development programme. The study grappled with the question of how teachers 'take up the pedagogical practices' of teacher education programmes and curriculum policies. It built on work by Christie et al. (2000) who found that teachers continue to practise traditional teaching methods despite their exposure to strategies for facilitating learner-centred approaches. The researchers distinguished between the substance and form of learner-centred practices by investigating the extent to which teachers addressed the key principles of learner-centred approaches like respect for learner diversity and incorporating constructivist approaches to learning (referred to as 'substance'). The researchers explored the strategies (referred to as 'form') that these teachers used to implement learner-centred approaches which included a range of questioning and scaffolding techniques. They argued that these strategies could be implemented "without the up-take of learner-centred teaching principles underpinning the teacher development programme"(Brodie et al, 2002, p. 557).

Similarly, in a report on promoting quality education in low-income countries (Barrett, Ali & Clegg, 2007) analysed the impact of the rise of learner-centred and outcomes-based pedagogies in South Africa on FET pedagogies. It highlighted the difficulties of teaching large classes and presented several debates related to the tension between learner-centred pedagogies and structured pedagogies. The authors argued against an oversimplification of these debates by dichotomising teacher and learner centredness, especially in low-income contexts where learning may be jeopardised by poor teaching. Teachers in poorly resourced schools with large classes used a wide range of pedagogical strategies including talking to the whole class from the front, question-and-answer sessions, structured reading and writing individual exercises and group discussions.

When it comes to understanding how teachers and learners perceive student performance, a study was conducted by Tsanwani, Harding, Engelbrecht and Maree (2014) about perceived factors that facilitate learners' performance in mathematics. Ten rural schools participated in the study at government schools, representing both high-performing and low-performing schools in mathematics. Data were collected from learner focus group interviews and individual teacher interviews. Perceptions pointed to factors such as learners' and teachers' commitment and motivation, attitudes and self-concept, learners' career prospects, learners' perceptions of peers and teachers and teachers' perceptions of learners. Findings pointed to student characteristics (such as self-perception and motivation), classroom characteristics (including quality of instruction, resources and teaching), and school characteristics to do with the context of schooling. Learners from high-performing schools shared common characteristics, such as being very positive about themselves and their ability to do mathematics, being well motivated and knowing what they wanted to do after grade 12. While such results are interesting, it is difficult to draw conclusions about the reasons for the higher or lower performance. The conclusion was that the application of sound teaching and learning principles fostered an environment where pupils were motivated to reach their full potential regardless of resources and conditions.

Interestingly, Barkhuizen (1998) found in a study, 'Discovering Learners' Perceptions of ESL teaching and learning activities', that the students preferred the more traditional rather than communicative or critical approaches, believing that it taught them better English and would benefit them when they left school. He argued that it is important for teachers to be aware of their learners' perceptions of their learning experiences in ESL classes, and he proposed a variety of reading and writing/reflective activities. Although not the focus of this chapter, it is worth including the study by Bester and Brand (2013) on the effects of technology on learner attention and achievement in the classroom. Lessons in Geography, English and Mathematics were presented to an experimental and a control group. In all three learning areas the application of technology instruction resulted in a significant difference between the average achievement of the learners who received technology instruction during the lesson and those who received normal verbal instruction.

The above-mentioned studies explored learners' perceptions of learning, and the effect of technology on learner achievement in the classroom but did not focus on the learners' activities as much as on the external factors that affected learner achievement.

Chapter 6

Conclusion

There was an overriding sense while engaging in our systematic review of a range of research studies on teaching and learning in South African schools, that many of the selected research papers over the past two decades have not turned their attention to the inner workings of student learning and engagement. Instead, they have focused on a wide range of external and internal factors that enhance or constrain learner achievement and success which we have presented in the five main themes: socio-economic conditions affecting learning, culture of teaching and learning in schools, the effects of curriculum change, teacher activities and learner activities.

Despite the array of research methods used in these studies, we noticed that there is an absence in the reporting about the actual learning that takes place in the classroom. A number of studies drew conclusions about learning based on teachers' and learners' perceptions, rather than on empirical evidence about learning, or learners' actual achievement, or activities (see for example Yolisa (2012) and Ramnarain (2014). This raises questions as to whether studies of teacher and learner perceptions can tell us anything other than what teachers think. It therefore becomes difficult to make claims about the impact on learning itself. Those studies recognise the complex web of factors that influence learning such as Weeks (2012) and Zulu (2004), but nevertheless fail to grapple with how learners actively learn. The studies that focused on the socio-ecconomic factors that influence teaching and learning (Carrim, 2011; Howie, 2003; Legotlo et al., 2002; Smith, 2011; Spaull, 2013) all concur that learners' access to resources in their communities (outside the school) had a large impact on their achievement in schools. It was also found that the school culture affected learners achievement, with school violence, noise and overcrowding adversely affecting learning. These findings corroborate Todd et al.'s (2005) finding that only after distal factors such as the school context and school culture are realised will proximal factors relating to the teachers' practices such as good feedback, and goal setting, and good quality teaching have a positive impact on learning.

It was interesting that a number of studies pointed to the need to address gaps in teacher training, for example Gouws (2007), Nompula (2012) and Todd and Mason (2005) which all highlighted the need to change teacher training. The book study conducted by Nassimbeni and Desmond (2011) found that even when materials become available to teachers, teachers cannot be expected to use them effectively without intensive training. It was difficult to find research papers that grappled with what it means to learn in a discipline and how the nature of teaching and learning is understood in different disciplinary contexts. Much of the research on learning in disciplines is focused on learning in Science and Maths, with a few studies exploring language learning, and two studies on learning in the arts and one study on religious education. On the basis of her extensive literature review on teaching and learning in primary schools, Hoadley (2012) also reported on the limited capacity of small-scale studies to show the impact of teaching and learning on learner achievement. She recognised their value in determining indicators for successful outputs, and we agree with her recommendation to implement large-scale longitudinal or mixed methods studies.

This systematic review has found that research on learning and teaching rarely gives insight into *how* learning takes place, and how the learners engage with the course pedagogies and materials to build content knowledge. The focus in existing research is on theories of teaching and learning, and what the teachers do, or teachers' and learners' perceptions. We argue for a more complex approach for addressing these gaps by investigating and comparing teachers' perceptions with what is actually happening. These research processes will build on and promote innovative teaching practices in South African classrooms.

References

Aldridge, J.M, Laugksh, Rüdiger C., Mampone, A., Seopa & Fraser, Barry J. (2006). Development and Validation of an Instrument to Monitor the Implementation of Outcomes-based Learning Environments in Science Classrooms in South Africa. *International Journal of Science Education*, 28(1), 45-70. https://doi.org/10.1080/09500690500239987

Barkhuizen, G. (1998). Discovering Learners' Perceptions of ESL Classroom Teaching/Learning Activities in a South African Context. *TESOL Quarterly*, 32(1), 85-108. https://doi.org/10.2307/3587903

Barrett, A., Ali, S., Clegg, J., Hinostroza, J., Lowe, J., Nikel, J., Novelli, M., Oduro, G., Pillay, M., Tikly, L., &, G. Yu. (2007). Initiatives to improve the quality of teaching and learning: a review of recent literature. EdQual Working Paper no. 11. Bristol: EdQual.

Botha, E.M. (2012). Turning the tide: creating Professional Learning Communities (PLC) to improve teaching practice and learning in South African public schools. *Africa Education Review* 9(2), 395-411. https://doi.org/10.1080/18146627.2012.722405

Brodie, K., Lelliott, A., & Davis, H. (2002). Forms and substance in learner-centred teaching: teachers' take-up from an in-service programme in South Africa. *Teaching and Teacher Education*, 18(5), 541-559. https://doi.org/10.1016/S0742-051X(02)00015-X

Carrim, N. (2011). Modes of participation and conceptions of children in South African Education. *Perspectives in Education*, 29(1),74-82.

Chidester, D. (2003). Religion Education in South Africa: Teaching and Learning About Religion, Religions, and Religious Diversity. *British Journal of Religious Education*, 25(4), 261-278. https://doi.org/10.1080/0141620030250402

Chisholm, L., Hoadley, U., & wa Kivilu, M. (2005). *Educator Workload in South Africa*. Final report prepared for the Education Labour Relations Council, Pretoria: Child, Youth & Family Development, Human Sciences Research Council.

Chisholm, L., & Leyendecker, R. (2008). Curriculum reform in post-1990s sub-Saharan Africa. *International Journal of Educational Development*, 28, 195-205. https://doi.org/10.1016/j.ijedudev.2007.04.003

Christie, P. (1998). Schools as (Dis)Organisations: the 'breakdown of the culture of learning and teaching' in South African schools. *Cambridge Journal of Education*, 28(3), 283-300. https://doi.org/10.1080/0305764980280303

Christie, P., Butler & Potterton. (2007). *Report to the minister of education ministerial committee on schools that work*. South African Department of Education, available online: http://www.education.uct.ac.za/sites/default/files/image_tool/images/104/schoolsthatwork.pdf. Site accessed on 15 August 2019.

Chux, G.I., Saphetha, A.G., Henrie, O.B., & Robertson, K.T. (2013). Teacher job satisfaction and learner performance in South Africa. *Journal of Economics and Behavioral Studies*, 5(12), 838-850. https://doi.org/10.22610/jebs.v5i12.457

Gouws, F.E. (2007. Teaching and learning through multiple intelligences in the outcomes-based education classroom. *Africa Education Review*, 4(2), 60-74. https://doi.org/10.1080/18146620701652705

Hoadley, U. (2012). *What do we know about teaching and learning in South African primary schools?* Carnegie III Conference, University of Cape Town, Cape Town. https://doi.org/10.1080/16823206.2012.745725

Howie, S. J. (2003). Language and other background factors affecting secondary pupils' performance in Mathematics in South Africa. *African Journal of Research in Mathematics, Science and Technology Education*, 7:1, 1-20. https://doi.org/10.1080/10288457.2003.10740545

Legotlo, M.W., Maaga, M.P, Sebego M.G., et al. (2002). Perceptions of stakeholders on causes of poor performance in Grade 12 in a province in South Africa. *South African Journal of Education*, 22(2), 113- 118.

Muthivhi, A.E., & Kriger, S. (2019). Music instruction and reading performance: Conceptual transfer in learning and development. *South African Journal of Childhood Education*, 9(1), a544. https://doi.org/10.4102/sajce.v9i1.544

Nassimbeni, M., & Desmond, S. (2011). Availability of books as a factor in reading, teaching and learning behaviour, in twenty disadvantaged primary schools in South Africa. *South African Journal of Libraries and Information Science*, 77(2), 95-104. https://doi.org/10.7553/77-2-52

Naude, M., & Meier, C. (2019). Elements of the physical learning environment that impact on the teaching and learning in South African Grade 1 classrooms. *South African Journal of Education*, 39(1), 1-11. https://doi.org/10.15700/saje.v39n1a1342

Nkhoma, P.M. (2002). What successful black South African students consider as factors of their success. *Educational Studies in Mathematics*, 50, 103-113. https://doi.org/10.1023/A:1020509528995

Nompula, Y. (2012). An investigation of strategies for integrated learning experiences and instruction in the teaching of creative art subjects. *South African Journal of Education*, 32, 293-306. https://doi.org/10.15700/saje.v32n3a579

Nykiel-Herbert, B. (2004). Mis-constructing knowledge; the case of learner-centered pedagogy in South Africa. *Prospects, XXXIV*, (3), 249-265. https://doi.org/10.1007/s11125-004-5306-x

Ramnarain, U.D. (2014). Teachers' perceptions of inquiry-based learning in urban, suburban, township and rural high schools: The context-specificity of science curriculum implementation in South Africa. *Teaching and Teacher Education*, 38, 65-75. https://doi.org/10.1016/j.tate.2013.11.003

Reeves, C., & Muller, J. (2005). Picking up the pace: variation in the structure and organisation of learning school mathematics. *Journal of Education*, 37, 1-28.

Schweisfurth, M. (2011). *Learner-centred education in developing country contexts: From solution to problem?* Avaliable online at https://www.semanticscholar.org/paper/Learner-centred-education-in-developing-country-to Schweisfurth/925b69f91d6b580eaa7b18c678edb14f1ed3ab88. Accessed on 15 August 2019.

Spaull, N. (2013). Poverty & privilege: Primary school inequality in South Africa. *International Journal of Educational Development*, 33, 436-447. https://doi.org/10.1016/j.ijedudev.2012.09.009

Taylor, N., & Moyana, J. (2005). Khanyisa Education Support Programme: Baseline Study Part 1: communities, schools and classrooms. *JET Education Services*, Johannesburg.

Todd, A., & Mason, M. (2005). Enhancing learning in South African schools: strategies beyond outcomes-based education. *International Journal of Educational Development*, 25, 221-235. https://doi.org/10.1016/j.ijedudev.2004.08.003

Tsanwani A., Harding, A., Engelbrecht, J., & Maree, K. (2014). Perceptions of teachers and learners about factors that facilitate learners' performance in Mathematics in South Africa. *African Journal of Research in Mathematics, Science and Technology Education*, (18)1, 40-51. https://doi.org/10.1080/10288457.2014.884262

Webb, P. (2009). Towards an Integrated Learning Strategies Approach to Promoting Scientific Literacy in the South African Context. *International Journal of Environmental & Science Education*, 4(3), 313-334.

Weeks, F.H. (2012). The quest for a culture of learning: A South African schools perspective. *South African Journal of Education*, 32,1-14. https://doi.org/10.15700/saje.v32n1a565

Zulu, B.M., Urbani, G. & Van der Merwe, A. (2004). Violence as an impediment to a culture of teaching and learning in some South African schools. *South African Journal of Education*, 24(2), 170-175.

CHAPTER 7

Science teacher professional development in post-apartheid South Africa: A systematic review of the literature on basic education
Elaosi Vhurumuku
Email: elaosi.vhurumuku@wits.ac.za
School of Education, University of the Witwatersrand

Abstract

This systematic review analysed and synthesised the research done on effective science teacher professional development (PD) in post-apartheid South Africa, for the period 1994 to 2019, focusing on basic education. It investigated the efficacy of professional development models, with the aim of identifying models which positively impacted on science teachers and had the potential to improve teaching effectiveness. It also explored the issue of how South African researchers and education practioners evaluated the effectiveness of PD. Twenty articles were selected for analysis from electronic search of data bases. The findings reveal that 13 (65%) of the 20 analysed studies concluded that PD had a positive impact on participating teachers. Seven studies (35%) were either inconclusive or concluded that PD was ineffective. While researchers and education practioners have 'successfully' used a variety of PD models, the training and cascading models were the most popular. The results also show that, for all the reviewed studies, the evaluations of the effectiveness of PD only focused on what happened to the teacher and completely ignored determining the impact on students' learning outcomes, performance and achievement. It is recommended that future evaluations of science teacher PD efforts should take into account the effect or impact of the PD on students' learning outcomes, performance and achievement.

Keywords: science teacher, professional development, teaching effectiveness, evaluation, student learning

Introduction

Globally, it is now generally accepted that the success of educational programmes and reform initiatives largely hinges on the quality and effectiveness of teachers. It is also unanimously accepted that student learning and achievement can only be improved if teachers have the requisite knowledge and pedagogical skills, which enable them to be effective practioners. There is an underlying assumption that outcomes for students can be improved through effective professional development of teachers (Doig & Groves, 2011; Garet, Porter & Desimone et al., 2001; Guskey, 2002; Darling-Hammond, Hyler, & Gardner, 2017). Professional development of teachers is often synonymous or conflated with teacher professional learning or in-service education or staff development. Grosemans, Boon, Verclairen et al. (2015) argue that professional development for teachers is necessary because society is constantly changing; meaning that teachers also have to change and/or reform their teaching knowledge, practices, skills, attitudes and beliefs in order to continue transforming the students' learning outcomes. In many parts of the world the changing socio-economic, political, ideological contexts and professional environments have resulted in unprecedented financial investment in effective teacher professional development. Effective teacher professional development (PD) is about involving teachers in learning that results in them changing and/or reforming their teaching practices, skills, attitudes and beliefs so as to transform the learning outcomes of students (Darling-Hammond et.al., 2017; Guskey, 2002).

While there appears to be agreement that teacher PD can result in improved teaching effectiveness, there is dissensus around issues of how effective professional development should be done and what should be its features. These contestations are made more complicated by the lack of a generally agreed-upon understanding of what it is which should be called effective teaching (Goe, Bell, & Little, 2008; Patrick & Smart, 1996). For more than fifty years, the landscape of research on teacher professional development and effective teaching has been dominated by the questions: What is it that should constitute effective teacher professional development? Which models of professional development result in improved teaching practices? How can the effectiveness of teacher professional development be determined? What is effective teaching and how can it be characterised? And does teacher professional development improve teacher effectiveness?

In science education, research focusing on investigating the relationship between teacher professional development and instructional effectiveness has been going on for almost eight decades (see, Capps, Crawford, & Constas, 2012.; Yoon et al., 2007; Guskey, 2010; Guskey & Huberman, 1995; Thair & Treagust, 2003; Villegas-Reimers, 2003; Van Veen, Zwart, & Meirink, 2012; Buczynski & Hansen, 2010; Lumpe, Czerniak, Haney et al., 2012; DeBoer, 1991; Wilson, 2013). This research can be stranded into several foci, including: the effect of professional development (PD) programmes or interventions on science teachers' teaching practices (e.g. Supovitz & Turner, 2000; Capps, Crawford, & Constas, 2012); examining the effect of teacher professional development models on teacher knowledge and practices (e.g. Jimoyiannis, 2010; Heller, Daehler, & Wong et al., 2012); investigating the effectiveness of professionally developed teachers in implementing new or reformed science curricula and programmes (e.g. Wilson, 2013; Penuel, Fishman, & Yamaguchi et al., 2007); the effect of professional development on teachers' self-efficacy, attitudes and beliefs (e.g. Lumpe, Czerniak, & Haney et al., 2012; Carleton, Fitch, & Krockover, 2007; Tosun, 2000); factors that can facilitate or impede teacher engagement with PD (Kervin, 2007; Opfer &

Pedder, 2011); and the effect of professional development on teachers' pedagogical content knowledge (PCK) (e.g. Van Driel & Berry, 2012; Appleton, 2008).

Within this realm, the terrain of discourse has been dominated by contestations concerning how to evaluate the effectiveness of professional development. For example, it has been argued that the evaluation of the effectiveness of PD should be based not on determinations and measurements of what happens to teachers, e.g. improvements in their content and pedagogical knowledge, etc.; but focus more on student learning outcomes as the underlying endeavour (Earley & Porritt, 2014; Guskey, 2002).

Given the arguments surrounding teacher professional development and its effectiveness, the current systematic review focuses on this topic. It follows the footsteps of Guskey and Yoon (2009), who carried out a synthesis of the research literature focusing on the relationship between teacher professional development and student achievement as an indicator of PD effectiveness. In interrogating this issue, their review addressed questions about: the relationship between professional development and student learning; the validity of evidence justifying that relationship; and what should be called truly effective professional development? To date, in addition to this work, several systematic reviews focusing on effective professional development of teachers have been undertaken internationally (see for example, Vangrieken, Meredith, & Packer et al., 2017; Yoon, Duncan, & Lee, 2007; Trede, Macklin, & Bridges, 2012; Steinert, Mann, & Centeno et al., 2006; Luneta, 2012). None of these reviews, however, explicitly focuses on analysing and synthesising the research on effective professional development of science teachers. The systematic review being presented in this chapter is the first to do so. In addition, the current review is the first on this topic to be done in South Africa focusing on basic education.

Purpose of the review

This review's major focus is exploring, analysing and synthesising the research literature on effective science teacher professional development and its evaluation in post-apartheid South Africa. Only the research done in basic education in South Africa between the years 1994 and 2019 is considered. For South Africa, the demise of apartheid in 1994 brought about political, economic and social changes, which were accompanied by changes in the education system (Vandeyar & Killen, 2007) including transformation of school science curricula. School science curricula changes brought about a necessity for teacher professional development. It is in the light of this background that the focus of the current review was limited to research done during and after 1994.

In science education, systematic reviews are increasingly being used to explicitly answer specific questions based on cumulated research evidence. Polanin, Maynard and Dell (2017) argue that, systematic analysis, appraisal and summarisation of burgeoning research literature can lead to the generation of new knowledge as well as inform policy and practice. This supports Hargreaves (1996), who suggests that in similar fashion to what is done in medical research, systematic reviews can be used in educational research to contribute to theory and practice through answering questions about what works and what does not.

As indicated, the major goal of this review is to determine the efficacy of professional development models in improving science teachers' classroom effectiveness as determined by student learning outcomes. Through this determination, and focusing on research in basic education in post-apartheid South Africa, the review attends to answering questions about what science teacher professional development models have been effective and how the effectiveness of PD has been measured. The research questions that guided this review were:

- Which professional development models have resulted in improving teaching effectiveness for science teachers?
- How have South African researchers determined the effectiveness of science teacher professional development?

It is important to point out that, in the context of this review, basic education refers to education in primary and secondary schools as well as tertiary education and vocational training. This means the search for literature on effective teacher professional development covered these levels of the South African education system. The review's focus was on research done on practising, in-service and pre-service science teachers including lecturers and professors involved in science teacher education. The focus was on school science education and tertiary science teacher education. Science teaching was taken to encompass the teaching of Natural Science, Physical Science, Chemistry, Physics and Life Sciences/Biology at primary and secondary schools as well as tertiary and vocational science teacher education. Teacher professional development and teaching effectiveness in such fields as medicine, engineering and environmental science, were excluded from the review.

Given the focus of this review, it is fitting to briefly examine some theoretical and conceptual tenets on effective professional development and teaching effectiveness.

Effective teacher professional development

Rationales for teacher professional development

In the present epoch of the Anthropocene, the demands made on both education and teachers have made effective teacher professional development a major focus of systemic reform initiatives around the globe (Garet, Porter, & Desimone et al., 2001; Bhattacharya, Roehrig, Kern, & Howard, 2014). The political, social, economic and environmental challenges society is facing in the Anthropocene, has generated new expectations of teachers. Anthropogenic challenges include such issues as: climate change, global warming, the greenhouse effect, deforestation, drug abuse, environmental degradation, species extinction, sustainable use of natural resources, democratisation, and HIV/AIDS.

While it is true to say that science teacher professional development should desirably be a continuous and lifelong endeavour (Ryan, 2003; Nicholls, 2000), the reality is that in most cases teacher PD has largely been driven and necessitated as a reaction to challenges and changes and/or reforms in the educational milieu. These include PD of teachers as a response to: science education curriculum changes, reforms and innovations – with PD aimed at capacitating teachers to implement new or reformed curricula, e. g. incorporating new subjects and/or new content requiring new social and technical competencies (Wilson, 2013; Penuel, Fishman, & Yamaguchi et al., 2007); efforts to mitigate anthropogenic challenges (Hestness, McDonald, & Breslyn et al., 2014); efforts to remediate identified teacher deficiencies e.g. poor subject knowledge mastery (Bayar, 2014); for certification of unqualified and qualified teachers (Ono & Ferreira, 2010); and advancements in information and communication technologies, which lead to the introduction of new technology-based teaching approaches and strategies (Mouza, 2002; Brinkerhoff, 2006).

In addition to these factors science teacher PD has also been driven by efforts to demonstrate the efficacy of underpinning theoretical models, orientations and paradigms. Examples of this include: research focusing on professional development of teachers' pedagogical content knowledge (PCK) (Van Driel1 & Berry, 2012; Doering, Veletsianos, & Scharber et al., 2009), teacher professional development as part of action research (McNiff, 2010), and demonstrating the role that teacher communities (TCs) can play in effective professional development (Boone, 2010; Vangrieken, Meredith & Packer et al., 2017). Generally, irrespective of the rationale for PD, its major goal is bringing about changes in the knowledge, skills, attitudes, beliefs and values of teachers, which in turn are assumed to change or improve classroom practices, resulting in the logical consequence of change or improvement in the learning outcomes for students. As already noted, teacher professional development is associated with teacher learning which brings about change in the classroom (Guskey, 2003; Garet, Porter, & Desimone et al., 2001).

Models of teacher professional development

Teacher professional development can be organised and structured in a variety of ways based on a wide spectrum of rationales. Bayar (2014) categorises teacher professional development into traditional and non-traditional. Traditional teacher professional development is organised and structured around short workshops (one day, one week or one month), conferences and seminars. This type of PD has been castigated by many researchers for being too brief, disjointed and out of tandem with the state of reality in the classrooms (Ono & Ferreira, 2010). Non-traditional teacher professional development is about organising programmes and/or activities, which include mentoring, coaching, peer collaboration, observation and reflections, participation in a network of teachers, clusters of teachers, individual or collaborative research focusing on a topic of professional interest, reading professional literature, engaging in informal dialogue with peers on how to improve teaching, and participation in teacher communities of practice (TCP).

Table 7.1 *Models of continuous professional development*

Model	Characteristics and theoretical underpinnings	Delivery actions and activities
Training Model	-skills-based, technocratic view of teaching -centralized and transmissive -focus on introducing new knowledge/skills -teacher must achieve pre-determined standards	-Expert delivers knowledge and skills to teacher -Delivery at the institution or outside sites
Award-bearing Model	-emphasises, the completion of award-bearing programmes or courses of study -focuses on classroom practice	-teacher attends or does courses which lead to recognition or accreditation by, for example, professional bodies
Deficit Model	-aimed at addressing perceived deficits in teacher performance through remedial action -linked to performance management	-teacher attends a course or program focusing on remediating perceived weaknesses
Cascade Model	-teachers attending 'training events' and then cascading or disseminating the information to colleagues -training-the-trainer to ensure that the message flows down from experts and specialists -focus on developing knowledge and skills -technicist view of teaching, where skills and knowledge are given priority over attitudes and values	-teachers attend workshops, courses and training events and then cascade or disseminate information learnt to colleagues
Standards-based Model	-based on behaviourist perspectives of teaching and learning, focusing on the competence of individual teachers and resultant rewards -emphasis on the 'professional actions', as a measure of achievement of standards or competencies -standards and competencies to be achieved are centrally determined	-teacher achievement of standards or competencies are externally assessed and evaluated

Model	Characteristics and theoretical underpinnings	Delivery actions and activities
Coaching/ Mentoring Model	-experienced teacher mentors or coaches the novice teacher -novice does apprenticeship under tutelage of mentor - can be hierarchical or collegial - can be based on transmission or transformative view of learning about teaching	-experienced teacher mentors or coaches the novice teacher
Community of Practice Model	-involves two or more teachers who form a professional community to learn about practice -based on social theory of learning -teachers involved in: mutual engagement, understanding and tuning [their] enterprise; and developing repertoire, styles and discourses	-teachers participate in learning communities and improve their knowledge and skills
Action Research Model	-main aim is practitioner development and transformation -teachers acting as researchers critically examine their practices with a view to improving the quality of teaching -teachers' understanding of the situation, as well as the practice, within the situation	-teachers research on their practices to improve teaching and learning
Transformative Model	-combination of practices and conditions -integration of the range of models described above -a tenacious balance of power relations and accommodation of stakeholder interests	-uses approaches and actions in the other eight models

A summary based on Kennedy A. (2005). Models of Continuing Professional Development: a framework for analysis. *Journal of In-service Education*, Volume 31, Number 2, pp. 236-247)

Within these domains teacher PD can be continuous or non-continuous. Continuous teacher professional development (CTPD) is ongoing and based on the principle that teachers need to make learning about teaching a lifelong endeavour. It is about unremittingly enhancing the knowledge and skills of teachers through ongoing orientation, training, support, reflection and review (Coetzer, 2001; Kennedy, 2005). With non-continuous PD, the orientation, training and support is intermittently done, sometimes only once in the working life of the teacher. This type of PD is usually done as a direct response to factors in the educational milieu.

It is argued that, to a very large extent, the success and effectiveness of teacher PD depends on how it is organised, structured and implemented. In the literature several descriptions and classifications of continuous professional development (CPD) models are found (see for example, Dede, 2006; Heller, Daehler, & Wong et al., 2012; Kennedy, 2005). For this review, the description and classification by Kennedy (2005) is used as a lens for the analysis mainly because of its simplicity and comprehensiveness. According to Kennedy (2005) CPD can be done using models which fall into nine broad categories. While the models are comprehensive, they are neither necessarily exhaustive nor exclusive. Table 7.1 shows a summary of these models.

Evaluating the effectiveness of teacher professional development
Darling-Hammond, Hyler and Gardner (2017) describe effective PD as one which: focuses on content subject matter and pedagogy; incorporates active learning; supports teacher collaboration; uses models of effective practice; provides coaching and expert support; offers feedback and reflection; and is of sustained duration. In addition to this, it is argued that an effective PD activity should: have an establishing clarity of its purpose at the outset; include a clear focus on student learning outcomes; specify its focus and goal with clear timescales; have an understanding of the current practice at the start of the activity/project; make participants' feel ownership of the activity; and have a clear understanding of how to evaluate the impact (Earley & Porritt, 2014).

Nonetheless, it has been pointed out that there is dissensus around what it is that should be done in evaluating the effectiveness of teacher professional development. This is pertinent because there are many models of evaluating PD and its effectiveness – all of them proclaiming truth (see for example, King, 2014; Earley & Porritt, 2014; Bubb, 2013). Earley and Porritt (2014) posit that much of the evaluation of PD done by school leaders, practitioners, policy-makers and researchers is simplistic, impressionistic and untrustworthy as it is based on simple measures (e.g. post-event evaluation forms or a 'happy sheet', questionnaires and interviews). They suggest that the evaluation of the effectiveness of PD should be based on elements focusing on the intended outcomes and the impact on student learning. This supports Pedder, Opfer and McCormick et al. (2010) who argue that evaluation of PD should focus on adequately specified learning outcomes for teachers, which must be made explicit from the beginning. These outcomes must be sufficiently linked to student learning outcomes, school improvement and teacher self-evaluations. In essence, the determination of the effectiveness of PD is about gathering asserted or substantiated evidence on these aspects, in order to precisely ascertain the impact of the PD process (Earley & Porritt, 2014).

Guskey (2002) contends that the focus of evaluating the effectiveness of PD should be on learning outcomes for students. However, she flags some pillars on which evaluation of the impact of PD should be built. According to Guskey (2002) the impact of PD can be evaluated through determining: its impact on students' learning outcomes (effect on experience, attainment and achievement of students); its impact on participants' (teachers') learning; its impact on participants' (teachers') use of new knowledge and skills; the participants' (teachers') own evaluations and reflections of the PD; and whether the organisation (e.g. the school) changes in terms of practices and support of the teaching and learning process. Building on

Guskey's (2002) and other works (for example, Bubb & Earley, 2010; Ofsted, 2010; Bubb, 2013), Earley and Porritt (2014) argue that the key issues in evaluating the impact and hence the effectiveness of PD is to know whether PD has made a difference to teachers, students and the organisation (precisely the school). While they accept that in evaluating the effect of PD, it is important to determine the changes and improvements in teachers' subject matter knowledge, planning, pedagogy, teaching skills, attitudes, beliefs and values; they emphasise that student learning outcomes should be at the core of PD evaluation. As they correctly articulate, the purpose of professional development should from the outset be to improve the learning for students. Consequently, evaluation of the effectiveness of PD should be focused on determining whether there is a difference between the performances of students before teachers underwent PD and after they have gone through a PD activity or programme.

Teaching effectiveness

As previously noted, it is generally accepted that the most critical determinant of student performance and achievement is the quality or effectiveness of the teacher (Darling-Hammond, 2000; Muijs & Reynolds, 2001). Although there is this unanimity, there are gruesome quarrels around the issues of: what it is that should be called effective teaching, and how teaching effectiveness should be evaluated or measured. Coggshall (2007) asserts that these ponderous but divergent eruditions arise because of the existence of a multiplicity of perspectives on what makes good teaching and how to gauge it in a valid way. The diversity of perspectives is an inevitable consequence of the existence of a surplus of stakeholders in education. These stakeholders include politicians, policy makers, parents, teachers, students, and researchers. Each of these interested parties advocates for different conceptions of effective teaching and its evaluation based on political, ideological, socio-economic, and paradigmatic orientations and aspirations.

Darling-Hammond (2010) describes an effective teacher as one who is: generally intelligent and can organise, explain and communicate ideas, has strong pedagogical content knowledge, shows an understanding of learners and their learning and can cater for differentiation, and adapt and modify his/her teaching to cater for student needs. From the literature (see for example, Sammons, 2006; Pretorius, 2012; Muijs & Reynolds, 2001) effective teaching has also been pronounced as involving: catering for differentiation in the classroom; being able to deliver lessons with clarity; keeping students motivated; setting high standards for student achievement; showing good classroom management skills; being able to appropriately sequence the content; showing mastery of questioning skills and techniques; ability to plan and use teaching and learning resources appropriately;

ability to monitor student understanding formatively and summatively; and working collaboratively with peers. All these aspects focus only on the teacher.

Several scholars, however, argue that it is problematic to determine teaching effectiveness by solely focusing on the teacher or only on student learning and achievement as measured by standardised test scores (e.g. Fenstermacher & Richardson, 2005; Goe, Bell & Little, 2008). They contend that the effectiveness of the teacher depends on a matrix of variables, which include: the quality of the student, availability of teaching and learning resources, the physical learning environment, administrative support, student motivation and the nature of the curriculum. Based on this, Goe, Bell and Little (2008), advocate for a consensually arrived at definition of teacher effectiveness, which is comprehensive and a composite of these factors. They recommend that the determination of teaching effectiveness should be based on a weighted fusion of the following: classroom observation of the teacher; evaluation of the teacher by peers including school principals; use of instructional artifacts which are structured protocols used to analyse such things as the quality of instruction, lesson plans, teacher assignments and tests, and students' written work; a teaching portfolio which documents teaching behaviours and responsibilities; teacher self-report measures; student evaluations of the teacher; and a value-added model, which is a calculation of the teacher's contribution to student achievement as measured by test scores.

Method

Literature search and selection procedure

The literature search team for this review consisted of the author and two research assistants. Bearman, Smith and Carbone et al. (2012) suggest that in order for systematic reviews to answer the targeted research questions, they need to use explicit inclusion and exclusion benchmarks, transparent search strategies, clear data analyses procedures as well as synthesise all the available evidence. The literature searches and selection procedure adapted was based on a blend of the approaches described by Van Lankveld, Schoonenboom and Volman et al. (2017), Bennett et al. (2005) and Bearman (2012). A synopsis of this adoption summates into the sequence shown in Figure 7.1.

First, the study title was formulated and research questions identified. Second, inclusion and exclusion criteria were formulated. Inclusion or exclusion of articles for review was based on the following criteria:

Teacher professional development focus: Only empirical research articles that focused on teacher professional development in basic education at the primary and secondary schools as well as tertiary teacher education and vocational teacher training were to be included.

Science teacher professional development: Only empirical research articles that focused on science teacher professional development in basic education were considered. Articles also focusing on the professional development of Natural Science, Physical Science, Chemistry, Physics and Life Sciences/Biology teachers in basic education were considered. Articles focusing solely on teacher professional development in other disciplines, such as environmental science, technology, engineering, medicine and mathematics were excluded. Articles which involved science and mathematics teachers were included.

Geographical location of the research: Only empirical studies, quantitative or qualitative, done in South Africa were considered for selection.

Article publication period: Only empirical research articles published in referred journals and conference proceedings between 1994 and 2019 were considered.

Teaching effectiveness: Only articles that referred to determining the impact of PD on teachers' knowledge, skills, practices, beliefs, attitudes and values, teacher effectiveness/quality and/or the effectiveness of professional development were selected.

Third, based on the title and research questions, the following search phrases, terms and words were formulated and used alone or in combination: 'South Africa development of science teacher content knowledge', 'teacher professional development teaching effectiveness', 'South Africa science teacher professional development teaching effectiveness', 'South Africa science teacher professional development teacher quality', 'science teacher professional learning and effectiveness', 'teacher professional development, 'science teacher professional development', 'South Africa effectiveness of professional development', 'South Africa science teacher professional development', 'South Africa professional training teaching effectiveness', 'science teacher quality', 'in-service professional development science', 'in-service science teacher training South Africa', 'professional development basic education South Africa', 'physical science teaching South Africa', 'natural sciences teaching South Africa', 'Biology teaching South Africa', 'Life sciences teachers South Africa', 'Chemistry teaching professional development South Africa', 'Physics teaching professional development South Africa', and 'teacher development and effectiveness South Africa'.

Using these search phrases, terms and words, a search for potentially relevant articles was done using electronic searching. This included use of Google Scholar, extensive searches of all relevant education databases such as: ERIC, EBSCO, Academic Search Ultimate, Abstracts, WITS library bibliography databases, Ingenta and SCOPUS. The literature search looked for published work focusing on referred journals and conference proceedings, including online publications. Masters and Doctoral dissertations published online were not considered.

Fourth, screening and classification of studies was done applying the inclusion and exclusion criteria to identify potentially relevant studies. This stage also involved looking at article titles and reading and coding abstracts. Fifth: full text reading and screening of articles applying inclusion and exclusion criteria. Sixth: in-depth reading of screened articles and summarisation of each study's work including study goal, theoretical framework, study design, data-collection methods and major findings. Seventh: Analysing the study findings to extract the key data from the studies and making decisions about answering the review questions regarding the impact and/or effectiveness of science teacher professional development and how the impact of PD and teaching effectiveness were determined.

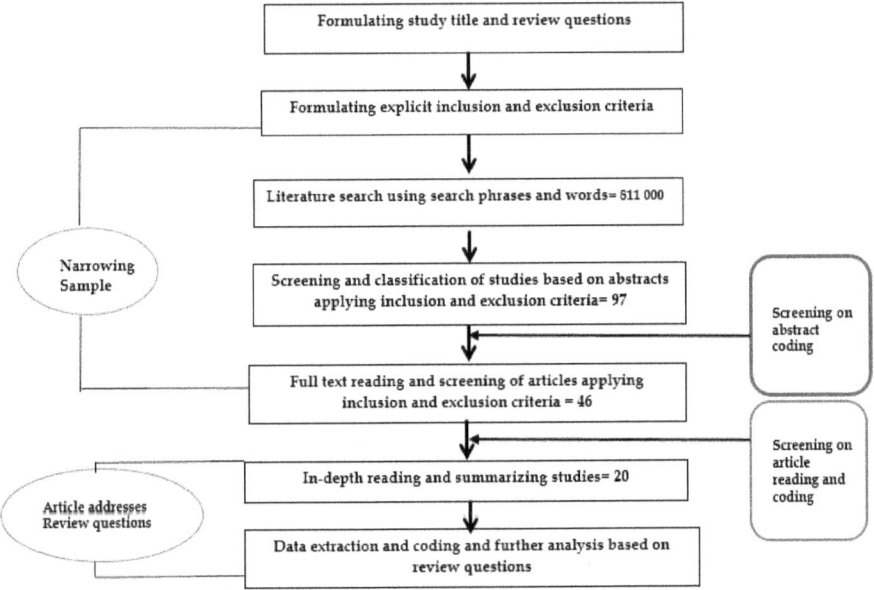

Figure 7.1 *A summary of the literature search and selection procedure (Adapted from Van Lankveld, Schoonenboom & Volman et al., 2017; Bennett et al., 2005 & Bearman, 2012)*

Analysis and synthesis

In order to organise and interpret the literature, a descriptive and qualitative analysis and synthesis was done along the approaches followed by Van Lankveld, Schoonenboom and Volman et al. (2017) and Vangrieken, Meredith and Packer et al. (2017). This translated into a fusion of thematic (De Rijdt, Stes, & Van der Vleuten et al., 2013) and narrative analysis (Thomas & Harden, 2008). First the team members read and coded the abstracts in order to get the major themes of each article. They then discussed their coding. These resulted in the exclusion of some articles as they were adjudged not to meet the inclusion criteria, and were irrelevant to answering the review questions. Twenty articles were identified as relevant to answering the study questions.

Second, all the 20 screened and selected articles were read in-depth and the main study features summarised in an inventory. For each article the following characteristics were captured: Author(s); Article Title; Year of Publication; Journal/Book; Study aims/objectives/questions; Theoretical/conceptual framework; Research design; Sample characteristics; Professional development model used; Rationale for the PD; Method used to evaluate effectiveness of PD; Outcome of the PD; Method used to determine teaching effectiveness; Major findings; and Conclusion(s). The assignment of studies to PD models was guided by the description and classification by Kennedy (2005) (see Table 7.1). Each of the three members of the research team independently read the selected articles and produced an inventory. The team members then came together to review decisions, compare inventories and come to consensual agreement regarding the assignment of characteristics to a study. In this way the rigour, credibility, transferability, dependability, and confirmability of the data were assured (Maxwell, 1992). Third, an iterative comparison was made of the summarised results in order to check for regularities and patterns and determining whether the findings were relevant to answering the review questions (Van Lankveld, Schoonenboom, & Volman et al., 2017). Fourth, each of the articles was re-read in-depth in order to identify sections, paragraphs and lines which contained information related to answering the research questions for the review (Vangrieken, Meredith, & Packer et al., 2017). The following themes were used: Professional development model (research Question 1); Method of evaluating impact or effectiveness of PD (Research questions 1 and 2); Method of determining teaching effectiveness (Research question 2); measuring teacher competencies (Research questions 1 and 2); and determining student outcomes (Research questions 1 and 2).

Results

Overview of studies included in the review
Before addressing the research questions, which is done in the discussion section, it is fitting to give an overview of the studies included in this review. In doing so, key elements and characteristics essential for answering the research questions are teased out. In Table 7.2 the key features and characteristics of the studies analysed for this review are summarised, with the numbers of studies given. In addition to this table a description of the review results is given. This description captures the following aspects: the methodological approaches used in the studies – including the data collection and analysis procedures; an outline of the major rationale(s) for the undertaken professional developments; the types of PD models used; a narration of the approaches and strategies used to determine the effectiveness of the PD (i.e. how the impact or effectiveness of PD was evaluated); and the outcome(s) (major findings and conclusions) of the studies.

The methodological approaches used in the studies

In general, all the reviewed studies reported on the impact of professional development on the content and pedagogical knowledge, skills, practices, attitudes and beliefs of participating teachers. Of the twenty reviewed studies, twelve or 60% employed qualitative research methodology. Six studies (30%) utilised a combination of quantitative and qualitative methodology. Two studies (10%) were quantitative, with one of these utilising an experimental design. Three of the reviewed studies (Mavhunga & Rollnick, 2016; Pitjeng-Mosabala & Rollnick, 2018; Mavhunga & Rollnick, 2013) were PD interventions involving pre-service/novice secondary school teachers. The rest of the studies involved practising primary and/or secondary school teachers. Across the studies the dominant methods of data collection are: using questionnaires, pre- and post-intervention questionnaires and interviews, teacher reflective journals, lesson observations and teacher self-evaluations.

Table 7.2 *A summary of the main features and characteristics of the reviewed studies*

Model	Methodological Approach(es)			Study Rationales							Outcome(s) of PD			Summary of Major Finding(s)
	Qualitative	Quantitative	Mixed	Improve teachers classroom practices	Improve content and pedagogical knowledge	Skills to implement new science curricula	To demonstrate the efficacy of a PD model	Teacher focus	Evaluation of the impact effectiveness of PD	Student learning focus	Positive	Negative	Inconclusive	
Cascade Model	4	1	1	6	2	0	2	6	0	3	1	2		Improvement in half the studies negative. and inconclusive for the other half
Training Model	3	0	3	3	4	0	0	6	0	4	1	1		Improvement in four studies negative, and inconclusive for two studies
Action Research Model	2	0	1	3	0	3	3	3	0	2	1	0		Positive and negative result
Community of Practice Model	2	0	0	2	0	0	2	2	0	1	0	1		Positive and inconclusive result
Coaching/Mentoring Model	0	1	0	1	0	1	1	1	0	1	0	0		One positive result
Deficit Model	0	0	1	1	1	0	0	1	0	1	0	0		One positive result
Transformative Model	1	0	0	1	0	0	1	1	0	1	0	0		One positive result
Totals	12	2	6	20	7	4	9	20	0	13	3	4		

Chapter 7

The rationales for professional development

Four major reasons or rationales flesh out as having been the drivers of the research. For some studies, more than one driver was identified. All the studies mention the need to improve teachers' classroom practices as a goal of PD. Within this recognition the need to change teachers' beliefs and attitudes is also acknowledged (e.g. Onwu & Mogari, 2004; Kriek & Grayson, 2009). One of the dominant motivations cited is the need to improve the quality of science teachers' content and pedagogical knowledge. Seven of the twenty reviewed articles give this reason as a justification for study. Examples of these include: Mavhunga and Rollnick (2016), Pitjeng-Mosabala and Rollnick (2018), and Mogari et al. (2016). For these studies, there is an inherent assumption that there is a deficit in the teachers' knowledge which needs addressing.

Four studies appear to have been driven by the necessity to equip teachers with the requisite knowledge and skills to implement new science curricula (see, Singh-Pillay & Samuel, 2017; Onwu & Mogari, 2004; Bantwini, 2009; Ono & Ferreira, 2010). Suffice to mention that post-apartheid South Africa has experienced three major waves of curriculum reform. First was the Curriculum 2005 (C2005), introduced in 1997, which became the Revised National Curriculum Statement (RNCS) in 2002. This was followed by the National Curriculum Statement (NCS) of 2007, and the current Curriculum and Assessment Policy Statements (CAPS), which was introduced in 2012. The studies by Onwu and Mogari (2004), Ono and Ferreira (2010) and Bantwini (2009), for example, were in response to challenges faced by teachers in implementing outcomes-based education, adopted after independence as part of decolonising education. They sought to equip teachers with the requisite content knowledge and skills to change their teaching ways in line with the Revised National Curriculum Statement (RNCS) introduced in 2002. The study by Singh-Pillay and Samuel (2017) focused on the implementation of all three curricula including the CAPS of 2012.

Nine of the twenty studies are categorised as having been motivated fully or in part by the desire to demonstrate the efficacy of a professional development model or try out a 'new' PD model (see, Aldridge, Fraser, & Sebela, 2004; Reed, Davis, & Nyabanyaba, 2002; Harvey, 1999; Mbowane, Rian de Villiers, & Braun, 2017; Mokhele, 2013; Jita & Mokhele, 2014; Ndlalane & Jita, 2009; Ono & Ferreira, 2010; Bantwini, 2009). Of these studies, three are attempts to show that action research is an effective approach to PD (Ono & Ferreira, 2010; Reed, Davis, & Nyabanyaba, 2002; Aldridge, Fraser, & Sebela, 2004). Two of the nine studies are efforts to use the teacher communities of practice (TCP) model to: improve teachers' PCK, resulting in changes in classroom practices (Ndlalane & Jita, 2009); and to alter the knowledge, beliefs and practices of teachers (Jita & Mokhele, 2014). One study (Mbowane, Rian de Villiers, & Braun, 2017) investigated the effect of teacher attendance of science fairs on their professional identity and professional development, including their pedagogical knowledge and insight into inquiry-based learning approaches as well as topic-specific PCK. This was categorised as following the cascade model of PD since teachers who attended the fair were expected to disseminate information learnt to colleagues and to students (Kennedy, 2005).

Identified types of PD models

Overall, based on the descriptions and classification by Kennedy (2005), the reviewed studies were categorised as falling under the following PD models: Cascade Model-6 (30%); Training Model-6 (30 %); Action Research Model-3 (15%); Community of Practice Model-2 (10%); Deficit Model-1 (5%); Coaching/Mentoring Model-1 (5%); and Transformative Model-1 (5%). This categorisation was done using Kennedy's (2005) framework, irrespective of the fact that some of the studies made claims to implementing a new PD model (e.g. Kriek & Grayson, 2009; Mokhele, 2013; Jita & Mokhele, 2014). For example, Kriek and Grayson (2009) tried out what they call a Holistic Professional Development (HPD) model, in which the intervention started with a baseline study, and offered a developed, year-long Physics course that was taught through workshops and distance learning. Their study sample consisted of 12 teachers from rural schools in Limpopo Province. To evaluate the PD effectiveness of this model they analysed data from assignments, teachers' journal entries, pre- and post-tests, examination scripts, workshop evaluation forms, classroom observations and interviews. They concluded that the application of the HPD model resulted in improvements in content knowledge, teaching approaches, and professional attitudes of the participating teachers. However, when the HPD is carefully scrutinised it reveals features and characteristics of Kennedy's (2005) transformative model. This is so because a combination of practices and conditions as well as integration of at least two models is evident. In this instance the intervention was provided through workshops and distance education, which are features of the Training Model; and peer support which has the characteristics of the Community of Practice Model. In similar vein, Ono and Ferreira (2010) tried out a PD model, rooted in the Japanese learning study project, which falls under the umbrella of the action research model with the difference that it was being experimented in a South African context. Another study, also categorised under the action research model, is by Aldridge, Fraser and Sebela (2004), whose ancestry is the Australian learning environments project (Fraser, 1998; Taylor, Fraser & Fisher, 1997). This study aimed to help teachers implement more constructivist practices in their classrooms.

Evaluation of the impact/effectiveness of PD

Without exception all the reviewed studies evaluated the impact of PD, and hence its effectiveness, by focusing on the teacher. The most common approaches to evaluation of effectiveness identified include: using teacher questionnaires

– including validated instruments to assess shifts in PCK or TSPCK; learner questionnaires; post-event evaluation forms or 'happy sheets', teacher self-report measures; pre- and post-tests – including assignments and examinations; observing teachers' lessons schedules; interviewing teachers; and analysing teachers' reflective journals. For all the reviewed studies, all or some of these data sources were used to evaluate the effectiveness/impact of the PD specifically focusing on determining teacher changes or shifts in: subject matter and pedagogical knowledge, classroom practices, teaching skills, beliefs and attitudes. This is said, albeit that the study by Aldridge, Fraser, and Sebela (2004), administered a modified version of the Constructivist Learning Environment Survey (CLES) (Taylor, Fraser, & Fisher, 1997) to assess students' perceptions of whether there was a change in the classroom teaching as a result of the teacher going through an action research PD programme. The CLES is based on the assumption that students' perceptions of what happens in the classroom are a valid and reliable indicator of the teaching process. Taylor, Fraser, and Fisher (1997) suggest that teacher-researchers can validly employ it to monitor the development of constructivist approaches to teaching in science classrooms. This instrument has been used in many studies around the world (e.g. Ozkal, Tekkaya & Cakiroglu et al., 2009; Ahmad, Ching, & Yahaya et al., 2015). However, given the spirit of the current review, it is argued that this kind of evaluation still focuses on the teacher, as the CLES is in essence an evaluation of the teacher by students. It fails to indicate whether there are shifts in students' performance and achievements as a result of the teacher's participation in PD.

Outcomes of the PD

Overall, thirteen (65 %) of the twenty reviewed studies show that there was a shift or a change in science teachers' content and pedagogical knowledge, teaching skills, classroom practices, beliefs and attitudes as a result of their involvement in PD. Three studies (15%) report that the PD was not successful in improving or changing teachers' content and pedagogical knowledge, teaching skills, classroom practices, beliefs and attitudes. The results of the other four studies (20%) can be described as inconclusive because, either the data was insufficient to provide a concrete support for the efficacy of the PD model or the findings gave mixed signals.

Discussion

The aim of this systematic review was to determine which professional development models are effective in developing science teachers and how the effectiveness of PD has been evaluated focusing on research in basic education in post-apartheid South Africa.

The findings suggest that in post-apartheid South Africa, a wide range of teacher PD models are used by researchers and practitioners. Furthermore, based on the reviewed studies, the results show that, overall, PD can in general have a positive impact on the teachers who participate in PD. The majority of the studies (65 %) point towards PD having improved or shifted the participating science teachers' content and pedagogical knowledge, teaching skills, classroom practices, beliefs and attitudes. These findings also show that without exception, researchers have evaluated the effectiveness of PD models focusing on determining changes and shifts happening to the teacher.

An interesting observation is that all the PD models tried out in South Africa have features and characteristics evident of a European/Western progeny (Johnson, Hodges & Monk, 2000). This remains so, irrespective of the fact some of the studies in the current review made attempts to modify the models to suit the South African context (e.g. Kriek & Grayson, 2009; Mokhele, 2013; Jita & Mokhele, 2014; Ono & Ferreira, 2010). In spite of these efforts the models largely remained the same Western models as described by Kennedy (2005). Johnson, Hodges and Monk (2000) have warned that Northern/Western ideas and paradigms of PD are unsuitable for modelling practices and challenges facing post-colonial countries. The centrality of Western hegemony in PD efforts is an affront to the processes of decolonisation and transformation of South Africa's science education. Chinn (2007) laments the damaging effects of Western hegemonic influence on teacher PD and suggests the use of critical indigenous knowledge based approaches. He argues that PD, which employs decolonising methodologies articulated through indigenous knowledge systems (IKS), has the potential to nurture teachers' awareness of linkages among their personal experiences, cultural practices, beliefs and values, and teaching and learning.

Having made these general observations, it is appropriate to address the review's research questions.

The effectiveness of teacher professional development models

Based on the reviewed studies, it appears that, in South Africa, PD has in general positively impacted on the teachers. The validity of this statement, however, should be taken with a measure. This is so because when the findings of this review are closely scrutinised and unpacked, this validity diminishes. According to these findings, the most popular and effective models are the cascade and training models with a combined total of seven studies showing that PD has a positive impact on teachers' knowledge, practices, skills etc. Other models which showed successes in at least one study are: action research, community of practice, coaching/mentoring, deficit, and transformative. None of the reviewed studies could confidently be categorised into two of Kennedy's (2005) models. These are the award-bearing model, and the standard-based model.

In answering the first of this review's research questions, it can be suggested that, generally, all the PD models used in the reviewed studies show success in effective PD of science teachers in South Africa. This is so because in the majority of cases, the results of the PD process were positive. Such a broad generalisation, however, is difficult to sustain for two reasons. First, the number of reviewed studies (20) is too small to confidently support such a sweeping statement or claim. The paucity of research on this topic suggests that more studies need to be done to get a clearer picture. The fact that 35% of the studies were either negative or inconclusive decreases the assurance with which such a generalisation can be made. The second reason has to do with how the effectiveness of PD was evaluated, which leads to the second research question.

Evaluation of the effectiveness of science teacher professional development
As shown, the data analysis reveals that all the reviewed studies evaluated the effectiveness of PD, based on attributes which have to do with the teacher. Those studies which claim effectiveness of the PD process do so on the basis of changes or shifts in teachers' subject matter and pedagogical knowledge, classroom practices, teaching skills, beliefs and attitudes. There is an underlying assumption, that these observed changes or shifts are indicators not only of the impact of PD on teachers but also the effectiveness of PD. In turn, effective PD is presumed to translate into effective teaching.

It has been argued that determining improvements in student performance and achievement should be at the centre of the evaluation of the effectiveness of teacher PD (Earley & Porritt, 2014; Pedder, Opfer, & McCormick et al., 2010). It was also suggested that the achievement of effective evaluation of PD involves a balanced assessment of changes or shifts in: student learning outcomes, teacher knowledge, practices and efficacy, and a plethora of factors in the teaching and learning environment. The greatest weight of this equilibrium, however, should be given to determining improvements in student performance and achievement. Given that all the studies in this review focused evaluation of effectiveness of PD by determining what happens to the teacher, it is argued that no definitive conclusion can be arrived at regarding the effectiveness of the employed PD models. The approaches to evaluating effectiveness of PD used by the studies covered by the current review can be described as simplistic, impressionistic and untrustworthy as they are based on simple measures (Earley & Porritt, 2014). In other words, it is difficult to arrive at a conclusion regarding the efficacy of a PD model without factoring in the impact or effect that PD has had on improving the performance and achievement of students. The implications are that South African researchers and education practioners need to seriously consider making assessment of student gains a part of evaluation of the effectiveness of PD. This is in line with the current thinking on PD evaluation (Pedder, Opfer, & McCormick et al., 2010).

Conclusions and recommendations

This systematic review has shown that in South Africa, several teacher professional development models have been tried on in-service and practising teachers. These models are: cascading, training, action research, community of practice, coaching/mentoring, deficit, and transformative. The results of the analysis reveal that in the majority of cases the models have been successful in improving the participating teachers' content and pedagogical knowledge, teaching practices, skills, beliefs and attitudes. The efficacy of these models should, however, be considered with caution because of the methods the researchers used to evaluate the effectiveness of PD. It is recommended that future evaluations of science teacher PD efforts should take into account the effect or impact of the PD on students' learning outcomes, performance and achievement. In order to achieve this, the design of PD and its evaluation should take the form of longitudinal studies, where the impact of the teachers' PD is monitored over time.

References

Ahmad, C.N.C., Ching, W.C., Yahaya, A., & Abdullah, M.F.N.L. (2015). Relationship between constructivist learning environments and educational facility in science classrooms. *Procedia-Social and Behavioral Sciences*, 191, 1952-1957. https://doi.org/10.1016/j.sbspro.2015.04.672

Appleton, K. (2008). Developing science pedagogical content knowledge through mentoring elementary teachers. *Journal of Science Teacher Education*, 19(6), 523-545. https://doi.org/10.1007/s10972-008-9109-4

Bantwini, B.D. (2009). District professional development models as a way to introduce primary-school teachers to natural science curriculum reforms in one district in South Africa. *Journal of Education for Teaching*, 35(2), 169-182. https://doi.org/10.1080/02607470902771094

Bayar, A. (2014). The Components of Effective Professional Development Activities in Terms of Teachers' Perspective. Online Submission, 6(2), 319-327. https://doi.org/10.15345/iojes.2014.02.006

Bearman, M., Smith, C.D., Carbone, A., Slade, S., Baik, C., Hughes-Warrington, M., & Neumann, D.L. (2012). Systematic review methodology in higher education. *Higher Education Research & Development*, 31(5), 625-640. https://doi.org/10.1080/07294360.2012.702735

Bennett, J., Lubben, F., Hogarth, S., & Campbell, B. (2005). Systematic reviews of research in science education: rigour or rigidity? *International Journal of Science Education*, 27(4), 387-406. https://doi.org/10.1080/0950069042000323719

Bhattacharya, D., Roehrig, G., Kern, A., & Howard, M. (2014). Teacher professional development in the Anthropocene. Future Earth – Advancing Civic Understanding of the Anthropocene, 19-30. https://doi.org/10.1002/9781118854280.ch3

Brinkerhoff, J. (2006). Effects of a long-duration, professional development academy on technology skills, computer self-efficacy, and technology integration beliefs and practices. *Journal of research on technology in education*, 39(1), 22-43. https://doi.org/10.1080/15391523.2006.10782471

Capps, D.K., Crawford, B.A., & Constas, M.A. (2012). A review of empirical literatureon inquiry professional development: Alignment with best practices and a critique of the findings. *Journal of Science Teacher Education*, 23(3), 291-318. https://doi.org/10.1007/s10972-012-9275-2

Carleton, L.E., Fitch, J.C., & Krockover, G.H. (2007, October). An in-service teacher education program's effect on teacher efficacy and attitudes. In *The Educational Forum*, . 72(1), 46-62. Taylor & Francis Group. https://doi.org/10.1080/00131720701603628

Chinn, P.W. (2007). Decolonizing methodologies and indigenous knowledge: The role of culture, place and personal experience in professional development. *Journal of Research in Science Teaching*, 44(9), 1247-1268. https://doi.org/10.1002/tea.20192

Darling-Hammond, L. (2010). Evaluating teacher effectiveness: How teacher performance assessments can measure and improve teaching. Center for American Progress.

Dede, C. (2006). *Online professional development for teachers: Emerging models and methods*. Harvard Education Press, 8 Story Street, First Floor, Cambridge, MA 02138, A brief history of science teacher professional development initiative in Indonesia and the implications for centralised teacher development. *International Journal of Educational Development*, 23(2), 201-213. https://doi.org/10.1016/S0738-0593(02)00014-7

Doering, A., Veletsianos, G., Scharber, C., & Miller, C. (2009). Using the technological, pedagogical, and content knowledge framework to design online learning environments and professional development. *Journal of Educational Computing Research*, 41(3), 319-346. https://doi.org/10.2190/EC.41.3.d

Doyle, W. (1977). 4: Paradigms for research on teacher effectiveness. *Review of Research in Education*, 5(1), 163-198. https://doi.org/10.3102/0091732X005001163

Fernandez, C., & Yoshida, M. (2012). *Lesson study: A Japanese approach to improving mathematics teaching and learning*. London: Routledge. https://doi.org/10.4324/9781410610867

Fraser, B.J. (1998). Classroom environment instruments: Development, validity and applications. *Learning Environments Research*, 1(1), 7-34. https://doi.org/10.1023/A:1009932514731

Garet, M.S., Porter, A.C., Desimone, L., Birman, B.F., & Yoon, K.S. (2001). What makes professional development effective? Results from a national sample of teachers. *American Educational Research Journal*, 38(4), 915-945. https://doi.org/10.1023/A:1009932514731

Gast, I., Schildkamp, K., & Van der Veen, J. T. (2017). Team-based professional development interventions in higher education: A systematic review. *Review of Educational research*, 87(4), 736-767. https://doi.org/10.3102/0034654317704306

Guskey, T.R. (2003). What makes professional development effective? *Phi delta kappan*, 84(10), 748-750. https://doi.org/10.1177/003172170308401007

Guskey, T.R., & Huberman, M. (1995). *Professional development in education: New paradigms and practices.* New York: Teachers College Press, ISBN-0-8077-3425.

Guskey, T.R., & Yoon, K.S. (2009). What works in professional development? *Phi delta kappan,* 90(7), 495-500. https://doi.org/10.1177/003172170909000709

Hargreaves, D. (1996). *Teaching as a research-based profession: possibilities and prospects.* Teacher Training Agency Annual Lecture, The Teacher Training Agency, London.

Heller, J.I., Daehler, K.R., Wong, N., Shinohara, M., & Miratrix, L.W. (2012). Differential effects of three professional development models on teacher knowledge and student achievement in elementary science. *Journal of Research in Science Teaching,* 49(3), 333-362. https://doi.org/10.1002/tea.21004

Hestness, E., McDonald, R.C., Breslyn, W., McGinnis, J.R., & Mouza, C. (2014). Science teacher professional development in climate change education informed by the Next Generation Science Standards. *Journal of Geoscience Education,* 62(3), 319-329. https://doi.org/10.5408/13-049.1

Jimoyiannis, A. (2010). Designing and implementing an integrated technological pedagogical science knowledge framework for science teachers professional development. *Computers & Education,* 55(3), 1259-1269. https://doi.org/10.1016/j.compedu.2010.05.022

Jita, L.C., & Mokhele, M.L. (2014). When teacher clusters work: selected experiences of South African teachers with the cluster approach to professional development. *South African Journal of Education,* 34(2). https://doi.org/10.15700/201412071132

Johnson, S., Hodges, M., & Monk, M. (2000). Teacher development and change in South Africa: A critique of the appropriateness of transfer of northern/western practice. Compare: *A Journal of Comparative and International Education,* 30(2), 179-192. https://doi.org/10.1080/713657456

King, F. (2014). Evaluating the impact of teacher professional development: An evidence-based framework. *Professional Development in Education,* 40(1), 89-111. https://doi.org/10.1080/19415257.2013.823099

Lumpe, A., Czerniak, C., Haney, J., & Beltyukova, S. (2012). Beliefs about teaching science: The relationship between elementary teachers' participation in professional development and student achievement. *International Journal of Science Education,* 34(2), 153-166. https://doi.org/10.1080/09500693.2010.551222

Maxwell, J. (1992). Understanding and validity in qualitative research. *Harvard Educational Review*, 62(3), 279-301. https://doi.org/10.17763/haer.62.3.8323320856251826

Mbowane, C.K., De Villiers, J.J.R, & Braun, M.W.H. (2017). Teacher participation in science fairs as professional development in South Africa. *South African Journal of Science*, 113(7/8). https://doi.org/10.17159/sajs.2017/20160364

McNiff, J. (2010). Action research for professional development: Concise advice for new action researchers. Dorset: September Books.

Mogari, D., Kriek, J., & Atagana, H. (2016). Designing a teacher development programme for improving the content knowledge of grade 12 mathematics and science teachers. *SAARMSTE Conference Proceedings*, January 2016.

Mokhele, M. (2013). Empowering Teachers: An Alternative Model for Professional Development in South Africa, *Journal of Social Sciences*, 34:1, 73-81. https://doi.org/10.1080/09718923.2013.11893119

Mokhele, M.L., & Jita, L.C. (2010). South African teachers' perspectives on continuing professional development: a case study of the Mpumalanga Secondary Science Initiative. *Procedia-Social and Behavioral Sciences*, 9, 1762-1766. https://doi.org/10.1016/j.sbspro.2010.12.396

Mouza, C. (2002). Learning to teach with new technology: Implications for professional development. *Journal of Research on Computing in Education*, 35(2), 272-289. https://doi.org/10.1080/15391523.2002.10782386

Ndlalane, T.C., & Jita, L.C. (2009). Teacher clusters in South Africa: Opportunities and constraints for teacher development and change. *Perspectives in Education*, 27(1), 58-68.

Nicholls, G. (2000). Professional development, teaching, and lifelong learning: the implications for higher education. *International Journal of Lifelong Education*, 19(4), 370-377. https://doi.org/10.1080/02601370050110419

Ono, Y., & Ferreira, J. (2010). A case study of continuing teacher professional development through lesson study in South Africa. *South African Journal of Education*, 30(1). https://doi.org/10.15700/saje.v30n1a320

Onwu, G.O., & Mogari, D. (2004). Professional development for outcomes-based education curriculum implementation: the case of UNIVEMALASHI, South Africa. *Journal of Education for Teaching*, 30(2), 161-177. https://doi.org/10.1080/0260747042000229771

Ozkal, K., Tekkaya, C., Cakiroglu, J., & Sungur, S. (2009). A conceptual model of relationships among constructivist learning environment perceptions, epistemological beliefs, and learning approaches. *Learning and Individual Differences*, 19(1), 71-79. https://doi.org/10.1016/j.lindif.2008.05.005

Pedder, D., Opfer, V.D., McCormick, R., & Storey, A. (2010). 'Schools and continuing professional development in England – State of the nation' research study: Policy context, aims and design. *The Curriculum Journal*, 21(4), 365-394. https://doi.org/10.1080/09585176.2010.529637

Penuel, W.R., Fishman, B.J., Yamaguchi, R., & Gallagher, L.P. (2007). What makes professional development effective? Strategies that foster curriculum implementation. *American Educational Research Journal*, 44(4), 921-958. https://doi.org/10.3102/0002831207308221

Steinert, Y., Mann, K., Centeno, A., Dolmans, D., Spencer, J., Gelula, M., & Prideaux, D. (2006). A systematic review of faculty development initiatives designed to improve teaching effectiveness in medical education: BEME Guide No. 8. *Medical Teacher*, 28(6), 497-526. https://doi.org/10.1080/01421590600902976

Supovitz, J.A., & Turner, H.M. (2000). The effects of professional development on science teaching practices and classroom culture. *Journal of Research in Science Teaching*, 37(9), 963-980. https://doi.org/10.1002/1098-2736(200011)37:9<963::AID-TEA6>3.0.CO;2-0

Taylor, P.C., Fraser, B.J., & Fisher, D.L. (1997). Monitoring constructivist classroom learning environments. *International Journal of Educational Research*, 27(4), 293-302. https://doi.org/10.1016/S0883-0355(97)90011-2

Thair, M., & Treagust, D. F. (2003). A brief history of a science teacher professional development initiative in Indonesia and the implications for centralised teacher development. *International Journal of Educational Development*, 23(2), 201-213. https://doi.org/10.1016/S0738-0593(02)00014-7

Tosun, T. (2000). The impact of prior science course experience and achievement on the science teaching self-efficacy of preservice elementary teachers. *Journal of Elementary Science Education*, 12(2), 21-31. https://doi.org/10.1007/BF03173597

Trede, F., Macklin, R., & Bridges, D. (2012). Professional identity development: a review of the higher education literature. *Studies in Higher Education*, 37(3), 365-384. https://doi.org/10.1080/03075079.2010.521237

Vandeyar, S., & Killen, R. (2007). Educators' conceptions and practice of classroom assessments in post-apartheid South Africa. *South African Journal of Education*, 27(1), 101-115.

Van Driel, J.H., & Berry, A. (2012). Teacher professional development focusing on pedagogical content knowledge. *Educational Researcher*, 41(1), 26-28. https://doi.org/10.3102/0013189X11431010

Vangrieken, K., Meredith, C., Packer, T., & Kyndt, E. (2017). Teacher communities as a context for professional development: A systematic review. *Teaching and Teacher Education*, 61, 47-59. https://doi.org/10.1016/j.tate.2016.10.001

Van Lankveld, T., Schoonenboom, J., Volman, M., Croiset, G., & Beishuizen, J. (2017). Developing a teacher identity in the university context: A systematic review of the literature. *Higher Education Research & Development*, 36(2), 325-342. https://doi.org/10.1080/07294360.2016.1208154

Villegas-Reimers, E. (2003). Teacher professional development: an international review of the literature. Paris: International Institute for Educational Planning.

Wilson, S.M. (2013). Professional development for science teachers. *Science*, 340(6130), 310-313. https://doi.org/10.1126/science.1230725

Yoon, K.S., Duncan, T., Lee, S.W.Y., Scarloss, B., & Shapley, K.L. (2007). Reviewing the Evidence on How Teacher Professional Development Affects Student Achievement. Issues & Answers. REL 2007-No. 033. Regional Educational Laboratory Southwest (NJ1).

Chapter 8

Dealing with difference: A scoping review of disability in education in South Africa

Judith McKenzie, Brian Watermeyer (Disability Studies Division, Department of Health and Rehabilitation Sciences, University of Cape Town), and Kyla Meyerson (Desmond Tutu TB Centre, Department of Paediatrics and Child Health, Stellenbosch University)

Keywords: Inclusive education, special education, disability, impairment

Introduction

In this chapter we will consider the access and participation of children with disabilities in basic education in South Africa, within an inclusive education policy framework. We begin by setting the scene with a brief background to how disability has been viewed historically in the basic education arena and providing a theoretical framework for our ensuing discussion and analysis. Thereafter, we outline the scoping review methodology upon which this analysis will be based. It is our aim to provide a critical perspective on addressing impairment and disability within inclusive education, while querying how we, in our national dispensation, deal with diversity more broadly. One important issue within this inquiry relates to the role of special schools in our education system.

Background and rationale

The history of education for children with disabilities in South Africa is marked with racist and ableist assumptions. Schooling was segregated based on both disability and race, as in the early 1960s legislation was passed bringing special schools for particular race groups under the control of the departments of Coloured Affairs, Indian Affairs and Bantu Education. Such legislation also distinguished between which disabilities merited special education, differentiated in terms of race. The Bantu Special Education Act no 24 of 1964 specifically addressed special schooling for disabled children classed as Bantu. Notably, this piece of legislation expressly excluded service provision to black children with mild to moderate intellectual disability (then mental handicap), while such provision was made for white children (McKenzie, 2010).

With the advent of democracy in South Africa, a consultative process over several years resulted in the development of Education White Paper 6: *Special Needs Education, Building an Inclusive Education and Training System* (EWP6), which outlines education policy for children with disabilities. This policy aimed to address the post-apartheid configuration of special education, which reflected racial inequity, limited educational access and, of course, segregation of children with disabilities. It also recognised that disability was one of many barriers to learning that required urgent attention. In order to achieve these goals, the vision of an inclusive education system was adopted – a dispensation in which all children would learn together within a seamless system of support that would address not only disability but also a range of barriers to learning arising from poverty, inequality and other social conditions (Department of Education [DoE], 2001).

Regrettably however, it is no exaggeration to say that currently children and youth with disabilities face a crisis of education. In South Africa, the national prevalence rate of disability among 5- to 9-year-olds is 10.8%, while in the 10 to 14 age group it is 4.1%, and 2.6% for 15- to 19-year-olds, which comes to a total of 718 409 children of school-going age who have disabilities according to the census data (Statistics South Africa, 2014). However, the Department of Basic Education (DBE) (2016) notes that there are 117 477 learners with special needs in their programmes (Department of Basic Education, 2016), some 600 000 less than would be expected according to the census. Furthermore, even those who are in school do not experience success on par with their non-disabled peers. According to the DBE National Senior Certificate (NSC) 2018 Examination Report (Department of Basic Education, 2018), 624 733 learners wrote matric in 2018, of which 3 856 were learners with special educational needs – that is 0,6% of the total, a figure completely out of line with disability prevalence, even when one factors in that children with intellectual disability are unlikely to be following the NSC route. Given the current crisis, and the fact that in 2001, the EWP6 set a 20-year target to achieve its stipulated goals, this chapter on education of children with disabilities is timely as the 2021 deadline approaches, and the progress toward these goals can be critically assessed.

At time of writing, research work in disability and education in South Africa remains severely challenged by a lack of sufficiently specific baseline data in key areas, beginning with locality and prevalence of forms of childhood disability. Further, available research data on a variety of issues regarding disability in education is patchy and incoherent, leaving both scope and need for a substantial, integrated future research agenda. While theoretical ideas from the global arena are of great use, locally specific knowledge, such as that pertaining to cultural issues in disability inclusion, issues in teacher training, or the local availability of assistive technology and accessible learning and teaching materials, is essential. Thus, part of our aim here is the identification of strategically important gaps in our understanding, to inform a research agenda with developmental relevance.

Aims and objectives of the chapter

In this chapter we explore the effects of implementation of inclusive education policy as expressed in EWP6, in relation to the right to education and reasonable accommodation of children with disabilities – rights mandated in the Constitution and the United Nations Convention on the Rights of Persons with Disabilities (Republic of South Africa 1996, United Nations 2006). To do this, we provide a disability studies in education (DSE) lens as a starting point. The essence of such an approach is to acknowledge disability as a human rights issue that requires environmental and social accommodations in all sectors, but significantly within basic education as the gateway to lifelong learning and participation (Connor, 2019). DSE reminds us that we need to move away from essentialist concepts of disability as bodily deficit requiring medical attention, and to rather contextualise disability within political and social spheres. At the same time, the self-representation and privileging of voices of disabled people and their families must be prioritised if we are to address issues of social justice and provide meaningful and equitable educational opportunities. Such an approach assumes competence rather than incompetence (Connor, 2019). Within this framework we will identify existing research on: disability in initial teaching education; inclusive education policy specifically applied to disability; the status and function of special schools; attitudes to disability; and patterns of referral. Further, we will develop a better understanding of why learners with disabilities are at increased risk of exclusion and explore the transformative potential of disability inclusion across the education system.

Methodological approach

We used a scoping review to explore the existing literature about education of children with disabilities in South Africa. A scoping review, like its better-know counterpart – a systematic review – is an approach to evidence synthesis (Munn et al., 2018). The scoping review is a recent development in the field of evidence synthesis (Munn et al., 2018). Similarly to systematic reviews, scoping reviews are used to synthesise data in a structured manner (Arksey & O'Malley, 2005; Munn et al., 2018). A key difference between a systematic review and a scoping review is their underlying rationale (Munn et al., 2018; Peters, Heunis, Kigozi, Osoba, & Van der Walt, 2015). Unlike systematic reviews, which aim to produce a critically appraised answer to a research question, scoping reviews aim to outline a body of literature on a given topic (Munn et al., 2018; Peters et al., 2015).

A scoping review is a process of mapping the existing literature on a specific topic in a structured manner (Arksey & O'Malley, 2005). As a result, scoping reviews are suitable for exploratory projects as they are used to determine the overall state of research on a given topic by highlighting the types of evidence available, summarising the main sources of literature, as well as identifying the gaps in the literature (Arksey & O'Malley, 2005; Peters et al., 2015). Due to the structured nature of the scoping review, a strength of this methodology is its ability to generate reproducible results and thus, minimise potential bias (Sucharew & Macaluso, 2019). However, a weakness of the scoping review methodology is its failure to assess the quality of the evidence of the mapped-out literature (which is the primary task of the systematic review; Arksey & O'Malley, 2005).

We followed the guidelines of a scoping review proposed by the Joanna Briggs Institute (JBI; Aromataris & Munn, 2020; Peters et al., 2015). The framework originally proposed by Arksey and O'Malley (2005) and then further refined by Levac, Colquhoun and O'Brien (2010) underpins the methodology proposed by JBI (Aromataris & Munn, 2020; Peters et al., 2015). The methodological steps proposed by JBI, and that we adopted for this study, are as follows: (i) defining the research objectives; (ii) developing the inclusion criteria for study selection in alignment with the research objectives; (iii) planning the approach to study selection, data extraction and presentation of the evidence; (iv) searching for the studies; (v) selecting studies; (vi) extracting the data; (vii) analysing evidence; (viii) presenting the results as well as (ix) addressing the research objectives and drawing the conclusions (Aromataris & Munn, 2020).

Search strategy and selection criteria
We developed a comprehensive literature search using the population, concept, context (PCC) strategy with the elements being: Children with disability (population) in education policy (concept) enacted in South African schools (context). We used the following specific keyword combinations to conduct our search: "South Africa" AND ((children) OR (learners)) AND ((intellectual disability) OR (physical disability) OR (visual impairment) OR (blind) OR (hearing impairment) OR (deaf)) AND ((special education) OR (inclusive education)) AND ((education) OR (schooling)). The search term, South Africa, was restricted to abstracts only. We did not limit the date range and all studies had to be conducted in English. Databases included: ERIC, Education Database, Academic Search Premier, SAGE online and Africa-wide information.

We included grey literature in the search, as there have been several such reports addressing this topic within South Africa, notably by Section 27, an NGO and Human Rights Watch (Fish-Hodgson and Khumalo, 2016; Human Rights Watch, 2015). Grey literature has been defined as literature, excluding books and journal articles, which has been acquired and identified through measures other than commercial outlets or electronic databases (Bonato, 2018). We operationalised grey literature as a Google search using the same key words limiting the search to the first 50 outputs organised by relevance. Our final search produced reports by government, NGOs and NPOs as well as academic theses. We included outputs that reported on basic education of children with disabilities in South Africa. Studies were excluded if they (i) were conducted in Africa but not South Africa; (ii) were related to disability but not to education; and (iii) were irrelevant database returns.

Screening and data abstraction

We imported search results from each database into separate sheets in a Microsoft Excel document. The results were organised according to title, author(s), year of publication and journal title. We removed duplicates within each database. Thereafter, we combined the data from the five sheets into a single sheet and removed duplicates between the databases. One reviewer (KM) applied the exclusion criteria during the title screening. Any uncertainties were discussed with the senior reviewers (JM and BW). Thereafter, during the abstract screening, all reviewers (JM, BW and KM) read through the abstracts and, using the same exclusion criteria, decided whether to include each study.

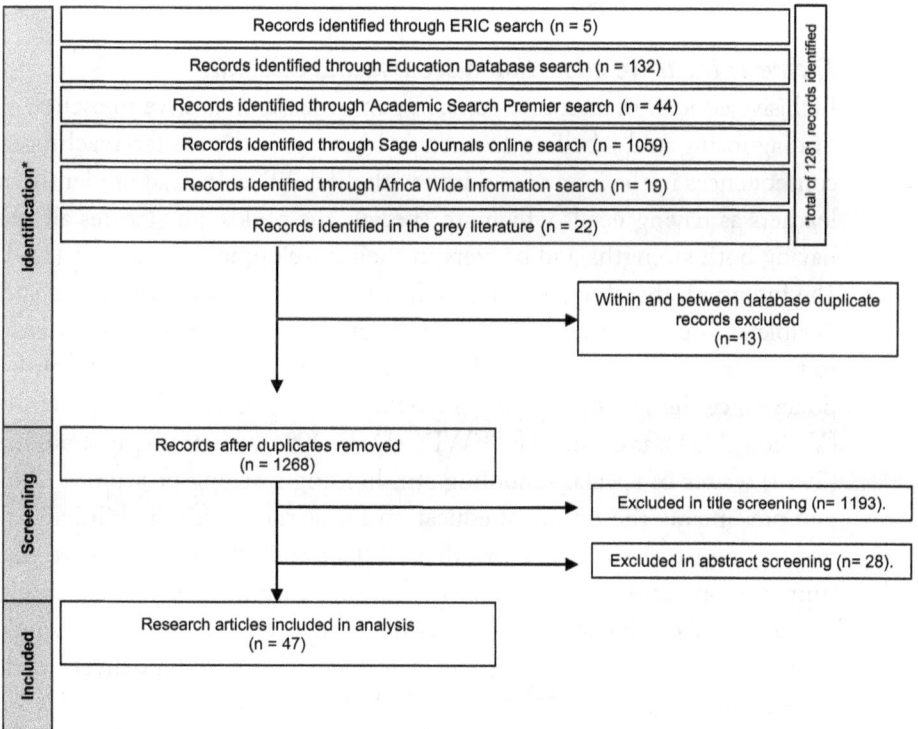

Figure 8.1 *Flow chart representing article selection [add in]*

Data analysis

Once the final database was concluded, the researchers were delegated the responsibility to read and report on a certain number of articles each. We identified the major trends of the literature and allocated these to each of the authors who then prepared a brief summary to share with the others. Based on this review they divided the papers into six themes (see Appendix 1 for the full list of papers and their allocation to themes):

Theme 1: Inclusive education discourse and disability
Theme 2: Teaching and learning
Theme 3: Parents' perspectives
Theme 4: Disability, race and special education
Theme 5: Human rights
Theme 6: Teacher education

In the balance of the paper, we reviewed the resultant store of literature under these themes. The authors then reviewed the analysis in its totality, drew conclusions about the education of children with disabilities, and made suggestions for future research.

Thematic categories

Theme 1: Inclusive education discourse and disability

Inclusive education discourse rests, in part at least, on a drive to eschew practices of diagnosing and labelling learners, which has had such far-reaching negative consequences in the lives of children with disabilities. Instead of identifying some learners as having needs which are 'special', the philosophy locates all learners as having both strengths and barriers in their developmental journeys (DoE, 2001). The intention, therefore, is to create learning environments which are sufficiently flexible and receptive, as well as carefully created and managed, in order to attune to the learning styles of all children. These ideals have been part of South African policy since the 1990s, implying a de-emphasising of the role of special schooling (Walton, 2011), as outlined by EWP6 (DoE, 2001). Interestingly though, Naicker (2014) writes of special schooling still holding a strong position in the present, and presumably the future, of education for learners with disabilities. At time of writing, South Africa has more than 400 special schools, which are marked by immense operational challenges. In fact, the current reality in this sector bears out many of the harshest criticisms that proponents of inclusion would direct at special education, including low standards of curriculum delivery and limited subject choices (DSD, DWCPD & UNICEF, 2012).

The idea that inclusion – that is, non-segregation – builds social cohesion and breaks barriers of difference is self-evidently true. Yet, debates on the practical implementation of inclusion have at times drawn more on ideology than pedagogical knowledge regarding the diverse needs of learners. From a legal perspective, Ngwena (2014) notes how many countries sign international conventions such as the UNCRPD (2006) for strategic geopolitical reasons, rather than through a sincere intention to fulfil their prescripts. Further, he points to the distinction between formal equality and substantive equality. The former is a largely cosmetic gesture, while the latter (which is demanded by the Constitution) requires actions from the State for its full realisation. This distinction would seem to coincide with the contrast between inclusion which is enacted in a superficial, un-considered manner, and practices which meaningfully afford all learners the means and opportunity to participate fully in education.

As the intention of inclusive education is to address all forms of barriers to learning, including poverty, cultural and linguistic difference, community problems such as violence and abuse, as well as disability, the challenge is immense. Walton (2011) notes correctly that a society such as ours, with a history of institutional discrimination based on race, gender, ethnicity and class, could not reasonably expect its teachers and communities to simply leave behind the impressions left by that legacy on individuals and relationships. To achieve inclusion, therefore, teachers are required to continually interrogate beliefs and practices which maintain old divisions; this is no easy task, for which many would assume they need specialised training and the support of therapeutic and other professionals. Pather (2011), however, opposes this sober perspective, arguing that an 'expert model' – one which relies on specialised professionals – will always underpin a 'learner deficit' rather than a 'system deficit' model, reifying difference, perhaps most notably in the lives of learners with disabilities. But in the attempt to avoid the labelling and isolation of disability, there is a concern that identifiable impairment-specific learning needs are glossed over.

This concern is highlighted in the case of Deaf education, where ample evidence shows the painful consequences of government's inability to provide essential, specialised teaching expertise – primarily, teachers who are fluent in South African Sign Language (SASL) (Storbeck & Martin, 2010). The abject failure of government to provide such capacity even at special schools puts the idea of success across a nation of, aspirationally at least, full-service schools in a most worrying light. To these writers, the DBE's manner of implementing inclusive education reflects 'an ignorance of the experiences and needs of deaf and hard of hearing learners in inclusive settings' (ibid.; Peel, 2004). Evidence regarding the dysfunctionality of essential services at special schools for visually impaired learners carries similar implications for more inclusive settings (Section 27, 2015). If learners' impairment-specific needs cannot be met in special schools whose raison d'être is to meet these needs, then what are the chances for these needs being met within full service and inclusive schools? At a further extreme, it required a judgment by the Cape High Court in 2010 for learners with severe to profound intellectual disability (SPID) to be admitted to the education system at all – until that point government's (in)actions had rested on the discredited and oppressive belief that such children are 'ineducable' (McKenzie et al., 2017; Molteno, 2006). The high prevalence of complex and multiple disabilities in this group provides an example of a need for specialised teaching and challenges the limits of inclusion and how we think about the right to belong in one's community.

While it is essential in low-resource settings to mobilise and value the coping, innovation and creativity of inclusive teachers, a question arises regarding the possible danger of idealising their work in a manner which tacitly condones state neglect. Evidence suggests that principals who are motivated, and teachers who have sufficient training, are key variables, but also that barriers to inclusion are sometimes better overcome in rural, poor schools where communities are more consciously interdependent (Walton, 2011). The study by Pather (2011), noted earlier, provides data from a low-resourced high school in KwaZulu-Natal, which accepts and includes a high proportion of learners with disabilities from a nearby special primary school. While the picture painted by this study is very hopeful indeed and presented in the context of an inclusive education position which is suspicious of 'expert knowledge', questions arise around validating the 'independence' of learners with disabilities in overcoming barriers to essential resources such as transportation.

Taking a squarely critical view of the 'optimistic' inclusive education discourse, civil society organisation Section 27 declares that inclusive education in South Africa is 'in crisis', 'rebutting' government's 'good story' which obscures the daily violation of the rights of learners with disabilities. Supporting this cautionary view, Du Toit & Forlin (2009) provide a thorough description of the very real constraints on successful inclusion which our damaged education system affords, including teachers with little understanding of inclusive principles, extremely poor general literacy and numeracy among learners, low levels of parent involvement in schools, little culture of reading and learning support of children in families, and communities that face multiple forms of adversity which limit human and material resources for education. Unfortunately, this lack of quality education is often framed as a debate between inclusive and special education, with the frequent assumption that special education delivers better education than inclusive education for learners with disability because their "high support needs" are addressed in special schools. However as discussed above, this is simply not the case. This simple binary – between special and inclusive – results in limited thinking around two mutually exclusive options and is strongly challenged by these authors.

Theme 2: Teaching and learning

A section of the literature was concerned with impairment-specific pedagogies, focusing on a range of disabilities including learning disabilities (see for example, Harmston, Strong, & Evans, 2001; Howgego, Miles, & Myers, 2014; Rohleder & Swartz, 2009); intellectual disabilities (see for example, Brown, Howcroft, & Jacobs, 2009; Ellman et al., 2004; McKenzie, Pillay, Duvenhage, Du Plessis, & Jelsma, 2017; Nyokangi & Phasha, 2016; Phasha & Nyokangi, 2012; Sethosa, 2001); and hearing impairments (see for example, Collair, 2001; Holness, n.d.; Jairaj, 1996; Kilian, 2001; Peel, 2004; Ram, 1998; Storbeck, 2012; Van Dijk, Hugo, & Louw, 2004). However, there were notably few studies conducted on teaching strategies for children with visual impairments (see for example, Baboo, 2011; Devenish, 2000).

Of the studies on teaching and learning in the context of disability, the majority focused on inclusive facilities. For example, Reenen and Karusseit (2017) identified the ideal ambient level of a classroom for children with sensory, language and learning impairments. Some of these studies reflected on improvements to school facilities. For example, Devenish (2000) reflected on the developments to the library at a special school in KwaZulu-Natal that is now more accessible to children with visual impairments. On the other hand, Baboo (2011) highlighted that the accessibility needs of the learners with visual impairments at a mainstream school in the Western Cape were only partially met. Kempen & Steyn (2017) described a teacher development programme in a school for children with intellectual disability.

Surprisingly, the number of studies on teaching strategies in the context of basic education and disabilities was limited. In our review, it seems as if Van Staden (2013) and Harmston et al. (2001) are the only two studies to report on teaching interventions. Van Staden (2013) tested whether a balanced reading approach intervention improved deaf children's reading and vocabulary skills, and Harmston et al. (2001) explored the benefits of pen-pal writing correspondence for children with learning disabilities.

Theme 3: Parents' perspectives

The perspective of parents was significant in the literature reviewed. Parents have been a driving force advocating for inclusion of children with disabilities globally, and South Africa is no different (Engelbrecht, Oswald, Swart, Kitching, & Eloff, 2005). The papers identified in this theme recognise and describe the legal and policy bases for parental advocacy for values of equity, individual rights, and freedom of choice in the education of their children (De Sas Kropiwnicki, Elphick, J., & Elphick, R. 2014; Engelbrecht et al., 2005; Erasmus et al., 2016; McKenzie et al., 2018).

Access to education remains a stumbling block. Entry into mainstream schools in pursuit of inclusive education presented difficulties which often required fierce advocacy from parents, to the extent that some expressed the concern that the levels of conflict around admission might subsequently impact upon their children's sense of belonging within that environment (Engelbrecht et al., 2005). This also applied to admission to special schools as noted by De Sas Kropiwnicki et al. (2014):

> *"Poor coordination between professionals and different government departments left caregivers frustrated and feeling helpless. To expedite state processes, some*

caregivers paid exorbitant amounts to private therapists to assess their children. Even with the necessary documentation in hand, caregivers approached an average of three to seven different schools seeking admission." (p. 362)

Having gained entry into the education system, concerns were expressed about the quality of education, with parents of children in inclusive settings being prepared to compromise on academic achievement in pursuit of social inclusion (Engelbrecht et al., 2005). In special schools there were concerns with a lack of progression from one grade to the next, as well as inadequate academic development, even when the child moved up grades, which was expressed most clearly by parents of children who are Deaf (De Sas Kropiwnicki et al., 2014; McKenzie et al., 2018).

Another area of concern was the relationship between parents and professionals. While parents are supposed to exercise choice in their child's schooling (Republic of South Africa, 1996), this is often undermined by a power imbalance between departmental officials and parents, especially those who are poor, black and female (De Sas Kropiwnicki et al., 2014). The relationship is dependent on how the various partners perceive the rights of the child to education. The demands placed on the teacher appeared to vary according to whether the parents understood the inclusion of their child as a right or a privilege. In the former case, they have higher expectations of the teacher, and in the latter are willing to take on some of the teacher's work (Engelbrecht et al., 2005). In special schools, teachers often expressed scepticism about the capacity and willingness of parents to be involved in their child's education, and partnerships between parents and professionals were marked by unequal power relationships favouring teachers (McKenzie et al., 2018). In order to address this, parents emphasised the importance of school leadership, and the attitudes of teachers, which could possibly be addressed through further training (Engelbrecht et al., 2005).

Financial issues were found to be a huge burden on poor families such as those interviewed in an informal settlement by De Sas Kropiwnicki et al. (2014). The families struggled with transport costs and higher fees at special schools (none of which have no-fee school status as they draw from a range of quintiles as well as medical costs). When children are placed in the mainstream parents are often requested to provide a classroom assistant at their own expense (Human Rights Watch, 2015). In addition, they feared for the safety of their children who might be targets for bullying in school or the wider community (De Sas Kropiwnicki et al., 2014; Erasmus et al., 2016). This is compounded by generally unsafe communities, where gang violence and crime impact upon all children, but presents difficulties for children with disabilities on their journeys to and from school (Human Rights Watch, 2015; McKenzie et al., 2018).

Despite these challenges, parents demonstrated agency and activism in support of their children. Many had adopted a rights discourse and honed their knowledge of enabling policies to make the right to education a reality. Although it is not entirely clear from the literature, we would suggest that there is a tendency for parents from more affluent communities to support inclusive education (Engelbrecht et al., 2005) and those from poorer areas to work toward special schools where they feel that their children will be safe (De Sas Kropiwnicki et al., 2014). For parents of children who are deaf or blind the major concern is for quality education wherever it is delivered, but with the provisos that the communication between child and family is maintained, and that the school placement does not have a negative effect on their child's behaviour (McKenzie et al., 2018). The value of parents' support groups, as well as advocacy agencies that guide their work, became very clear, with some parents expressing that they could not have continued without this backing (De Sas Kropiwnicki et al., 2014; Engelbrecht et al., 2005).

Theme 4: Disability, race and special education

This theme recognises that inclusive education has its roots in the need to redress racial inequity under apartheid, both in the general education system (where education for black children was deliberately of a low quality and not compulsory), and in the special education system (where there was minimal provision for black children) (Nkabinde, 1993). In terms of special education provision, the Van Wyk Report of 1967 was viewed as a milestone for children with intellectual disability, as it advocated for educational provision for children with an IQ below 50. However, this provision only applied to white children (Molteno, 2006). There were different race-based implications for learners with different forms of impairment, for example, Deaf education involved different sign languages across segregated race groups, and discussion of the notion of 'double oppression' (Ram, 1998).

Schools for children with sensory or mobility impairments were initially more racially integrated, as they were supported by charitable and faith-based organisations. For example, after an early period of racially integrated settings, schools for the Deaf were segregated by race after 1948. As a result of the homeland policy, several additional schools for African Deaf children were established throughout South Africa. The racial segregation was mirrored in educational approaches – oralist (spoken word) policies were implemented in white schools as the more expensive and elitist approach and a manual, sign language system of instruction in black, Coloured, and Indian schools, as the simpler, less expensive option. Ironically, the split disadvantaged the white deaf child given that oral instruction had limited success compared to sign (Storbeck & Martin, 2010). However, Deaf education in separate schools meant different sign languages developed, hampering communication within the Deaf population and the development of a Deaf identity, such that a black Deaf child would find themselves completely isolated within their community (Ram, 1998). Overall, for black disabled children there was a double disadvantage due to apartheid and disability, resulting in many receiving hardly any services at all (Fish-Hodgson & Khumalo, 2016).

The situation in special education only mirrored what was occurring in the general education system where, due to a lack of compulsory, free education, and racial inequality, there were dismal educational outcomes for all black children. The situation in the general education system was described as one where: "The majority of black students are academically retarded due to the inadequate and imbalanced educational and socio-political systems" (Nkabinde, 1993; p.107).

In this context, special education policy in the democratic era extended way beyond disability, aiming to address educational disadvantage across the broader population as well. Special education in separate specials schools was viewed as an unaffordable luxury, and inclusive education was seen as the only way to address special educational needs cost-effectively (Nkabinde, 1993). Nevertheless, special schools were retained in inclusive education policy without sufficient thought as to how the two systems would be linked from operational and budgetary perspectives, despite a clear outline of their place within a systemic policy of educational support (Human Rights Watch, 2015). This is currently reflected in the low investment for children with disabilities in inclusive schools relative to special schools combined with an overall increase in budgets for new special schools in all provinces (Human Rights Watch, 2015). However, Rule and Modipa (2011) collected data on the memories of education of a cohort of adults with disabilities in KZN, finding that all had experiences of schooling which were negative or harmful. The logic of inclusive education policy involved learners with disabilities having access to the mainstream, with specialised provision in special schools only when strictly necessary (Fish-Hodgson & Khumalo, 2015, 2016, 2017, Human Rights Watch, 2015). This implies that special schools are a necessary deviation from the inclusion principle only called upon to offer high levels of support. The literature examined in this review indicates that these schools are not able to fulfil this function for the reasons noted below.

Teachers in special schools are not trained to meet children's needs, with specific mention being made to lack of proficiency in braille (Fish-Hodgson & Khumalo 2015; McKenzie et al., 2018); SASL (McKenzie et al., 2018; Storbeck & Martin, 2010), and augmentative and alternative communication (Bornman & Alant, 1996). Budgets for maintaining infrastructure and purchasing specialised learning and teaching materials are not used effectively, and a conditional grant that was promised in EWP6 for special schools' development did not materialise (Fish-Hodgson & Khumalo, 2015; Fish-Hodgson & Khumalo, 2016). Due to complex and slow admission processes, children with disabilities tend to be much older when they enter the education system, and both take longer and are less likely to complete their education when compared to their able-bodied peers (Human

Rights Watch, 2015). There is often a restricted subject choice in special schools, as skilled teachers are not available, or are simply unwilling to make the necessary adaptations for children who are deaf or blind (Fish-Hodgson & Khumalo, 2016; Human Rights Watch, 2015; McKenzie et al., 2018).

Since special schools serve a wide catchment area and many of their learners cannot use transport independently, there are often elaborate transport arrangements which take up a large chunk of the child's day (Fish-Hodgson & Khumalo, 2015; 2016). Those who live too far away from the school are accommodated in hostels, which are often understaffed (Human Rights Watch, 2015) and have poor infrastructure with limited recreational facilities for the children (Fish-Hodgson & Khumalo, 2015, McKenzie et al., 2018). There are also reports of pervasive abuse and neglect (Human Rights Watch, 2015). Despite this, many parents are eager to enrol their children in special schools because of the often-hostile environment in mainstream schools. However, as we have seen, as many as 600 000 children remain excluded altogether from the education system, in many cases due to being unable to attend special schools due to long waiting lists and excessive financial burdens for transport and school fees (Human Rights Watch, 2015).

Children with severe and multiple disability are most often excluded from education, even by special schools, and very few of these schools are willing to address issues such as incontinence (Human Rights Watch, 2015). Government's failure to maintain high functional standards at special schools, especially regarding the provision of properly trained teachers and adequate support staff and therapeutic professionals, has created conditions for abuse and neglect of learners. For example, Nyokangi and Phasha (2016) report on the high incidence of sexual assault suffered by female learners with mild intellectual disability in a special school in Gauteng (Nyokangi & Phasha, 2016; Phasha & Nyokangi, 2013). Rohleder and Swartz (2009) note oppressive discourses surrounding intellectual disability in their analysis of HIV awareness teaching provided to special school learners, emphasising how cultural judgments related to HIV infection and sexual behaviour interact with disability stereotypes in a manner which endangers the rights and health of young people with intellectual disability.

Theme 5: Human rights
A large proportion of literature in this theme revolves around the history of the right to education of children with disabilities in South Africa (Engelbrecht, Oswald, Swart, Kitching, & Eloff, 2005; McKenzie, Pillay, Duvenhage, Du Plessis, & Jelsma, 2017; Ngwena, 2014). Up until 2010, the constitution of South Africa cast children with severe to profound intellectual disability as uneducable and thereby denied them equal access to education (McKenzie et al., 2017). In 2010, the High Court instructed the government to provide children with severe to

profound intellectual disabilities with appropriate educational opportunities which they had previously been denied. Although there has been progress in the educational provision of children with disabilities, implementation has been slow (McKenzie et al., 2017). Overall, many children with disabilities in South Africa still do not receive the basic right to education (Engelbrecht et al., 2005).

Against this backdrop of exclusionary policies, parents of children with disabilities have increasingly advocated equality of access to basic education. In a study by Erasmus, Bornman, and Dada (2014), parents of children with disabilities ranked the right to education as equally valuable as their children's right to safety – and these rights above rights of access to medical services; love and understanding; and freedom of speech. Advocacy has primarily revolved around access to inclusive education (Engelbrecht et al., 2005).

Although parents' advocacy for inclusive education was grounded in an attempt to secure children's education, both literature and the condition of mainstream and special education in South Africa begs the question of which of these two approaches is to children's benefit or not. As highlighted by Engelbrecht et al. (2005), "the development of inclusive educational practices in South Africa clearly does not always reflect the values of equity and individual rights" (p. 474). For example, if a child is accepted into a mainstream school because of obligations required by law, but the school does not cater for the child's needs, then the rights of the child are invariably not being met (Engelbrecht et al., 2005).

One of the later shifts to improve children's access to basic education has been the implementation of the 'National Strategy on Screening, Identification, Assessment and Support' (the SIAS Strategy). Some writers, such as Ngwena (2014) argue that the SIAS strategy, which is used to determine a child's capacities to be included in mainstream education, is a contradiction to the inherent principles of inclusive education. Ngwena (2014) believes that the SIAS Strategy does not serve the rights of children with disabilities to education – that is, on an equal basis with others in the communities in which they live. Others, like McKenzie et al. (2017), are in favour of the SIAS Strategy to provide information on the learning needs of children and to assist with planning education appropriate to their needs.

Theme 6: Teacher education
In the apartheid era there was a discrepancy between the training of teachers in the different educational departments. Black African teachers received much shorter and less rigorous training such that huge differences in the quality of teaching on a racial basis were evident by the end of apartheid (Nkabinde, 1993). This posed a challenge to teacher education for inclusion, as conservative chalk-and-talk methods had become entrenched (Walton & Lloyd, 2012). As regards special education, all 14 white universities offered training in special education, but this

was not reflected in any of the black universities (Nkabinde, 1993). EWP 6 states that teachers are the most important resource for inclusive education and that adequate training and professional development is critical (Walton & Lloyd, 2012).

The required shift has proceeded in a somewhat arbitrary manner. Some universities have introduced modules on inclusive education in initial teacher education. In the British Council Report it was noted that 28 percent of teacher education courses included modules that address inclusive education and that the majority of these courses adopt what they call the "silo" approach, where inclusive education modules are presented separately (Majoko & Phasha, 2018). This is in contrast to integrative approaches where inclusive education permeates all courses (Walton & Lloyd, 2012). While this increase in inclusive education training does not meet the need, it has been accompanied by the closure of special needs courses across all universities such that very few teacher special education courses exist from those 14 noted by Nkabinde (1993) above (McKenzie et al., 2018).

There is evidence of continuing professional development such as courses for teachers in schools for children with moderate intellectual disability (Kempen & Steyn, 2017) and recommendations are made for in-service education of teachers by educational audiologists (Van Dijk, Hugo, & Louw, 2004). However, there is a resounding consensus from a host of sources that specific training for teachers in dealing with severe disabilities is completely inadequate and needs to be developed urgently. This consensus confirms that inclusive education training is insufficient to deal with the specific problems of children with visual (Fish-Hodgson & Khumalo, 2016; Human Rights Watch, 2015; McKenzie et al., 2018), hearing (Storbeck & Martin, 2010; Van Dijk et al., 2004) and intellectual impairments (Bornman & Alant, 1996; Kempen & Steyn, 2017; McKenzie et al., 2018).

It appears that any such training would be best conducted in such a way as develops collaboration, agency, and teacher empowerment (Kempen & Steyn, 2017; McKenzie et al., 2018; Walton & Lloyd, 2012). According to a study based on identifying the needs of learners with disabilities the following aspects are recommended: knowledge about the nature of the impairment and specific teaching strategies; skills in the selection and use of assistive devices and the ability to use these devices across the curriculum; and specialist skills in teaching Braille, SASL and alternative and augmentative communication. This needs to be accompanied by a knowledge of disability rights and understanding of how families and children respond to the challenges that disability poses (McKenzie et al., 2018).

Conclusions

The research in South Africa on the needs of children with disabilities is largely subsumed within inclusive education research. While special schools are retained in the system, there is no research within our review that supports their usefulness, which is a significant gap in the literature. While this review may appear to be very critical of special schools and may not reflect day-to-day experiences of schools that are well-run, and which meet the needs of their learners, such experiences are not reflected currently in the research record. Where there is good practice in special schools, and in inclusive settings too, this should be highlighted to increase understanding of which elements contribute to quality education for children with disabilities. Similarly, there is little evidence presented for effective teaching and learning practices – a potential area for further research.

It is apparent that access and quality remain significant issues for children with disabilities, and parents have their work cut out for them in challenging the system in this regard. As is true of all areas of South African life, apartheid has left its stamp in multiple ways, not least of which is the need to address huge backlogs which then overshadow and compound disability-related learning needs.

It is clear that there is a dire shortage of specialist skills within the education system, whether these be located in special, full-service or ordinary schools. Given the overall poor performance of special schools, innovative ways of distributing these skills over an inclusive education system need to be explored. Some suggestions which have been adopted in the education of children with severe to profound intellectual disability include the creation of teams of therapists, teachers, and psychologists (McKenzie et al., 2017). Teacher education cannot only focus on inclusive education in general but must include impairment-specific skills in an incremental manner according to the learners with whom the teacher is working within a specific classroom. This implies that the necessary teaching skills will change over time, and thus continuing professional development would be a critical component in ensuring learners with disabilities are taught by suitably trained teachers.

The division between special and ordinary schools is perhaps one way in which systemic deficit is maintained. We need to question the ways in which this distinction provides a means for looking away from disability in the archaic and infamous apartheid principle of "separate but equal" (Lalvani et al., 2015). We need to give serious consideration as to where we place disability within a diversity framework and to what extent social justice can be served with segregated education systems.

In sum, the area of disability in education in South Africa remains under-researched, which is extremely problematic, given the urgent and extreme crisis of exclusion which we face. Research which highlights best practice in disability inclusion is crucial, as well as exploration of how such work can be effectively upscaled. Teacher training, and how to address the skills deficit, is another key area. Broadly, the implementation of EWP6 has failed for many reasons, but one central one is the failure of government to create budget mechanisms to provide for a host of essential resources, from infrastructure and technology to the capacitation of district-based support teams and the training of teachers and education officials. Until staff at all levels fully understand the requirements of the Constitution regarding the imperative toward inclusion, as well as the directives laid out in EWP6 for their work, there will be no clarity about what must be aimed for, let alone how to achieve it. There is much work to be done.

References

Review articles

Baboo, N. (2011). A Case Study of A Neighbourhood School That Included Two Learners Who are Blind (master's thesis). University of the Western Cape. Retrieved from https://pdfs.semanticscholar.org/a2c5/439d228d29d3492f4b57fbb80b2e851cf394.pdf

Bonato, S. (2018*). Searching the grey literature: A handbook for searching reports, working papers, and other unpublished research.* London: Medical Library Association.

Bornman, J., & Alant, E. (1996). Nonspeaking Children in Schools For Children With Severe Mental Disabilities in The Greater Pretoria Area: Implications For Speech-Language Therapists. *The South African Journal of Communication Disorders*. 43(February), 53-61. https://doi.org/10.4102/sajcd.v43i1.238

Brown, O., Howcroft, G., & Jacobs, T. (2009). The coping orientation and resources of teachers educating learners with intellectual disabilities. *South African Journal of Psychology*, 39(4), 448-459. https://doi.org/10.1177/008124630903900406

Collair, L. J. (2001). *Indicators of successful inclusion of a learner who is deaf in a mainstream class* (Doctoral dissertation, Stellenbosch: Stellenbosch University).

De Sas Kropiwnicki, Z.O., Elphick, J., & Elphick, R. (2014). Standing by themselves: Caregivers' strategies to ensure the right to education for children with disabilities in Orange Farm, South Africa. *Childhood*, 21(3), 354-68. https://doi.org/10.1177/0907568214526263

Devenish, P. (2000). Creating a Book Culture In a Special Needs School With Specific Reference to Visually Impaired Learners. In *International Association of School Librarianship. Selected Papers from the... Annual Conference* (p. 1). International Association of School Librarianship.

Du Toit, P., & Forlin, C. (2009). Cultural transformation for inclusion, what is needed? A South African perspective. *School Psychology International*, 30(6), 644-666. https://doi.org/10.1177/0143034309107081

Ellman, B. (2004). *The experiences of teachers in including learners with intellectual disabilities* (Doctoral dissertation, Stellenbosch: Stellenbosch University).

Engelbrecht, P., Oswald, M., Swart, E., Kitching, A., & Eloff, I. (2005). Parents' Experiences of Their Rights in the Implementation of Inclusive Education in South Africa. *School Psychology International*, 26(4), 459-477. https://doi.org/10.1177/0143034305059021

Erasmus, A., Bornman, J., & Dada, S. (2014). Afrikaans-speaking parents' perceptions of the rights of their children with mild to moderate intellectual disabilities: A descriptive investigation. *Journal of Child Health Care*, 20(2), 234-242. https://doi.org/10.1177/1367493515569326

Fish-Hodgson, T., & Khumalo, S. (2015). Left in the dark: Failure to provide access to quality education to blind and partially sighted learners in South Africa. *Section 27* (Vol. 23).

Fish-Hodgson, T.F., & Khumalo, S. (2016). Too many children left behind: exclusion in the South African inclusive education system, with a focus on Umkhanyakude District, Kwazulu-Natal, (July). Retrieved from http://section27.org.za/wp-content/uploads/2016/08/Umkhanyakude-Report-Final-08082016-1.pdf

Harmston, K., Strong, C., & Evans, D. (2001). Writing to South Africa: International Pen-Pal Correspondence for Student with Language-Learning Disabilities. *The Council for Exceptional Children*. https://doi.org/10.1177/004005990103300307

Holness, W. (2016). The Development and Use of Sign Language in South African Schools: The Denial of Inclusive Education. *Afr. Disability Rts. YB, 4*, 141.

Howgego, C., Miles, S., & Myers, J. (2014). Inclusive Learning: Children with disabilities and difficulties in learning. *Health and Education Advice and Resource Team*, 22(7), 663-667.

Human Rights Watch, H.R. (2015). "Complicit in Exclusion" South Africa's Failure to Guarantee an Inclusive Education for Children with Disabilities.

Jairaj, S. (1996). The inclusion of a deaf learner in a regular school? a case study., (December). Retrieved from http://researchspace.ukzn.ac.za/xmlui/handle/10413/3191

Kempen, M.E., & Steyn, G.M. (2017). An Investigation of Teachers' Collaborative Learning in a Continuous Professional Development Programme in South African Special Schools. *Journal of Asian and African Studies*, 52(2), 157-171. https://doi.org/10.1177/0021909615570950

Kilian, D. (2001). English literacy as a second language in deaf grade one children: a bilingual-bicultural perspective on the pedagogy of initial reading. University of Witwatersrand.

McKenzie, J.A., Pillay, S.G., Duvenhage, C.M., Du Plessis, E., & Jelsma, J.M. (2017). Implementation of Educational Provision for Children with Severe to Profound Intellectual Disability in the Western Cape: From Rights to Reality. *International Journal of Disability, Development and Education*, 64(6), 596-611. https://doi.org/10.1080/1034912X.2017.1313394

McKenzie, J., Kelly, J., & Shanda, N. (2018). Starting where we are: Situational analysis of the educational needs of learners with severe to profound sensory or intellectual impairments in South Africa. *Disability Innovations Africa*.

Molteno, C. (2006). Education and intellectual disability in South Africa. *Journal of Child and Adolescent Mental Health*, 18(2).

Naicker, S. (2014). Special education today in South Africa. Advances in Special Education. https://doi.org/10.1108/S0270-401320140000028020

Ngwena, C.G. (2014). Human right to inclusive education: Exploring a double discourse of inclusive education using South Africa as a case study. *Netherlands Quarterly of Human Rights*, 31(4), 473-504. https://doi.org/10.1177/016934411303100405

Nkabinde, Z. (1993). The role of special education in changing South Africa. *The Journal of Special Education*, 27(1), 107-114. https://doi.org/10.1177/002246699302700107

Nyokangi, D., & Phasha, N. (2016). Factors Contributing to Sexual Violence at Selected Schools for Learners with Mild Intellectual Disability in South Africa. *Journal of Applied Research in Intellectual Disabilities*, 29(3), 231-241. https://doi.org/10.1111/jar.12173

Pather, S. (2011). Evidence on inclusion and support for learners with disabilities in mainstream schools in South Africa: Off the policy radar? *International Journal of Inclusive Education*, 15(10), 1103-117. https://doi.org/10.1080/13603116.2011.555075

Peel, E. (2004). Inclusive practice in South Africa: a deaf education perspective. University of Witwatersrand. Retrieved from http://0-search.ebscohost.com.innopac.wits.ac.za/login.aspx?direct=true&db=awn&AN=NX0160508&site=ehost-live&scope=site&scope=cite

Phasha, T.N., & Nyokangi, D. (2012). School-Based Sexual Violence Among Female Learners with Mild Intellectual Disability in South Africa. *Violence Against Women*, 18(3), 309-321. https://doi.org/10.1177/1077801212444578

Ram, A. (1998). *An investigation into the social identity of the South African deaf community: Implications for the education of deaf learners*. University of KwaZulu-Natal.

Rohleder, P., & Swartz, L. (2009). Providing sex education to persons with learning disabilities in the era of HIV/AIDS: Tensions between discourses of human rights and restriction. *Journal of Health Psychology*, 14(4), 601-610. https://doi.org/10.1177/1359105309103579

Rule, P., & Modipa, T.R. (2012). "We must believe in ourselves": Attitudes and experiences of adult learners with disabilities in KwaZulu-Natal, South Africa. *Adult Education Quarterly*, 62(2), 138-58. https://doi.org/10.1177/0741713611400303

Sethosa, M. (2001). Assisting teachers to support mildly intellectually disabled learners in the foundation phase in accordance with the policy of inclusion, (June). Retrieved from http://uir.unisa.ac.za/handle/10500/17719

Storbeck, C. (2012). A Professional Development Programme for Teachers of the Deaf. Teaching for all: Mainstreaming Inclusive Education in South Africa. (2018). The state of inclusive education in South Africa and the implications for teacher training programmes. Research Report December 2018.

UNICEF. (2012). Children with Disabilities in South Africa, 6-103. Retrieved from http://www.wcpd.gov.za/

Van Dijk, C., Hugo, R., & Louw, B. (2004). The needs of teachers of children with hearing loss within the inclusive education system. *The South African Journal of Communication Disorders. Die Suid-Afrikaanse Tydskrif vir Kommunikasieafwykings*, 51(6), 23-44. https://doi.org/10.4102/sajcd.v51i1.208

Van Reenen, C., & Karusseit, C. (2017). Classroom acoustics as a consideration for inclusive education in South Africa. *South African Journal of Communication Disorders*, 64(1), 1-15. https://doi.org/10.4102/sajcd.v64i1.550

Van Staden, A. (2013). An evaluation of an intervention using sign language and multi-sensory coding to support word learning and reading comprehension of deaf signing children. *Child Language Teaching and Therapy*, 29(3), 305-318. https://doi.org/10.1177/0265659013479961

Walton, E. (2011). Using literature as a strategy to promote inclusivity in high school classrooms. *Intervention in School and Clinic*, 47(4), 224-233. https://doi.org/10.1177/1053451211424604

Walton, E., & Lloyd, G. (2012). From clinic to classroom: A model of teacher education for inclusion. *Perspectives in Education*, 30(2), 62-70.

Additional references

Aromataris, E., & Munn, Z. (2020). *JBI manual for evidence synthesis*. Australia: JBI. Available from https://synthesismanual.jbi.global. https://doi.org/10.46658/JBIMES-20-01

Connor, D. (2019). Why is Special Education So Afraid of Disability Studies? Analyzing Attacks of Disdain and Distortion from Leaders in the Field. *Journal of Curriculum Theorizing*, 34(1), 10-21.

Department of Education (2001). Education White Paper 6. *Special needs education: Building an inclusive education and training system.* D. o. Education. Pretoria, Government Printer.

Department of Basic Education (2016). Education Statistics in South Africa 2014. B. Education. Pretoria Department of Basic Education.

Department of Basic Education (2018). NSC 2018 Examination Report. B. Education. Pretoria, Department of Basic Education.

Lalvani, Priya, Broderick Alicia A., Fine, Michelle, Jacobowitz, Tina, & Michelli, Nicholas. (2015). Teacher education, Exclusion, and the implicit ideology of Separate but Equal: An invitation to a dialogue. *Education, Citizenship and Social Justice*, 10(2), 168-183. https://doi.org/10.1177/1746197915583935

McKenzie, J. (2010). Constructing the intellectually disabled person as a subject of education: A discourse analysis using Q-methodology. Unpublished PhD thesis Grahamstown, Rhodes University.

Munn, Z., Peters, M.D.J., Stern, C., Tufanaru, C., McArthur, A., & Aromataris, E. (2018). Systematic review or scoping review? Guidance for authors when choosing between a systematic or scoping review approach. *BMC Medical Research Methodology*, 18(1), 1-7. https://doi.org/10.1186/s12874-018-0611-x

Republic of South Africa (1996). *The Constitution Act No. 108 of 1996.* Pretoria, Government Printer.

Republic of South Africa (1996). *South African Schools Act, no. 84 of 1996.* Government Gazette 377(17579).

Statistics South Africa (2014). *Profile of persons with disabilities in South Africa.* Pretoria, Statistics South Africa.

Sucharew, H., & Macaluso, M. (2019). Methods for research evidence synthesis: The scoping review approach. *Journal of Hospital Medicine*, 14(7), 416-418. https://doi.org/10.12788/jhm.3248

United Nations (2006). Convention on the rights of Persons with Disabilities. Retrieved 2 September, 2008, from http://www.un.org/disabilities/.

Appendix 8.1 *List of reviewed articles according to theme*

Theme 1: Inclusive education discourse and disability	1	Du Toit, P., & Forlin, C. (2009). Cultural transformation for inclusion, what is needed? A South African perspective. *School Psychology International*, 30(6), 644-666. https://doi.org/10.1177/0143034309107081
	2	DSD, DWCPD and UNICEF. 2012. *Children with Disabilities in South Africa: A Situation* Analysis: 2001-2011. Pretoria: Department of Social Development/Department of Women, Children and People with Disabilities/UNICEF
	3	Fish-Hodgson, T.F., & Khumalo, S. (2016). Too many children left behind: exclusion in the South African inclusive education system, with a focus on Umkhanyakude District, Kwazulu-Natal, (July). Retrieved from http://section27.org.za/wp-content/uploads/2016/08/Umkhanyakude-Report-Final-08082016-1.pdf
	4	Khumalo, S., & Hodgson, T.F. (2017). The right to basic education for children with disabilities. *Basic Education Rights Handbook – Education Rights in South Africa*, 105-127.
	5	McKenzie, J.A., Pillay, S.G., Duvenhage, C.M., Du Plessis, E., & Jelsma, J.M. (2017). Implementation of Educational Provision for Children with Severe to Profound Intellectual Disability in the Western Cape: From Rights to Reality. *International Journal of Disability, Development and Education*, 64(6), 596-611. https://doi.org/10.1080/1034912X.2017.1313394
	6	Molteno, C. (2006). Education and intellectual disability in South Africa. *Journal of Child and Adolescent Mental Health*, 18(2). https://doi.org/10.2989/17280580609486620
	7	Naicker, S. (2014). Special education today in South Africa. *Advances in Special Education*. https://doi.org/10.1108/S0270-401320140000028020
	8	Ngwena, C. G. (2014). Human right to inclusive education: Exploring a double discourse of inclusive education using South Africa as a case study. *Netherlands Quarterly of Human Rights*, 31(4), 473-504.
	9	Nkabinde, Z. (1993). The role of special education in changing South Africa. *The Journal of Special Education*, 27(1), 107-114.
	10	Pather, S. (2011). Evidence on inclusion and support for learners with disabilities in mainstream schools in South Africa: Off the policy radar? *International Journal of Inclusive Education*, 15(10), 1103-1117. https://doi.org/10.1080/13603116.2011.555075
	11	Peel, E. (2004). Inclusive practice in South Africa: a deaf education perspective. University of Witwatersrand. Retrieved from http://0-search.ebscohost.com.innopac.wits.ac.za/login.aspx?direct=true&db=awn&AN=NX0160508&site=ehost-live&scope=site&scope=cite
	12	Walton, E. (2010). Getting Inclusion Right in South Africa. *Intervention in School and Clinic*, 46(4), 240-245. https://doi.org/10.1177/1053451210389033
	13	Storbeck, C., & Martin, D. (2010). South African deaf education and the deaf community. *American annals of the deaf*, 155(4), 488-490..
	14	Storbeck, C. (2012). *A Professional Development Programme for Teachers of the Deaf*. Teaching for all: Mainstreaming Inclusive Education in South Africa. (2018). The state of inclusive education in South Africa and the implications for teacher training programmes: Research Report December 2018.

	15	Baboo, N. (2011). A Case Study of A Neighbourhood School That Included Two Learners Who are (Masters thesis, University of Western Cape, Bellville, South Africa). Retrieved from https://pdfs.semanticscholar.org/a2c5/439d228d29d3492f4b5 7fbb80b2e851cf.394.pdf
	16	Bornman, J., & Alant, E. (1996). Nonspeaking Children in Schools For Children With Severe Mental Disabilities in The Greater Pretoria Area: Implications For Speech-Language Therapists. *The South African Journal of Communication Disorders*, 43(February), 53-61.
	17	Collair, L. (2001). Indicators of Successful Inclusion of a Learner Who is Deaf in a Mainstream Class. Stellenbosch University.
	18	Devenish, P. (2000). Creating a Book Culture in a Special Needs School with Specific Reference to Visually Impaired Learners, 1-14.
	19	Harmston, K., Strong, C., & Evans, D. (2001). Writing to South Africa: International Pen-Pal Correspondence for Student with Language-Learning Disabilities. The Council for Exceptional Children.
	20	Howgego, C., Miles, S., & Myers, J. (2014). Inclusive Learning: Children with disabilities and difficulties in learning. *Health and Education Advice and Resource Team*, 22(7), 663-667.
Theme 2: Teaching and Learning	21	Jairaj, S. (1996). The inclusion of a deaf learner in a regular school? a case study., (December). Retrieved from http://researchspace.ukzn.ac.za/xmlui/handle/10413 /3191
	22	Kilian, D. (2001). English literacy as a second language in deaf grade one children: a bilingual-bicultural perspective on the pedagogy of initial reading. University of Witwatersrand.
	23	Loewenstein, H. (2005). Support for Learners with Intellectual Disabilities in the Transition to Secondary Schools. *Educational Psychology*, (December).
	24	McCallum, R. S. (2017). Context for nonverbal assessment of intelligence and related abilities. In *Handbook of nonverbal assessment* (pp. 3-19). Springer, Cham.
	25	McKenzie, J., Kelly, J., & Shanda, N. (2018). Starting where we are: Situational analysis of the educational needs of learners with severe to profound sensory or intellectual impairments in South Africa. *Disability Innovations Africa*.
	26	Nel, M. (2019). Voices from the field: Early Childhood inclusion in South Africa. *Young Exceptional Children*, 22(1), 3–5. https://doi.org/10.1177/1096250617742599
	27	Reenen, C. Van, & Karusseit, C. (2017). Classroom acoustics as a consideration for inclusive education in South Africa. *South African Journal of Communication Disorders*, 64(1), 1-15.
	28	Sethosa, M. (2001). Assisting teachers to support mildly intellectually disabled learners in the foundation phase in accordance with the policy of inclusion, (June). Retrieved from http://uir.unisa.ac.za/handle/10500/17719
	29	Van Staden, A. (2013). An evaluation of an intervention using sign language and multi-sensory coding to support word learning and reading comprehension of deaf signing children. *Child Language Teaching and Therapy*, 29(3), 305-318. https://doi.org /10.1177/0265659013479961
	30	Walton, E. (2011). Using literature as a strategy to promote inclusivity in high school classrooms. *Intervention in School and Clinic*, 47(4), 224-233. https://doi.org/10.1177 /1053451211424604

Theme 3: Parents' Perspectives	31	De Sas Kropiwnicki, Z.O., Elphick, J., & Elphick, R. (2014). Standing by themselves: Caregivers' strategies to ensure the right to education for children with disabilities in Orange Farm, South Africa. *Childhood*, 21(3), 354-368. https://doi.org/10.1177/0907568214526263
	32	Engelbrecht, P., Oswald, M., Swart, E., Kitching, A., & Eloff, I. (2005). Parents' Experiences of Their Rights in the Implementation of Inclusive Education in South Africa. *School Psychology International*, 26(4), 459-477. https://doi.org/10.1177/0143034305059021
	33	McKenzie, J., Kelly, J., & Shanda, N. (2018). Starting where we are: Situational analysis of the educational needs of learners with severe to profound sensory or intellectual impairments in South Africa. *Disability Innovations Africa*.
	34	Bornman, J., & Alant, E. (1996). Nonspeaking Children in Schools For Children With Severe Mental Disabilities in the Greater Pretoria Area: Implications For Speech-Language Therapists. *The South African Journal of Communication Disorders*, 43 (February), 53-61.
Theme 4: Disability, race and special education	35	Fish-Hodgson, T., & Khumalo, S. (2015). Left in the dark: Failure to provide access to quality education to blind and partially sighted learners in South Africa. *Section 27* (Vol. 23).
	36	Fish-Hodgson, T.F., & Khumalo, S. (2016). Too many children left behind: exclusion in the South African inclusive education system, with a focus on Umkhanyakude District, Kwazulu-Natal, (July). Retrieved from http://section27.org.za/wp-content/uploads/2016/08/Umkhanyakude-Report-Final-08082016-1.pdf
	37	Human Rights Watch, H. R. (2015). *"Complicit in Exclusion" South Africa's Failure to Guarantee an Inclusive Education for Children with Disabilities*.
	38	Khumalo, S., & Hodgson, T. F. (2017). The right to basic education for children with disabilities. *Basic Education Rights Handbook – Education Rights in South Africa*, 105-127.
	39	McKenzie, J., Kelly, J., & Shanda, N. (2018). Starting where we are: Situational analysis of the educational needs of learners with severe to profound sensory or intellectual impairments in South Africa. *Disability Innovations Africa*.
	40	Molteno, C. (2006). Education and intellectual disability in South Africa. *Journal of Child and Adolescent Mental Health*, 18(2). https://doi.org/10.2989/17280580609486620
	41	Nkabinde, Z. (1993). The role of special education in changing South Africa. *The Journal of Special Education*, 27(1), 107-114.
	42	Nyokangi, D., & Phasha, N. (2016). Factors Contributing to Sexual Violence at Selected Schools for Learners with Mild Intellectual Disability in South Africa. *Journal of Applied Research in Intellectual Disabilities*, 29(3), 231-241. https://doi.org/10.1111/jar.12173
	43	Phasha, T.N., & Nyokangi, D. (2012). School-Based Sexual Violence Among Female Learners with Mild Intellectual Disability in South Africa. *Violence Against Women*, 18(3), 309-321. https://doi.org/10.1177/1077801212444578
	44	Ram, A. (1998). An investigation into the social identity of the South African deaf community: Implications for the education of deaf learners. University of Natal.
	45	Rule, P., & Modipa, T.R. (2012). "We must believe in ourselves": Attitudes and experiences of adult learners with disabilities in KwaZulu-Natal, South Africa. *Adult Education Quarterly*, 62(2), 138-158. https://doi.org/10.1177/0741713611400303
	46	Rohleder, P., & Swartz, L. (2009). Providing sex education to persons with learning disabilities in the era of HIV/AIDS: Tensions between discourses of human rights and restriction. *Journal of Health Psychology*, 14(4), 601-610. https://doi.org/10.1177/1359105309103579
	47	Storbeck, C., & Martin, D. (2010). South African deaf education and the deaf community. *American annals of the deaf*, 155(4), 488-490.

Theme 5: Human Rights	48	De Sas Kropiwnicki, Z.O., Elphick, J., & Elphick, R. (2014). Standing by themselves: Caregivers' strategies to ensure the right to education for children with disabilities in Orange Farm, South Africa. *Childhood*, 21(3), 354-368. https://doi.org/10.1177/0907568214526263
	49	Engelbrecht, P., Oswald, M., Swart, E., Kitching, A., & Eloff, I. (2005). Parents' Experiences of Their Rights in the Implementation of Inclusive Education in South Africa. *School Psychology International*, 26(4), 459-477. https://doi.org/10.1177/0143034305059021
	50	Erasmus, A., Bornman, J., & Dada, S. (2014). Afrikaans-speaking parents' perceptions of the rights of their children with mild to moderate intellectual disabilities: A descriptive investigation. *Journal of Child Health Care*, 20(2), 234-242. https://doi.org/10.1177/1367493515556932
	51	Fish-Hodgson, T.F., & Khumalo, S. (2016). Too many children left behind: exclusion in the South African inclusive education system, with a focus on Umkhanyakude District, Kwazulu-Natal, (July). Retrieved from http://section27.org.za/wp-content/uploads/2016/08/Umkhanyakude-Report-Final-08082016-1.pdf
	52	McKenzie, J.A., Pillay, S.G., Duvenhage, C.M., Du Plessis, E., & Jelsma, J.M. (2017). Implementation of Educational Provision for Children with Severe to Profound Intellectual Disability in the Western Cape: From Rights to Reality. *International Journal of Disability, Development and Education*, 64(6), 596-611. https://doi.org/10.1080/1034912X.2017.1313394
	53	McKenzie, J., Kelly, J., & Shanda, N. (2018). Starting where we are: Situational analysis of the educational needs of learners with severe to profound sensory or intellectual impairments in South Africa. *Disability Innovations Africa*.
	54	Ngwena, C.G. (2014). Human right to inclusive education: Exploring a double discourse of inclusive education using South Africa as a case study. *Netherlands Quarterly of Human Rights*, 31(4), 473-504.

Theme 6: Teacher Education	55	Brown, O., Howcroft, G., & Jacobs, T. (2009). The coping orientation and resources of teachers educating learners with intellectual disabilities. *South African Journal of Psychology*, 39(4), 448-459. https://doi.org/10.1177/008124630903900406
	56	Ellman, B. (2004). *The experiences of teachers in including learners with intellectual disabilities* (Doctoral dissertation, Stellenbosch: Stellenbosch University).
	57	Eloff, I., & Kgwete, L. K. (2007). South African teachers' voices on support in inclusive education. *Childhood Education*, 83(6), 351-355.
	58	Kempen, M.E., & Steyn, G.M. (2017). An Investigation of Teachers' Collaborative Learning in a Continuous Professional Development Programme in South African Special Schools. *Journal of Asian and African Studies*, 52(2), 157-171. https://doi.org/10.1177/0021909615570950
	59	McCallum, R. S. (2017). Context for nonverbal assessment of intelligence and related abilities. In *Handbook of nonverbal assessment* (pp. 3-19). Springer, Cham.
	60	McKenzie, J., Kelly, J., & Shanda, N. (2018). Starting where we are: Situational analysis of the educational needs of learners with severe to profound sensory or intellectual impairments in South Africa. *Disability Innovations Africa*.
	61	Naicker, S. (2014). Special education today in South Africa. Advances in Special Education. https://doi.org/10.1108/S0270-401320140000028020
	62	Sethosa, M. (2001). Assisting teachers to support mildly intellectually disabled learners in the foundation phase in accordance with the policy of inclusion, (June). Retrieved from http://uir.unisa.ac.za/handle/10500/17719
	63	Storbeck, C. (2012). A Professional Development Programme for Teachers of the Deaf. Teaching for all: Mainstreaming Inclusive Education in South Africa. (2018). The state of inclusive education in South Africa and the implications for teacher training programmes: *Research Report December 2018*.
	64	Van Dijk, C., Hugo, R., & Louw, B. (2004). The needs of teachers of children with hearing loss within the inclusive education system. *The South African Journal of Communication Disorders. Die Suid-Afrikaanse Tydskrif vir Kommunikasieafwykings*, 51(6), 23-44.
	65	Walton, E., & Lloyd, G. (2012). From clinic to classroom: A model of teacher education for inclusion. *Perspectives in Education*, 30(2), 62-70.

CHAPTER 9

Research on mathematics teacher knowledge in Southern Africa: A 2010-2018 systematic review

Judah P. Makonye
Mathematics Education Division, University of the Witwatersrand School of Education, University of the Witwatersrand
Email: Judah.Makonye@wits.ac.za

Abstract

This systematic review focuses on the research of mathematics knowledge for teaching (MKT) in Southern Africa. MKT is an emerging research theme propounded by Ball et al. (2008) to explain how pedagogical content knowledge (PCK) can be extended to teaching mathematics. The review considered journal articles published in specialist mathematics education journals in Sothern Africa and other educational journals where mathematics education research is published. Focusing on the years 2010 to 2018 inclusive, the review uses the MKT framework to code the articles. The review shows that research in MKT is ongoing. The knowledge of content and students (KC&S) and knowledge of content and teaching (KC&T) domains are well researched but of particular concern is the low research on the specialised content knowledge (SCK) domain, which is central to teachers' unpacking of mathematics concepts to make then meaningful to learners and avoid rote learning. In addition, common content knowledge (CCK) is shown to be under-researched in a context where this domain underlines the mathematics under-achievement trap in South Africa. The review also shows that research on an important component of KC&S; learner errors and misconceptions is being published more in the Pythagoras journal, while the ARJMSTE journal is only beginning to publish on that theme. Also, publications of the research favour former white universities while other researchers from other South African universities and the region lag behind. Publication on MKT in top-end international mathematics education journals by Southern African authors is growing but still limited to a few mathematics education researchers linked to the privileged former white universities. Recommendations for practice, policy and further research are proffered.

Keywords: Systematic research, mathematics professionally situated knowledge, Southern Africa

Background and rationale

This systematic review article is guided by the Campbell review protocol evidence' (Campbell Collaboration, 2001). The overarching aim of Campbell reviews is 'to gather, summarize and integrate empirical research to help people understand the evidence' (Campbell Collaboration, 2001, p.3). Inevitably, this review is partial as it is drawn from publications selected from research in the Southern Africa mathematics education space.

Systematic reviews of mathematics education research are common overseas but are not as numerous in Southern Africa. Krainer and Goffree (1999) undertook a systematic review of mathematics education research in the European Union. Krainer and Goffree (1999) differentiated four categories of research in mathematics education which are; research in perspectives for teacher education, research on the context of teacher education, research on teacher education, and on research as teacher education. They argued that "the results of the research can be used as a basis for improving learning environments in teacher education" (Krainer & Goffree, 1999, p.233). This systematic review focuses on the category of 'research on teacher education' in Southern Africa. Therefore, it attempts to answer the broad question; 'What kind of knowledge and skills a person needs to be a "good" mathematics teacher?' (Sanchez Mario, 2011, p.2) in Southern Africa.

Earlier research regarded teacher mathematical content knowledge as the most important knowledge for a mathematics teacher but in recent times, there is widespread agreement that mathematics content knowledge alone is insufficient to effect learner outcomes. Current research discounts the opinion that a teacher's content knowledge would readily transform to good teaching and learning. Now other kinds of mathematical teacher knowledge and skills, regarded as Professionally Situated Knowledge (PSK) (Manizade & Martinovic, 2016) have been identified for one to be a good teacher; such as knowledge of content and knowledge of students (KC&S) and specialized content knowledge (SCK) (Ball, Thames & Phelps, 2008).

In the USA, the second International handbook on research in mathematics education (Bishop, Clemence, Keitel & Leung, 2003) introduced the theme; 'research on teacher knowledge'. It was observed that teaching mathematics required specialist knowledge that was not generally available in many teacher education curricula. In South Africa, Adler (2005) argued for rich mathematics tasks as critical in developing mathematics teachers' specialist knowledge for teaching mathematics. This theme for specialist knowledge for teaching mathematics has grown today to be quite important as embodied by PCK (Shulman, 1986), Mathematics Knowledge for Teaching (MKT) (Ball, 2008) and PSK (Manizade & Martinovic, 2016).

Adler (2005) reported on the massification of access to education not only in South Africa but across the world, where access to education has become a human rights issue. She argued that for quality mathematics education to succeed, then research for teachers to have the know-how to teach mathematics was imperative. Adler made a review on mathematics education research based on the SAARMSTE conference proceedings (1993-2002). She noted that most of the research was on single teachers and their classes; there were very few large-scale studies on teacher education. Only 14 out of 143 papers that is 9.8% at the conference proceedings were on research on teacher knowledge. This author will comment later in the analysis if there is any change in the years after Adler's study post 2002. It was also noted that despite a decade of a democratically elected government, apartheid's legacy and increasing disparity in society continued unabated in a country where education is regarded as a major catalyst for social change.

Later in 2009, another review of research in mathematics education covering the years 2000–2006 (Venkat, Adler, Rollnick, Setati, & Vhurumuku, 2009) was published. Following that, another review was done for research in mathematics education in Southern Africa for the years 2007-2015 (Pournara, Hodgen, Adler & Pillay, 2015). That review explored, 'the relationship between the published research and policy and practice in mathematics education, and the extent to which the spread of research was inter-connected and so accumulating' (Adler, Alshwaikh, Essack & Gcsamba, 2017; p.1). Noted was 'an established, albeit relatively young and also fragile, field of mathematics education research in the country, with biases towards small qualitative studies at the secondary level, and a relatively small quantitative research' (p.1). The results showed an increasingly strong mathematics education research community in Southern Africa. Also noted was an increase in research on primary mathematics teaching and learning.

The continuous reviews on research in mathematics education in South Africa are very important in marking trends in the field; however, they are quite general. This review adds to these reviews in that it focuses on an emerging topic in mathematics education, that is teacher knowledge for teaching mathematics. This topic augments PCK first established by Shulman (1986) and has of recent times become eminent in mathematics education. Therefore in a way this review traces its development in the past 10 years.

Problem Scoping: Mathematics teacher knowledge problem in South Africa

The theme of teacher knowledge is becoming increasingly important in educational research (de Clercq & Shalem, 2015). In Clercq and Shalem (2015)'s review of educational research in South Africa, these authors concluded that for the improvement of South African education, research was imperative on the theme; 'deeper teacher knowledge of subject matter and subject knowledge for teaching' (p. 25).

For some time, educational researchers around the world (see for example Porrance, 2000; Chall & Jacobs, 2003) have reported on disadvantaged, low socioeconomic status learners' fourth-grade slump. This scenario is common in South Africa in that from grade 4 disadvantaged learners' performance in mathematics begins to retard. This scenario is referred to as 'Education in Crisis' (Fleisch, 2008). It is shown that once this slump begins, learners retrogressively fall behind the mathematics curriculum with little hope of catching up. Learners' retrogression is proportional to their grade with the mathematics achievement gap between learners increasing exponentially between learners of the same cohort. Consequently, while some learners might have a chronological age of twelve or thirteen years for example, in terms of mathematics, most may operate at the age of a nine-year-old. The grade 4 slump discussed here results in a disproportionate number of learners who drop mathematics as a school subject or opt to study mathematical literacy. This scenario demonstrates that the journey to an equitable society where education acts as the main catalyst for repair, redress and reform (Adler & Pillay, 2016) is still a long one. This is because the lack of proper school mathematics qualifications limits children's chances of a bright career, since mathematics is a gate-keeper to the most important professions. Thus while education at its most noble stage aims to be the great equalizer, it is a myth because in effect it maintains if not increases social inequality.

In this systematic research, I regard the teachers' mathematics teaching knowledge as a factor that can ameliorate the learners' challenges described above. Firstly, the teachers' Pedagogical Content Knowledge (PCK) (Shulman, 1986/1987) in teaching mathematics is neither well-articulated nor systematic. PCK is the knowledge that teachers develop as they transform content knowledge for teaching. Secondly, teachers' teaching is curriculum centred, mainly driven by CAPS prescriptions rather than learner-centred approaches in that teachers rarely take into account or listen (Davis, 1997) to the difficulties that learners face in learning mathematics, mainly their current concepts and misconceptions. In research circles, it is now widely agreed that although subject matter content knowledge is vital for teachers, it is not enough for a teacher to teach a subject effectively (Mavhunga & Rollnick, 2013). What teachers need is Mathematics Knowledge for Teaching (MKT) (Ball, Thames & Phelps, 2008) to teach mathematics in ways that take into account the most helpful mathematical presentations (termed Specialised Content Knowledge (SCK)), together with learners' current mathematics conceptions and misconceptions (termed Knowledge of Content and Knowledge of Students (KC&S) to make mathematics understandable to their learners. As Pournara, Sanders, Adler and Hodgen (2016) have noted, much research done on South African mathematics education shows what the learners cannot do.

The ultimate aim of any educational research is to affect positive changes in learners, particularly those from disadvantaged backgrounds. As Hargreaves

(1999) argues, the bar for educational research is low when compared to other fields such as medicine. There seems to be little accountability in educational research as educational researchers seem to focus on theoretical knowledge quite divorced from the practical needs of teachers and learners in the classroom. Teachers require hands-on practical knowledge they can apply to solve their day-to-day mathematics teaching challenges, and policymakers as well. This issue is highlighted particularly in South Africa where learner under-achievement in mathematics is commonplace. What important research findings over the years can be gleaned to advise practitioners, policymakers and researchers on this issue?

In medicine, there is an unremitting systematic review of research so that the best research informs practice for the betterment of patients. On the other hand, in education, such urgency to adopt research findings into teaching practice is not assured because there is no such systematic research to mark advances in research in teaching and learning. Educational researchers, mainly in universities and teachers in the schools seem to work parallel to each other instead of collaborating. I argue that in Southern Africa; for research to impact practice, isolating High Leverage Mathematics Teaching Practices (HLMTP) (Ball, Thames & Phelps, 2008) from research needs to come to the fore and be shared. HLMTPs are those teaching practices that maximise mathematics learner outcomes from a supposedly 'minimum' effort. Therefore good research results need to be identified and shared through systematic research. Other researchers recommend that for good research uptake to be effective, research advocates such as change agents and opinion leaders are necessary. Yet others have argued that the 'carrot and stick' technique is helpful; that if practitioners are given funding and rewards for implementing research findings or are sanctioned for not doing so then good research can impact teaching and learning.

Mathematics education research in Southern Africa

Since the dawn of democracy in 1994, considerable research in mathematics education has been undertaken in Southern Africa to promote equity and reverse the effects of apartheid. Most of that research has been spearheaded by organisations such Association of Mathematics Teachers of South Africa (AMESA) nationally, and Southern Africa Association of Research Mathematics Science and Technology Education (SAARMSTE) regionally. At international levels, organisations such as the International Commission of Mathematics Education (ICME) and the International Group of Psychology of Mathematics Education (PME). All these research organizations hold periodic research conferences where researchers showcase their research and there is knowledge interchange. The National Research Foundation (NRF) of South Africa in collaboration with universities and other research institutions play a big role in funding and encouraging educational research. In this research, the publications in international mathematics education journals will be excluded mainly because of time and expense. Also, I focus on research within reach of practitioners, policymakers and academics mainly in Southern Africa.

Purpose of the review

This article aims to do a systematic review of research on mathematics teacher knowledge in Southern Africa from 2010-2018 inclusive.

In pursuant to the aim, several questions are explored in this review;

- What high-level mathematics teaching practices (HLMTP) in terms of MKT (Ball, et al., 2008)'s domains have been published on mathematics teacher knowledge by Southern African researchers in Southern African and international journals?
- What gaps continue to exist in mathematics teacher knowledge to boost the teaching and learning of mathematics in Southern Africa? What do we seem to know quite well about mathematics teacher knowledge in Southern Africa and what do we not know so well?
- What outcomes of the review on research on mathematics teacher knowledge in Southern Africa are meaningful to policy; practice and further research?

Methodological approach and data collection

The purpose of the methods section of a protocol is to describe operationally how the review was conducted. Content analysis methodology on data from published journal articles drove the systematic review.

The criteria for inclusion and exclusion of studies in the review is discussed in the following. The review included the publications on mathematics teacher knowledge at basic education level in Southern Africa. These were:

- 2010-2018 (inclusive) publications in specialist Southern African mathematics education journals. These are Pythagoras and African Research Journal in Mathematics, Science and Technology Education (ARJMSTE),
- Other educational journals in Southern Africa namely, South African Journal of Education, Perspectives in Education, African Educational Review, Journal of Educational Studies and Education as Change
- Top-end international mathematics education journals such as Educational Studies in Mathematics, ZDM, International Journal of Science and Mathematics Education

The database mainly used is SABINET; a South African based database that includes educational research journals of mainly African origin. SABINET is subscribed to by my institution's library so I could readily access the journals without due payment. However, other journals such as African Educational Review are not on SABINET but were readily accessible online without payment. Other journals, such as Education as Change at present do not have the years 2010-2016 online or on SABINET so it was difficult to access some of its publications during these years. I also accessed Google Scholar and Researchgate. Google Scholar was quite helpful as I could readily read the abstracts of the articles to help me with coding. There was also hand search of journals on the internet.

The search words that were used include; mathematics teacher content knowledge, teacher knowledge, mathematics teacher methodology, pedagogical content knowledge, mathematics lesson preparation, teaching mathematics; methods of teaching mathematics, errors and misconceptions in mathematics. This list is not exhaustive.

The relevance decisions were based on readings of research topics, abstracts and recommendations of the research. The reliability and validity of the decisions for inclusion were based on whether the research was on mathematics teacher knowledge at basic education level in South Africa. I excluded any research published by researchers in or outside Southern Africa that does not explicitly focus on teaching and learning mathematics in Southern Africa at basic education level.

Rationale for choosing the sources

The main database used to select the journal articles is SABINET. SABINET is a South African based research database. It stores most of the African research articles including in education. In particular, this database is accessed through my institution's library. Therefore, there was ready access to the journals and the articles. Without this facility, it would have been quite challenging because most sources require payment.

Description of methods used in the component studies

No systematic review can do everything particularly due to limitations of funding as well as time. Further, this systematic review on research in mathematics education in Southern Africa required at most 8000 words. These constraints dictated that only what is possible could be done. As such, within the time and resources, the review was done based mainly on the publications on the main mathematics education journals in Southern Africa as well as other general education journals in Southern Africa that also published articles in mathematics education although on a smaller scale. Notwithstanding these limitations, the author believes a good review was possible because the selection of the journals was good. This is supported in probability theory which asserts that a well select small sample can be highly informative of the behaviour of the population which does not improve through using a larger sample.

Analytical framework

For reviewing research on mathematical teacher knowledge in Southern Africa the Ball et al. (2008) framework will be used.

MKT covers both the domains of traditional pedagogical content knowledge of mathematics content and knowledge of students (KCS), as well as, knowledge of content and teaching (KCT). The other domains of mathematics knowledge for teaching centering on subject matter knowledge are common content knowledge (CCK), or simply content knowledge comparable to the mathematics that other professions different from teaching also use mathematics. Then there is specialised content knowledge (SCK). This is content knowledge which is special for teachers to understand how mathematics content can be broken down or represented so that learners can understand it; this knowledge is relevant to teachers in their day to day work as they explain concepts to learners (Ball et al., 2008). Such knowledge is not required in other professions. Manizade and Martinovi (2016) regard all these as professionally situated knowledge (PSK). Journal articles from major educational journals in Southern Africa were used as the source of data on research on MKT. Examples of how the coding was done using this protocol are given in the following. Besides, the topic, the coding was done after studying the abstract, research questions, findings and recommendations of each study.

Findings and discussion

The analysis of the journal articles was done based on the object of the six MKT domains. The analysis was based firstly on the number of publications per year per journal over the 2010-2018 period. Secondly, it was done overally on the number of articles on each MKT domain over the period, thirdly it was done on the number of publications on the topic; learner errors and misconceptions per journal, and fourthly the affiliations of the first author.

Table 9.1 *Number of papers from South African universities on PCK and MKT (2010-2018)*

	CCK				SCK				HCK				KC&S					KC&T				KCur				
Year	AJ	PY	Others	Tt	AJ	PY	Others	Tt	AJ	PY	Others	Tt	Total	PY	Others	Tt	Tt	AJ	PY	Others	Tt	AJ	PY	Others	Tt	Total
2010	0	2	0	2	1	9	3	15	0	1	0	1	29	5	2	9	9	1	9	3	15	0	1	0	1	29
2011	0	1	0	1	5	0	1	6	0	0	1	1	10	0	1	2	2	5	0	1	6	0	0	1	1	10
2012	2	1	0	3	4	2	1	7	0	0	0	0	38	7	5	15	15	4	2	1	7	0	0	0	0	38
2013	0	0	3	4	4	4	8	16	0	1	3	4	37	2	4	11	11	4	4	8	16	0	1	3	4	37
2014	0	0	0	0	6	2	3	11	0	0	0	0	23	2	5	10	10	6	2	3	11	0	0	0	0	23
2015	1	1	1	3	5	1	6	11	0	0	0	0	27	6	1	9	9	5	1	6	11	0	0	0	0	27
2016	0	1	0	1	4	0	3	7	0	0	0	0	22	4	1	10	10	4	0	3	7	0	0	0	0	22
2017	0	1	0	1	2	1	3	6	1	0	0	1	18	1	1	7	7	2	1	3	6	1	0	0	1	18
2018	1	0	1	2	1	2	0	3	1	0	0	1	17	5	1	9	9	1	2	0	3	1	0	0	1	17

Year	CCK				SCK				HCK				KC&S				KC&T				KCur				Total
	AJ	PY	Others	Tt	AJ	PY	Others	Tt	AJ	PY	Others	Tt	Total	PY	Others	Tt	AJ	PY	Others	Tt	AJ	PY	Others	Tt	
2019	0	0	0	0	0	1	0	1	0	0	0	0	5	0	2	2	2	0	1	0	1	0	0	0	0	5
Total	4	7	3	14	32	22	15	69	2	2	1	5	182	32	9	69	69	32	22	15	69	2	2	1	5	221

(Source: ARJMSTE, Pythagoras and South African Journal of Education)

Key to Acronyms in Table 9.1

AJ	African Research Journal in Mathematics, Science and Technology Education
PY	Pythagoras
Others	Other educational journals in Southern Africa namely, South African Journal of Education, Perspectives in Education, African Educational Review, Journal of Educational Studies and Education as Change
Tt	Total
CCK	Common Content Knowledge
SCK	Specialist Content Knowledge
HCK	Horizon Content Knowledge
KC&S	Knowledge of Content and Students
KC&T	Knowledge of Content and Teaching
KCur	Knowledge of Content and Curriculum

Emerging patterns on the number of publications per journal over the period

This trend is shown in Table 9.1. Most of the research was published in the years 2012 and 2013. However, the research is still alive and current over the general period.

Trends on research on different MKT domains over the period

Bar graph showing number of articles published under different mathematics teacher knowledges for teaching (2010-2019)

Figure 9.2 *Frequencies of segments of research on MKT (2010-2018)*

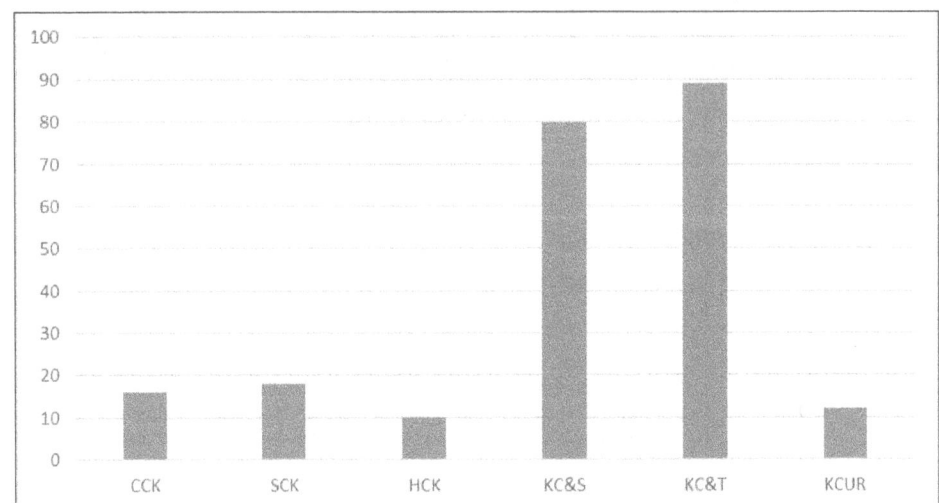

From this fig. 9.2, we note that:
- The mathematics knowledge for teaching segments most researched fall under PCK and are KC&S and KC&T.
- The least researched is KCUR and HCK.
- The year 2012 was the year in which these segments of mathematics knowledge for teaching were most researched.
- The year 2011 was a year in which these knowledges were least researched.

In general, over the period 2010-2018, there was a slight decline in researching these mathematical knowledges. Although the quantity of research on the teaching and learning of mathematics has not changed much over the years, it is important to note that the MKT terms such as SCK or KC&S are imposed on the research by this author. These terms only started to appear around 2012. It is important to point out that the terms PCK and MKT though important and beginning to be widespread, are not pervasive in research in mathematics education literature in Southern Africa. Few researchers in Southern Africa seem to use these terms in their research even up to today.

This review regards this as a gap. This is because researchers need this language of description to take the research into the teaching and learning of mathematics further.

Mathematics teacher knowledge research published abroad by Southern African Researchers

As to publishing on the theme, mathematics teacher knowledge by southern African researchers, I found the following statistics (Table 9.2);

Table 9.2 *Mathematics Teacher Knowledge Theme Publications by Journal by Southern African Mathematics Education Researchers*

Journal Name	Number of Articles	Themes and authors
Educational Studies in Mathematics	4	teacher practice, leveraging research on classroom discourse, mathematising, learner errors and misconceptions (these are mainly from researchers linked to a top South African university)
Journal of Mathematics Teacher Education	0	
International Journal of Science and Mathematics Education	2	teacher knowledge of function concept (from a Zimbabwean author) mathematics knowledge for teaching (from a Kenyan and South African author)
For the learning of mathematics	0	
Journal for research in mathematics education	0	
Journal of mathematics behavior	4	(these are mainly from researchers linked to a top South African university)
ZDM	1	(researcher linked to a top South African university)

The statistics shown above concern some of the most influential mathematics education journals in the world concerning this systematic research. In general, only eminent mathematics education researchers can publish in those journals. The data show that publishing abroad on the theme; mathematics teacher knowledge by Southern African authors is these journals exists, but is limited. Where it exists, it is concentrated on established researchers from one or two leading South African universities. There are one or two contributions from researchers outside South Africa, namely Kenya and Zimbabwe. But these researchers were in some way trained in South Africa.

Research on errors and misconceptions

Research on learner errors and misconceptions is central to building mathematics PCK and therefore professionally situated knowledge (PSK). It is critical because learner mathematical errors and misconceptions explain the concept images learners build of the mathematics concepts and skills that they experience in doing mathematics. It is key for teachers to understand them (pedagogical thinking), to probe and elicit learners to engage with (pedagogical action) in teaching if the learning of mathematics is to be taken forward. Researching on learner errors and misconceptions therefore and acting on the knowledge of how learners view mathematics empowers mathematics teachers.

The review considered the major mathematics education journals of Southern Africa; African Journal of Research in Mathematics, Science and Technology

Education (ARJMSTE) and Pythagoras, in conjunction with research on learner mathematics errors and misconceptions.

The Pythagoras journal published 22 articles. ARJMSTE had 5 articles over the period under review, 2010-2018 (see fig 9.3).

Figure 9.3 *Number and proportion of articles relating to research on errors and misconceptions in two Southern African mathematics education journals*

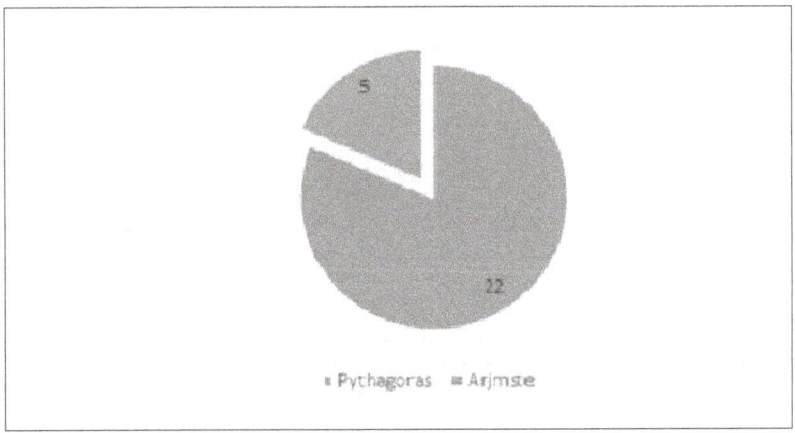

A closer look over the period shows that in most years Pythagoras published articles on this theme consistently. However, ARJMSTE seems to be picking up on this though slowly (see figs. 9.3 and 9.4). The amount of publications on this theme has serious implications on MKT and therefore improving equity in mathematics education.

Figure 9.4 *Number of articles on errors and misconceptions research in Pythagoras versus ARJMSTE*

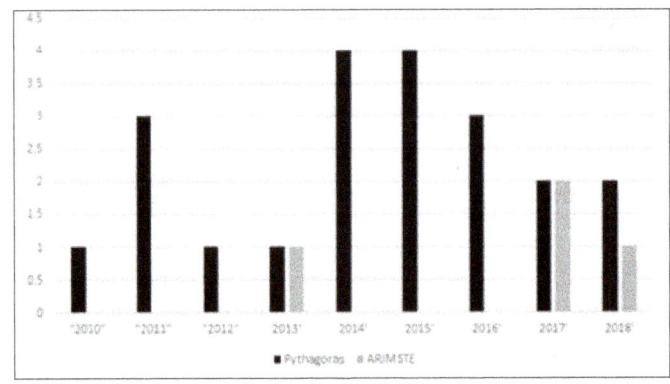

Other trends

Also to note is that some topics such as teacher and students' perceptions of mathematics are persistent, though not many have persisted over that time. The same applies to Rasch analysis, as well as research on research. These research topics are also persistent though sporadic in those years.

Who does research on mathematics teacher knowledge? Journal articles and first author affiliation

This analysis is done for local and international publications.

Local Publications

It is important to also review which authors are publishing on mathematics teacher knowledge. On this issue, the review only considered the ARJMSTE journal. This was because this journal particularly focuses on research in mathematics education alongside science and technology education drawing participants from Southern Africa Development Community region composed of the countries; South Africa, Zimbabwe, Botswana, Angola, Democratic Republic of Congo, Malawi, Zambia, Namibia, Mozambique, Madagascar Lesotho and Swaziland. Also considered was the individual universities in South Africa in terms of publication and other publishers from overseas.

Figure 9.5 *Number of articles published and first author affiliation in the ARJMSTE journal*

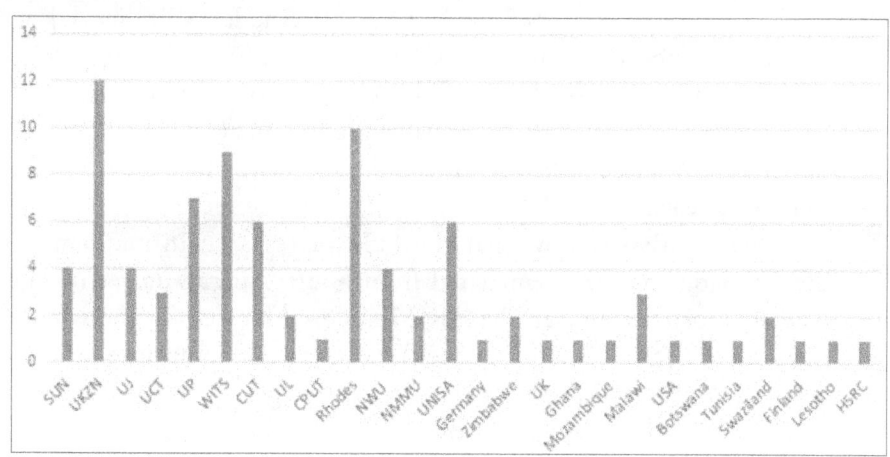

Key to Fig. 9.5

Acronym	Full Name
SUN	University of Stellenbosch
UKZN	University of KwaZulu-Natal
UJ	University of Johannesburg
UCT	University of Cape Town
WITS	University of the Witwatersrand
CUT	Central University of Technology

Acronym	Full Name
UNISA	University of South Africa
UL	University of Limpopo
CPUT	Cape Peninsula University of Technology
RHODES	Rhodes University
NWU	North-West University
NMMU	Nelson Mandela University
VUT	Vaal University of Technology
UP	University of Pretoria

Fig. 9.5 shows the number of first authors for mathematics teacher knowledge articles in ARJMSTE over the period 2010-2018 and their affiliation. In reading this data, it is important to notice that the movement of researchers from one institution to another is quite fluid. A number of these researchers moved from one university to another. This often occurs if an academic publishes as a post-doc in one university but then moves on to another when they get full jobs at other institutions in South Africa. Also to note is that South Africa employs several academics born from many other African countries such as Zimbabwe and Nigeria. Such academics' publications are included in the South African universities statistics and are not included in their (former) home countries.

Four universities topped the list; UKZN, Rhodes, Wits and UP respectively. CUT, Stellenbosch, Unisa, UJ, NWU followed. For universities of technology CUT was top, also noted was CPUT. Outside South Africa, Malawi, Swaziland and Zimbabwe together had 7 research articles, an average of two articles, among other few SADC countries. USA, Tunisia, Germany, Finland and Ghana produced one article each.

These statistics show that the bulk of research in mathematics teacher knowledge (over 90%) emanated from South African universities. This result is disproportionate given the ARJMSTE is a journal for the whole Southern Africa and not South Africa alone. This shows the dominance of South African researchers in mathematics education in the region. Perhaps a key factor in this is the National Research Foundation (NRF) which supports research in South Africa through the funding it provides. Comparable research funding support is not readily available in other Southern African countries. However, funding alone does not explain research activity in the region. South Africa has twenty-six (n=26) universities with virtually all of them except one or two involved in teacher education. The above data show only thirteen universities involved in research in mathematics teacher knowledge in ARJMSTE. So in South Africa, many universities are not research-active in this area. Their academics hardly contribute to research in mathematics education as this data shows.

International publications

In summary, if we consider publications in local and international journals on the theme mathematical teacher knowledge we find that very few South African researchers are doing that. It is being done by a few authors that can be counted on one hand in the whole South(ern) Africa.

Summary of strong evidence in the area

The strong evidence we have is that;

- Research in mathematics knowledge for teaching is ongoing. In the past ten years, it has been published almost consistently in the major journals of South Africa
- Research on mathematics teacher knowledge is many driven by former white universities
- Research on a major element of learner mathematics errors and misconceptions is mainly published in the Pythagoras journal. ARJMSTE is slowly picking up on this theme.

Summary of persistent gaps

- Research in mathematics teacher knowledges in most Southern African countries such as Zimbabwe, Lesotho, Swaziland, Botswana, Mozambique, and Malawi is very low. For other Southern African countries, publications are almost non- existent. These are worrying trends in mathematics education research given that these countries have many universities.
- Research in teacher knowledges up to now is being down but it seems implicit. Researchers are encouraged to use appropriate language of description in their research, such as Common Content Knowledge (CCK), Specialist Content Knowledge (SCK), Horizon Content Knowledge (HCK); Knowledge of Content and Students (KC&S), Knowledge of Content and Teaching (KC&T), Knowledge of Content and Curriculum (KC&Cur) among other so that there is deeper research for the teaching and learning of mathematics.
- CCK has always been assumed as the most portent knowledge for effecting learner outcomes and is often a given in research in mathematics education. In this review it is under-researched
- The data show strongly a very low level of research on SCK, and this is to be noted
- The review also shows that there are no mathematics education research journals in mathematics outside South Africa. In South Africa, there are only two mathematics education specialist journals. The second of these is

not purely mathematics education but caters also for science and technology education research.

- The authorship of the articles under review shows that to a large extent it is concentrated in a few universities such as UKZN, UP, SUN, WITS, Rhodes, UJ, NWU and CUT. These are historically white universities. Given that South Africa has more than twenty universities and universities of technology that train teachers, this shows that there are very limited activities in those universities. The universities that are not research active are historically black universities.

Recommendations for further research, policy and practice

In general there in research in teacher knowledges under the review period, but the problem is that there is no language of description to unify the research. What is recommended is to have this research more focused on mathematics content knowledge and PCK, particularly SCK which is important in unpacking mathematical meaning to learners. This is important to advance the research in the teaching and learning of mathematics, particularly for specific mathematics topics. It is known that SCK is a component of High Leverage Mathematics Teaching Practices (HLMT) of which minimum effort leverages much students' learning.

The research inactivity of academics in many universities in South Africa, particularly black universities and many others in the SADC region needs to be investigated so that these colleagues participation must be taken aboard.

Research in a very important type of teacher knowledge, the Specialised Content Knowledge (SCK) is very low. This study recommends the increase of this research in Southern Africa.

Further notes

- This review is an independent work done by the author. The author is highly aware that this review may have made some errors and omissions on the data and its analysis. The author is open to the improvement of the accuracy of this review. Readers may contact him with their comments on the email address; Judah.Makonye@wits.ac.za
- This review will be updated after five years in 2024. If possible, this author plans to do the review.
- I acknowledge Professor Felix Maringe, Head of Wits School of Education who encouraged us and supported us to do this review.

There is no conflict of interest in doing this review either personal, political, academic and other possible conflicts, as well as financial conflicts.

References

Adler, J. (2005). Holding the past, living the present and creating research on mathematics teacher education. *Researching mathematics education in South Africa*, 163.

Arksey, H., & O'Malley, L. (2005). Scoping studies: Towards a methodological framework. *International Journal of Social Research Methodology*, 8(1), 19-32. https://doi.org/10.1080/1364557032000119616

Ball, D.L., Thames, M.H., & Phelps, G. (2008). Content knowledge for teaching: What makes it special? *Journal of Teacher Education*, 59(5), 389-407. https://doi.org/10.1177/0022487108324554

Bansilal, S., Mkhwanazi, T., & Brijlall, D. (2014). An exploration of the common content knowledge of high school mathematics teachers. *Perspectives in Education*, 32(1), 34-50.

Bishop, A., Clements, M.K., Keitel-Kreidt, C., Kilpatrick, J., & Leung, F.K.S. (Eds.). (2003). *Second international handbook of mathematics education*, (Vol. 10). Springer Science & Business Media. https://doi.org/10.1007/978-94-010-0273-8

The Campbell Collaboration. (2001). *Guidelines for preparation of review protocols*. Retrieved from https://www.campbellcollaboration.org/ 13th June, 2019

Chall, J.S., & Jacobs, V.A. (2003). *Poor children's fourth-grade slump. All about adolescent literacy*. Retrieved from http://www.adlit.org/article/13995/ November 9, 2011.

de Clercq, F., & Shalem, Y. (2015). Teacher knowledge and professional development. In F. Maringe and M. Prew (Eds.), *Twenty years of education transformation in Gauteng 1994 to 2014*. Cape Town: African Minds, GDE.

Fleisch, B. (2008). *Primary education in crisis: Why South African schoolchildren underachieve in reading and mathematics*. Cape Town, South Africa: Juta.

Hanneke, R., Asada, Y., Lieberman, L., Neubauer, L.C., & Fagen, M. (2017). *The scoping review method: Mapping the literature in "structural change" public health interventions*. N.Y.: SAGE Publications Ltd. https://doi.org/10.4135/9781473999008

Hargreaves, D. (1999) The knowledge creating school. *British Journal of Educational Studies*, 47, 2, 122–144. https://doi.org/10.1111/1467-8527.00107

Hemsley-Brown, J.V., & Sharp, C. (2004). The use of research to improve professional practice: a systematic review of the literature. Oxford: *Oxford Review of Education*. https://doi.org/10.1080/0305498032000153025

Krainer, K., & Goffree, F. (1999). Investigations into teacher education: Trends, future research, and collaboration. *On research in teacher education*, 223-242. https://doi.org/10.1023/A:1009996502053

Long, C., Debba, R., & Bansilal, S. (2014). An investigation of mathematical literacy assessment supported by an application of Rasch measurement. *Pythagoras*, 35(1), 1-17. https://doi.org/10.4102/pythagoras.v35i1.235

Makonye, J.P. (2017). Pre-service mathematics student teachers' conceptions of nominal and effective interest rates. *Pythagoras*, 38(1), 1-10. https://doi.org/10.4102/pythagoras.v38i1.307

Manizade, A.G., & Martinovic, D. (2016). Developing an interactive instrument for evaluating teachers' professionally situated knowledge in geometry and measurement. In *International perspectives on teaching and learning mathematics with virtual manipulatives* (pp. 323-342). Springer, Cham. https://doi.org/10.1007/978-3-319-32718-1_14

Maoto, S., Masha, K., & Maphutha, K. (2016). Where is the bigger picture in the teaching and learning of mathematics?. *Pythagoras*, 37(1), 1-8. https://doi.org/10.4102/pythagoras.v37i1.338

Mavhunga, E., & Rollnick, M. (2013). Improving PCK of chemical equilibrium in pre-service teachers. *African Journal of Research in Mathematics, Science and Technology Education*, 17(1-2), 113-125. https://doi.org/10.1080/10288457.2013.828406

Mavhunga, E., & Rollnick, M. (2016). Teacher- or learner-centred? Science teacher beliefs related to topic-specific pedagogical content knowledge: A South African case study. *Research in Science Education*, 46(6), 831-855. https://doi.org/10.1007/s11165-015-9483-9

Mays, N., Roberts, E. & Popay, J. (2001). Synthesizing research evidence. In N. Fulop, P. Allen, A. Clarke, & N. Black (Eds.). *Studying the Organisation and Delivery of Health Services* (pp. 188–219). London: Routledge.

Mellor, K., Clark, R., & Essien, A.A. (2018). Affordances for learning linear functions: A comparative study of two textbooks from South Africa and Germany. *Pythagoras*, 39(1), 1-12. https://doi.org/10.4102/pythagoras.v39i1.378

Molefe, N., & Brodie, K. (2010). Teaching mathematics in the context of curriculum change. *Pythagoras*, 2010, 71, 33. https://doi.org/10.4102/pythagoras.v0i71.5

Moru, E.K., Qhobela, M., Wetsi, P., & Nchejane, J. (2014). Teacher knowledge of error analysis in differential calculus. *Pythagoras*, 35(2), 1-10. https://doi.org/10.4102/pythagoras.v35i2.263

Porrance, E.P. (2000). The millennium: A time for looking forward and looking back. *The International Journal of Creativity & Problem Solving*, 10(1), 5-19.

Pournara, C., Hodgen, J., Adler, J., & Pillay, V. (2015). Can improving teachers' knowledge of mathematics lead to gains in learners' attainment in Mathematics? *South African Journal of Education*, 35(3), 1-10. https://doi.org/10.15700/saje.v35n3a1083

Sanchez, M. (2011). *A review of research trends in mathematics teacher education*. Retrieved from http://www.repositoriodigital.ipn.mx/handle/123456789/11811 20 June 2019.

Shalem, Y., Sapire, I., & Huntley, B. (2013). Mapping onto the mathematics curriculum – an opportunity for teachers to learn. *Pythagoras*, 34(1), 1-10. https://doi.org/10.4102/pythagoras.v34i1.195

Shulman, L. (1987). Knowledge and teaching: Foundations of the new reform. *Harvard Educational Review*, 57(1), 1-23. https://doi.org/10.17763/haer.57.1.j463w79r56455411

Shulman, L.S. (1986). Those who understand: Knowledge growth in teaching. *Educational Researcher*, 15(2), 4-14. https://doi.org/10.3102/0013189X015002004

Vithal, R., Adler, J., & Keitel, C. (Eds.). (2005). *Researching mathematics education in South Africa: Perspectives, practices and possibilities*. HSRC Press.

Wessels, H. (2014). Number sense of final year pre-service primary school teachers. *Pythagoras*, 35(1), 1-9. https://doi.org/10.4102/pythagoras.v35i1.244

Appendix 9.1

ARTICLE	CODE AND THE REASON
Teacher knowledge of *error* analysis in differential calculus : original research Authors: Eunice K. Moru, Makomosela Qhobela, Poka Wetsi and John Nchejane Source: *Pythagoras* 35, pp. 1 - 10 (2014) http://dx.doi.org/10.4102/pythagoras.v35i2.263	KCS: Research on learner errors takes into account students' thinking and this is related to a content area of calculus
Pre-service mathematics student teachers' conceptions of nominal and effective interest rates Author Judah P. Makonye Source: *Pythagoras* 38, pp. 1 - 10 (2017) http://dx.doi.org/10.4102/pythagoras.v38i1.307	KCS: Research on learner conceptions which takes into account students' thinking; these can involve misconceptions related to a content area of financial mathematics
Affordances for learning linear functions: a comparative study of two textbooks from South Africa and Germany Authors: Kathryn Mellor, Robyn Clark and Anthony A. Essien	KCT: This research encompasses a special way of teaching a particular mathematics topic
Mapping onto the mathematics curriculum – an opportunity for teachers to learn : original research Authors: Yael Shalem, Ingrid Sapire and Belinda Huntley Source: *Pythagoras* 34, pp. 1 - 10 (2013) http://dx.doi.org/10.4102/pythagoras.v34i1.195	Kcur: This is research on the mathematics curriculum
Teaching mathematics in the context of curriculum change Authors: Nico Molefe and Karin Brodie Source: *Pythagoras* 2010, pp. 33 - 12 (2010) https://doi.org/10.4102/pythagoras.v0i71.5	This is research on the mathematics curriculum and teaching mathematics
Number sense of final year pre-service primary school teachers : original research Author Helena Wessels Source: *Pythagoras* 35, pp. 1 - 9 (2014) http://dx.doi.org/10.4102/pythagoras.v35i1.244	SCK: This research works on deeper understanding of the concept number by teacher students
Where is the bigger picture in the teaching and learning of mathematics? Authors: Satsope Maoto, Kwena Masha and Kgaladi Maphutha Source: *Pythagoras* 37, pp. 1 - 8 (2016) http://dx.doi.org /10.4102/pythagoras.v37i1.338	HCK: This article researches connections between mathematics topics
An exploration of the common *content knowledge* of high school *mathematics teachers* Authors: Sarah Bansilal, Thokozani Mkhwanazi and Deonarain Brijlall Source: *Perspectives in Education* 32, pp. 34 - 50 (2014)	CCK; This is about common content knowledge of mathematics of secondary school teachers
An investigation of Mathematical Literacy assessment supported by an application of *Rasch* measurement: original research Authors: Caroline Long, Sarah Bansilal and Rajan Debba Source: *Pythagoras* 35, pp 1 - 17 (2014) http://dx.doi.org/10.4102/pythagoras.v35i1.235	Articles like this one were excluded in the study, but commented on as it is on assessment

CHAPTER 10

Systematic literature review of literacy and reading in South Africa

Geeta Motilal

Abstract

This chapter reports on a critical literature review of scholarship in literacy and reading in South Africa from 2010 to 2020 that draws on critical discourse analysis. Key issues, trends, and criticisms in the field are discussed. A three-staged methodology has been utilised; which starts with searching educational databases to locate literature focused on Literacy and Reading scholarship. Each article and data is then categorised. The second stage was the development of schemata to interpret the complexity of issues related to research design. The third stage involves the examination of literacy-focused empirical studies and theoretical papers in scholarly journals to reveal trends in the questions that researchers find interesting enough to pursue, the theories they find useful, and the kinds of interactions that capture their attention. The findings demonstrate that Literacy and Reading scholarship has been conducted in many areas of literacy studies, including policy, academic writing, the preparation of literacy teachers, professional development, textbook content, curricular design, assessment, and bilingual education. The review also found evidence of impact and identifies directions for future scholarship.

Introduction

The goal of this chapter is to provide a review of literature in Literacy and Reading in South Africa. This review is concerned with the capacity to find, understand, critically appraise, share and act on evidence based on research conducted in the country.

Methodology

The methods that were used to identify literature were to firstly scope the literature for studies related to Literacy and Reading and then proceed to do a Google and Google Scholar search on the desktop. Two categories of literature were sought, one on Literacy research and the other on Reading research done nationally. In most cases the literature is categorised into particular ideas and organised in chronological order starting with the earliest dates possible. It includes consideration of the nature and status of research literacy and knowledge mobilisation; where the research was conducted; the questions surrounding each research; the concepts and practices of finding, understanding, sharing and acting on research; developments in education research philosophies and communicating and presenting research reviews; the rise of evidence-based policy and practice; the questions of the review; the research methodologies in the area; what we know from the research; what we don't quite know in the areas of focus and major implications for the future. It draws on the expertise of researchers in the field of Literacy and Reading research.

To establish a reliable evidence base for recommendations, my approach to the literature review was that of a scoping review. Scoping studies comprehensively review available literature to 'map' critical ideas within a topic guided by one or more general research questions (Levac, Colquhoun & O'Brien, 2010). This methodology is especially useful in researching complex topics. Researchers can undertake a scoping study to examine the extent, range, and nature of research activity, determine the value of undertaking a full systematic review, summarise and disseminate research findings, or identify gaps in the existing literature (Arksey & O'Malley's, 2005). Scoping studies may be particularly relevant to disciplines with emerging evidence, such as the research in South Africa around Literacy and Reading in which the paucity of randomised controlled trials and research in critical areas make it difficult for researchers to undertake systematic reviews. In these situations, scoping studies are ideal because researchers can incorporate a range of study designs in both published and grey literature, address questions beyond those related to intervention effectiveness, and generate findings that can complement the findings of existing research (Arksey & O'Malley's, 2005).

There were some stakeholder consultations as this was an important strategy to begin the search with, to improve the quality and uptake of the review and to enhance the study results. This review followed Arksey and O'Malley's (2005) five stages: identifying research questions; identifying relevant studies; study selection; charting the data; and collating, summarising and reporting results. In this review most of the studies used predominantly qualitative data, but used some quantitative data to show findings and results.

The review was driven by the following general questions:

1. What literature exists around Literacy and Reading in South Africa?
2. What is literature around Literacy and Reading informing us about?
3. What are the gaps in Literacy and Reading research and what are the implications for future research?

These questions broadly capture the research, the issues and challenges facing research and some attempt to address these issues in South Africa. To ensure that the review followed the five statges, I scoped the literature searching for studies related to Literacy and Reading and then proceeded to screen the studies. I then described and mapped an outline of each study and thereafter evaluated each study in a descriptive frame. Studies were selected on their appropriateness to the topic and questions. The selected studies were then synthesised and gaps identified. This was then followed by a set of implications and conclusions.

Affordances and constraints of the review

Scoping studies offer some affordances and constraints of gathering evidence. I found that scoping study research questions is broad in nature as the focus is on summarising breadth of evidence. Arksey and O'Malley (2005) acknowledge the need to maintain a broad scope to research questions. However, I found that my research questions, although broad, lacked the direction, clarity, and focus needed to inform subsequent stages of the research process, such as identifying studies and making decisions about study inclusion. The broad research question should have included a clearly articulated scope of inquiry (Levac et al, 2010).

While the strength of scoping studies includes the breadth and depth, or comprehensiveness, of evidence covered in a given field, practical issues related to time, funding, and access to resources often require researchers to consider the balance between feasibility, breadth, and comprehensiveness. This search strategy yielded a vast amount of literature, making it difficult to determine how in-depth to carry out the information synthesis and how in-depth to report due to page constraints. This resulted in a concise deep dive to capture the gist of the research. Although Arksey and O'Malley (2005) identify these concerns and provide some suggestions to support these decisions, I also struggled with the trade-off between breadth and comprehensiveness and feasibility in our scoping studies. As such, I ensured that decisions surrounding feasibility did not compromise my ability to keep to the broad research questions or achieve the goal of the chapter (Levac et al, 2010).

Arksey and O'Malley (2005) provide suggestions to manage the time-consuming process of determining which studies to include in a scoping study. I experienced this stage as more iterative and requiring additional steps as I began the search. Due to the time constraints and working from home with inconsistent access to articles also contributed to these iterative steps. This stage involved extracting data from included studies. Based on my experiences, I was uncertain about the nature and extent of information to extract from the included studies, with the result that I used my own experience in the field to extract research that I thought would be useful to influence future research. It has been criticised for rarely providing methodological detail about how results were achieved and this was one of the constraints for this research (Levac etal, 2010).

Literacy and reading

Learning to read can be a joyful and natural process. In 1908, Huey wrote concerning children who learn to read by themselves: "they grow into it as they learned to talk, with no special instruction or purposed method, and usually such readers are our best and most natural readers" (p. 330). The beginning of literacy and of literacy failure, especially in view of a long history of language learning as a natural process, yet also of continued public anxiety about falling literacy standards, brings into focus the concerns regarding literacy and reading as the search for success goes on.

Holdaway (1979) generates a remarkable congruency and balance between theory and practice, insight and respect for the language learning potential of young children. Anyone who has been following language learning theory and research for the past decade will not be surprised by this theoretical stance on literacy as a developmental, natural process rather than as a skills item-oriented product, nor by his strong emphasis on a language environment which is invitational and emulative rather than prescriptive and instructional. The recurring belief suggested by Holdaway is that "literacy begins with immersion in an environment in which the skill is used in a purposeful, active, and meaningful way" (p. 107).

Literacy and reading theories frameworks

Notwithstanding Holdaway's view of looking at literacy, the evidence from some studies shows that other theories of literacy and learning have come to the fore and are being used as a theoretical framework by researchers in more recent studies. The social learning perspective is extremely popular among reading researchers. Many current research and classroom practices in literacy instruction are built upon the premise of this perspective, which encompass theories such as the socio-linguistic theory, socio-cultural theories, social constructivism and critical literacy theories amongst others. A large number of scholars in the field of literacy and reading, especially more recent researchers, tend to use the social learning perspective to interpret their data.

The socio-linguistic theory is often seen in studies that examine language in relation to children's reading development. According to Tracey & Morrow (2006) very often the focus of these studies is on parents', teachers' or peers' language use and its impact on children's literacy skills.

There is reasonable evidence that researchers use the socio-cultural theory to understand the effects of the broad concept of culture on literacy learning and literacy learning in the community. This perspective is becoming more popular with researchers in South Africa due to the lack of diversity and indigenous and decolonised knowledge to inform literacy learning around the diverse cultural population.

Perry (2012) contends that the socio-cultural perspectives on literacy include various theories focused on the myriad ways in which people use literacy in context, which include a strong emphasis on power relations of which some are literacy as social practice, multiliteracies and critical literacy. According to Perry (2012) these theories also have important differences, and many in the field of literacy do not clearly differentiate among them (Perry, 2012).

The South African literacy and reading landscape

The importance of literacy has become more evident in the last 50 years since the United Nations (UN) declared literacy to be a basic human right along with the right to adequate food, health care and housing. The ability to read and write effectively is a basic right for children and becomes more important as the "knowledge economy" increases (Freire, 1970; World Bank, 2006). In South Africa the characteristic of African education changed from Bantustan and separatist education under the apartheid regime to education in the newly formed democratic South Africa. Education and, more importantly, literacy in the school curriculum began to assume more importance for the majority of African people who moved from education in the home languages or African languages to the use of a second language as media in the new democracy (Mazonde, 2003). In his paper, Mazonde brings to the fore problems associated with using a second language as the main language for learning. The origins of the use of second languages in African education are of course historical, ethnographical and political (Mazonde, 2003).

The new national language-in-education policy of South Africa mandates the use of English as the medium of instruction (MoI) for all students from Grade 4 onwards. Despite an ongoing debate about the benefits of mother-tongue education on student success, and the unintended outcome of excessive mother-tongue code-switching in classes where English is deemed a barrier to learning, the reality is that for the majority of secondary school students, English is the default MoI even in classes where, for an overwhelming majority of students and educators, English is a second, third or even foreign language. To some extent, this offers an explanation for the poor English literacy development of a large majority of secondary school students in South Africa. A consequence of this reality is that unequal opportunities for learning are presented to these students, which also results in unequal learning outcomes. In such cases, an inability to develop more advanced English academic literacy skills becomes an indicator for academic marginalisation, exclusion and alienation at secondary school level and later at tertiary level. Mazonde's (2003) literature reveals the difficulties African learners face in understanding the basic concepts when taught in a foreign language – especially a language, which is not used in their home environment. It also shows how culture comes up strongly to present a barrier for African students when they are forced to learn in a foreign language which is based on values and metaphors different from theirs (Mazonde, 2003). He strongly emphasises pedagogical supply of teachers and the lack of educators to firstly converse in the language of instruction, and secondly, the lack of training to teach a foreign language.

Twenty-five years later, after achieving democracy, there is significant transformation in the South African education system but inequalities in the provision of literacy in education to all its citizens remain a conundrum. This has become evident in a number of assessment results – a fact captured by a number of researchers in South Africa. Literacy research has become increasingly important since the results of a series of post-democratic, national and international literacy evaluations and reports. It has become evident that there are continuing low levels of literacy proficiency in South African primary schools during the post-democratic period (Fleisch, 2008; Howie, Venter, Van Staden, Zimmerman, Long, Scherman and Archer, 2007; Howie, Van Staden, Tshele, Dowse and Zimmerman, 2012; Howie, Combrinck, Roux, Tshele, Mokoena, Palance, 2017; Taylor, 2013; Spaull, 2013; 2016). These evaluations found that the majority of Grade 3 children were reading below grade level and that 95% of Grade 5 learners read with exceptionally low levels of comprehension compared with other participating countries and that 78% of Grade 4 children cannot read for meaning (Howie et al., 2007; 2012; 2016). These findings have led to the belief that South Africa has a literacy crisis where learners could not access learning because of the their literacy levels. Various researchers (Fleisch, 2009; Spaull, 2013; Taylor, 2013) in education in South Africa consider education to be in 'crisis'. A number of International tests such as the SACMEQ 111 (2013), TIMMSS (2015) and PIRLS (2016) provide a picture of the crisis. The PIRLS (2016) report indicates that the biggest developmental challenge facing South Africa is the large number of children who do not learn to read for meaning in the early years of school (Motilal & Fleisch, 2020).

In fact, over the past decade, Motilal and Fleisch (2020) in their article state that there has been a growing recognition that a substantial proportion of South African school children perform one or more years below acceptable levels of achievement, particularly in key subjects such as English First Additional Language and Mathematics (as cited in the NEEDU report, 2014; Spaull, 2013; Taylor, 2014). Spaull (2015) argues convincingly that school children who are academically behind in the Foundation Phase are likely to fall further and further behind their peers as they progress through the school system. According to him this is clearly not a conventional 'remedial' problem, in which a small number of individuals in a class have specific learning barriers or challenges. The learning deficits are systemic, often affecting almost all the learners in the majority of disadvantaged schools (Spaull, 2015).

The United Nations Educational, Scientific and Cultural Organization (UNESCO) on the other hand listed South Africa as having a literacy rate of

93% but beyond the mechanical ability to identify words, the picture is much bleaker. According to their research released by the University of Pretoria eight out of ten Grade 4 pupils "still cannot read at an appropriate level" (PIRLS, 2016). In a statement Combrinck (2017) states that learners are expected to understand the language of learning well enough to read and understand study textbooks and other written material. However, a switch to English as the medium of instruction in Grade 4 for all learners exacerbates the problem. Learners are expected to move from Learning to Read to Reading to Learn in this crucial transition from Foundation Phase to Intermediate Phase in the South African system of education. Thus the question arises as to what is going wrong despite the many curriculum changes and the various attempts to change the situation through a number of intervention programmes. What is literature pointing to as being the gap that cannot address this so-called "crisis"?

Causal factors of literacy and reading challenges

There is evidence in a research conducted by Mudzielwana (2011) on the Causal Factors of Low Level Reading Standards in the Foundation Phase among Primary School Learners in South Africa indicating that there are some key factors affecting the low level of reading ability among learners and provides possible intervention strategies to address them. The study recognises that education experts and academics alike agree that the ability to read is necessary for effective communication, solving of practical life problems, and critical for the wellbeing of an individual. The study empirically investigated, evaluated and understood the factors responsible for low level of reading standards in the Foundation Phase among South African primary school learners. The study utilised a combination of theoretical frameworks and qualitative techniques to explore teachers' perception and understanding of causal factors related to low level of reading standards. The findings of the study showed that there were a number of factors that contributed to the low level of reading standards amongst the learners. These include, among others, the implementation of the National Curriculum Statement (NCS), Foundations for Learning Campaign (FFLC), inappropriate use of methodology in the teaching of reading, multi-grade teaching approach and multilingualism. The study pointed out some intervention strategies that teachers suggested for the improvement of reading amongst the learners (Mudzielwana, 2011).

Boakye (2015) highlights in a research into the social dimension of reading literacy development in South Africa – 'Bridging inequalities among the various language groups' – that different communities, such as language groups and different socio-economic status (SES) families, widely acknowledge the practice of literacy in different ways. Certain language communities of low SES observe literacy interactions differently from the traditional "schooled literacy", which may influence learners' reading literacy. However, this link between language communities, SES and reading literacy has not been extensively researched, especially in the South African context where there are 11 official languages and wide socio-economic disparities. The research examined students' social literacy in relation to their reading literacy levels, and revealed that the literacy gap between indigenous South African language (ISAL) speakers, a number of whom are from low SES families, and speakers of English and Afrikaans is further widened at the tertiary level due to the mismatch between the social literacy practices of the different language groups and the education system that operates in the country. Recommendations are made on how educators could employ strategies such as social relevance and culturally sensitive teaching to bridge the academic literacy gap among the language groups (Boayke, 2015).

Agreeing with Mudzielwana's (2011) research and identifying other challenges to literacy and reading is a research by Nel, Mohagi, Krog and Stephens (2016) on Pre-school literacy teaching in Early Childhood Education (ECD) inclusive classrooms which is crucial in preparing learners for the transition to formal literacy teaching and learning. Their research describes a collaborative exploratory research project between a university in South Africa and one in China, in order to gain an overview of early literacy teaching and learning in the two countries. In the case of South Africa, the focus was on Grade R literacy teaching and learning. Teacher participants in three rural schools, three township schools and four inner-city schools in Mpumalanga and Gauteng were purposively selected. Data were gathered by means of open-ended questions in a questionnaire, individual interviews with Heads of Departments (HODs) and classroom observations. The research identifies persistent challenges such as limited resources, low socio-economic conditions and English as the language of learning and teaching (LoLT). Other barriers to learning were highlighted together with inadequate teaching strategies used to implement the Curriculum Assessment Policy Statement (CAPS) (Nel et al., 2016).

Reading as oral performance

In an article by Rule and Land (2017) it is argued that we have lost the plot in South African reading Education and to find the plot we need to move beyond the predominant mode of reading as oral performance, where the emphasis is "accuracy and pronunciation" rather than "reading as comprehension of meaning in text" (2017, p 1.) They indicate that reading research in South Africa has been mainly conducted in schools where it is mainly concerned with oratorical approaches to reading and should move beyond that to higher education institutions where reading is fundamental to learning. Their research, using a case study approach, was conducted in a learning community comprising a school and an Adult Basic

Education and Training Centre. They suggest that "developing the way in which teachers understand the teaching of reading and transforming the teaching practices of those who teach as they were taught in the education system of the apartheid era are key to improving the teaching of reading" (Rule & Land, 2017, p. 1) In a study conducted by Taylor (2014) he states that a common finding in school-based research is that teachers simply do not have knowledge of effective reading pedagogies and as a result cannot teach reading effectively in spite of their efforts to do so (Taylor, 2014). Motilal and Fleisch (2020) agree with this as they found in their research that despite using the EGRS triple cocktail programme that is provided, teachers find it difficult to implement lesson plans and reading strategies in a well-informed and engaging way.

Literacy as a social practice

Another research of 'Children Engagement with Literacy: A study of Literacy Practices at a multilingual classroom in Cape Town by Prosper (2016) reports on the early literacy activities which children engage with at school to develop multi-competences. It draws on an understanding of literacy as a social practice given the intricacies related to a particular literacy event. In this paper literacy is understood beyond reading and writing ability in order to widen the scope for early literacy learners to explore with literacy. The data was collected through ethnographic case study design from a grade three class using observation and document analysis. The class teacher became a resource as she used linguistic competence in English, Afrikaans and isiXhosa to teach literacy in different situations. The data shows that language should be seen as a resource for teaching and learning literacy instead of seeing it as a problem and barrier to the learning process. Home language can be an instrument through which children develop cognitive skills for learning. The paper concludes that, despite the efforts to support learners to become multi-literate, teachers' competence in different languages is necessary to facilitate the acquisition of multilingual skills (Prosper, 2016).

Role of the family in literacy and reading development

The role of the parent in enhancing literacy and reading development is another critical component to the success of literacy in the country. A number of international studies (Hill, 2012) point to the importance of parental involvement in the education of the literate child. Parents' involvement with their children's education usually depends on their social, cultural and linguistic capital (Bourdieu, 1986). It is imperative that differentiated parent outreach strategies are included in literacy and reading plans depending on the context and the community. A few small-scale studies were concentrated around this issue.

Overett and Donald (2011) conducted one such study on parental involvement in 'Paired reading strategies and the effects of a parent involvement programme in a disadvantaged community in South Africa' (Overett & Donald, 2011). This study was conducted in an educationally disadvantaged South African community where the effectiveness of a paired reading parent involvement programme, which stressed interaction around reading as a means of mediating meaning, was evaluated. The research aimed to evaluate whether reading accuracy, comprehension and attitude were promoted through involving parents and other family members as mediators in a process of paired reading. Further, it aimed to elucidate interactive ecosystemic effects across family, school and community levels. Two complete grade four classes (29 and 32 children respectively) served as comparison groups (average age: 9 years 7 months). The methods used were to test the significance of the improvement in reading accuracy and comprehension (Neale Analysis of Reading Ability: Neale, 1966) and attitude (Elementary Reading Attitude Survey: McKenna & Kear, 1990) for the experimental group relative to the control, where one-tailed t-tests for independent samples on the respective pre-test/post-test difference scores were applied. The results showed that statistically significant improvements in reading accuracy and comprehension, as well as reading attitude and involvement, were demonstrated. A broad ecosystemic analysis suggested that positive relationships between children and significant others in the family were nurtured and other children in the family were benefiting. Interactions between family and school, and school and the local community library, were also enhanced. The study emphasised the importance of developing mediation insights and skills in parent involvement programmes, and the place of ecosystemic analysis in understanding the social dynamics involved in such programmes.

Aitchison and Land conducted studies in 2005 and 2011 on 'Family Literacy, Bringing literacy home', which placed emphasis on the importance of bringing literacy into the family environment. Learning families with school children and adults reading at home confirms the importance of family reading activities. It is evident that where children learnt and read together with parents in the home environment, the children found reading more enjoyable and performed better at reading in school.

Another research in 2016 conducted by Le Roux and Gertruida looked into the role of family literacy programmes to support emergent literacy in young learners. The collaboration between the parents and the school has a powerful influence on a child's literacy development. The research showed that home-school partnerships to support young learners' emergent literacy development are weak in South Africa. Research into family literacy in South Africa is particularly important due to many socio-economic factors impacting negatively on family life and on children's literacy development. The South African education system lacks a dedicated policy for the promotion of family literacy. Against this background the study investigated the role of family literacy programmes in supporting emergent literacy among young children. A literature study on family literacy and family-school-community partnerships to support literacy framed an empirical inquiry following an interpretivist approach, using an action research design and qualitative techniques of data collection. The research used the Wordworks Home-School Partnerships programme for implementation and the programme was modified through the design and inclusion of a children's component. A multicultural independent primary school situated in Pretoria, South Africa was selected through a combination of purposeful and convenience sampling. A small-scale study employing the school principal, four Foundation Phase teachers and seven families including nine children, participated in the study. Criteria for family inclusion were that the participating families should have at least one child enrolled in Grade R and at least one parent should agree to attend the full six-week duration of the modified Wordworks School-Family Partnerships programme. Data was gathered during parallel sessions from parents, children and teacher-facilitators through multiple techniques: observation, interviews, feedback sessions, artefacts and journals. Data was analysed according to qualitative principles and the findings were presented in a narrative format substantiated by verbatim quotations. Key findings indicated a greater sense of community among the families and the teachers, improved quality of parent-child interactions; parents' improved knowledge of emergent literacy skills and improved confidence in supporting their children with early literacy development. The medium-term impact of the programme includes benefits for the whole school, the teaching staff, parent body and children. Based on the findings of the literature study and the implementation of the family literacy programme through action research, recommendations were made to improve school-family partnerships with a view to supporting emergent literacy development among young learners (Le Roux, Sarlina Gertruida, 2016).

Reading ability and academic performance

When it comes to reading, Motilal & Fleisch (2020) in their research claim that reading is critical for primary school learners. The ability to decode texts and read with meaning is a critical skill for learners to navigate learning. Literacy and reading provides learners with the ability to understand what teachers are teaching: develop conceptual understanding; and to adapt to different teaching approaches and reading materials (Motilal & Fleisch, 2020). Researching what works and what does not in a reading programme is another important area that requires much input. A number of different components of Literacy and Language referred to as the "Big Five" by Snow (1991) which comprise of: Background Knowledge; Oral Language and Vocabulary; Book Knowledge and Print Concepts; Alphabet Knowledge and Early Writing; and Phonological Awareness, can be researched to provide expert knowledge in these critical areas. Snow (1991) states that considerable research now suggests that, in addition to the phonemic awareness skills which support early decoding, skilled reading also requires more general oral language competencies, particularly those involving the use of decontextualised language.

Early literacy development occurs as children become increasingly proficient in cognitive processes that support skilled reading. Prominent among these skills is the development of phonological knowledge. Early reading is characterised by a process through which spoken language is mapped onto phonological sounds that are associated with alphabetic characters and assembled together into words. This is where neuroscience and the application of the brain and cognitive ability to the promotion of literacy development and prevention of reading disability begin to play a critical role. Much research is required in terms of neuroscience to understand how the development of literacy skills and reading ability involves understanding how the brain becomes proficient in early acquisition skills, phonological processing, decoding, the development of neuroanatomy of reading, comprehension and reading disabilities. Research is scant in these areas while research on the brain science has advanced.

Pretorius's (2008) research titled 'Reading ability and academic performance in South Africa: Are we fiddling while Rome is burning?' reports on two studies which investigated the relationship between reading skill and academic performance at undergraduate level. The findings showed clear and consistent differences in reading ability between the different academic groups, with reading skills improving the higher the academic group. The findings indicate that many additional language (AL) students have serious reading comprehension problems, which means that they have ineffective and limited access to the rich sources of declarative knowledge provided by print-based materials in the learning context. Reading is important in the learning context not only because it affords readers independent access to information in an increasingly information-driven society, but more importantly because it is a powerful learning tool, a means of constructing meaning and acquiring new knowledge. If developing countries aim to produce independent learners, then serious attention will need to be given to improving the reading skills of students and to creating a culture of reading. Reading is not simply an additional tool that students need at tertiary level – it constitutes the very process whereby learning occurs (Pretorius, 2008).

In another research by Pretorius and Klapwijk (2016) called 'Reading Comprehension in South African schools: Are teachers Getting it, and getting it right?' They contend that much research exists about South African learners' low literacy and numeracy levels and about poorly performing schools. By contrast, there are far fewer detailed descriptions of instructional practices and what teachers are actually doing in their classrooms, and far less evidence exists of in-depth research attempts to understand in what way and why teachers may experience problems with the teaching of reading literacy, particularly reading comprehension. Their article aimed to contribute to narrowing that gap by reviewing recent South African research on classroom comprehension instruction and obtaining information from teachers about how they perceive themselves as readers, what their teaching context is, what they claim to be doing about reading in their classrooms, and to match these responses with Annual National Assessment (ANA) results at their schools. Data were obtained through a quantitative questionnaire from 159 teachers at 30 schools across three provinces. The results show that many teachers are not themselves immersed in rich reading practices; many teachers claim to be doing more than is reflected in their schools' literacy results, and in general teachers don't seem to have a clear understanding of reading concepts, reading development and reading methodology (Pretorius & Klapwijk, 2016).

More of this type of research on instructional practices and using qualitative research is coming to the fore in recent years.

Another research by Pretorius and Spaull (2016) is called 'Exploring relationships between oral reading fluency and reading comprehension amongst English second-language readers in South Africa'. In their article they state that most analyses of oral reading fluency (ORF) are based on first-language (L1) reading, and the norms that have been developed in English are based on first-language reading data. This is problematic for developing countries where many children are learning in English as a second language. The aim of this study was to model the relationship between English reading fluency and comprehension among rural English-second-language learners (ESL) in South Africa. They used data collected in 2013 by the National Education and Evaluation Development Unit in South Africa. This survey tested 4 697 Grade 5 students from 214 schools across rural areas in South Africa. A sub-sample of 1 772 students was selected for an Oral Reading Fluency (ORF) test. For these students there exist data on both reading comprehension and reading fluency. Although a number of studies have analysed the relationship between fluency and comprehension, none have been conducted on a large-scale for ESL learners in a developing country such as South Africa. The present research contributes to the literature by analysing the size, significance and uniformity of this relationship for ESL learners in South Africa. Preliminary findings indicate a threshold at 70 words-read-correct-per-minute, which is lower than the typically used threshold of 90 words-read-correct-per-minute of English first-language (Pretorius & Spaull, 2016).

To this end the Department of Education has implemented several interventions to combat the Literacy and Reading challenges. Gauteng Primary Literacy and Mathematics Strategy [GPLMS] in Gauteng, Early Grade Reading Study [EGRS] 1 in the North West province, EGRS 11 in Mpumalanga, National

Education and Collaboration Trust (NECT) and Primary School Reading Improvement Programme [PSRIP]) are programmes initiated in an attempt to improve learner outcomes related to Literacy and Reading. South Africa has introduced multiple small- and large-scale intervention programmes to alleviate the huge reading deficit "crisis" and produced important research in this area. The Early Grade Reading Study initiative is one of these programmes, which is a large-scale intervention to improve basic learning and reading skills among second-language learners in primary school in South Africa. It has evolved considerably over the past 10 years since its inception.

Emanating from the EGRS are several papers including a research article by Fleisch, Pather and Motilal (2017) which was a qualitative study that concentrated on instructional practices and was titled 'The patterns and prevalence of monosyllabic three-letter-word spelling errors made by South African English First Additional Language learners'. The growing evidence of systematic underachievement of South African primary school learners in reading in English as the first additional language promoted this research. There is a small but growing literature that provides insights – that is, causes, patterns and prevalence – of this phenomenon. Through a secondary analysis of a spelling component of a literacy test that was administered as an end-line assessment for a randomised control trial, this research provided new evidence for and insight into the patterns and prevalence of English language spelling errors made by Grade 4 second-language learners. The study specifically coded errors on four monosyllabic three-letter words for 2 500 Grade 4 learners tested individually at the end of the second term in 2014. Three distinct linguistic error patterns were identified. The most frequent error patterns involved the incorrect use of the vowel grapheme. For example, bed was spelled 'bad'. The second pattern related to common errors associated with the transfer of linguistic, orthographic patterns from the first language (isiZulu). The final pattern suggests that between 6% and 8% of learners were struggling to make the basic phoneme–grapheme connection. This pattern, however, would need to be confirmed with oral interviews. The implications of these error patterns are discussed.

Nkomo's (2018) research covered another view of the research on Literacy and Reading. She looked at Grade 3 learners' imagined identities as readers revealed through their drawings which resonates with Olshansky's book on the use of multimodalities in the teaching of Literacy. There has been limited attention towards the affective aspect in literacy development; yet, reading attitude, an affective component, is a significant element within literacy instruction. This makes a compelling case for investigating Grade 3 learners' attitudes towards reading. In this study, a situational analysis was conducted as Phase 1 of the research process before implementing a responsive reading programme at a primary school in Grahamstown, South Africa. In an effort to explore Grade 3 learners' attitudes, experiences and perspectives about reading, the study adopted the use of drawings, which is a child-centred approach. Learners were required to draw their perspectives or experiences about reading. In analysing the drawings, a range of semiotic theorists were integrated. Findings of the study indicate that by using drawings as a methodological tool, learners were able to provide detailed insights about their daily experiences with reading, attitudes towards reading and their varied individual views about reading. Such information gathered was vital for future consideration when implementing a responsive and extensive reading programme (Nkomo, 2018).

Reading and teacher education in South Africa

Bharuthram's (2012) study claims that over the past two decades much has been written in the literature about the importance of reading and the importance of teaching students reading strategies to improve their reading comprehension. Reading is one of the most important academic tasks encountered and required by students. In higher education, students are exposed to a number of texts, readings and textbooks that require independent reading. At this level they are expected to comprehend what they read so that they can analyse, critique, evaluate and synthesise information from various sources. However, according to this study, many students entering higher education are not adequately prepared to meet these challenges. What is important to note is that this article highlights the importance of teaching students reading strategies across the curriculum in order to improve their reading comprehension, thereby enhancing their chances of academic success not only in school but also at tertiary level. The implications of this research for policy makers and academics in higher education institutions are outlined and some suggestions are made (Bharuthram, 2012).

According to Henning (2016) there was a notable increase in research articles in the early years of schooling, more especially on the teaching of initial reading and of mathematics. In the first issue of the 2011 *South African Journal of Childhood Education*, most of the articles, according to Henning (2016) focused on language and reading. The Strenthening of Foundation Phase Teacher Education Programme helped to produce more much-needed submissions to journals dealing with Literacy and Reading issues. This notable increase can be attributed to articles coming from university specialists in language and reading and one of the suggestions that came out of most of the publications was the need for more research on the teaching of literacy and mathematics. Following on this came the Primary School Teacher Education project (PrimTed) which is another intervention by the Department of Education to increase research and produce much-needed knowledge regarding Literacy, Language and Reading.

It was during these consultations about teacher education for reading instruction that Henning came to the conclusion that literacy education research may be stymied by its bifocal nature: (1) young children first learn *to* read and (2) then progress to read *for* learning. This seems to be a simplistic and linear distinction of reading and Henning (2016) states that it separates reading competence into periods of mechanical skills and reading for understanding as a main ingredient of learning. The learning of the graphological/graphemic bytes of reading is already oriented to comprehension and the current separation may be a false dichotomy. Understanding, or comprehension, means that a reader is able to construct some meaning derived from her sound awareness (including prosody) (Halliday, 2013). Snow, Griffin and Burns (2005, 9) said, simply, that '(r)eading is, at its basis, about language and about thinking'.

Summary of findings

This scoping review provided a synthesis of literature from researchers based primarily in higher institutions but research was also carried out in schools, higher education institutions and home settings. Although many descriptive papers were included in this scoping review, they were important to include, as the topic was relatively broad. It is necessary to expand our understanding of what constitutes evidence; and what knowledge and value is contributed by colloquial evidence (Culyer & Lomas, 2006). However, the acceptance of colloquial evidence presents other challenges – what papers should be excluded, how to extract data from them and then analyse the results?

E-research has been described as the use of advanced information and communication technology (ICT) such as broadband communication networks, software and infrastructure services that enable secure connections and interoperatability, information data management and collaboration tools to support research activities (Allan, 2009). Technology has tremendous potential to assist complex research endeavours especially when researchers are geographically distributed, span many disciplines (Sagotsky et al., 2008) and are hampered by certain restrictions such as a lockdown due to COVID-19. According to Allan (2009) Virtual Research Environments (VREs) can help researchers conduct and manage the complexity of research activities through the provision of a secure and trustworthy infrastructure to support large- and small-scale teams (Allan, 2009).

South Africa's classrooms in both schools and higher education institutions are increasingly diverse with the majority of students coming from a second-language background and diverse contexts into the educational scenario requiring sophisticated language and literacy knowledge and skills both in the educational institutions and their place of employment. This chapter captures the main points, which are critical to the goal of the study and captures succinctly the nature and status of research and knowledge mobilisation. It was concerned with the capacity to find, understand, critically appraise, share and act on evidence and to identify essential gaps in research that are important for further studies and to produce critical knowledge required that would help to improve the teaching of Literacy and Reading in South Africa.

It considered research in both Literacy and Reading in respect of the South African landscape, causal factors to literacy and reading challenges, reading as an oral performance, literacy as a social practice, the role of family in literacy and reading development, reading ability and academic performance, and reading and teacher education where research is situated.

Gaps in literature and implications for future research

In the light of the above research studies that were reviewed it is recognisable that there are several implications for students, educators and researchers who work in Literacy and Reading in South Africa. It gives a semblance of research in the country around topics that are researched but it also shows where gaps exists. Related studies are based on similar topics.

In a recent literature review conducted by Biesman-Simons, Dixon, Pretorius, & Reed (2020) on 'Pitfalls and possibilities in literacy research: A review of South African literacy studies, 2004-2018' the authors evaluated literature from two annotated bibliographies. They used examples of 70 quantitative and qualitative studies and critically analysed these studies. Their findings showed that weaknesses were evident in the research reviewed and suggested greater consideration is needed to lay sound methodological foundations for quality literacy research. According to them three methodological issues underlying local literacy research that require greater attention are research design, selection and use of literature and research rigour. According to them high-quality research examples are referenced but, for ethical reasons, examples of what they consider to be flawed research are described generally. In their article they offer guidelines for addressing these pitfalls that, in their view, contribute to research of limited quality (Biesman-Simons et al., 2020).

Given the challenges in Literacy and Reading, extensive research is required to expound on the link between language communities, SES, reading literacy, writing literacy, digital literacies and multimodal literacies, especially in the South African context where there are 11 official languages and wide socio-economic disparities. Another gap that exists is the mismatch between the social literacy practices of the different language groups and the education system that operates in the country. Thus drastic measures need to be taken at all levels to improve the overall literacy and reading levels of all South African learners and hence inevitably of students entering higher education institutions. Robust and rigorous research is needed to enhance the production of knowledge in all of these spheres of Literacy and Reading.

The advances in cognitive neuroscience and brain development in reading and the importance of executive function for early reading development and education require much more research to ascertain how the brain works with Literacy and Reading development. Because executive function and its associated brain developments parallel reading acquisition, work in executive function has profound implications for fostering the successful development of reading skills, including pre-reading skills, word reading, and reading comprehension. Instruction and strategies that help children learn to manage the multiple features of spoken and printed language will help ensure that children develop the reading-specific executive functions that will enable them to manage the complexities of reading processes throughout their lives.

Teaching pedagogies lack ideas on what works and what does not with a result that research in knowledge, skills, methodologies and strategies are required. Future research should attempt to understand in what way and why teachers may experience problems with the teaching of reading literacy, particularly reading comprehension. To this end, different activities, both interactive and cooperative, and instructional strategies require particular research in varying contexts.

Another area of literacy is the effect digital literacies increasingly have on the promotion and teaching of literacy skills and reading. Given the era of the pandemic and COVID-19 lockdown provides researchers with an opportunity to research how literacy and reading can be promoted using Online Platforms and the Funds of Knowledge available in the home and children's immediate environment.

Conclusion

Drawing on a variety of articles indicated that many of the studies conducted are small-scale studies, which predominate research in literacy in South Africa. This chapter is not intended as a comprehensive guide, but can be useful to teachers, supervisors, postgraduate students and early career researchers currently undertaking, or planning to undertake, literacy research and writing for publication in Literacy and Reading.

References

Aitchison, J., & Land, S. (2005). *Bringing literacy home*: Family Literacy Conference Proceedings. Pietermaritzburg: The Centre for Adult Education.

Allan, R. (2009). *Virtual research environments: from portals to research environments*. Oxford: Chandos Publishing. https://doi.org/10.1533/9781780630144

Arksey, H. & O'Malley, L. (2005). Scoping studies: towards a methodological framework. *International Journal of Social Research Methodology* 8, 19-32. https://doi.org/10.1080/1364557032000119616

Bharuthram, S. (2012). Making a case for the teaching of reading across the curriculum in higher education. *South African Journal of Education*, 32(2), 205-214. https://doi.org/10.15700/saje.v32n2a557

Biesman-Simons, C., Dixon, K., Pretorius, E., & Reed, Y. (2020). Pitfalls and possibilities in literacy research: A review of South African literacy studies, 2004–2018. *Reading & Writing*, 11(1), 1-9. https://doi.org/10.4102/rw.v11i1.238

Boakye, N. (2015). The social dimension of reading literacy development in South Africa: Bridging inequalities among the various language groups. *International Journal of the Sociology of Language, 2015*, (234), 133-156. https://doi.org/10.1515/ijsl-2015-0008

Bourdieu, P. (1986). The forms of capital. In J.G. Richardson (Ed.), *Handbook of theory and research for the sociology of education* (pp. 241-258). New York, NY: Greenwood Press.

Combrinck, C. from UP: TimesLive (06 December 2017, 07:13). *Read it and weep: SA kids struggle with literacy.*

Culyer, A.J., & Lomas, J. (2006). Deliberative processes and evidence-informed decision-making in health care: do they work and how might we know? *Evidence and Policy* 2, 357-71. https://doi.org/10.1332/174426406778023658

Dixon-Woods, M. (2011). Systematic reviews and qualitative methods. In D. Silverman (Ed.), *Qualitative research*. London: Sage.

Fleisch, B. (2008). *Primary education in crisis: Why South African schoolchildren underachieve in reading and mathematics*. Juta and Company Ltd.

Fleisch, B., Pather, K., & Motilal, G. (2017). *South African Journal of Childhood Education* 7(1), a481. https://doi.org/10.4102/sajce.v7i1.481

Freire, P. (1970*). Pedagogy of the oppressed* (MB Ramos, Trans.). New York: Continuum, 2007.

Grønmo, L.S., Lindquist, M., Arora, A., & Mullis, I. V. (2015). TIMSS 2015 mathematics framework. *TIMSS*, 11-27.//timssandpirls.bc.edu/timss2015/downloads/t15_fw_chap1.pdf Retrieved 23 August 2020

Halliday, M.A.K., & Matthiessen, C.M. (2013). *Halliday's introduction to functional grammar*. Routledge. https://doi.org/10.4324/9780203431269

Henning, E. (2016). Reading as learning in the primary school. *South African Journal of Childhood Education*, 6(1), 6. https://doi.org/10.4102/sajce.v6i1.504

Hill, S. (2006). *Developing early literacy: Assessment and teaching*. Eleanor Curtain Publishing.

Holdaway, D. (1979). *The foundations of literacy* (Vol. 138). Sydney: Ashton Scholastic.

Howie, S.J., Combrinck, C., Roux, K., Tshele, M., Mokoena, G., & McLeod Palane, N. (2017). *PIRLS Literacy 2016: Progress in International Reading Literacy Study (PIRLS) 2016: South African children's reading literacy achievement*. Centre for Evaluation and Assessment (CEA).

Howie, S., Van Staden, S., Tshele, M., Dowse, C., & Zimmerman, L. (2012). *Progress In International Reading Literacy Study 2011. South African children's reading literacy achievement: Summary report*.

Howie, S.J., Venter, E., Van Staden, S., Zimmerman, L., Long, C., Du Toit, C.M., ... & Archer, E. (2007). *PIRLS 2006 summary report: South African children's reading achievement*. Centre for Evaluation and Assessment (CEA).

Huey, E.B. (1908). *The psychology and pedagogy of reading*. The Macmillan Company.

Le Roux, S.G. (2016). *The role of family literacy programmes to support emergent literacy in young learners* (Doctoral dissertation).

Levac, D., Colquhoun, H., & O'Brien, K.K. (2010): Scoping studies: advancing the methodology. *Implementation Science* 5, 1-9. https://doi.org/10.1186/1748-5908-5-69

Motilal, G.B., & Fleisch, B. (2020). The triple cocktail programme to improve the teaching of reading: Types of engagement. *South African Journal of Childhood Education*, 10(1), 13. https://doi.org/10.4102/sajce.v10i1.709

Mudzielwana, N. (2011). Causal Factors of Low Level Reading Standards in the Foundation Phase among Primary School Learners in South Africa. Department of Early Childhood Education, University of Venda. *Journal of Research in Education and Society*, 2(1), April 2011.

Nkomo, S.A. (2018). 'Grade 3 learners' imagined identities as readers revealed through their drawings', *Reading & Writing* 9(1), a163. https://doi.org/10.4102/rw.v9i1.163

Overet, J., & Donald. D. (2011) Paired reading: effects of a parent involvement programme in a disadvantaged community in South Africa. https://doi.org/10.1111/j.2044-8279.1998.tb01296.x

Perry, K.H. (2012). What Is Literacy? A Critical Overview of Sociocultural Perspectives. *Journal of Language and Literacy Education*, 8(1), 50-71.

PIRLS. 2015. Retrieved from http://timss.bc.edu/ (accessed June 2015)

Pretorius E.J. (2008). Reading ability and academic performance in South Africa: Are we fiddling while Rome is burning? Pages 169-196 | Published online: 31 May 2008. https://doi.org/10.1080/10228190208566183

Pretorius, E.J., & Klapwijk, N.M. (2016). Reading comprehension in South African schools: Are teachers getting it, and getting it right? *Per Linguam: a Journal of Language Learning= Per Linguam: Tydskrif vir Taalaanleer*, 32(1), 1-20. https://doi.org/10.5785/32-1-627

Pretorius, E.J., & Spaull, N. (2016). Exploring relationships between oral reading fluency and reading comprehension amongst English second language readers in South Africa. *Reading and Writing*, 29(7), 1449-1471. https://doi.org/10.1007/s11145-016-9645-9

Prosper, A. (2017). Children Engagement with Literacy: A Study of Literacy Practices at a Multilingual Classroom in Cape Town, South Africa. *Huria: Journal of the Open University of Tanzania*, 24(1), 140-162.

Rule, P., & Land, S. (2017). Finding the plot in South African reading education. *Reading & Writing*, 8(1), 1-8. https://doi.org/10.4102/rw.v8i1.121

SACMEQ. 2015. The Southern and Eastern Africa Consortium for Monitoring Educational Quality. Retrieved from http://www.sacmeq.org/?q=about-us (accessed June 2015)

SACMEQ II. 'Visualization of research results on the quality of education', Southern and Eastern Africa Consortium for Monitoring Educational Quality viewed 1 June 2011, from http://www.sacmeq.org/?q=research-Visualization

Sagotsky, J.A., Zhang, L., Wang, Z., Martin, S., & Deisboeck, T.S. 2008. Life sciences and the web: a new era for collaboration. *Molecular Systems Biology*, 4, 1-10. https://doi.org/10.1038/msb.2008.39

Snow, C.E. (1991). The theoretical basis for relationships between language and literacy in development. *Journal of Research in Childhood education*, 6(1), 5-10. https://doi.org/10.1080/02568549109594817

Snow, C.E., Griffin, P.E., & Burns, M. (2005). *Knowledge to support the teaching of reading: Preparing teachers for a changing world*. Jossey-Bass.

Spaull, N. (2013). *South Africa's education crisis: The quality of education in South Africa 1994-2011*. Johannesburg: Centre for Development and Enterprise, 1-65.

Spaull, N. (2015). Schooling in South Africa: How low-quality education becomes a poverty trap. *South African Child Gauge*, 12, 34-41.

Taylor, N. (2014). *Initial teacher education research project: An examination of aspects of initial teacher education curricula at five higher education institutions.* Summary report. Johannesburg South Africa: JET Education Services.

Tracey, D.H., & Morrow, L.M. (2006). *Lenses on reading: An introduction to theories and models.* New York: Guilford.

World Bank. Africa Regional Office. Office of the Chief Economist, World Bank. Africa Regional Office. Operational Quality, Knowledge Services, & World Bank. Development Data Group. (2006). *Africa development indicators.* World Bank Publications.

CHAPTER 11

Imperatives for educational improvement in South Africa's basic education system

Felix Maringe and Otilia Chiramba

Abstract

In this final chapter of the book, we attempt to synthesise the evidence for what needs to be done to enhance the quality of several aspects of basic education in South Africa. The enduring phenomenon of poverty that afflicts most schools in the country is an indictment of a systemic paralysis of unprecedented proportions in the sector. This phenomenon is exacerbated by the unabated widening of school and educational inequalities and deepening poverty differentials between schools that serve different racial and socio-economic groups in South Africa. While there is a substantial body of research on the impact of poverty in education, there remains a dearth of evidence that evaluates the impact of post-democracy interventions introduced to circumvent the effects of poverty on schooling.

The effectiveness of teaching and learning in mathematics, languages and science is also presented as a significant concern in South African schools. Challenges range from weaknesses in specialisation amongst educators, poor training, and inadequate resources, through to ineffective pedagogical approaches deployed by educators in schools. While the school system relies heavily on research undertaken by university academics, there is evidence that some researchers appear to lack theoretical robustness in their approaches. Research in the field of basic education, therefore, tends to be limited in size and scope, and more critically, is seldom adequately theoretically grounded.

Despite leadership being acknowledged as critical for school improvement and success, school leadership in South Africa remains devoid of training for incumbents. Although ongoing professional development for school principals takes place, much of it lacks approaches that are context-specific, and very little is known about the leadership roles and needs of middle managers in South African schools. There is also a shortage of broader research on basic education in South Africa. For example, we don't know enough about how teachers utilise teaching and learning time, how they present conceptual ideas, how children learn to read and write and how learners develop mathematical literacy, amongst other similar issues. This book also highlights the notion of professional development of teachers. While there is abundant evidence of a wide range of professional development programmes in schools, little is understood about how these are conducted, and even less is known about how and if these programmes are having the desired impact.

Finally, the chapter presents evidence for the progress that has been made in promoting physical access in schools. The extent to which schools are sufficiently empowered to promote epistemological access remains a significant concern in many cases. The sector is thus presented as one with no shortage of good intentions, but with insufficient research capacity to influence much-needed change and improvement across all schools.

Evidence from the systematic reviews reported in this book

In Chapter 1, we provided the context of the state of basic education in South Africa. We argued that there is growth in evidence-based practice and research-led development that informs decision-making in education in general and basic education in South Africa in particular. However, despite the noted improvements, the legacy of apartheid continues to persist in education. The chapter identifies, in broad terms, aspects of the basic education system that are poorly performing. These tend to fall into the broad areas of poverty, inequality and socio-economic conditions, all of which, separately and collectively, interact to repress children's epistemological access.

Although the apartheid regime was discontinued in 1994, we highlighted the existence of two systems of education, one that serves the rich communities and the other that serves the underprivileged minority. We analysed the concept of the systematic review as a highly valued evidence-gathering process and discussed its usefulness as the agreed methodological approach for work presented in this book. Further, the purpose of the first chapter was to highlight the planned contribution to the knowledge base by the subsequent chapters: to conduct a systematic review in nine different areas in basic education. We argued that the methodology of the systematic review was most likely to provide the best evidence available in South Africa upon which school improvement and learning outcomes could be enhanced. The first chapter provided a synopsis of each of the subsequent chapters, outlining the purpose and how a systematic review was carried out in each.

In Chapter 2, Besharati, Fleisch and Tsotsotso conducted a meta-analysis of local studies that have not been captured in existing international reviews, providing insights into the impact of various programmes and policies on language, mathematics and science learning in South African public schools. They concluded that international reviews are biased because they give prominence to studies from the global north. The meta-analysis revealed serious weaknesses in the South African education system, despite twenty-five years of reform effort. The chapter plays a significant role in highlighting and discussing the three major areas of research, policy and methodology, and how context and study design have huge impacts on the effect reported in various programme evaluations. The authors suggested that more empirical evidence is needed in the context of South Africa's education sector, particularly the use of rigorous counterfactual evaluations. Moreover, reflecting a bias for quantitative research, they recommended that local researchers should pay more attention to sampling processes and to qualitative studies.

In Chapter 3, Chikoko and Mthembu discussed the notion of poverty and its impact on basic education in South Africa. They found that poverty remains one of the most significant barriers in learners' attainment of basic education milestones. They acknowledged a range of government interventions that have been implemented to mitigate the impact of poverty in schools. Key interventions include:

- Free school uniforms for poor children
- Free school meals for poor children
- Fee-free education for poor children
- Supervised homework in school

More targeted literacy development programmes have also been introduced in schools, with variable results. For example, some steps taken such as reading literacy and other landmark education policies, have failed due to poverty and difficulties in fully implementing the policies owing to poor contexts. The authors recommended a framework that aims to eradicate two barriers simultaneously. The first struggle should be against poverty and the second should be concerned with crafting and implementing ways to improve the quality of education. They also advocated a drastic shift from deficit-based to asset-based thinking.

In Chapter 4, De Clercq and Shalem critically examined eight reviews and evaluation studies, noting two significant factors, amongst others. Firstly, those studies did not engage sufficiently with the theoretical dimensions underpinning their interventions. The authors argued that theoretical frameworks are essential, especially when researchers seek to contribute to the knowledge base on successful intervention programmes and policies. Secondly, the authors discovered that factors outside the formal education system related to students' socio-economic status, as well as factors revealed by emergent cognitive neuroscience research, all play a significant role. The chapter concluded by suggesting a framework that engages with the limited role of learning in society, and learning theories that recognise the psychological processes of cognitive development and wellbeing for effective school improvement interventions.

In Chapter 5, Bush and Glover reviewed literature on school leadership with the aim of discovering how policy and practice are reflected in published research outputs. In their systematic review, they identified significant evidence about the

nature of school leadership in South Africa, through a critical review of twelve themes:
- School leadership policy
- Leadership styles and models
- Leadership roles, including principals, deputy principals and heads of departments
- School management teams
- Curriculum management and instructional leadership
- Management of finance and resources
- School governance
- Leadership and management of people
- Leadership and diversity, including gender, race and ethnicity
- Leadership culture and structures
- Leadership and student outcomes
- Leadership preparation and development

The authors considered four variables, namely context, differences, school type and relationships, which contribute significantly to understanding school leadership literature in South Africa. Their literature review revealed that the data is uneven, with some of the twelve themes remaining underdeveloped. For example, much research is conducted about school principals, but we know less about other leadership roles such as deputy principals, heads of department and school management teams. Furthermore, research is concentrated in Gauteng and the Western Cape, with little research in other provinces, particularly the rural areas. The authors presented critical recommendations on the need for more substantial research in two areas: firstly, on the themes and topics where there is limited evidence; and secondly on large-scale projects, comparative cross-cultural studies and observational studies of educational leadership practice. The chapter concluded by outlining a framework of evidence which suggests why South African schools underperform.

In Chapter 6, the systematic review by Dison and Kearney revealed two insights. Firstly, there is a lack of extensive research that examines teaching and learning in the classroom. Secondly, quoting Hoadley's (2012) review of South African primary schools, they highlighted the strengths and limitations of teaching and learning studies in terms of their methodologies and consistency of findings. Their systematic review of Basic Education and Training (BET) and Further Education and Training (FET) over a period of twenty-five years provides further insights, for example, instead of paying attention to the learning process and the inner

workings of student learning and engagement, research on learning tends to focus on the influence of external and internal factors such as:
- Socio-economic conditions affecting learning
- Culture of teaching and learning in schools
- Effects of curriculum change
- Teacher activities
- Learner activities

The authors bemoan the fact that they found it very difficult to locate research that deals with what it means to learn in a particular discipline, or how the nature of teaching and learning is understood in different discipline contexts. Some studies make it difficult to claim anything about the impact of learning because they are based on teachers' and learners' perceptions, rather than on empirical evidence about learning, or learners' actual achievement or activities. The authors concluded by recommending the need for large-scale longitudinal or mixed-methods research studies to understand learning and its processes to promote innovative teaching and learning.

In Chapter 7, Vhurumuku presented critical insights based on a systematic review of twenty articles. He noted that research on professional development has dwelt much on the quality and effectiveness of teachers. Although professional development is considered vital, it is not clear how it should be done effectively, nor what major features it should comprise. This chapter addressed the following two questions:

- Which professional development models have resulted in improving teaching effectiveness for science teachers?
- How have South African researchers determined the effectiveness of science teacher professional development?

The twenty articles reviewed were selected based on five themes designed to capture and answer the above questions:

- Professional development models used
- Methods of evaluating impact or effectiveness
- Methods of determining teaching effectiveness
- Measuring teacher competencies
- Determining student outcomes

The findings revealed that in general, professional development has a positive impact on participating teachers. Although most of the studies confirmed this, a few studies were either inconclusive or showed professional development to be ineffective. Findings also revealed a surfeit of concentration of professional development on the teachers, at the expense of determining the impact on student learning outcomes, performance and achievement. As a result, the chapter recommended decolonising methodologies articulated through indigenous knowledge systems. Priority should also be given to assessing student learning outcomes to enhance professional development initiatives.

In Chapter 8, McKenzie, Watermeyer and Meyerson provided insights about access and participation for children with disabilities. The selected papers for review were based on six themes:

- Inclusive education discourse and disability
- Teaching and learning
- Parents' perspectives
- Disability, race and special education
- Human rights
- Teacher education

The authors discovered that research on children with disabilities has, to a large extent, concentrated on inclusive education, with less attention being paid to the other five areas listed above. They, therefore, advocated the need for further research in those areas, including research that highlights best practice in educational provision for children with disabilities. Moreover, teacher training and how to address the skills deficit should be treated as crucial. The authors noted that most people seem to be ignorant about inclusive education. Hence, they suggested processes to raise awareness regarding constitutional provisions for inclusive education, as well as the directives laid out in Education White Paper (EWP) 6.

In Chapter 9, Makonye explored how Ball et al.'s (2008) pedagogical content knowledge (PCK) analytical framework can be extended to the teaching of mathematics. Makonye argued that mathematics knowledge for teaching comprises six domains:

1. Common content knowledge
2. Specialist content knowledge
3. Horizon content knowledge
4. Knowledge of content and students
5. Knowledge of content and teaching
6. Knowledge of content and the curriculum

The author synthesised five significant findings:

- Research about teacher mathematics knowledge is deficient in some southern African countries and does not exist at all in others.

- Researchers lack the appropriate language to describe various teacher knowledges as exemplified in the six domains.
- Common content knowledge is the least researched, yet it is the most important, especially in affecting learner outcomes.
- There is a lack of mathematics education journals in South Africa and internationally.
- The concentration of articles in South Africa is in universities formerly occupied by whites only.

The author highlighted the need for more focused research on mathematics content knowledge according to the PCK framework, particularly specialised content knowledge (SCK), which is important in unpacking mathematical meaning for learners. He also recommended that more research should be conducted in the broader southern African region.

In Chapter 10 Motilal was concerned with the capacity to find, understand, critically appraise, share and act on evidence based on research conducted in the country. Through the scoping review, she answered three critical questions. Findings indicated that there are challenges in literacy and reading. She, therefore, recommended for extensive research to expound on the link between language communities, socioeconomic status, reading literacy, writing literacy, digital literacies and multimodal literacies, especially in the South African context where there are eleven official languages and wide socio-economic disparities. Secondly, she discovered that there is a mismatch between the social literacy practices of the different language groups and the education system that operates in the country. She advocated for drastic measures to be taken at all levels to improve the overall literacy and reading levels of all South African learners. Furthermore, she highlighted the need for robust and rigorous research to enhance the production of knowledge in all of these spheres of literacy and reading.

Conclusion

In summary, we began this chapter by reflecting on the role of education in development. We argued that a sound education is at the heart of the proper functioning of the three basic means of production i.e. the human, financial and land dimensions in any economy; thus education is at the centre of economic and social growth. We further argued that although South Africa allocates a large proportion of its budget to education, the country performs poorly compared to the rest of the world (measured via several international instruments), including countries with lower GDPs and those that do not invest much in education. As a result of this misalignment between financing and performance, we advocated a serious review of the basic education sector. In response to this crisis, we hypothesised that the following five significant elements are closely linked to school improvement and need to be improved themselves: human capacity development, leadership and management in schools, deployment and utilisation of educational resources, learner outcomes and interrogation of poverty in the sector.

We also compared pre- and post-apartheid systems of education and argued that during apartheid, various forms of violence were exerted on local populations. Sadly, the effects of these violations persist in South Africa's democratic education system. We argued that whilst the country has achieved almost 100% physical access to schools, a great deal still needs to be done to promote epistemological access to basic education in South Africa.

The evidence from the systematic reviews in this book has highlighted various gaps in the literature. Below we highlight five key recommendations, which we refer to as imperatives for improving schooling and educational outcomes in South Africa. We have deliberately presented them as a list, to emphasise the high priority that we consider should be given to them.

Key recommendations

The separate chapters in this book provide valuable insights into the working of critical aspects of basic education in South Africa. We, however, synthesise these into the following five key areas:

1. **The need to develop frameworks for interrogating poverty in schools, including evaluating the impact of post-democratic interventions aimed to reduce poverty in schools**

Three dimensions of school poverty appear to be at the forefront of the debates in this area. The first is material poverty (Ferguson, 2008; Kabir and Ahmed, 2019; Raffo et al., 2007) that has necessitated key interventions such as school uniform policy, free school meals and food support to child-headed families. The second is economic poverty (Bhorat and van der Westhuizen, 2010), which is closely related to the first, but specifically refers to the challenges faced by low-income families. Such challenges include lack of access to financial resources, scarce reading materials, limited study spaces and above all, limited parental support for cognitive growth, amongst others. The third dimension is epistemological poverty (du Plooy and Zilindile, 2014), which includes phenomena such as lack of socio-cognitive capital (Roser and Ortiz-Ospina, 2013) to deal with the requirements of formal schooling by poor learners, the poverty of epistemological support in poor schools due to frequent teacher absence, uneven distribution of good teachers in schools, which has a substantial impact on poor schools, and the poor state of infrastructural support in these poor schools. These factors combine to depress cognitive development in learners, increase school dropout, influence poor learning outcomes, and generally ensure the recycling and reproduction of poverty, socially, cognitively, culturally and intergenerationally amongst the poor (McLanahan, 2009). There seems to be a need to explore how it is that, despite the interventions over the last 25 years following the demise of apartheid, learners from poor households continue to finish schooling with insecure learning outcomes, contribute the most to the wastage phenomena in schools, and have the lowest progression rates to higher forms of learning and meaningful employment opportunities. We can learn from other international interventions, especially in South America, but also from the more developed world where reducing school poverty has a longer history. A starting point could be for the Department of Basic Education to sponsor a systematic review of poverty-alleviating strategies in different countries to see what has and has not worked and why.

2. The need to interrogate inequalities in knowledge distribution

The evidence across most of the systematic reviews captured in this book identifies two fundamental issues that relate to knowledge and power dynamics in an unequal world (Chirwa, 2020). The first issue is the limited presence of South African research in mainstream publications. This is reflected in the dominance of global north research in the reference lists of the research captured for this book. In part, this might reflect the developmental status of knowledge in the global south. But it might also reveal deliberate mechanisms for marginalising knowledge from the global south, a process that was a major strategy for exerting power and dominance in the colonial and colonisation processes (Roser and Ortiz-Ospina, 2013; Evans, 2014). This may call for a more vigorous pursuit of the goals of decolonisation of knowledge, which entails more support for local research and publication, and stronger motivation for turning the gaze of research and theory from dominant Western epistemes to more local and indigenous epistemes. The effort cannot be left to individual researchers to muster; there will be a need for a significant national shake-up, both in terms of prioritising the decolonising of knowledge and education as key strategic goals, and in terms of supporting research that seeks to support these goals. The need for supporting research that interrogates issues of coloniality, the reproduction of intergenerational poverty and inequality and the perpetual dependency of developing nations on the developed world must be a major impetus for change and transformation not just in basic education, but across different areas of human endeavour.

The second issue is the over-representation of deductive forms of research, which lay emphasis on hypothesis testing, and the limited representation of inductive research that seeks to draw on in-depth understandings and experiences of phenomena by those who engage with reform and school interventions in the most valued research outlets (Eyisi, 2016; Sale et al., 2002). This too has its roots in the long-standing tradition of the superiority of quantitative knowledge over all other forms of knowledge and especially over qualitative data, which some describe as spurious hearsay and gossip (Layder, 2013). Also, many qualitative studies tend to be small-scale case studies that have limited application beyond their specific contexts, reproducibility and generalisability and can thus add limited value to policy reform and strategic change aimed at systemic-level transformation. However, the need for such studies is gradually being recognised, especially as they provide enhanced and nuanced understandings of systemic issues and challenges, which are needed in informing more successful transformation and its implementation (Brannen, 2005).

3. The need to develop a stronger focus on language, literacy and numeracy teaching especially in the early learning phases

The research by both Motilal and Fleisch et al. in this book specifically points to substantial gaps in language, literacy and numeracy teaching in basic education in South African schools. Three specific issues seem to have strong relevance to the improvement of basic education in South Africa.

First is the question of language-of-instruction in the early grades. Policy in South Africa requires that learners be instructed in their mother tongue in the first two grades of schooling. The problem is that in many cosmopolitan areas, especially, learners come from a variety of mother-tongue spaces. There are eleven official languages in South Africa and sometimes, classrooms have children from all these language backgrounds. This stretches the capacity of schools to have teachers who can teach in all the official languages and could also compromise the cherished goals and values of inclusivity in education. In the end, schools tend to teach all children in the language of the majority in specific areas of the country. Besides, schools have a choice about the language of instruction. Most schools choose between English and Afrikaans, and the local languages are only taught as subjects, rather than mediums of instruction (Makalela, 2019). Research also appears to show that most parents in South Africa prefer their children to be taught in English rather than through local languages (Gordon and Harvey, 2019), a reflection of the impact of colonialism and the persistent coloniality of being amongst the citizens of the country.

The third aspect is related to the effectiveness of methodologies used in teaching literacy and numeracy in schools. In a review undertaken by Nag et al. (2014) for the period 1990 to 2013 in several developing country contexts, it was established that rote and surface learning, chorus, copywriting and drill were the most prevalent instructional techniques used for teaching numeracy and literacy. Phonological awareness was rarely developed in learners in early grade teaching, despite its acknowledged centrality to facilitating reading and understanding of text. Similarly, Vale et al. (2016) draw attention to substantial constraints in numeracy teaching and learning in developing country contexts. Key barriers include teacher deficits in mathematical content, poor understanding of mathematical pedagogical skills, large class sizes and limited teaching and learning resources (Askew, 2013).

There seems to be an urgent need for supporting multiple research thrusts around recapacitating teachers with both content and pedagogical knowledge skills in both areas of literacy and numeracy teaching in the early grades in South African schools.

4. The need to increase teacher awareness and competency in dealing with the idea of inclusive education

Inclusive education in South Africa is an integral part of the overall transformational agenda in schools. Emanating directly from the Constitution of the country and supported by various pieces of legislation, the imperatives of establishing an equal, non-segregated and non-sexist society are cherished goals. Inclusion, thus, has a high-profile presence in teacher education and more broadly, in schools in South Africa. However, as Sayed et al., (2003) have noted, the notion of inclusion is mired in intractable debates about its meaning, its priorities and, more importantly, in the efficacy of its associated strategies. Inclusion is thus a slippery concept. It comes with a lot of promise for righting the wrongs of the past, for delivering equal opportunities especially to previously disadvantaged communities, and for ensuring equal treatment and access to resources amongst groups with different identities such as disabled learners, gendered identities, and learners from disadvantaged and marginalised backgrounds, amongst others.

The major problem in dealing with issues of inclusive practice seems to be the challenge of striking a balance between creating opportunities for marginalised groups without disadvantaging other groups. For example, teaching special groups of learners separately from mainstream groups can be exclusionary in its own way. On the other hand, integrating the learners in mainstream teaching and learning formations carries its own burdens of managing differentiated learning support in a common environment and the risk of short-changing other learners who need different forms of support.

In South African schools, students from poor socio-economic backgrounds, such as those from rural schools, experience multiple challenges. First, the middle-class culture that characterises many schools is a threat to their process of integrating into the citizenry of the institutions. Many come to school without having used a computer or laptop, and they need time to be socialised into the high-tech learning environment before they can productively engage with the learning. They could very quickly be left behind given the fast pace of curriculum instruction in many schools. In South Africa, almost 40% of students who start year one, do not complete their full years of compulsory education. Approximately 80% of these students are from disadvantaged backgrounds characterised by the infliction of multiple deprivations. To that end, we can argue that while schools have created substantially more opportunities for disadvantaged learners through promoting greater physical access, the equality of epistemological access remains an issue of great concern. As such, the South African schools cannot be said to be providing cognitive justice to all their students.

The question of integrating learners with various forms of disabilities is also a very thorny issue in basic education in South Africa. While there are important philosophical and ideological arguments for mainstreaming learners from all backgrounds in the same schools and environments, there are substantial challenges confronting schools and teachers with respect to providing cognitively and socially just educational experiences to all. The practice of integrating learners from all walks of life in the same teaching environments has the potential to create new forms of exclusion which may negate the overall purpose of inclusive education.

5. A need to explore more effective distributed leadership development modalities

Three significant challenges are worth mentioning in the basic education sector in South Africa. Leadership is a highly significant contributor to school improvement in its broadest sense and to learner outcomes specifically. Apart from the influence of good teachers, leadership exerts the second most significant influence of the success of schools and their learners. But good leaders do not grow on trees; they are made by the systems that need them. In South Africa though, as indeed in many other places across the world, and especially in developing nations, school leaders are assumed to grow organically without formal investment in the systems and the people expected to become leaders. There is no formal training of school principals as they are expected to emerge from the crop of experienced teachers in the schools. In 1995, almost 60% of teachers in South Africa were either under-qualified or unqualified to teach in schools. Yet this pool forms the source of future leaders in the system. The Advanced Certificate in Education (ACE), which has now been redeveloped to an Advanced Diploma in Education (ADE), has been the flagship programme for reskilling and capacitating school leadership/principalship in South Africa. There has not been any formal evaluation of the impact of this programme in the country, something which is now overdue.

A second substantial challenge with school leadership in South Africa is the question of age. Most principals are in the 50-65 year age group, and there is not an adequate pipeline ready to take over when these leaders retire.

Third, school leadership development in South Africa places little or no emphasis on distributed leadership layers below the principal role. The principals alone have limited capacity to drive school improvement without the involvement of deputy heads, heads of departments, leader leadership groups and parent leadership groups. Relatively little leadership training exists to cultivate effective distributed school leadership in South Africa. This is an area requiring dedicated attention to enhance the quality of school improvement in the country.

A sound and effective education system is critical for the development of nations. The evidence presented in this book clearly shows that basic education in South Africa remains in a state of crisis. Despite the transition to democracy and significant investment in education, learner outcomes continue to trace the contours of race and privilege. The changes that have been introduced since 1994 do not reflect sufficient epistemological and ontological transformation. Amongst the many issues raised in specific chapters, this book identifies three critical areas of transitioning to a more decolonised education system: revitalised language, literacy and numeracy programmes, especially in the early grade learning phases; stronger teacher training for enhancing content and pedagogical competences, including greater attention to the intractable issues of inclusive educational programmes; and a distributed leadership training approach that goes beyond a focus on school principalship.

We hope readers and policymakers, other researchers and postgraduate students will find the ideas and suggestions in this book a sound basis for developing new ideas and new programmes of research and development in basic education in South Africa.

References

Askew, M. (2013). Mediating learning number bonds through a Vygotskian lens of scientific concepts. *South African Journal of Childhood Education*, 3(2), 1-20. https://doi.org/10.4102/sajce.v3i2.37

Ball, D. L., Thames, M. H., & Phelps, G. C. (2008). Content knowledge for teaching: What makes it special? *Journal of Teacher Education*, 59(5), 389-407. https://doi.org/10.1177/0022487108324554

Bhorat, H., & van der Westhuizen, C. (2010). Poverty, inequality and the nature of economic growth in South Africa. In: Misra-Dexter, N., & February, J. (eds.). *Testing democracy: Which way is South Africa going?* pp. 46-70. Cape Town: Idasa.

Brannen, J. (2005). Mixing methods: The entry of qualitative and quantitative approaches into the research process. *International Journal of Social Research Methodology*, 8(3), 173-184. https://doi.org/10.1080/13645570500154642

Chirwa, G. C. (2020). "Who knows more, and why?" Explaining socioeconomic-related inequality in knowledge about HIV in Malawi. *Scientific African*, 7, e00213. https://doi.org/10.1016/j.sciaf.2019.e00213

Du Plooy, L., & Zilindile, M. (2014). Problematising the concept epistemological access with regard to foundation phase education towards quality schooling. *South African Journal of Childhood Education*, 4(1), 187-201. https://doi.org/10.4102/sajce.v4i1.51

Evans, V. (2014). *The language myth: Why language is not an instinct*. Cambridge: Cambridge University Press. https://doi.org/10.1017/CBO9781107358300

Eyisi, D. (2016). The usefulness of qualitative and quantitative approaches and methods in researching problem-solving ability in science education curriculum. *Journal of Education and Practice*, 7(15), 91-100.

Ferguson, I. (2008). *Reclaiming social work: Challenging neo-liberalism and promoting social justice.* London: SAGE Publications Ltd.

Gordon, S. L., & Harvey, J. (2019). Choice of language in education: do we know what South Africans want? *Language and Education*, 33(3), 226-243. https://doi.org/10.1080/09500782.2018.1488865

Hoadley, C. (2012). What is a community of practice and how can we support it? In: Lund, S., & Jonassen, D. (Eds.). *Theoretical foundations of learning environments* (2nd ed., pp. 286-300). New York, NY: Routledge.

Kabir, M. A., & Ahmed, A. (2019). An empirical approach to understanding the lower-middle and upper-middle income traps. *International Journal of Development Issues*, 18(2), 171-190. https://doi.org/10.1108/IJDI-09-2018-0138

Layder, D. (ed.). (2013). Qualitative data & mixed strategies. In: *Doing Excellent Small-Scale Research*, pp. 70-94. London: SAGE publications Ltd. https://doi.org/10.4135/9781473913936.n5

Makalela, L. (2019). Uncovering the universals of ubuntu translanguaging in classroom discourses. *Classroom Discourse*, 10(3-4), 237-251. https://doi.org/10.1080/19463014.2019.1631198

McLanahan, S. (2009). Fragile families and the reproduction of poverty. *The Annals of the American Academy of Political and Social Science*, 621(1), 111-131. https://doi.org/10.1177/0002716208324862

Nag, S., Chiat, S., Torgerson, C., & Snowling, M. J. (2014). *Literacy, foundation learning and assessment in developing countries*. Department for International Development. [Online]. Available from: https://eppi.ioe.ac.uk/cms/Portals/0/PDF%20reviews%20and%20summaries/Literacy%202014%20Nag%20report.pdf?ver=2014-04-24-134404-340

Raffo, C., Dyson, D., Gunter, H. M., Hall, D., Jones, L., & Kalambouka, A. (2007). *Education and poverty: A critical review of theory, policy and practice*. Education and Poverty Programme, Joseph Rowntree Foundation, York.

Roser, M., & Ortiz-Ospina, E. (2013). *Global extreme poverty*. [Online]. Available from: https://ourworldindata.org/extreme-poverty#citation.

Sale, J. E. M., Lohfeld, L. H., & Brazil, K. (2002). Revisiting the quantitative-qualitative debate: Implications for mixed-methods research. *Quality & Quantity*, 36(1), 43-53. https://doi.org/10.1023/A:1014301607592

Sayed, Y., Soudien, C., & Carrim, N. (2003). Discourses of exclusion and inclusion in the South: Limits and possibilities. *Journal of Educational Change*, 4(3), 231-248. https://doi.org/10.1023/B:JEDU.0000006162.07375.aa

Vale, C., Atweh, B., Averill, R., & Skourdoumbis, A. (2016). Equity, social justice and ethics in mathematics education. In: Makar, K., Dole, S., Visnovska, J., Goos, M., Bennison, A., & Fry, K. (Eds.). *Research in Mathematics Education in Australasia 2012–2015* (pp. 97-118). Singapore: Springer. https://doi.org/10.1007/978-981-10-1419-2_6

www.ingramcontent.com/pod-product-compliance
Lightning Source LLC
Chambersburg PA
CBHW080602170426
43196CB00017B/2879